Entertainment
&Society

This book is dedicated to our families:
to Shay's son, Ryan; daughter, Aubyn; and grandson, Sage;
and to Cynthia's parents, Jack and Judy; sister, Christine; and
grandmother, Trudy, who have contributed countless hours of entertainment to our lives.

Entertainment &Society

Audiences, Trends, and Impacts

2003

Shay Sayre & Cynthia King

California State University, Fullerton

SAGE Publications
International Educational and Professional Publisher
Thousand Oaks ▪ London ▪ New Delhi

For information:

Sage Publications, Inc.
2455 Teller Road
Thousand Oaks, California 91320
E-mail: order@sagepub.com

Sage Publications Ltd.
6 Bonhill Street
London EC2A 4PU
United Kingdom

Sage Publications India Pvt. Ltd.
B-42 Panchsheel Enclave
Post Box 4109
New Delhi 110-017 India

Printed in the United States of America

Library of Congress Cataloging-in-Publication Data

Sayre, Shay.
Entertainment & society: audience, trends, and impact / Shay Sayre and Cynthia M. King.
    p. cm.
Includes bibliographical references and index.
ISBN 0-7619-2548-1 (pbk.)
   1. Performing arts-Social aspects. 2. Amusements-Social aspects.
I. Title: Entertainment & Society. II. King, Cynthia M. III. Title.
PN1590.S6 S29 2003
791—dc21

                               2002153077

Printed on acid-free paper

03   04   05   10 9 8 7 6 5 4 3 2 1

Acquiring Editor:	Al Bruckner
Editorial Assistant:	MaryAnn Vail
Copy Editor:	Meredith L. Brittain
Typesetter:	C&M Digitals (P) Ltd.
Indexer:	Molly Hall
Cover Designer:	Michelle Lee

Acknowledgments

We are extremely grateful for the support and inspiration for this text contributed by mentors and colleagues, including Dolf Zillmann, formerly at the University of Alabama; Bryant Jennings, University of Alabama; Peter Vorderer, University of Southern California; and Patrice Oppliger, La Salle University. We would also like to acknowledge Jennifer Johnson and Meredith Brittain for their thoughtful feedback and thorough editing, and Tom Phipps for serving as our text sketch artist and illustrator. Thanks also to the reviewers, who provided many insightful comments, and to our students, who played an invaluable role in inspiring and refining the contents of this text.

Contents

Foreword

No matter which country you go to and which cultures you encounter, what seems to be most striking today is how important entertainment has become almost all over the globe. Particularly in the Western World, but increasingly everywhere else, people spend more of their time, money, and—perhaps most importantly—more of their attention on entertainment than ever before. The media play a predominant role in providing us with this ever-increasing variety of entertainment possibilities: to be amused, to have fun and pleasure, to be delighted and enlightened, and sometimes even to grieve and suffer. Questions of life and death, of love and hate, of success and failure, and of security and danger keep us busy almost daily when they are packaged as entertainment. Interestingly enough, we seem to become involved and absorbed with these issues deliberately, willingly, happily, and even eagerly.

There is no doubt that this is the Age of Entertainment. But the question is: What does this age mean for our society? What does entertainment do for us and to us? Does entertainment make this world more pleasurable, more livable, after all, or does it only create more problems? Does it help or hinder our efforts to learn and understand? Does entertainment motivate us to face difficult and challenging issues that are hard to comprehend or does it make us lazy and distract us from more important aspects of our lives? Quite frankly, we really don't know yet. These questions, however, seem to be of critical importance for our understanding of modern times, making it all the more alarming that, to date, we have fallen short on answering them.

To put these questions into more concrete examples,

☆ Why is it that even though people may claim that they watch television only when they have nothing better to do, so many of us still spend more time watching TV than engaging in almost any other leisure activity?

☆ Why do adolescents complain about not having enough time to do their homework as they slowly watch the minutes tick away, yet they almost completely forget about time and space when they become immersed in an entertaining video game?

☆ And why do so many people claim to suffer from "information overload," becoming easily distracted and confused by the sheer volume, variety, and complexity of today's media messages, and yet they are still able to easily follow and remain attentive to their own favorite television programs, video games, and the like that are just as varied and complex?

These questions would certainly appear to be appropriate topics of inquiry for scholars in areas such as communication, psychology, or sociology. However, entertainment research does not yet exist as an established academic field of study. Considering the prominence of entertainment in our daily lives, it is perplexing that the academic effort to deal with this phenomenon has remained rather weak. This may be the case, at least in part, because people believe that they already know the answers. Answers like *We are so spoiled in our own lives that any additional excitement can come only from the fake, over-the-top world of entertainment*. Or *We are so bored or distressed by our own lives that we need to escape our daily routines by entering those rather glorious worlds inhabited by the rich and famous, where we can be voyeurs to their successes and scandals*. We even pretend to know what entertainment does to us: It distracts us from real social and political problems, it manipulates us and makes us even more irrational, or, it fosters our social learning by allowing us to vicariously experience things we might not encounter in our own lives. Some of these answers are merely questionable speculations; others are potentially more constructive suppositions. Some of these proposed answers might be easily tested while others might prove to be more challenging.

These conjectures are not necessarily mutually exclusive, but they do place different emphasis on various aspects of entertainment, with different levels of precision, and certainly with different explanatory power. Most of these notions have at least been introduced, and a few have more thoroughly explored, in academic literature. Some propositions reflect writings by Aristotle; others lean on Plato. Scholars who are familiar with the debate between Christianity and hedonism in the 16th and 17th centuries argue differently from those who are influenced by the so-called Frankfurt School of Social Sciences and their more recent followers within the Cultural or Critical Studies approach in the Humanities. Even those who are not familiar with any of these formal schools of thought often hold strong convictions about the danger and blessings of entertainment, simply because of its increasing prominence and relevance in our daily lives.

Only recently, slowly from the 1970s on, have academics started to rigorously study entertainment by running experiments, conducting surveys, and implementing longitudinal studies that look at these phenomena over a certain period of time. While academia was hesitant to appreciate these endeavors for quite some time, scientific journals in areas such as communication, psychology, and sociology have now started to accept publications on these issues. Theories of action, of cognition, and of emotion have been developed and applied to entertainment; innovative research design and measures have been invented and used. As a result, we are also finally beginning to see the introduction of texts that synthesize and review various areas of this promising body of entertainment theories and research. However, we are still far from understanding what entertainment means to us and what it does to us on a larger scale. And, much more specific, rigorous and creative research in different labs and different social settings all around the globe will be necessary before we will be able to sufficiently answer these questions.

It is encouraging to see the growing number of texts that address the study of entertainment. However, most of these texts remain geared to a more advanced audience of academics and graduate students who are already well-versed in the basic theories of communication, psychology, sociology, and related disciplines that are driving contemporary entertainment research. That is why *Entertainment & Society: Audiences, Trends, and Impact* makes for such a welcome addition to entertainment literature. I am encouraged by the authors' effort to introduce entertainment as a meaningful topic of study for a more general audience.

Of course, a book like this will not be able to compensate for all the gaps that still exist in our understanding of entertainment, and this text doesn't pretend to do so. However, what a book like this can do is to put entertainment on the agenda for those who are interested in understanding our times. It introduces us to the various questions and even to the approaches and perspectives that will eventually lead to some answers. This book is written from the viewpoint of those who know the world of entertainment and who are particularly familiar with what is going on in Southern California, where entertainment has chosen its capitol. It is written for anyone and everyone with a general interest in understanding that world as well as those who eventually may decide to devote their time and attention to the academic study of entertainment.

—Peter Vorderer

Introduction

GENERAL OVERVIEW

We live in an entertainment society. In the morning, we wake up to the radio playing our favorite music or morning show. When we get to work or school, we amuse ourselves while we sit at our desks by thumbing through magazines, playing handheld video games, or surfing the Internet. When we are running errands, we often shop and eat at locations that bear closer resemblance to tropical getaways and cartoon adventures than to traditional retail stores and restaurants. And when we get a speeding ticket while we are running those errands, we go to comedy traffic school. By combining a little ambiance and perhaps some live music with a double caramel latté, we have even managed to turn a task as mundane as getting a cup of coffee into an engaging, entertaining activity.

In contemporary industrialized societies, we have entered an era where everything is entertainment and entertainment is everything. Entertainment is discussed in many texts as it relates to specific disciplines, but few books have explored entertainment as the central focus of inquiry. Given its seemingly pervasive presence in society, we felt that it was high time that entertainment received top billing. Thus, we embarked upon writing a text that takes a closer look at the dawning age of entertainment.

A society's books, music, films, television programs, games, and other forms of entertainment both shape and reflect the history, culture, beliefs, experiences, and concerns of the people of that society. Therefore, the study of entertainment is also a study of the history, culture, beliefs, experiences, and concerns of the audiences it entertains. In this book, we explore the nature of entertainment from a variety of perspectives. We reflect on what entertainment is and how it has evolved over the centuries. We review contemporary entertainment trends in an effort to understand both their origins and their implications. We question who likes what and why to understand audiences and their preferences, and we examine how the entertainment industries—indeed, all industries—have learned to cater to these preferences. We also consider the impacts that different entertainment trends may have on both audiences and institutions.

The text offers an interdisciplinary approach to the study of entertainment. Our discussion draws from social scientific and humanistic theory and research found in sociology, psychology, communications, economics, marketing, and cultural anthropology, among other fields. Throughout this book, we trace the numerous ways that developments in entertainment have been shaped by the social, cultural, technological, political, economic, and legal realities that existed at the time. In turn, we also note the many ways in which those realities and, perhaps most importantly, our perceptions of those realities are shaped by the entertainment we consume.

INTENDED AUDIENCE

Entertainment & Society was written as an introductory text for general audiences. It is primarily intended for use as an undergraduate or lower-level graduate text for courses that focus specifically on the study of entertainment or popular culture more generally. Its interdisciplinary nature makes it an appropriate text for inquiry and instruction in a wide range of fields, including American Studies, Communications, Liberal Studies, Psychology, Sociology, and related disciplines. Readers need not have any previous background or instruction in any of these fields; all of the theories and concepts readers need to understand are explained in the text. However, readers who are more familiar with one or more of these disciplines will also benefit from this book because they will see how general ideas and concepts can be adapted to the study of entertainment. Because entertainment has become so pervasive in our lives, we believe that this text may be particularly well suited for general education courses designed to introduce some of these disciplines to wider audiences.

PART OVERVIEWS

The book is divided into four parts. The first and last parts focus on general factors that are related to many different forms of entertainment, whereas the middle two parts provide a more in-depth focus on specific categories of entertainment.

Part I: Spotlight Up (Chapters 1 through 5)

In this first part of our text, we present topics related to understanding the role of entertainment in our modern society. Chapter 1 defines entertainment and introduces readers to forms of leisure and the notion of play. Next we trace the development of entertainment from its live forms through mediated technology. Finally, we introduce social theory and take a closer look at entertainment-focused media.

In Chapter 2, we focus on the business of entertainment and the attention economy that drives it. We introduce the concepts of branding and consumption, and we discuss the psychology of attention as it applies to entertainment. This chapter explores the international market for entertainment, and we take a closer look at the leadership qualities necessary to be an entertainment mogul.

Entertainment audiences are the topic of Chapter 3, which includes both live and mediated audience types. We look at audience segments and characterizations, revealing that we are all audiences all of the time. Spectacle and narcissism are presented for their roles in shopping and fandom. We discuss audience research and the changing nature of today's audiences. Finally, we take a closer look at enthusiasts, fans, and fanatics of sports entertainment.

In Chapter 4, we ground entertainment in the theory of drama. Built on the pleasure principle, drama is the driving force of most forms of entertainment. We discuss drama's appeal, and we take a look at why people watch each form of drama—tragedy, mystery, humor and comedy, violence and horror. We explore contemporary entertainment trends—including time manipulation, genre blending, reality programming, and interactivity—and take a closer look at Showtime Interactive TV.

Our introduction to entertainment would not be complete without a discussion of the effects of entertainment on society. Chapter 5 examines the history of media effects theories, presents research methods used to measure those effects, and identifies current theories. We also discuss the impact of entertainment effects, including such factors as stereotyping, role models, sex, drugs, and violence. Finally, we take a closer look at how entertainment has been used as a tool for social change by focusing on how popular U.S. television programs were used to combat drunk driving.

Part II: Entertainment Media (Chapters 6 through 9)

Media are a driving force in contemporary entertainment. This part presents a chronology of the development of traditional forms of media entertainment, from print to television.

In Chapter 6, we cover the original form of mass media—print. Best-selling fiction and nonfiction, mystery novels, children's books, and coffee table volumes are featured first. Next we present newspapers and magazines in their various forms and variety, with a special focus on cartoons and comic strips. We also trace developments in print venues and media following the September 11, 2001, terrorist attack, and we examine political satire and cartoon commentary.

Chapter 7 focuses on the roles of music and radio as entertainment vehicles. We discuss jazz, electronics, hip hop, and pop music in terms of their currency and culture. We examine how recorded music and the record industry promote music, and we explore how technological developments—such as the Internet and changing governmental regulations—are profoundly influencing trends in music entertainment. We discuss live music and music videos, and we also reflect on the appeal and impact of music for the audiences it entertains. Finally, the lawsuit of Pearl Jam versus Ticketmaster gets a closer look.

Film is the focus of Chapter 8. We take note of the ways government regulation, trends in ownership, and new technology have shaped film entertainment. Animated films and female warriors are what's up at the movies. We reflect on violence and the celebrity society that film created, and we preview coming attractions for Hollywood. The evolution of advertising gets a closer look as we examine the rise of product placements.

In Chapter 9, we see what's on television. We explore the structure of the television industry and its impact on entertainment offerings. We examine television shows of reality, games, talk, news, and religion, and their respective audiences. We present television trends and programming nuances and discuss the effects of TV viewing. We take a closer look at television as radio by reviewing cable music offerings.

Part III: Live Performances, Amusement, and Recreation (Chapters 10 through 13)

Part III highlights forms of entertainment that can be enjoyed in person, including live performances as well as other forms of amusement and recreation, including gaming, sports, and travel. Chapter 10 investigates forms of classical performance (such as drama, musicals, opera, and orchestral concerts) and types of popular performance (such as rock concerts, comedy clubs, magic, the circus, and rodeos). The chapter concludes with a closer look at what motivates performing arts audiences.

Audiences worldwide amuse themselves in urban centers of entertainment, such as Las Vegas and Monaco. In Chapter 11, we investigate games of challenge and chance, including the game theory that drives them. We explore the topic of video games—their technology, cultural impact, and trends. Gambling's mini-history is woven into a discussion of casinos, e-gambling, and lotteries. We take a closer look at the use of psychographics to promote the lottery in states throughout the United States.

Although sports can be a form of recreation, we focus primarily on audiences who amuse themselves watching sports in Chapter 12. We present sports as drama and spotlight sports fans, sponsorship, media coverage, and extreme sports. We compare sports to religion, fanaticism, and politics, and we touch on fan violence. We profile sports heroes and icons, and take a closer look at the Anaheim Angels' efforts to "Show Us the Monkey."

Adventure and recreation can best be viewed in the context of travel and tourism. Chapter 13 traces the origins of travel and characterizes modern tourism by types. Tourists as guests and the hosts who receive them are discussed. We investigate tourist destinations, roadside attractions, and souvenirs. We overview the tourism industry, and we explore real versus staged spaces and experiences. We identify new and emerging tourism markets, and we introduce theoretical approaches to tourism. We also explore tourism's effect on our global environment, and we take a closer look at a beach city's tourism problems and opportunities.

Part IV: The Grand Finale (Chapters 14 through 16)

Traditionally, many forms of entertainment ended with a grand finale, where individual performers, acts, and elements would all join together for an over-the-top, action-packed closing number. Today, however, we rarely must wait for the finale—instead, all entertainment is grand. From beginning to end, entertainment products, services, and performances pack in as much as they can to keep audiences happy. Many of the chapters in the previous three parts allude to the ways in which different types of entertainment and entertainment genres have joined forces to become bigger, bolder, and presumably better than ever. We have also shown ways that entertainment borrows from and blends with aspects of larger society. This convergence represents a predominant characteristic of today's entertainment. The chapters in Part IV all highlight key trends that reflect the blending, converging, and redefining of various forms of entertainment.

Chapter 14 shows how reality is simulated by the clever use of symbols and signs that reflect a particular theme. We see how theming can bring together a wide range of entertainment products and services into a cohesive whole. We explore themed spaces created for shopping, restaurants, and retailing, and we discuss themed places like neighborhoods, cities, and parks. To further illustrate the theming concept, we take a closer look at the theming of the Outback Steakhouse.

Postmodern entertainment is the topic of Chapter 15. After characterizing postmodernism, we explore how boundaries have been blurred and broken between high art and popular culture, entertainment and everyday life. We show how hyper-reality has invaded marketing, our lifestyles, and our physical spaces. We present architecture, museums, cinema, and video examples of postmodernism, and we take a closer look at the buildings of architect Frank Gehry.

In Chapter 16, we wrap up our study of entertainment with a focus on futuretainment. This chapter explores the convergence of different media technologies into new media and considers possible implications for future entertainment trends. We discuss types of new media, with a focus on the Internet. We reveal the ways in which the adult entertainment and gaming industries have fueled the development of new media, and we examine futuretainment audiences and isolate key characteristics of new media as predictors for the future of entertainment. We conclude our study of entertainment and society by taking a closer look at PricewaterhouseCoopers' predictions for futuretainment. We hope that you will find our exploration of the book's topics intriguing, and perhaps even entertaining.

1

That's Entertainment!

Along the highway of life, everything is a roadside attraction.

—Tom Robbins

In this new millennium, Americans view entertainment as a fact of life. We are transitioning into an "experience economy" where we each become part of the commercial marketplace.[1] Today, the entertainment industry packages experiences, access to simulated worlds, and virtual realities. Americans and Europeans gladly admit to spending a very large portion of their income for entertainment. Because a large proportion of human activity is centered on entertainment, it is an important element of society. Entertainment drives social behavior and, as such, it deserves to be studied for its contributions, its significance, and its effects.

WHAT ENTERTAINMENT IS AND WHAT IT ISN'T

The word *entertainment* has Latin roots—*inter* (among) plus *tenere* (to hold)—that mean "to hold the attention of" or "agreeably diverting." Over the years it has come to refer to a constructed product designed to stimulate a mass audience in an agreeable way in exchange for money. Entertainment can be a live or mediated experience that has been intentionally created, capitalized, promoted, maintained, and evolved. In other words, entertainment is created on purpose by someone for someone else. Entertainment is easily located, accessed, and consumed. And of course, entertainment is also attractive, stimulating, sensory, emotional, social, and moral to a mass audience.

And it is a business with specific components, as explained here. Entertainment always exists as a product or service. As a thing, it has an existence, so you can find it, go to it, and purchase it. When we attend performances and events, we are witnessing *live* entertainment. When we receive entertainment in print or electronically, it is said to be *mediated*. Entertainment involves both full and partial dedication. Television and film are industries completely dedicated to creating entertainment as a product. Other industries, such as advertising, use entertainment as an addition to their other services.

Entertainment is always *constructed,* meaning that it is put together with conscious intent. Entertainment is produced with a design and awareness of what it is and what it does. We identify six characteristics of its construction:

1. Entertainment is provided by highly trained experts and experienced professionals who act with a team of contributors.

2. Most entertainment products are the result of multiple inputs from a range of people.

3. Entertainment is usually controlled by a single dominant person or central figure— such as a producer, director, or writer—who organizes and makes decisions.

4. Entertainment is a web of symbols that are shaped, molded, and polished to add to the audience's experience.

5. Most entertainment products rely on technology to maximize their effectiveness.

6. Marketing promotions tell audiences how to experience entertainment before they actually access the product.

Of course, entertainment products are designed to give pleasure, but one of their primary purposes is to attract audiences. To draw, grow, and maintain audiences, entertainment must stimulate agreeable effects for its users. As a capitalist product, entertainment is developed to make money—there is always a bottom line to consider. Secondarily, entertainment may elicit strong emotions, may teach us what we don't know, and can help us escape from real-life experiences into simulated or vicarious ones.

If it sounds to you as if entertainment is everything, you're almost correct. It is part of our everyday life, but there are a few things that it is not.

Entertainment is *not*

1. *art,* although it may aspire to and attain the level of art at times.

2. *ordinary life;* it has a different feel, time, and emotion associated with it.

3. *truth,* because it makes use of whatever will be most stimulating and whatever will make for a better experience.

4. *intellectual thought;* rather, it is more like simple and familiar thought with a touch of surprise.

5. *moral,* because entertainment won't be judged as good or bad for people—just entertaining.

Entertainment Relationships

Entertainment is a product to which we are introduced and develop an understanding of in *growth stages*. We begin as *ignorants* with no exposure and, like illiterates, we are unable to interpret the experience. As *novices* we learn about entertainment and eventually become *aficionados* who appreciate it at a higher level. Some of us become *fans* with strong attachments for the product. A few of us go behind the scene to become *researchers;* others become *epicureans* who prefer the best product available.

People who make judgments or those who evaluate the product and can explain their judgment criteria are called *critics*. *Simple critics* report their experience without explaining why; *true critics* understand different audiences and can explain, argue, and defend their judgment well enough to convince others to agree with them. People who generate original ideas that explain entertainment products and principles are *theorists*. They examine entertainment products from five perspectives: gender, economics, culture, media (the influence of their technological forms), and production. You'll be introduced to several theories later in the chapter.

Entertainment's four constituents are *producers,* who understand the process of putting products together; *creationists,* who are actively involved in creating a particular product; *promoters,* who sell the products, and *consumers,* who pay for entertainment's many products. As you will see in later chapters, consumers are audiences who develop and give away loyalty to a variety of entertainment product brands. Audience relationships are highly valued by the industry for their loyalty and support.

THE WORLD AT PLAY

> *[Leisure] is better than occupation and is its end; and therefore the question must be asked, What ought we to do when at leisure?*
>
> —Aristotle

The story of entertainment and its impact on modern society begins with the advent of *free time* or *leisure*. Leisure is time that is left over after basic survival needs have been met. Citizens of agrarian societies had little time away from their fields to spend in leisure activities; workers in the industrial age also spend most of their time hard at work. Leisure activity began as a way to reduce the drudgery of farming and labor. Songs were sung in fields to music produced with primitive instruments, such as drums and bone whistles. Musical festivities are recorded as early as Neolithic times. Factory workers escaped the dreariness of assembly lines by playing cards during breaks.

By its very nature, leisure is socially stratified—the rich are able to buy more free time than the poor. Because it is enjoyed only by people who can afford not to work, leisure activity was once confined to a few rich and powerful men. Social stratification is evident in ancient Egyptian stories of landowners who were amused by erotic dancers at lavish banquets, whereas the middle classes gathered in beer houses to pass along tales of adventure.

With the inception of private property, a privileged leisure class of men and women emerged with money to spend. Greece became the capital of grand society, generating painting, sculpture, and lyrical songs. Dining and drinking sessions were accompanied by dancing girls and magicians, who often played to scores of drunken guests. Greek aristocrats became the world's first "party animals." Still, only a small minority of men was so privileged; women, aliens, and slaves were not eligible for these elitist benefits.[2]

During the Roman Empire's prosperity during the 1st through 4th centuries, leisure became an entitlement of all levels of society. For unemployed restless citizens, leisure became a pacifier; for workers, it was a form of rejuvenation. Christianity dismantled the leisure state when Emperor Constantine proclaimed it Rome's official religion in 313. After the church began regulating activities, fairs were redesigned as religious festivals, theaters were closed, and actors left town.

Centuries later in America, leisure time was an outcome of the Industrial Revolution, when workers had increasing amounts of free time and could afford to pay for recreational activity. To meet this demand, the recreational service movement was initiated during the latter part of the 19th century and first several decades of the 20th century when recreational activity became a major industry in its own right. Premediated entertainment traces its beginnings to performance and games. Whether leisure activities were practiced as religious, mystical, or cultural rituals, they developed into the theater, games, and sporting events we enjoy today.

Forms of Leisure and the Notion of Play

> We find play everywhere as a quality of action which is different from "ordinary life."
>
> —Johan Huizinga

The way we pass our free time takes various forms, and terms for these forms help us understand their role in society. We refer to free time—time to use as we please—as *leisure,* which comes from a Latin word meaning "to be free." Leisure is activity performed for its own sake, an activity carried on apart from work, that is a function of social class. We engage in three types of leisure:

☆ *Recreation* consists of activities or experiences carried on within leisure, either because of satisfaction, pleasure, or creative enrichment. The recreation industry was developed to provide a way out of the boredom-fatigue cycle by enriching the play activities of youth and by expanding recreational activities for adults.

☆ *Entertainment* refers to a diverting performance—especially a public performance, such as a concert or drama—including the pleasure received from comedy or magic.

☆ *Amusement* is a pleasant diversion, such as a game or spectacle, especially the individual satisfaction derived from play.

Every form of leisure we enjoy today falls into one of these three categories. For instance, physically active adults may prefer recreational activities; other adults amuse themselves by gardening or seek escape through mediated entertainment, or simply enjoy leisurely shopping as a diversion from work. By listing your activities for a week, you'll get some insight into your personal entertainment category preferences.

As leisure time continued to proliferate, people concentrated on expanding the *notion of play*. According to Huizinga,[3] play existed even before culture itself, accompanying and nourishing culture from the beginning of civilization. He asserts that all the great archetypal activities in human society are permeated with play. In characterizing play as a cultural function that separates it from the context of ordinary life, he defined its main characteristics as follows (these traits are expanded upon in Chapter 11):

1. Play is a *voluntary* activity. No one forces us to play.

2. Play is set *apart from reality.* It is an interlude in the day that provides temporary satisfaction.

3. Play is *limited* in terms of its locality and duration. It has a beginning and an end.

4. Play is controlled or governed by *rules*.

5. Play has a sense of persistent social community. Sports fans are such a community.

6. Play promotes a sense of symbolic *secrecy.* It is different from everyday life.

7. Play is a *sacred and profound* activity. It involves rituals, ceremony, and a venue for symbolic representation.

Some aspects of contemporary play may assume different characteristics than those set forth by Huizinga. For instance, in the early 19th century, play was considered an *extramundane activity* because it was thought to provide people with the rewards that they could not find in work or in the consumption of the ordinary world. Yet today, much of our consumption of the ordinary world is filled with all forms of entertainment and play.

Contemporary play is an outgrowth of hedonism. As a facet of cultural movement, hedonism is a shaping force behind our individual pursuits of pure pleasure and immediate gratification. Influenced by the Romantic doctrine that values individualism, power, and sensitivity, hedonistic consumption designates a conceptual framework of leisure activity. Hedonism is expressed in activities such as game playing, shopping, and activities that are self-indulgent as well as pleasurable. As we investigate the development of entertainment, try to identify new aspects of play that add dimensions to its original conceptualization.

Play Theory

Play, viewed as an outgrowth of leisure-time activities, takes its meaning from the Latin word *ludenic,* which refers to games, recreation, contests, theater, and liturgical presentations.

Table 1.1   Classifications of Play

Dimensions	Agon Competition	Alea Chance	Mimicry Simulation	Ilinx Vertigo
PAIDEIA Kite flying	Racing Wrestling Athletics Boxing	Rhymes Heads/tails	Imitation Illusion Magic	Whirling Riding Swinging Waltzing
Solitaire	Chess			Carnival
	Billiards	Betting	Tag	Skiing

Crossword
    puzzles
	Football
	Sports
	    in general
		Roulette	Disguises
			Mountain
			    climbing	

LUDUS				Tightrope walking

SOURCE: From a classification of games developed by Caillois, R. (1961). *Man, play and games.* New York: Free Press. As adapted by Miller, D. L. (1970). *Gods and games: Toward a theory of play.* New York: Harper & Row.

According to William Stephenson,[4] the spirit of play is essential to the development of culture; stagecraft, the military, debate, politics, marriage rules, and so forth are all cultural aspects grounded in play.

Play can be characterized by four classes, each of which can be found in contemporary forms of entertainment:

☆ *Agon* is the principle of games involving two sides, such as football and chess.
☆ *Alea* refers to games of dice, roulette, lotteries, and chance.
☆ *Mimicry* includes acting and pretending.
☆ *Ilinx* is activity that produces dizziness such as that caused by swings, Ferris wheels, and dance.

Stephenson identified three ways of playing:

☆ *Wan* is a quietly sensual Chinese way of playing, such as evidenced in Kamasutra.
☆ *Paideia* is primitive, pure play of carefree gaiety and uncontrolled fantasy.
☆ *Ludus* is formal play, the type found in games with rules, conventions, and skill development.

Play dimensions can be conceptualized on a scale that moves from paideia (improvisation and freedom) to ludus (rules and orders), as shown in Table 1.1. The opposite of work, play teaches loyalty, competitiveness, and patience. Through play, we learn to construct order, conceive economy, check monotony, and establish equity.

Distinguishing play and leisure from work, play theory suggests that work deals with reality and production, whereas play provides self-satisfaction. According to the theory, play is pleasure, and pleasure is a concept at various levels: physiological pleasure (as when a good meal satisfies our hunger); an association with objects and the relationship between self and things (like riding a bicycle); objects themselves (such as favorite possessions); and communications-pleasure (for example, enjoying a film).

ALL THE WORLD IS A STAGE

In the 21st century, the notion of play is characterized by a dramatic worldview that originated from the ancient Greek theater and mythology and is embedded in every layer of Western culture. This worldview assumes a dramatic structure that pits protagonists against antagonists, providing conflicts to be released through denouement and catharsis. The elements of dramatic structure (see Chapter 4) shape our entertainment, as exemplified in sport, game, media, and, most of all, the theater. Modern entertainment can be traced back to live performance and gaming, where audiences were both participants and spectators. In this text, we present entertainment in two forms: *activity where we are spectators* watching others perform in an arena or on stage, and *activity of participation,* such as games and travel, where we become part of the performance.

In the next section, we trace entertainment as it has evolved and developed. Our abbreviated history provides highlights of leisure activities and performers prior to the 20th century—circus, jesters, and troubadours; theater, actors, and puppets; games and sports. For more details, you can consult the recommended readings and Web sites mentioned at the chapter's end.

Three Rings and a Big Top

In the best of times or the worst of times, entertainment has played a role in the leisure-time activities of global audiences. Providing amusement to fill leisure time, the circus and its performers were the forerunners of organized performance. We can trace the origins of Western entertainment back to the days of Pompeii's Rome, where pachyderms and performance were interspersed with chariot racing in what has come to be known as the circus. In keeping with the preferences of the day, Roman circuses featured athletes who fought to the death, dueling with animals and combative equestrians to entertain the masses. Caesar's audiences cheered for gladiators who fought wild animals and each other; his Circus Maximus accommodated 250,000 spectators.

For many of us, one of our first entertainment experiences was the circus, which was first developed in Europe. Unlike Roman circuses performed in an arena, British entertainers performed within an actual ring. During the 18th century, Sergeant Philip Astley, a British Cavalry officer and talented rider, roped off a field near London for a riding exhibition. He perfected the riding ring so he could stand on the back of a cantering horse and entertain small audiences. When he hired clowns to amuse the audience between performances, the circus as we know it was born. Astley covered part of the ring with a roof, added seats, and began advertising his amphitheater riding feats to the public. Later, tumbling, rope dancing, and juggling were added to the circus repertoire.

Performing feats of horsemanship, a cousin of George Washington brought the circus to Philadelphia, enhancing the programs with comic dances and tumbling. After the War of 1812, permanent equestrian shows were replaced by roaming shows that pitched their tents on village greens. These tents, designed and developed by Americans, became the original Big Top of later circuses. Old Bet, an African elephant purchased by a man named Bailey, was such a hit with townspeople and farmers that he accumulated exotic animals from ship captains and presented them in three rings within a tent.[5] From wagons to trucks and trains, the circus continued to reward audiences with its innovation and creativity.

Some of the most famous names in circus performance—animal trainer Clyde Beatty, clown Emmett Kelly, and the Escalante Family of aerialists—owe much of their notoriety to a circus publicist, Shirley O'Connor.[6] The owner of a Hollywood-based public relations and advertising firm, the 82-year-old O'Connor spent 36 years promoting the famous Ringling Brothers and Barnum & Bailey Circuses, where her husband was a ringmaster. Performers such as the Sheep-Headed Man, Flipper Boy, and the Two-Faced Man entertained the public every year as part of the traveling circus during its various routes across America.

Today, hybrid circus offshoots such as Cirque du Soleil have replaced clowns and calliopes with dancers and violins. And although the Big Top still travels to perform in America's major cities, traditional circuses are remnants of a bygone era. How many kids in your neighborhood today would ever think of running away to join the circus?

Comics, Poets, and Actors

Clowns' predecessors, called *jesters*, were small fellows charged with making royalty laugh. They would entertain the guests at parties or perform for kings in private. Dressed in garish colors and adorned with bells, jesters were a combination of puppeteer, juggler, tightrope walker, and official wit. Jesters were both applauded and punished by wealthy landowners who called upon them to perform at their whim in exchange for room and board.[7] Often rejected from courts as palace vermin, ousted jesters became sideshow attractions at fairs. Assuming the role of buffoon, jesters have appeared as characters in comedies by Shakespeare, Victor Hugo, and countless authors who portrayed them as rascals and vagabonds. These one-line comedians are predecessors of late-night techno-jesters such as Jay Leno and Dave Letterman.

Favored by the ladies of the court for their intellectual lyrics, poets called *troubadours* occasionally intervened in the political arena. They invented poems and verses for love lyrics that can be found today in manuscripts known as *chansonniers* (songbooks). Using dance songs with a refrain, troubadours told tales of love. Their songs, put to music in France, Spain, and Italy, are unharmonized melodies of which fewer than 300 survive today. Troubadours are credited with influencing all European lyrical poetry and, as such, are the first intellectual entertainers who performed off stage. Although most troubadour poems are attributed to specific writers, the musical scores remain anonymous.[8]

Other off-stage performers include touring groups who used trained animals and acrobatics to amuse the public during the dark ages. In medieval European courts, performers entertained kings and queens with humor and song. Displaced stage actors, or *histriones,* appeared on street corners and in ale houses as sword swallowers, fire eaters, and mimes. As recently as the 16th century, mimes acted in theatrical presentations of life and death.

Theater, one of the greatest contributions to leisure-time entertainment, was first performed in outdoor amphitheaters for thousands of Greeks. Dramatic festivals were so popular in Athens that business was suspended and prisoners were allowed to attend stage performances. When brought to a raised stage, performances became professional productions. Some of the first stage performers began as clowns. Pierrot, a white clown who performed as the good conscience of a character, began signifying the "good guy" in the 16th century Commedia dell' Arte of Paris. Playing the evil conscience of characters, *harlequins* of the same era wore diamond costumes and masks. In 19th century England, Grimaldi, a satirical character played by a woman, revolutionized male-dominated stage performance. The 20th century's most famous mime, Marcel Marceau, was renowned for his silence and gave mimes their present nonverbal performance mode. And after the Follies became the hit of Paris, women entertained audiences on stage with dance and song. In the American West, burlesque shows in saloons were a primary pastime for range-weary cowboys.

Often rivaling live actors were puppets, whose origins date back to India about 4,000 years ago. Early puppets were tribal ritual masks with hinged jaws or jointed skulls used primarily for religious ceremonies. They evolved into figures with moving limbs and, by the 16th century, marionette operas were very popular in Europe. In the 1700s, hand puppets were used for children's shows.[9] In America, puppet stars appearing on early television included marionette Howdy Doody, ventriloquist's dummy Charlie McCarthy, hand puppet Lamb Chop, and the Muppets.

Playing to Win

Games are a form of play characterized by rules, competition, and one or more elements of physical skill, strategy, chance, and make-believe.[10] Long before there were staged performances, we learned how to amuse ourselves. Gaming began in 2000 B.C. in China as *Wei-qi* and in Japan as the game of Go. Lotteries—in the form of keno—helped to finance the Great Wall of China 3,000 years, ago. From the outskirts of medieval European cities to modern America, gaming has played an important role in the socialization of people.

Entertaining ourselves by playing games is an important aspect of amusement. In 18th-century England, parlor games such as blindman's bluff and charades were alternatives to social dancing. The board game backgammon can be traced to Rome before the birth of Christ. Chess, which came to the West from India, was popular as far back as 700 A.D. Card playing began in Spain about 1300 and, within 100 years, the four standard card suits (club, diamond, heart, and spade) were solidified in France. Between 1600 and 1850, cribbage, solitaire, bridge, and Chinese checkers made their debuts. By the early 20th century, Monopoly and Scrabble were popular; by 1970, Dungeons and Dragons hit the marketplace. In 18th century

Table 1.2   Pre-Media Entertainment Timeline

Century/Date	Country of Origin	Innovation
5000 B.C.	Asia Minor	Musical instruments
3000 B.C.	China	Lottery (keno)
2000 B.C.	Japan	Go board game
1st through 3rd century A.D.	Rome	Chariot races, gladiators
	Greece	Olympic games
	Italy	Morality plays
	Europe	Touring performers
	Italy	Chess
11th century	Spain, Italy	Troubadours
13th century	Spain	Card suits established
16th century	England	Theater, mimes
	Italy	Lottery prizes
	France	Harlequins
17th century	England	Puppets
	England	First public museum
18th century	America	Backgammon, billiards, Monopoly
	England	First woman acts on stage
	America	Big top circus
	France	Follies
	America	Chorus lines

New England, patrons of the British-style pub culture played sporting games such as billiards and shuffleboard, and participated in shooting contests. In the past several decades, arcades emerged as an important part of the gaming industry when they moved from dingy street fronts to regional malls. Today, video arcades gross billions of dollars annually.

Since their beginnings in Asia, lotteries have provided public funding for everything from food to weapons. Italy was the first country to award prize money for winners in 1530; not until 1612 did Americans see winnings from playing the lottery. Lottery profits helped fund the Colonial army in the Revolutionary War as well as most of the Ivy League colleges. New Hampshire began the first state-owned lottery in 1964, and today 38 states have followed the practice. Lotteries provide 250,000 jobs, and more than 240,000 retailers sell lottery products nationwide. Enthusiasts can even play one line at www.megawin.com.

One of the most popular forms of games is *spectator sports*. Home of the Olympic Games, Greece amused spectators with four-horse, 9-mile chariot races with up to 40 participants. Claudius devoted 93 holidays to sporting games; by the 4th century, almost every other day was dedicated to state-supported entertainment. Roman nobles and countrymen alike placed wagers as to who would win battles and discussed the day's events at public bathhouses. An overview of the development of entertainment activities before mass media is provided in Table 1.2.

As global audiences of spectators grew and participants of urban and rural performance increased, public entertainment venues played an important role in the development of modern society. But by the time the first radio broadcast was developed for transmission, audiences were ready and willing to allow some aspects of performance into their homes.

MASS-MEDIATED ENTERTAINMENT

Unlike live performance, mediated activity takes place primarily in the home. The withdrawal of audiences from public venues into private spaces not only changed the nature of entertainment, it also changed how we live our lives. With the arrival of electronic mass media, play shifted from an activity of participation to an activity of visual spectacle. Cable- and satellite-enhanced media entertainment enables users to choose from a plethora of programming to fit every taste and preference in American society.

Since AMC introduced the concept of "first-run movies" in 1959, the film industry has made celebrity the common currency of popular culture.[11] We feed on celebrity activity using every medium available to us. When we tire of chasing celebrity, we use the Internet to log on to our favorite Web sites for entertainment, education, and ecstasy. As the millennium turned, entertainment became a $480 billion industry, finding itself at the forefront of economic growth and cultural evolution.[12]

Today, technology drives many forms of entertainment, competing with but not depleting live performance. In fact, the emergence of theming (motifs communicated through mediated popular culture) has enhanced everyday experiences such as shopping and dining (for example, eating in a theme restaurant). The marriage of performance and technology is evident in concerts where philharmonic orchestras play to films, such as a recent Los Angeles concert performed in tandem with Looney Tunes classic cartoons.

Social Theory

The dramatic worldview, enculturated by mass media, can be explained with three social cognitive theories:

☆ *Framing theory*[13] argues that people use expectations to make sense of everyday life and that our expectations are based upon previous experience derived from media communications. Mass media are a social agent framing our expectations about a dramatic worldview of consumption. Every day we come into contact with hundreds of mediated messages from literature, music, television, and movies that convey a dramatic element influenced by Greek tragedy and comedy. Mass media influence us to believe in a dramatic structure that drives the conflicts and resolutions of our private and public lives.

☆ *Symbolic interactionism*[14] suggests that we give meanings to symbols that may eventually come to control our lives. This dramatic model of consumption represents a set of cultural symbols that are products of social interactions. Symbolic communication transmitted through mass media drives the process of dramatic enculturation. In other words, what we know of the world is a function of our prior communication experiences in that world.

☆   *Social construction of reality*[15] purports that we make sense of what goes on around us from what we learn as active participants in processing, reshaping, and storing pieces of information.

Mass media, then, provide a mechanism through which people seek their self-identities and engage in actual or vicarious behaviors of everyday life. Through media and their symbols, we make sense of our lives through the frame of a dramatic structure. This text views all types of leisure time and dramatic entertainment as play—activities that give people pleasure. Play provides something in common for us to talk about with other people, and sometimes play helps shake up society by being in the forefront of change (we're amused by clever advertising that persuades us to support a cause or buy a product).

As we continue to free ourselves from work, we become ever more engaged in all forms of activities of play. Theme parks, shopping malls, and tourist destinations are popular venues for entertaining consumers and travelers, blurring distinctions between the real and the simulated experience. As this book explores these and other modes of entertainment, *we focus on how "free time" has morphed into "all the time."* Transformed by mass media and seduced into a desire for experience, consuming audiences have entered the world of hyper-capitalism that is fueled by sought-after fantasy and fun.

FADE TO BLACK

From the beginning of time, people have looked to forms of entertainment to relieve the stresses of everyday toil. But only recently has entertainment become the primary activity of a population. In this century, America and most of Western Europe are consumed with the desire for adventure and all forms of leisure-time activities. We begin our day with a workout at the gym, play CDs on the way to work, use e-mail to contact our friends, play a few online games, catch a glimpse of the morning newspaper, listen to a radio talk show on the way home, eat in a theme restaurant, shop in a mega-mall, rent a video, see a movie or TV program, and read a mystery novel before falling asleep. Every activity outside of our jobs is a form of entertainment. Even advertisers promoting brands entertain us with commercials or elaborate promotions. We cannot avoid or escape encounters with entertainment. As you will see in the rest of this book, playfulness and pleasure seeking are everywhere. How does this proliferation of entertainment affect us? Read on.

🔍 A Closer Look

Profiles of Entertainment-Focused Media

Brill's Content. Monthly magazine

Steven Brill and his team of reporters provide insight into media-related issues. Stories range from presidential memoirs to newspaper takeovers to the diary of an unlikely game-show contestant who couldn't escape the media mania that is *Who Wants to Be a Millionaire*. Regular features include How They Got That Shot and Stuff We Like. Numerous editorial columns and a Report From the Ombudsman round out the contents of this incisive and sophisticated publication based in New York City. *$5.95 per issue.**

Entertainment Tonight (CBS).
Evening half hour television magazine

The network's answer to *Entertainment Weekly* (its print counterpart, described next), this program is dedicated to star gazing. Reporters speak with stars and show us clips and trailers of upcoming events in music, television, video, and film. *Free.*

Entertainment Weekly. Weekly magazine

Presented as an insider's view, this quasi-tabloid gives us Sound Bites and tips on a Hot Sheet each week, plus reviews and goings-on at the movies, on television, in books, in music, and on video. Stars are featured on the cover, and color photographs enhance the editorial content throughout the magazine. Graphics in this in-your-face glossy publication take you on a colorful merry-go-round of entertainment activities. *$2.99 per issue.*

ESPN. 24-hour sports network

From football to Frisbee, galloping to golf, or racing to rowing, this network provides sports enthusiasts with live games, match recaps, and previews of upcoming events. *Subscription channel.*

Fade In: The First Word in Film.
Monthly magazine

Graphically sophisticated, this magazine presents interviews, features such as "The Top 100 People in Hollywood (you need to know)," behind-the-scenes stories, and previews of films, print media, and soundtracks. Visit them online at www.fadeinonline.com. *$4.95 per issue.*

Inside the Actor's Studio (Bravo).
Weekly television interview

During this hour-long interview with film stars, acting students ask questions of the guests, many of whom attended the New York City training academy. Paul Newman, Julie Roberts, and Dennis Hopper are among guests who reveal the secrets to their success and talk frankly about the film business. *Subscription channel.*

Interview. Monthly magazine

Thick, matte-finished pages present conversations with film stars, designers, politicians, and just about everyone who is anyone. Sprinkled liberally among the interviews are movie news, music's latest hits, comedy corner, *View,* and fashion details. Upscale ads and great commercial photography make this a pictorial delight for readers who enjoy off-the-wall reading material. Antifeminist critic Camille Paglia, for instance, philosophizes about blondes and why they have more fun. A bargain at *$2.95 per issue.*

New York Times: Arts, Leisure,
Movies, and Performing Arts sections

Every Sunday, two hefty sections of reviews and in-depth analyses of what's happening in the arts feature comments and photographs by journalism's finest. Readers learn what's playing and what's hot, what's good and what's not. Reviews by experts in each field provide entertaining and informative reading for people interested in all forms of entertainment. *$4.00 for the entire Sunday newspaper.*

Rolling Stone. Bimonthly magazine

A hip, trendy publication that's been around long enough to be trusted for "all the news that fits"(the magazine's motto) into the world of music, movies, and television. Random news ribbons color page borders and, like static electricity, photos and copy come together to spark the latest developments in entertainment gossip. *$4.95 per issue.*

Talk. 24 issues per year

In spite of its glitzy format, this publication provides some depth of analysis and investigation on a variety of topics, including entertainment, foreign affairs, society, social studies (trading cards), city journal (travel), talking culture (television), book city, horoscope, and money talks. In one

August 2000 story, the writer wonders what Sartre, the connoisseur of selfhood, would have made of the phenomenon of celebrity. In another, we are told about the re-invention of Daryl Hannah. Then we learn about the next big thing—plus-sized models—who bring fat to the forefront of fashion. *$3.50 per issue.*

Travel Channel. Television network devoted to destinations of interest

Whether you're interested in desert islands, mountain resorts, or ocean cruises, this channel has it all. Advertisers are providers of vacation hotels, airlines, and rental cars, and they often make special offers for channel viewers. *Subscription channel.*

Variety. Weekly trade publication of film industry

Founded in 1905, this international entertainment weekly provides timely industry news as well as special issues, such as "Scrapbook of the Century," with 100 of the most famous mega-stars, moments, and mavens. If you want to read what members of the film industry read, this publication by Cahners Business Information is a must. *$6.95 per issue.*

Wall Street Journal: Weekend Journal of travel, Hollywood, art, and sports

Each Friday, this newspaper presents reviews and discussions of what's current in four areas. A business perspective drives the conservative publication's viewpoints on matters of interest to everyone who has the means to participate in the events available nationwide. *$1.00 per issue*

Wired. Monthly magazine

For some of the best ads and editorial in the age of technology, this magazine is the one to buy. From its forward-looking cover to its glossy photographic text, *Wired* is the essence of the present. Features include Design Is a Chain Reaction, columns such as Zip Drive and Schwag Bag, and the following departments: Rants and Raves, Electric Word, Fetish, Must Read, Infoporn, Street Cred (consumer reviews), Best, New Money, and Verge (creative sparks). *$4.95 per issue.*

*Prices are as of 2001. Note that single-issue prices are always higher than subscription rates.

DISCUSSION AND REVIEW

1. How does Huizinga's notion of play differ from contemporary play?

2. What social theory best describes the communication aspect of entertainment?

3. What roles have theorists and critics played in entertainment development?

4. Take another look at the characteristics of play as conceived by Huizinga. Which of these traits are not appropriate for a contemporary interpretation of play? What characteristics would you add to this list to better characterize play of the 21st century?

5. How has the Eastern play form *wan* been incorporated into Western society? What entertainment genres are rooted in *wan*?

EXERCISES

1. Argue for or against the statement that "all of life is a paid-for experience" by citing, in written arguments, authors who agree and disagree. After presenting both sides, pick one and defend your choice.

2. Keep a 2-week diary of all the forms of entertainment in which you participate and classify them according to the leisure-time categories presented in this chapter. What is the ratio of your paid-for to free activities? What conclusions can you make from this exercise?

RECOMMENDED READINGS AND WEB SITES

McKechnie, S. (1969). *Popular entertainment through the ages*. New York: Benjamin Blom.
O'Connor, S. C. (2000). *Life is a circus*. Philadelphia: Xlibris Press.
Rifkin, J. (2000). *The age of access*. New York: Penguin Putnam.
www.ew.com, *Entertainment Weekly*'s home page

2

The Business of Entertainment

Entertainment—not autos, not steel, not financial services—is fast becoming the driving wheel of the new world economy. . . . An infusion of entertainment content, what I call the E-Factor, is increasingly playing a fundamental role in determining which stores we shop at, what airline we fly, the restaurant where we eat, what clothes we wear, which pots we cook with, which computer we use. Is there a line between "real" business and entertainment? Not anymore.

—Michael J. Wolf[16]

Entertainment is the fastest-growing sector of the global economy. In the United States, entertainment ranks ahead of clothing and health care as a percentage of household spending (entertainment 5.4%, clothes 5.2%, health care 5.2%). Each year Americans spend at least 120 billion hours and more than $150 billion on legal forms of entertainment. Because "entertainment" spans a diverse set of industries, it is difficult to place a dollar figure on the revenue entertainment generates. Some figures estimate that in the United States, entertainment is a more than $480 billion industry, including domestic and international business. That figure does not include tourism or consumer electronics such as television sets and VCRs which, many would argue, are bought primarily for entertainment.[17]

The question, then, is: Why is the entertainment sector outpacing growth in other industries? The simplest answer is: because it can. Economies grow with supply and demand, and, in the case of entertainment, we've seen rapid growth on both ends. Technological advances have increased both the quantity and quality of entertainment choices (the supply). Meanwhile, because other sectors of the economy were doing well, these industries may have flourished simply because people had more money to spend on entertainment "extras" (demand). However, even as world economies began to slow down at the beginning of the 21st century, entertainment industries remained relatively healthy.

Entertainment has blurred beyond its traditional boundaries into other sectors. You can find entertainment in hotels, restaurants, and shopping malls, on news programs, on web sites, and in classrooms. We are entering an age when entertainment touches every aspect of our lives. And, once again, the question is: Why? This chapter explores how economic, technological, and societal forces are shaping and are shaped by the evolution of entertainment.

THE ATTENTION ECONOMY

For several decades economists and futurists have argued that we have moved into a period completely different from the past era of factory-based mass production of material items. During that era, talk of money, prices, returns on investment, laws of supply and demand, and so on all made excellent sense. Today's economy, however, is said to be driven more by the production and exchange of information than by the production and exchange of material goods. The statistics documenting the information proliferation in our society are impressive. For example, a typical weekday edition of the *New York Times* contains more information than the average 17th-century Englishman encountered in a lifetime. In a mere ten-year span from 1980 to 1990, the worldwide production of books increased by 45%. And it is estimated that a new site emerges on the World Wide Web every minute.[18] Many names for the new era have been invoked: the Information Age, the Third Wave, the move toward cyberspace. Beginning with the advent of television and large mainframe computers and continuing with personal computers, the Internet, and wireless products, this era is fueled by revolutionary technological advances in electronic data and communication technology.

Some theorists, however, argue that it is not this abundance of information, but the competition for attention that this abundance creates, that drives the economy. Economist Michael Goldhaber uses the term "the attention economy" to describe this evolving era. He explains why he does not see information itself as a driving economic force:

> Information . . . would be an impossible basis for an economy, for one simple reason: economies are governed by what is scarce, and information, especially on the Net, is not only abundant, but overflowing. We are drowning in the stuff, and yet more and more comes at us daily. . . . What would be the incentive in organizing our lives around spewing out more information if there is already far too much?[19]

It is this overabundance, however, that leads to growing competition for what *IS* increasingly scarce, which is, of course, our attention. Consumers today have more choices than ever in everything from television programs to automobiles to breakfast cereals. Nowhere is this more evident than on the Internet. A few keystrokes will direct Net surfers to numerous Web site options for information on countless products, services, and topics. And yet, although our choices may be plentiful, our time and money are limited. It seems like everyone wants some of our time and money but, to get it, they must first break through the clutter and get our attention. As a result, "the attention age" and "the attention economy" have emerged as popular labels for this new era.

Like money, attention has *instrumental* value because it can get you other things that you might want. Persuasion is often described as a process, and attention is always the first step. Thus, many of those who want your attention may actually really want something else. For example, advertisers are vying for your attention so that they can try to persuade you to buy their products or services. A nonprofit organization may want your attention to persuade you to volunteer or to give money. Your friends may want your attention to persuade you to do them a favor, and so on. Attention, however, also has what is called *terminal value,* meaning that many people value it for its own sake. Consider what kids will do to get their parents' attention or, worse yet, what people are willing to do or say to get on tell-all, show-all talk shows. Even the phrase "pay attention" suggests that attention has inherent value. We value both the attention we give and the attention we receive.

The Entertainment Principle

Attention may be valuable, but money can't buy it, at least not directly. Even if you paid people thousands, even millions of dollars, they could not guarantee you their attention. Most of us can recall books we have tried to read, lectures we have tried to listen to, and programs we have tried to watch. We may have the best of intentions but, no matter how hard we try, there are times when our minds still begin to wander or, worse yet, we fall asleep.

And this, naturally, is where entertainment comes in. If something is boring, we don't pay attention to it. Entertainment captures attention. As a result, an attention economy is also an *entertainment economy*. Whether you are making a film or an advertisement, if you do not hold the interest of your audience—that is, if you do not entertain them—they will stop paying attention.

Ironically, although you may not be able to pay people to get their attention, you may be able to get them to pay you for it. People will pay you for entertainment. And as long as you keep people entertained, you will have their attention. Consumers pay for newspapers, magazines, and books to read, movies to watch, and music to listen to. But you had better have something really good to offer if you expect individuals to give you their attention *AND* their money.

Commerce and Entertainment: A Symbiotic Relationship

The entertainment business as we know it today would not exist without the corporations who have supported it, typically through advertising. Some estimates say 40% of the revenue stream for the entertainment industry comes from advertisements. Today, advertising serves as a primary source of revenue not only for newspapers, magazines, television, and radio stations, but also for Web sites and sporting events. With the emergence of product placements, even the film industry has managed to generate a revenue stream from advertising.

Keeping audiences entertained is not easy. What entertained audiences yesterday will not necessarily entertain them today. Each new book, movie, video game, or shopping mall must be bigger, bolder, better than the last. Of course, bigger, bolder, and better is usually more expensive, but audiences do not want to pay any more for entertainment today than they did yesterday. Although audiences will pay for entertainment, and even pay well, entertainment providers—those who produce the magazines, the movies, and the music—still often find it difficult to make a profit from the sales of that content alone. Newspapers and magazines, for example, rarely make money from publication sales. Their profits usually come from advertising revenues—from advertisers who pay to take advantage of the attention that the publication captures. In fact, the content that actually captures your attention is often provided for free. Broadcast television and radio have always been "free" for their audiences. And often performances such as concerts or sports events may even be "free." However, that free entertainment is provided in an effort to capture audience attention for advertisers. Similarly, concert venues and theaters often do not make a profit from ticket sales alone. Instead, they may make their money through concession sales—the drinks, popcorn, and T-shirts you buy while you are there. Thus, although corporations may not be able to buy our attention directly, they do so indirectly by covering the costs of the entertainment "bait" that will capture our attention for them.

THE BIZ

Nowhere is competition for attention more fierce than within the entertainment industries themselves. This competition has resulted in some interesting trends. In the 1990s, many entertainment-related organizations merged and diversified their businesses. Starting in 2002, some of these same companies began decreasing some of their holdings. Nonetheless, companies continued efforts to extend brands, infuse them with entertainment, and tailor them for audiences and consumers around the world. This section reviews these trends and explores the factors that have influenced them.

Mergers and Consolidations

At the writing of this text, the global media and entertainment market was dominated by eight transnational corporations, or TNCs: General Electric, AT&T/Liberty Media, Disney, AOL Time Warner, Sony, News Corporation, Viacom, and Vivendi Universal, plus one national corporation, Bertelsmann, the Germany-based conglomerate. Nearly all the major Hollywood studios are owned by one of these conglomerates, which in turn control the cable channels and TV networks that air the movies.[20] Take a look at Table 2.1 and see if you can match the corporations with their holdings. Companies such as America Online (AOL) and Time Warner merged, wedding old and new media technology for news and entertainment. Meanwhile, Disney's assets grew to include motion picture studios, a TV network, cable networks, a book publishing company, a magazine division, TV stations, retail stores, theme parks, and

Table 2.1	Match the Parent Company With Its Corporate Holding. In some cases, the parent company may outright own the entity; in other cases, it may only hold a major stock interest.

Parent Corporation	Corporate Holding (as of December 2002)
1. AOL Time Warner	A. ABC Television Network
2. AT&T/Liberty Media	B. Arista Records
3. Bertelsmann	C. 8 Mile (2002 film)
4. Disney	D. Blockbuster (video stores)
5. General Electric	E. NBC television network
6. News Corporation	F. Netscape Communications
7. Sony	G. Sprint PCS
8. Viacom	H. The Young and the Restless (TV soap opera)
9. Vivendi Universal	I. 20th Century Fox

Answers: 1F, 2G, 3B, 4A, 5E, 6I, 7H, 8D, 9C

merchandise. In many cases, combinations of these nine major media conglomerates even share ownership of various assets.

More Choices

Although many factors fueled the growth of these mega-corporations, the competition for attention certainly played a significant role. Thirty years ago our entertainment options were more limited. Television included only three networks and handfuls of local channels, and there were fewer radio stations, magazines, musical groups, amusement parks, and so on. As a result, companies that owned only one of these operations could capture a large portion of the entertainment market. With the emergence of cable television, specialty magazines, the Internet, and other developments, however, entertainment choices began to multiply. Thus, rather than compete with each other for audience attention, companies began to merge and consolidate.

Synergy

In spite of these partnerships, however, the competition for attention remains fierce. This battle is reflected in the growing costs in production, marketing, and promotional budgets. In 1987, it cost $28.4 million to develop, release and market an average feature film. In 1997, it cost $75.6 million. These numbers reflect an average 10% increase in costs every year, significantly higher than the rate of inflation.[21] Such high costs make it difficult for smaller companies to compete. Large companies with diverse holdings also gained leverage through synergistic partnerships. For example, when Disney launches a new film, it engages its publishing, merchandising, television, and theme park divisions to both promote the film and to develop related products.

Figure 2.1   Disney's Synergy at Work

After patrons exit Disney theme park attractions based on Disney-themed films, they are funneled into gift shops featuring Disney-themed merchandise.
©Reinhard Eisele/Corbis.

Consider the film *The Lion King*. Advertisements on Disney-owned television networks promote the film; the film promotes interest in *Lion King* toys, books, spinoff videos, television programs, theme park attractions, and even the theater production of *The Lion King*. Ultimately, each element reinforces and promotes the others. These cross-promotional efforts are not subtle. Indeed, nowhere are such efforts more blatant than they are at Disney's family-oriented theme parks, where the company's family-oriented films are brought to life with film-themed roller coasters and interactive multimedia shows, each with its own themed souvenir shop strategically located so that patrons must walk through it as they exit the attraction (see Figure 2.1).

Diversification

Media mega-corporations also enjoy another advantage. As already noted, to keep audiences' attention in today's market, you must continuously offer something new—bigger, better, more entertaining than what you offered yesterday. It is difficult to keep up with technological advances, and perhaps even harder to predict what audiences will like. Companies must take risks investing in new technology and new ideas, not knowing which ones will succeed and which will fail. It is hard for small companies with limited resources to take such gambles. By "not putting all their eggs in one basket," so to speak, it was argued that large companies with diverse holdings were better equipped to handle the uncertainty and fickleness of the entertainment industry.

Deregulation

Another reason that more entertainment companies have merged and consolidated in recent years may also have been simply because they could. Ironically, in years past, before we had so many different choices for entertainment—particularly media entertainment—many of these mergers and acquisitions would have been illegal. For years, the United States government had antitrust legislation with strict rules limiting ownership because leaders feared that monopolies—both horizontal and vertical—would threaten fair competition. *Monopolies* occur when a single company controls a significant portion of an industry. Industries typically have multiple levels. Some companies may produce the raw materials or resources that are used, other companies may build or develop those resources into products and services, and still other companies may distribute the products and services to audiences and customers. In the film industry, for example, writers develop scripts, studios produce the films, and theaters, rental and retail stores, and cable and television stations "distribute" the films to audiences.

Horizontal monopolies occur when a limited number of companies dominate a single level of an industry—for example, if one company or a very limited number of companies controlled all of the studios, all of the movie theaters, or all of the television stations. *Vertical monopolies* exist when a single company controls a slice of all levels of an industry—for example, if one company owned a talent agency that represents screenwriters, a film studio, and movie theaters, retail stores, television stations, and so on. Although monopolies were traditionally considered a threat in any economic sector, in the media, where many forms of traditional entertainment are found, they were considered particularly dangerous.

In the United States the media have always been considered "watchdogs" that help police the activities of government and industry. Early technology limited the number of outlets for key media. Bandwidth allowed for only a few television and radio stations, and even the number of movie theaters and print news publications was limited. Thus, in addition to concerns about monopolistic problems such as price fixing and restricted consumer choices, people feared that if only a few companies owned all the media outlets, the lack of competition might cause them to abandon their watchdog function and instead control news content and entertainment content for their own benefit.

Media industries, including entertainment, may have wanted to merge and consolidate, but the government would not allow it. In the 1980s, however, deregulation in all industries began to remove some of these restrictions. And, thanks to the introduction of cable, the Internet, and other advances, these barriers broke down even further as the proliferation of new media outlets reduced fears that a single entity might control public information. Although regulations are less strict than they once were, proposed mergers and acquisitions are still closely examined and sometimes denied because of monopolistic concerns. In spite of this scrutiny, feelings about today's mega-corporations are mixed. Advocates argue that consumers gain cheaper, better-integrated entertainment choices. Critics, meanwhile, argue that mega-corporations limit competition, which results in price fixing and reduced entertainment, news quality, and selection. Nonetheless, even most critics would grudgingly agree that these mega-corporations are exceedingly successful at one thing—capturing our attention.

Divestiture and Fragmentation

With an ever-changing economic and political environment, it is difficult to predict how these mega-corporations will fare. At the start of the new millennium, there were already signs that the strain of maintaining such vast empires might be taking its toll on some of these mega-corporations. In 2002, although some corporations continued to merge and grow their empires, others began to *divest,* or sell off, some of their holdings.[22] In October, 2002, Vivendi Universal entered negotiations to sell off most of its publication unit and was receiving pressure from interested buyers to sell its U.S. Universal entertainment holdings. Disney was looking for buyers for its sports franchises, the Anaheim Angels and the Mighty Ducks. AOL Time Warner was also considering selling "non-core" assets, including the company's three Atlanta-based sports franchises and its 50% holdings in the Comedy Central and Court TV cable channels. And Robert Murdoch's News Corporation was working on a deal to get rid of the corporation's stake in Madison Square Garden, MSG Network, the New York Knicks, the New York Liberty WNBA team, and the New York Rangers. In December 2002, *Washington Post* writer Frank Ahrens noted this trend of rapid change:

> Only two heady years ago, the buzzwords in the media industry were "merger" and "strategic acquisition," which were supposed to lead to "combined revenue"and "synergy." Today, the operative phrases are "sales" and "non-core assets," which the companies hope will lead to "debt reduction" and "strategic fit."[23]

Analysts pointed to slumping stock prices and a change in the synergistic value of some of these assets as the impetus for this downsizing. For example, in the case of sports franchise ownership, owning both a television network and a sports franchise was first seen as a way to gain leverage over cable systems for distribution of game broadcasts but, once that distribution was secured, dual ownership was no longer much of an advantage. As a result, many companies' calculations suggested that there was more money to be made in selling the franchises than in keeping them and, in a time of slumping economies, corporations become eager to take advantage of opportunities that might improve the bottom line for shareholder reports.

Converging technologies make it unlikely that there will be a complete reversal, where entertainment conglomerates fragment all of their various holdings back into independent companies under separate ownership. In addition, changes to FCC regulations in 2003 were expected to further relax restrictions on the number and variety of media outlets that one corporation can own, changes that were strongly supported by conglomerates such as Disney, Viacom, AOL Time Warner, News Corp. and other corporations eager to increase their holdings.[24] Thus, it is likely that we will continue to see more splintering and downsizing, but we may also see some more strategic mergers as big media companies continually search for a balance between diversification and streamlining.

Branding

Because competition for attention is so fierce, if you are able to capture an audience, you want to do all you can to keep it. Organizations will often try to leverage the attention they have captured through branding. Branding is critical to almost all industries. Companies such as Nike, Coca Cola, and Microsoft have worked hard to establish brand identities. A *brand* reflects a common thread that runs through a range of products, services, or concepts. At a minimum, that thread usually includes a shared corporate name and logo, but brands usually also extend beyond shared symbols to shared attributes, concepts, stories, philosophies, personalities, and goals.

Organizations use brands to differentiate themselves from their competitors. Consider car brands; BMW is usually associated with performance and luxury, whereas Volvo is identified with safety and practicality, and Honda is correlated with economy and reliability. When an organization places its brand on something, it is in a sense making a promise that specific brand expectations will be met. If the product or service delivers on the promise, the brand is reinforced. However, if consumer expectations are not met, the brand loses its value. If, for example, people buy Hondas with the expectation that they are more reliable than other brands of cars, and all its parts start to break, the brand begins to lose its value.

Brand Extension

After a brand identity is established, organizations can use branding as a shortcut cue to attract audiences and to avoid wasting time and money reintroducing the same attributes, concepts, and so on with each new product and service. And because audiences also want to avoid wasting their time, money, and attention, they usually welcome these branding short-cuts to aid their decision making. Organizations expand their brands by spreading them to new, but *fitted* areas that are appropriate and logical extensions for the brand concept. Thus, Nike, which started with athletic footwear, has expanded to other athletic wear and gear. Similarly, Microsoft, which started with office software, expanded first to other software markets, and then to other computer-related markets, including its most recent foray into the console gaming market with its introduction of the XBox.

Recognizing the power of branding, visionaries began to "brand" entertainment. Disney provides classic examples of branding. Disney wants people to associate their brand with quality, wholesome family entertainment and, although Disney has had its share of controversies, for the most part, people do make this association. Today, the Disney brand that originated with film animation has been extended to a variety of related enterprises including theme parks, hotels, merchandise, and cable stations—all of which strive to be consistent with the quality, wholesome family entertainment brand image.

In some cases, Disney simply extended its brand by expanding its operations into other industries, while in other cases it relied on strategic mergers, acquisitions, or partnerships.

The idea is that people will choose Disney movies, merchandise, or vacations because they would rather stick with a brand they trust than take a risk on an unknown entertainment provider. These branding strategies factor heavily into Disney's decision to pursue new projects. The fact that Disney produced movies titled *Angels in the Outfield* and *The Mighty Ducks* and purchased the professional sports franchises of the same names was no accident. Each new Disney film—*The Lion King, Toy Story, Monsters, Inc.*—becomes a sub-brand that is leveraged throughout Disney's network in merchandising, theme park attractions, television spinoffs, and so on.

Every advance in communication technology, from print to broadcast radio and television, to cable, and finally to the Internet, has provided the entertainment industry with more opportunities for brand extension. Disney is one brand that has capitalized on these advances by expanding its brand into home videos, television programming, and cable channels. At the other end of the spectrum, Playboy is another brand that took full advantage of these opportunities. Worldwide, Playboy is one of the most popular and widely recognized brands in adult entertainment. As technology advanced, the Playboy brand extended from the original magazine into Playboy videos, The Playboy Channel on cable, and Playboy novelty merchandise. With the advent of the Internet came the Playboy Web site, providing original content and serving as a portal to all other Playboy-branded entertainment. Other popular print media organizations, however, did not take advantage of these opportunities. Instead, new brands emerged to fill these niches. Today, it is not *Sports Illustrated* or *Time* or *Newsweek* that we watch on cable—it is ESPN and CNN.

Think Different(ly)

When Walt Disney first conceived of the idea for a theme park, there were many people who questioned his judgment. They could not see the connection between an amusement park and Disney's roots in film animation, but Walt found connections and capitalized on them. The animation of Walt Disney, who was always a dreamer, created new fantasy worlds for his audiences. Disney's theme parks brought these fantasies to life, allowing people to enter and play in worlds they could previously only watch on a screen. To see these connections required thinking differently, thinking outside the box. The same might be said for Playboy's expansion from print to electronic media. Although today such an expansion might seem to be a natural transition, at the time, it was quite a revolutionary move. Indeed, if such brand extension had been more obvious, we probably would have seen more print publications like *Time* and *Sports Illustrated* pursuing such expansion at that time.

Image Focused

Branding should be focused on image or personality, not on a specific product or service. The brand identity must be broad enough that it can be expanded in a variety of ways, yet specific enough that it will differentiate the brand from its competitors. In the 1980s, KROQ, a youth-oriented rock radio station in Southern California, successfully promoted its cutting-edge, contemporary rock image with the slogan "the ROQ of the '80s." However, as the '80s drew to a close, this slogan threatened the station's cutting-edge image. Foreseeing this problem, the station changed its slogan to "the ROQ of the '80s . . . and '90s." Eventually, however, they were forced to abandon the slogan entirely as the new millennium approached.

The focus on image instead of specific products, services, or eras explains why many organizations try to associate themselves with famous personalities. Celebrity endorsements can enhance branding by tying the image of the celebrity to the image of the brand. Athletes are brand favorites because they can help tie images of strength and success to products. Certain celebrities have distinct personalities and images that have been partnered with different organizations to enhance certain images: Arnold Schwarzenegger is associated with fitness, Oprah Winfrey is viewed as the embodiment of open sincerity, and Britney Spears conveys sexy youthfulness. Celebrity endorsements can be very powerful, but they must be approached wisely. To be successful, personalities must be consistent with the brands they endorse. Some things do not fit; for example, although Britney Spears is youthful, a high- profile partnership between Spears and Disney might not be the best fit for Disney's family-oriented image. Even with the best fit, celebrity endorsements still involve a certain amount of risk. Consider the case of Martha Stewart. As a long-lauded icon for tasteful style, Stewart was a popular product endorser. However, her reputation—and, as a consequence, the reputations of the products she endorsed—were severely questioned when serious concerns began to arise in 2002 regarding some of her financial dealings.

E-tizing Consumer Products

As the competition for attention has increased, it's not surprising that all industries are following the entertainment principle. Whereas film producers try to wow you with all-star casts and heart-stopping special effects, companies like Citibank and Ford Motor Company hire consultants to learn how they can incorporate entertainment into their businesses. Citibank launched an advertising campaign featuring Elton John with the slogan "Who says a bank can't rock and roll?" to try to add some excitement and personality to the mundane activity of banking. When Ford launched a new compact car, the Ford Focus, the company hired Lori Dolginoff, a public relations expert from the entertainment industry. Not satisfied with traditional publicity in trade magazines and the auto sections in newspapers, Ford executives also wanted their car featured in high-profile entertainment media such as MTV and key fashion magazines.

Today, products are launched with the same fanfare as feature films or Broadway plays. In 1990, Gillette launched its Sensor razor with an astronomical $175 million marketing blitz, including movielike teaser ads broadcast during the Super Bowl. Sensor captured 9% of the domestic market in the first year, doubled its share the next year, and increased sales by more than $1.2 billion in the first 5 years. In true mega-hit fashion, Gillette launched a sequel in 1998, investing $750 million in development costs and $300 million in an ad and promotional

Figure 2.2   Gillette's Mach 3

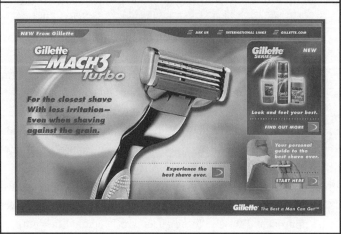

Gillette infuses dramatic Hollywood-type flair into its product promotions. For example, the Mach 3 was introduced as part of a space-age series of products.

campaign for the three-bladed, high-performance Mach3 (see Figure 2.2). The strategy worked. The Dow Jones News Service wrote,

> Everyone knows that Hollywood moguls have mastered the art of creating a buzz in the media. Just consider the movie *Titanic*. . . . But can anything approaching that kind of buzz be generated for something much more mundane than a movie—like, say, a new razor? Judging by Gillette's recent razzmatazz introduction of the Mach 3, the company's newest product, the answer appears to be yes.[25]

Windows jumped on the entertainment bandwagon in 1995 with the release of Windows 95. With a premiere-style launch, *The Tonight Show's* Jay Leno was the first to push the power button for the system, and he did it in front of thousands of reporters and guests. This "premiere" kicked off a 22-city promotional tour, including a Windows 95 box in Sydney Harbor that stood four stories tall. Anthony Edwards, of television's hit series *ER*, starred in a 30-minute Windows infoshow, and crop-circle–style patterns were painted in fields around Heathrow Airport for airline passengers to see.

It's a Small World After All: The International Entertainment Market

Today's entertainment is an international enterprise. The major Hollywood studios— all but one owned by the nine mega-conglomerates—make more than half of their money

Table 2.2 Who Owns the Movies?

The major Hollywood studios, all but one owned by the nine mega-conglomerates, make more than half of their money outside the United States. Here are the top four movies in selected countries in 1999, with ownership information.

Country	Films	Produced in	Film Company	Affiliated Media Conglomerate (if any)
Brazil	Titanic	U.S.	Fox/Paramount	NewsCorp/Viacom
	Armageddon	U.S.	BVI/Touchstone	Disney
	Devil's Advocate	U.S.	Warner Brothers	Time Warner
	The Mask of Zorro	U.S.	Sony Picture Entertainment	Sony
Japan	Titanic	U.S.	Fox/Paramount	NewsCorp/Viacom
	Deep Impact	U.S.	Paramount/ Dream Works	Viacom
	Pokémon	Japan	Sogakukan Productions Co., Ltd.	
	Godzilla	U.S.	Sony/TriStar	Sony
Russia	Titanic	U.S.	Fox/Paramount	NewsCorp/Viacom
	Armageddon	U.S.	Buena Vista/ Touchstone	Disney
	Godzilla	U.S.	Sony/TriStar	Sony
	Deep Impact	U.S.	Paramount/ Dream Works	Viacom
South Africa	Tomorrow Never Dies	U.S./U.K.	MGM/ United Artists	Disney
	Armageddon	U.S.	BVI/Touchstone	Disney
	There's Something About Mary	U.S.	20th Century Fox	NewsCorp
	Deep Impact	U.S.	Paramount/ Dream Works	Viacom

Adapted from McChesney, R. W. (1999, Nov. 29). The new global media: It's a small world of big conglomerates. *The Nation*. Retrieved March 24, 2002, from www.thenation.com/doc. mhtml?i=19991129&s=mcchesney

outside of the United States. As shown in Table 2.2, which identifies the top four movies in selected countries in 1999, American films are popular around the globe. Entertainment enterprises worldwide are growing, and many are also expanding their reach far beyond their own national borders. In the United Kingdom, the earnings of *Trainspotting* (film), Jamiroquai and the Spice Girls (musical artists), *Tomb Raider* (video game), *Teletubbies* and *Mr. Bean* (television programs), and *Miss Saigon* (musical) have created a trade surplus greater than the British steel industry.[26] One of the largest recording companies is also

British-owned, along with one Japanese, one German, one Canadian, and one American-owned corporation rounding out the music industry's "big five" companies.

In destination entertainment, nothing in Las Vegas surpasses the Crown Resort in Melbourne, Australia. With 5.3 million square feet, it has one of the largest casinos in the world, a 500-room hotel, 25 restaurants, 40 bars, 3 nightclubs, and a 2,000-seat theater. In Asia, cities such as Bangkok and Shanghai boast mega-plex malls with 15-plus movie screens, video arcades, discos, restaurants, and the full range of book, video, and movie stores that you would find in the United States or Western Europe. China appears particularly well poised for growth in the entertainment sector. Whereas the United States represents 4% of the worldwide audience, China is home to approximately 20%.

Industry expert Michael Wolf suggests that there is a critical difference between how entertainment developed in the United States and Western Europe and how it is evolving in today's developing countries. In the West, entertainment was at first seen as a luxury. Televisions, VCRs, and computers were items reserved for those with discretionary income. Adoption of new forms of entertainment and entertainment technology happened at a slower pace, as the innovations trickled down from the upper to the middle and lower classes. In today's world—even in many developing countries—entertainment is not seen as a luxury, but as a necessity. As entertainment offerings become a more integral part of our global society—tied closely to news, politics, and everyday life—to actively participate in this society, one must have access to these offerings. Thus, the pace of the "entertainmentization" of today's economies is accelerated, particularly in developing nations that are anxious to catch up with the rest of the world.

Recognizing this potential, leaders in the entertainment industry are investing heavily in opportunities in developing regions, predominantly in Asian countries such as China and India. Savvy leaders have learned, however, that you cannot always simply export Western entertainment products—you must adapt to your audiences. *Time*'s efforts to export its generic U.S. magazine were not well received, but Hearst's *Cosmopolitan* adapted to local audiences by using local editors who edited international content and added relevant local stories. These adaptations can be subtle. "With more than 36 editions of *Cosmopolitan* in more than a hundred countries," Wolf notes, "Hearst has found that women everywhere are interested in the same topics; sex, sex, and more sex—albeit in their own language."[27]

FOLLOWING THE RULES: THE DYNAMICS OF ATTENTION

A review of successful, contemporary entertainment reveals some of the key dynamics involved in capturing an audience's attention. This section highlights some of these dynamics in eight areas, including the importance of novelty and reinvention, exiting on top, people power, time considerations, solitude and shared community, hits and phenomena, alpha consumers, and barriers to entry.

Novelty and Reinvention

Perhaps the most important principle to remember is that what captures attention today may be ignored tomorrow. Audiences are fickle, so entertainers must constantly reinvent themselves and their entertainment. Journalists know that novelty captures the attention of news audiences. Indeed, the name "news" reflects an emphasis on delivering information that is new or different. Similarly, companies market their products as new and improved to gain and retain customers. Entertainers are no different. They know that novelty captures attention. Elvis Presley both shocked and delighted audiences when he introduced dirty dancing to rock and roll. Movies such as *Jurassic Park* and *The Matrix* attract attention with "new and improved" special effects. Although some audiences may have longer attention spans than others, all audiences eventually get tired of the same old thing and start looking for something new.

According to Mike Berry, Disney's senior vice president of operations, in the world of attention and entertainment, the rule "If it ain't broke, don't fix it" does not apply.[28] If something seems to be working, it is easy to become complacent. Writers, musicians, and other entertainers—even hotels and theme parks—may be tempted to stick with formulas and styles that have worked in the past, following the same routine until it "breaks" and they begin to lose their audiences. According to Berry, those who follow this policy may find it difficult if not impossible to win those audiences back again. Instead of waiting until it's "broke," Berry recommends continuously looking for ways to reinvent the old and make it new again.

Companies in the video game industry have learned the importance of reinvention the hard way. Although Atari was the first to put a game console on the market, it was Nintendo who dominated the market in the 1980s. In the 1990s, however, Nintendo began to lose market share first to Sega with its release of the game *Sonic The Hedgehog,* and then to Sony PlayStation's CD-only game console. Today competition in the gaming market is fierce. Not only do companies regularly introduce new games long before players have mastered the old ones, these new games often can be played only on new game consoles.

When Nintendo launched its new console, Nintendo GameCube, in November 2001, the company faced stiff competition not only from existing systems like Sega and Sony, but also from Microsoft, a new player in the console gaming industry, which launched its new console, the XBox, on November 15, 2001, beating Nintendo to the market by three days. Recognizing the importance of novelty and reinvention in this competitive marketplace, the head of Nintendo software development, Shiguru Miyamoto, tried to position the GameCube as a dynamic machine that would evolve instead of stagnate:

> In first thinking about Nintendo GameCube 3 years ago, we envisioned a system that would allow us to create entertainment which would surpass the common definitions of video gameplay. The engineers have given us just that—a machine that not only excels today, but will continue to break boundaries for years to come.[29]

The gaming industry continues to be fiercely competitive. As of October 2002, Nintendo's GameCube was ahead of Microsoft's XBox in projected global sales for 2002 with a 21%

market share compared to Microsoft's 16%. However, both continued to trail significantly behind Sony, whose PlayStation2 was projected to account for 63% of 2002 video console sales.[30]

In music, bands and recording artists whose success spans multiple decades (for example, the Beatles, the Rolling Stones, and Aerosmith) are often described as "reinventing" themselves. Some critics argue that if you listen to the varied sounds of these musicians, you can hear the precursors to many contemporary music trends, including such styles as rap and techno. In fact, rap stars Run-DMC and Public Enemy petitioned for rights to do remakes of some Beatles songs.[31] Other examples of reinvention include artists such as Madonna, Prince, and Sting, who have experimented with different sounds, looks, and names over the years, and bands such as Nirvana and Pearl Jam, who shifted from more traditional hard rock to leading the grunge/alternative movement. Even though audiences have been more receptive to some changes than others, these efforts at reinvention emphasize the value of novelty.

Consumers are drawn to entertainment offerings that are novel and different but, unfortunately, after the novelty wears off, attention may be lost. When consumer businesses begin behaving like entertainment businesses, they are likely to be treated like entertainment businesses. Thus, consumer products and services are also facing shorter life cycles guided by hits and fads. As Gillette and other companies have shown, even products as commonplace as razors must regularly reinvent themselves if they want to survive in the marketplace. This trend presents a problem for many enterprises. Consider the history of entertainment-infused themed restaurants, such as Rainforest Cafe and Planet Hollywood. Both had early success and then quickly faded. Kurt Barnard, of *Barnard's Retail Trend Report,* believes that novelty presents a problem for all themed stores and restaurants because "once you've seen it, you've seen it," he says. "A theme store cannot reinvent itself every four weeks."[32]

Exit on Top

To keep attention, you need to stay dynamic, and you have to be willing to take risks. For every novel concept or idea that succeeds, hundreds of others fail. And for the few that do make it, success is often short lived. As a result, entertainers and entertainment companies sometimes resemble day traders on the stock market as they try to "buy low," hoping to discover the next big entertainment trend, and then "sell high" at the pinnacle of success, right before attention begins to fade. This philosophy is reflected in many popular television sitcoms, such as *Seinfeld, Home Improvement,* and *Mad About You,* that went off the air while still receiving peak audience ratings. In explaining his decision to end his series, *Home Improvement* star Tim Allen said, "I don't like second encores. I don't like people who stay onstage too long."[33] And for good reason. Actors are most marketable when their program ratings are high, because that is when their ability to capture attention is maximized. Often actors leave successful programs to pursue new and different acting opportunities. Although it may be risky to leave a highly rated and high-paying program, actors who wait to look for new projects until after their program ratings drop risk not having any new or different opportunities to pursue. Furthermore, some believe that if you discontinue the show while it is still popular, it will do better in syndication (reruns) than if you wait until audiences have already "burned out" on the program.

The same logic applies to music. When radio stations play a song too frequently, audiences will often get sick of it. To guard against this problem, many stations do extensive marketing research, polling listeners to try to determine when audiences are beginning to "burn out" on a song. Of course, stations tend to play the most popular songs most often, and songs that are good, but perhaps not great, are played less frequently. As a result, top 10 songs sometimes come onto and go off of playlists quite quickly because of audience burnout, whereas many lower-rated songs may remain on play lists longer because they are played less frequently.

People Power

Just as reporters know that readers find stories more interesting when they appeal to human interest, advertisers and marketers know that people pay more attention to personal stories and individual testimonials—who did what and how others have been or might be affected—than to more impersonal facts or statistics. Similarly, filmmakers know that moviegoers often select a movie based more on the stars in the film than on the film's subject matter or plot. As you will learn in Chapter 4, entertainment is driven by drama, and drama is driven by human interest. In books, films, even sporting events, an audience's attention is held by audience members' interest in what is happening to whom and by the anticipation of what will happen to whom next.

People are valuable in an attention economy, some more than others. The more attention you capture, the more valuable you are. Consider Michael Jordan. In his last year with the Bulls alone, Jordan made millions because of his ability to capture the attention of sports fans worldwide. But his salary pales in comparison to the many millions of dollars he made from corporate sponsors because of his ability to capture the attention of their consumers.

Movie stars and athletes are not the only ones capturing attention. When you think of the company Microsoft, who do you think of? If you are like many people, you think of Bill Gates. The old adage that companies are only as valuable as the people who run them has renewed meaning. Economic theorist Michael Goldhaber demonstrates this point by making a comparison between Bill Gates and the late John D. Rockefeller, who served as leader and chief owner of the Standard Oil Trust almost a century ago. Goldhaber maintains that Rockefeller's wealth consisted chiefly of oil fields, oil wells, tanker cars, refiners, and other material things that would have been worth just as much if someone else had bought him out. Microsoft's value, on the other hand, is less tangible—it depends on new concepts and software that is yet to be completely designed. Rockefeller could have sold his interests and still kept about the same net worth, which is what monetary net worth is supposed to mean. But the share value of a company such as Microsoft, which depends on concepts and ideas, depends more on the brainpower behind those ideas.

This logic suggests that if Gates were to decide to sell out and buy control of the XYZ Corporation instead of staying at the helm of Microsoft, Microsoft stock would plummet, and XYZ's stock would rise. According to Goldhaber,

Despite the fact that the arena in which he made his mark happens to be business, it is already true that Gates' actual wealth, and that of many like him, is less in money or shares of stock than in attention."[34]

Thus, Goldhaber argues that business becomes a lively spectator sport. Just as we care about record breakers in football or basketball, we are interested in who heads lists such as the Forbes 400. And he argues that for some on those lists, the main motive for trying to earn still more boils down to wanting attention, wanting to be recognized as number one.

Although attention cannot be bought, it can be transferred. Attention will often "rub off" on things that are associated with it. Celebrity product endorsements (Elton John for CitiBank, Michael Jordan for Gatorade) and corporate sponsorships of entertainment venues (The Verizon Wireless Amphitheatre in California, Heinz Field in Pennsylvania) and events (Tostitos Fiesta Bowl, Hard Rock Cafe's sponsorship of Rockfest, a traveling rock festival) are based on the premise that the corporation will get to share the attention given the celebrities or events. Michael Jordan serves as one of the most convincing examples of the power of these alliances. *Fortune* magazine estimated that Michael Jordan had a $10 billion effect on the U.S. economy while he was playing in the National Basketball Association (NBA) from 1984 to 1998.[35] Jordan's name was a powerful marketing tool. By 1998, Jordan videos had made over $80 million. He had written or been the inspiration for 70 books totaling over $17 million in sales. Michael Jordan cologne had sales of $155 million, and his Hanes underwear exceed sales of $10 million annually. His debut feature movie, *Space Jam*, made $230 million in theaters and $209 million in video sales. These items alone combined to total $701 million in revenue. Jordan's impressive corporate alignments include companies such as Coke, General Mills (Wheaties), Wilson, McDonald's, Sara Lee (Hanes, Ball Park Franks), Upper Deck, WorldCom, CBS.SportsLine.com (Web site), Quaker Oats (Gatorade), Oakley (sunglasses), and Rayovac (batteries and lighting). Bill Schmidt, Gatorade's marketing director, explains Jordan's value: "We've gone into countries where they don't have a clue about what a sports beverage is, but they know Michael. He's instant validation. . . . We manage him like a brand."[36]

One of the corporations that most greatly benefited from the Jordan effect was Nike. Nike's Air Jordan brand made more than $130 million in shoe sales the first year. Over his career, it is estimated that Jordan will gross about $2.6 billion dollars for Nike. But Jordan's value to Nike goes well beyond sales. According to footwear analyst Jennifer Black, his impact on Nike's overall image is almost incalcuable:

> I've been doing this for 18 years, and I have not seen anything like the power of the name, and the ties to consumer, and the sales generated by him. Is it worth double the number he's done in sales? Maybe.[37]

Because attention is so valuable, events or individuals that are good at capturing attention are also highly valued. In fact, Goldhaber argues that attention can serve as currency, making money virtually obsolete. He reasons that the right attention from the right people

Figure 2.3   Michael Jordan

As one of the most successful celebrity endorsers of all time, Michael Jordan has been used to capture attention for everything from batteries to boxers.

can get you everything that money can buy, and even some things, such as attention itself, that money cannot buy. Companies offer celebrities free clothes to wear, food to eat, cars to drive, stays in hotels—all with the hope that consumers will give the same adoration and attention to the company's products and services that they give to the celebrity that endorses them. With the right sponsorships and endorsements, a celebrity like Michael Jordan could probably manage quite well without money. Of course, in today's economy, he gets plenty of that, too.

Time Won't Give Me Time

Once upon a time, analysts predicted that as technology increased, so would our leisure time as computers and other advances continued to do more and more of our work for us. Today it might seem comical, but critics once worried about what people would do with all of their free time. Of course, in reality, many of us may feel like we have less free time than ever. And time is what we want. Surveys show that if given the choice at work between more money and more time off, most people would take the time. This preference is even reflected in our gift giving. For example, although chocolate and roses still are ranked first as Valentine presents, studies found that more than one third of those surveyed give their Valentines gifts of time, such as catered meals, dry cleaning services, or certificates to a day spa.

Even though it may feel like we have less leisure time, studies comparing the total number of free hours that people report having today compared to past decades suggest that the amount of free time has actually remained fairly constant. One reason we may feel like we have less time is because of the many demands for our attention. In addition to work, family, friends, and school, we have organizations wanting us to spend time paying attention to them, listening to their sales pitches, buying their products, using their services, and signing their petitions. It is estimated that the average consumer is bombarded with as many as 3,000 advertising messages each day, all competing for attention.[38]

Similar to television programming, we budget our time into slots. But we only have so much time, so the more things we try to squeeze in, the smaller and smaller each time slot becomes. Because leisure time is a priority, most of us still manage to schedule in a fair amount of it, but instead of enjoying that time in a few long uninterrupted blocks, we break our free time up into smaller but more frequent time segments. And our entertainment preferences reflect these changes. We prefer short books or magazines to long ones. Instead of going to a video arcade and pumping quarters into a machine for several hours one Saturday afternoon, we play games on our Game Boy, sneaking in a few minutes here and there during our lunch breaks, between classes, and while we wait at the doctor's office. Instead of taking one 2- or 3-week vacation every year, we take a 1-week vacation and several long weekends. In the '90s, for the first time, more than half of all holiday trips were weekend trips, according to the Travel Industry Association of America.[39]

When you parcel your time in this way, you want to make the most of it, so you cram in all you can. Tourist organizations respond by packaging deals with airfare, rooms, meals, and sightseeing tours so travelers can maximize their time and money. Similarly, many entrepreneurs have found that they can build successful enterprises by making the chores we have to do more fun. Ventures such as comedy traffic schools, work seminars at mountain or beach resorts, and "shoppertainment" centers attract audiences by infusing entertainment into otherwise mundane tasks. Such time-sharing strategies allow individuals to get double duty—work and play—out of a single time segment, often for only a marginal increase in cost. Consider the costs—in terms of both time and money—of going to traffic school and a comedy show, or a 2-day work seminar and a weekend trip to the mountains, separately versus the costs of the combined offerings. Granted, comedy traffic schools and work retreats do not compare to the pure entertainment value of your favorite stand-up comedians and weekend getaways, but a little entertainment is usually better than none at all.

This time maximizing mentality is also reflected in the increasing popularity of simulated experiences and venues. Video games simulate all types of real experiences, including skiing, golfing, kayaking, flying planes, and even building cities. Water parks simulate beaches, complete with sand and waves. Perhaps the best examples of simulated environments are Las Vegas and Disney attractions, where you can tour Paris, China, Egyptian pyramids, and other wonders of the world without even leaving the country. Figure 2.4 shows Paris

Figure 2.4   Las Vegas, Nevada: The Ultimate Simulated Environment

Pictured here are the sights of Paris, France, re-created at the Hotel Paris, Las Vegas.
© Morton Beebe, S.F./Corbis.

Las Vegas, a themed casino that brings the sights, sounds, and tastes of Paris to the Nevada desert. Consistent with other entertainment trends, these attractions offer a better-than-nothing alternative for those who do not have the time or money to experience the real thing. However, these simulated experiences are often preferred even when the time and money costs are equivalent, or even higher, than costs for more authentic experiences. Instead of going outside and playing football, kids play it on Sega. People who live at the beach drive to water parks. International tourists visiting California bypass the authentic boardwalk at Santa Monica Pier, located only minutes away from the airport, to travel an hour inland to the boardwalk at Disney's California Adventure.

Although such behavior might seem puzzling, simulated environments do offer some advantages. Perhaps the biggest advantage is that they are more controlled. Simulated attractions extract and maximize the best, most popular attributes from the experiences they imitate. Real environments can be unpredictable. You go skiing, and a blizzard leaves you trapped in the lodge, or you go out on the slopes and break your leg on your first run. You go to the beach only to find that a ruptured sewage line has contaminated the water. You travel to Paris, France, as did one of the authors of this text, and all the museums are closed because government workers decide to go on strike. At the video arcade, however, broken bones are mended at the push of a button; at the water park, a set of chemically treated waves arrives onshore every 10 minutes, and nothing ever closes in Las Vegas. Although there are never any absolute guarantees in entertainment, because our time and money (not to mention our life spans) are limited, we look for ways to minimize our risks. And simulated, controlled entertainment experiences do just that.

Solitude and Shared Community

It is sometimes argued that in modern society, people have become more isolated from one another. Today, few families regularly gather around the dinner table to spend quality time together. Fast food and microwave meals make it easy for family members to fend for themselves and continue with their busy schedules. At work, face-to-face meetings are replaced by teleconferencing or email exchanges. Many people no longer go to a communal workplace at all, but instead telecommute from home offices. Many of the chores that used to bring us into contact with others, such as shopping and banking, and even education and exercise, can be conducted at home via the phone, the Internet, videos, or cable television. Thanks to increased urban and suburban sprawl, those who do venture out of their homes often find themselves spending more solitary hours sitting in traffic.

Although most of us welcome the conveniences of modern life, such isolation can make us feel a bit lonely. As a result, two opposing trends have emerged in entertainment. On one hand, because we spend more time alone, there is an increased demand for entertainment that people can enjoy when they are by themselves, such as video games, home videos, books, and magazines. On the other hand, there is also increased demand for shared entertainment experiences that help bring people together. Mega-plex shoppertainment centers create a renewed sense of community where people can come together in one place to socialize, run errands (buy shoes, switch cellular service providers, grab lunch) and have fun (listen to some live music, play video games, go to the movies).

When physically isolated from others, individuals can interact through virtual entertainment. Indeed, the most popular online video games are ones where players get to interact with each other. Online chat rooms, bulletin boards and special interest and hobby club Web sites also provide avenues for entertaining social interaction.

Hits and Phenomena

Every entertainer and entertainment business mogul shares the same aspirations to create the next big hit or phenomenon. In movies, it's the next *Jaws, Star Wars,* or *Titanic;* in television programs it's the next *Seinfeld;* in books it's the next *Harry Potter* or *Men Are From Mars, Women Are From Venus;* in toys it's the next Razor Scooter. Hits are not limited to entertainment, they are also found in other goods and services, such as Kinko's and the PalmPilot. According to entertainment industry strategist Michael Wolf, hits are driven by "high concepts," which are compelling ideas that can be expressed in simple thoughts.[40] It's *Seinfeld,* the show about nothing. It's expressing gender differences as different planets. It's putting a computer in the palm of your hand.

Wolf relates hits and phenomena to German philosopher Friedrich Hegel's concept of a "world historical person." Such a person is said to be so in touch with the times he or she can express the longings and desires of mass humanity. Leaders such as Abraham Lincoln, Martin Luther King, and Adolf Hitler are classic examples of world historical persons who shaped, reflected, and virtually embodied their eras. People feel connected to these individuals and they follow their lead. Similarly, according to Wolf, hits or phenomena might be considered to be world historical products in that they similarly express society's longings and desires. He argues that "hits transform mere commerce into a consumerist culture statement." People define themselves by the music they listen to, the programs they watch, the books they read, the clothes they wear. Hits are fueled by our desire to fit in, to be part of a group. If we haven't seen the latest blockbuster film and aren't wearing the "right" clothes, we feel left out. Our purchases and our entertainment choices give us a sense of belonging. They identify us as rebellious, goth teenagers, yuppie bikers, or soccer moms. Such labels help individuals define the lines between "us" and "them."

By definition, not everything can be a hit; in fact, hits are rare. As with all other products, entertainment marketers are looking for a *unique selling proposition (USP)*—something that sets them apart from and above the competition. In the case of most hits, the USP is not just a fancy gimmick, it delivers on its promise. In the competitive soft drink market, Mountain Dew was able to break from the pack by tying into extreme sports. Given that both soft drinks and extreme sports are youth-oriented, many soft drink brands might have liked to make this connection; however, the high caffeine content of Mountain Dew made the brand uniquely suited to capitalize on the "extreme" concept.

Alpha Consumers

Hits are set into motion by *alpha consumers*. Alphas are the trailblazers among different audiences and consumer groups. They are the first to try the latest market offerings, and they waste no time passing along their verdict to their peers: "I love it; you gotta get one," "Don't waste your money," or "Wait until it comes out on video." In a hit-driven society, marketers are anxious to reach alphas and eager to get their blessing. Reflecting the shift from mass to target marketing, efforts are focused on drawing the attention of key alphas or alpha groups who, it is hoped, will then capture the attention of the rest of the herd. In music, bands usually build followings by word of mouth. The bands or their agents try to secure gigs at venues such as Britain's King Tut's Wah Wah Hut in Glasgow, where other successful bands such as Oasis, Radiohead, and the Verve were discovered by key alpha fans. Recognizing the importance of the alphas, music label executives also frequent popular live music venues, scrutinizing the reactions of the alpha audience to try to determine a band's "hit" potential.

The production and marketing budgets of established entertainment conglomerates continue to grow as they battle to create the next entertainment phenomenon. Some experts, however, argue that the new focus on alpha consumers combined with key technological innovations can actually reduce the barriers to entry for new players on the entertainment market. The Internet has become a popular, low-budget option for reaching alpha consumers. Hits from relative unknowns such as the film *The Blair Witch Project* and the *South Park* precursor *The Spirit of Christmas* were born through this insider-based marketing strategy based on Internet buzz and circulation.

A movie, book, or any other product or service can often enjoy relative success when it is embraced wholeheartedly by one or more subcultures. Such phenomena are sometimes called *cult classics*. Popular among self-proclaimed "anticool" counter-culture teenagers and twenty-somethings, movies such as *The Rocky Horror Picture Show, Harold and Maude,* and *Clerks* are good examples of cult classics. It could be argued that Sue Grafton's alphabet mystery books (for example, *A is for Alibi*), popular among female mystery aficionados, and even Ben and Jerry's ice cream, fit the definition of cult classics in the sense that these classics have extremely loyal fans who identify with each other and with the "brand" in very personal ways.

Typically, however, for something to truly become an entertainment phenomenon, it must attract more than just a cult following. Major hits cross group boundaries, appealing to a wide range of audiences or consumers. The theatrical version of Disney's *The Lion King* became a hit when it became popular not just among regular theatergoers and their youngsters but among audiences of all ages and backgrounds. Similarly, the video game *Tetris* became a hit when moms, dads, and even grandparents began buying their own game units so they wouldn't have to fight their kids for the chance to play. Just as individual alphas can influence their individual groups, an entire group can become an alpha that in turn influences other groups. However, it is not always the same groups that are the first to discover new hits. Whereas middle-aged mothers led the way to the film *Bridges of Madison County*, their daughters led them to *Titanic*.

Barriers to Entry

Today, audiences have more options than ever—more movies, music, television stations, video games, amusement parks, and so on. With all these choices, the challenge to break through the clutter to become a hit might appear more daunting than ever.

And, in some ways, it is. Although novelty does have its appeal, we hesitate to try new things unless we are confident that we will like them. There are no guarantees in entertainment, but we still look for ways to minimize our risks. So we are more likely to go to movies that feature actors or directors or producers from films we have liked in the past. As a result, movies that do well at the box office invariably are followed by sequels. Chapter 6 discusses a similar pattern in publishing, where the same authors appear on bestseller lists year after year. Thus, success tends to breed success in these industries, and the rich do tend to get richer. And yet, as already noted, many recent hits, such as *The Blair Witch Project* and *South Park,* as well as J. K. Rowling's *Harry Potter* book series and products like Razor Scooters, did not come from well-established producers or writers. Some analysts argue that, even though more established producers do have a competitive advantage, technological advances have lowered production, marketing, and distribution barriers to allow at least a few unknowns the opportunity to enter the market.

FADE TO BLACK

The competition for attention has provided a new, empowered role for entertainment in today's economy. Entertainment trends both influence and are influenced by economic trends. And these trends evolve at a very rapid pace. This book was first conceived during the late '90s, when the economy was booming and investors were pouring their money into new technology, new products, and new entertainment resorts. At the start of the new millennium, however, while this book was being written, the economy began to take a significant downturn.

This downturn was exacerbated by the terrorist attacks of September 11, 2001. Travel and tourism was hit hard as people canceled trips and stayed closer to home. The television industry lost advertising revenue as regular programs were replaced with ad-free news broadcasts of the crisis. Several film productions were shelved, such as *Spider-Man,* which included footage of the World Trade Center's twin towers. Nonetheless, while some industries suffered setbacks, others prospered. Film box office overall ticket sales were up 44% the weekend after the attack ($54.1 million compared with $37.8 million from the same weekend the previous year).[41] Video rental revenue rose 30% to $156 million in the week after September 11 and remained high in the weeks that followed.[42] Audiences' entertainment preferences may have changed, and their spending power may have changed, but the demand for entertainment had not. It is difficult to say from month to month, much less from year to year, what entertainment or the economy will look like. But one can predict that entertainment trends will continue to reflect and shape larger economic and societal trends.

A Closer Look

Leadership Qualities:
What Does It Take to Be an Entertainment Mogul?[43]

Leaders in the media and entertainment industries are often referred to as *moguls*. The classic film *Citizen Kane* helped popularize the stereotype of the media mogul as calculating, dictatorial, ruthless, and insatiably ambitious, a combination of Genghis Khan and William Randolph Hearst. Of course, contemporary media moguls might dispute this stereotype. Indeed, many of today's moguls—the Murdochs, Turners, and Redstones—have developed their own unique business styles, but most do share one important characteristic—powerful leadership with a great deal of autonomy in decision making. Mogul management is also distinguished by several other important attributes, described in the following sections, that reflect this powerful, autonomous leadership style.

Educated Gut

To be a mogul, you need to know the industry. You need to read industry publications and know the important industry players. Moguls pay attention to their environment, taking note of what works and what fails, so they can learn from the experiences of others. In addition to this knowledge, most moguls seem to possess a global, intuitive sense of what works. Steven Spielberg, for example, has been credited with having an uncanny sense of when audiences are ready for escape (*Jaws, Raiders of the Lost Ark, ET, Jurassic Park*) and when they are ready for cathartic reality (*Schindler's List, Saving Private Ryan*). The emphasis, however, usually remains more on "educated" than on "gut" because even this intuitive sense is often sharpened, both consciously and unconsciously, by the knowledge gained from past successes and failures.

Educated Risk

Moguls are not afraid of risk. In gambling, you probably won't lose your shirt at the nickel slots, but you won't get rich there either. The same is true in business. To be successful, you must be willing to take some risks, and in entertainment, the stakes are high. Many people thought Ted Turner was taking a big risk when he bought the MGM and Hanna-Barbera libraries. He was cautioned that advertisers and audiences would not be interested in these dated productions, but Turner took the MGM films and created the backbone for the first network based neither on original programming nor on a patchwork of reruns. Turner efficiently took one resource, repurposed it, and created a network. He then turned around and did the same thing with the Hanna-Barbera cartoons, creating the Cartoon Network, a network that has enjoyed higher ratings than CNN, another successful Turner network. These risks that paid off reinforce the value of autonomous, mogul management. If Turner had needed unanimous corporate board support to move forward on these deals, they might never have happened.

Quick-Turn Artists

Because audience attention is so fickle, in entertainment you have to act quickly, or opportunities are lost. This fact again reflects the need for powerful, autonomous leadership. Moguls routinely make decisions of astronomically high dollar magnitudes that CEOs in other industries may never make. A studio head might decide that a film feels right according to his or her educated gut feelings and approve a decision that will trigger production and marketing efforts costing hundreds of millions of dollars. With investments of this magnitude, regular businesspeople would want to check and double-check everything to make sure that you weren't making a mistake, and probably rightly so. However, if moguls had to wade through typical levels of corporate bureaucratic approval with all the checks and double checks, one wonders if any films would ever be made.

Techno-Geeks

Although there are reports that some old-school moguls are so technically illiterate that their idea of Web surfing is to watch videotapes of Web search sessions that assistants have conducted for them, most moguls that are emerging today are exceedingly technologically savvy. Indeed, as entertainment trends are increasingly dictated by advances in communication, transportation, and production technology, today's moguls are often more geek than glamour. The new online moguls, such as AOL founder Steve Case, follow more in the footsteps of computer magnates Bill Gates and Steve Jobs than in those of traditional media moguls like Rupert Murdoch. Life changed for Steve Case, who started in an entry-level marketing job at Procter & Gamble, when he bought his first computer. Predominantly self-taught, Case built an empire playing with the possibilities of online content delivery.

Reinforcements

Moguls, in spite of their power, know their own strengths and weaknesses. They capitalize on their strengths and compensate for their weaknesses by surrounding themselves with good people and listening to them. Steve Case found a complement for his technological knowhow in Bob Pittman, the founder of MTV. Pittman had a strong history of finding new ways to sell creative content. There were music videos before MTV, but they served as little more than underused promotional pieces with occasional appearances in other television programs. With MTV, Pittman created a market for these videos among a youth audience that was starving for entertainment content, and when these young consumers tuned in, so did the advertisers.

Following this same logic, Case provided the technology that attracted an audience for AOL, and Pittman helped build partnerships with companies like Barnes & Noble, the Gap, J. Crew, Spiegel, and others interested in AOL's audience. In this brilliant arrangement, Pittman had AOL position its corporate sponsors' presence not as advertising, but as an added service providing information and online shopping opportunities for AOL subscribers. In essence, instead of creating more content to attract audiences and then soliciting advertising, AOL had its corporate sponsors create content for them, and the sponsors paid for the pleasure of doing so.

Taking a Punch

In entertainment, losing is more the norm than the exception. Most movies lose money. Most television shows never make it past their pilot.

Most songs never get played on the radio. Risk taking is just that—risky. As a result, the gambling analogy holds true; you need to know when to hold your cards and when to fold them. The more you have invested in a project, the more money you have out on the table, the harder it is to turn away. Moguls, however, have learned to accept their losses and move on.

Ted Turner once invested almost $50 million in something called the Checkout Channel. Based on the premise that most buying decisions are made in stores, the idea was to have advertiser-supported programming shown on monitors in checkout lines. Although the idea was good in theory, at the time it faced many problems in practice. With so much at stake, it would have been tempting to tough it out and try and make it work, but instead, Turner walked away from his multimillion-dollar investment and turned to other projects. Even moguls do not win every battle, but they know when to bail out so that losses are minimized. Ultimately, however, moguls become moguls because they win more often than they lose. There are many individuals in the entertainment industry who become rich or at least famous from one song, film, or product. Moguls, however, are not one-hit wonders. Their reputations are built through long track records of success.

Personality Driven

A mogul's personality becomes part of the brand. In new media, for example, Bill Gates's power nerd persona embodies the Microsoft brand. Many contemporary moguls, however, tend to be a bit looser and less conservative than their forerunners, reflecting a lightheartedness more consistent with the "fun" products and services they produce. Richard Branson from Surrey, England, has portrayed himself as the enthusiastic new kid on the block. Branson started with a mail-order music business in the 1970s that he called Virgin Records to emphasize the point that he and his employees were "virgins" in the music industry, meaning they weren't ruthless and hardened like more established music companies. Virgin Records was followed by Virgin Atlantic Airlines, Virgin Net, Virgin Hotels, Virgin Cola, Virgin Cinemas, Virgin Brides (full-service wedding planning), and Virgin Mega-stores. Branson's industries are diverse, but all reflect his fun, fresh personality and brand image.

Resourceful

Moguls understand that whoever has the resources has the power. In 1998, Thomas Middelhoff became the chairman of Bertelsmann, the third largest media corporation in the world. One of the first things he did was to spend an estimated $1.2 billion to acquire a major book publisher, Random

House, and another $330 million in a joint venture with Barnes & Noble to sell books online. His logic is that new media provide many promising distribution channels for entertainment—the Internet, CD-ROMs, DVDs, PDAs, and so on. However, the success of these channels will still be only as good as the entertainment content they have to distribute. Although some individuals are renouncing books as outdated media, Middelhoff sees them as a leading source of content for new media, whether it be for books on tape, on the Internet, on handheld devices, or as adapted screenplays for feature films or video shorts. Moguls see connections and opportunities where others do not. Jean-Marie Messier owned one of the largest water companies in the world, Messier's Compagnie Generale des Eaux, which pipes in water to millions of French consumers. Messier joined the media mogul ranks when he took advantage of the access he already had into millions of homes and added a digital line to his water pipes, creating a digital communication network alternative to France Telecom's monopoly.

Strange Bedfellows

Despite their ruthless image, moguls are more likely to make alliances with their adversaries than to destroy them. Viacom and Cinemax may battle for pay-TV viewers with Showtime/The Movie Channel and HBO/Cinemax, but they partnered 50-50 in Comedy Central, avoiding a bidding war for a limited pool of comedy talent. Music companies Warner and Sony similarly compete for listeners, but in the United Kingdom, these companies partnered in the Entertainment Network, which distributes both companies' music. Such alliances occur when two or more companies possess assets that will be more powerful in combination than they will in competition. By nature, each mogul wants to dominate the market, but moguls have learned that in today's market, alliances are often the only way to build the presence necessary to make a product or brand successful.

Thinkers and Dreamers

Contemporary entertainment moguls are born of varied backgrounds, from print media to television and film to computer networking and consumer goods. Regardless of their origin, however, moguls must be multifaceted. They are both whimsical dreamers and methodical thinkers. Old-school moguls like the Murdochs, Turners, and Redstones, and new-school moguls like the Gateses, Jobses, and Cases, rely equally on creativity, showmanship, and business savvy. They understand what audiences will like and give them the best possible entertainment at the best possible price while still turning a profit.

DISCUSSION AND REVIEW

1. Review the logic for the pronouncement that we have entered an entertainment economy. Do you agree with this assessment? What predictions would you make for the future regarding the relationship between entertainment and the economy?

2. Review the concepts and examples in the "Branding" section. Think of your favorite brands. They can be brands centrally focused on entertainment, like Disney, or only indirectly focused on entertainment, like Nike or Microsoft. Brainstorm ways these brands might extend into other entertainment offerings.

3. Review the principles of the dynamics of attention. Think of some of your favorite brands again, or think of your favorite films, games, bands, and so on and evaluate how they compare to these principles. Rules are often meant to be broken, so look for both consistencies as well as possible inconsistencies that may violate these principles.

4. Review the leadership qualities of entertainment moguls discussed in the "A Closer Look" section. Evaluate yourself in terms of these qualities. Do you have what it takes to be a mogul? Would you want to be a mogul?

EXERCISES

1. For one week, try to pay attention to the ways different individuals and organizations use entertainment to capture your attention. Examples might range from a friend or a teacher cracking a joke, to an entertaining advertisement, to a corporate-sponsored festival, to a giveaway for a new car during an intermission at a sporting event. List as many as you can identify.

2. Does success breed success? Do an Internet search to find a list of the 100 top-grossing movies. Determine how many of the films had sequels that followed. Count how many of the top-grossing films are sequels themselves. Look at the film directors. How many directors have more than one film on the list? Go to the bookstore and take a look at the current bestsellers. How many of the authors have had bestsellers before? Study top-selling video games, toys, and so on in the same manner. Examine the brands to see if there are any trends in which companies are producing "hits."

3. As noted in the chapter, an entertainment economy can change very quickly. Skim through the chapter again, and look for any claims that you think might already be outdated. Do some research to discover updated information on the statistics and information presented in this chapter (for example, statistics on entertainment's impact on the economy, the nine large conglomerates and their leaders, top-ranked films in different countries and who "owns" them). Make comparisons. Have there been any significant changes?

RECOMMENDED READINGS

Adler, R. P. (1997). *The future of advertising: New approaches to the attention economy.* Washington, D.C.: The Aspen Institute.

Goldhaber, M. H. (1997). Proceedings from "Economics of Digital Information," conference hosted by the Kennedy School of Government, Harvard University, Cambridge, MA, January 23-26.

McChesney, R. W. (1999, Nov. 29). The new global media: It's a Small world of big conglomerates. *The Nation.* Retrieved from www.thenation.com/doc.mhtml?i=19991129&s=mcchesney

Wolf, M. J. (1999). *The entertainment economy: How mega-media forces are transforming our lives.* New York: Random House.

3

Look Who's Watching

Understanding Entertainment Audiences

If people want to be entertained, they ought to go to the circus. They ought to go to the movies. Or they ought to go to the ballgame. I didn't sign on [as a moderator] to entertain people.

—Jim Lehrer, on his role as
moderator of the presidential debates

When we think about an audience, most of us visualize a group of people watching something on a field, screen, or stage. Most of us have been audience members with an active role in determining an activity's outcome. We may cheer or boo a live performance, and we may zip or zap electronic content. Either way, we have the power to determine what we want to see and hear. And if we don't like what we see or hear, we walk out or turn it off. That's just what happened during a highly publicized television debate between two presidential candidates in the 2000 election. The viewing audience, taking an active role, turned off the presidential debates that were moderated by PBS newscaster Jim Lehrer. Why? Because they were boring. As quoted at the beginning of the chapter, Lehrer kept to his serious mission, expecting audiences to put entertainment aside and focus on serious political issues. Instead, he was criticized for not providing a lively and entertaining debate. What he failed to recognize is that people in the 21st century expect to be entertained, even when it comes to issues as serious as choosing a president.

Audiences are both spectators and participants. As *spectators,* audiences are amused by actors and their props. Fans are spectators who watch athletes compete against one another. Spectators watch movies and TV to catch a glimpse of celebrities and stars. As *participants,* we challenge opponents by playing games of skill and chance. As travelers, we participate in exploring the unfamiliar; as tourists, we become actors in our own performances.

Participants come in two forms: passive and active. *Passive* participants include symphony goers who experience the event as pure spectators. In contrast, *active* participants, such as skiers or golfers, personally affect the performance experience. The connection that unites consumers with performance has two dimensions: *absorption* and *immersion.* Viewers of television drama are absorbed by the actions of others. Absorption is always performed from a distance. At the opposite of the spectrum, players who are immersed become physically part of the experience. Or, as with players of video games, become immersed in virtual reality.

Audiences are essential for the success of all types of performance. Without audiences, there would be no performance. Can you imagine scheduling a concert and no one coming? Attracting, engaging, and satisfying audiences are necessary activities for every aspect of entertainment. Yet, as important as audiences are, we don't understand as much about what motivates and affects audiences as we'd like to. Especially when we can't see them, such as in the case of mass media audiences—viewers, readers, and listeners. Because our knowledge about audiences is fragmented, the term *audience* itself has an abstract and debatable character. In this chapter, we discuss audiences as they evolved historically from *live audiences* to *mass mediated audiences* to *entertainment market segments.* Then we look at new audience trends and the role of audiences as market segments and their impact on society.

LIVE AUDIENCES

We have borrowed audience concepts from the ancient Greeks and Romans, who gathered for events in a fashion similar to today's. Public and popular events organized for education and entertainment were attended by people who chose to experience performance at a specific location and time. Although content varied, events such as fights, races, games, comedies, and circuses were typically held in urban areas for large publics. Members of ancient audiences had much in common with other viewers and often interacted with performers.

Characteristics of live audiences differentiate them from mediated audiences. Before the advent of mass media, all audiences experienced entertainment live. Culture was transmitted orally, engaging people in active support or participation in all forms of entertainment. We call such audiences *simple audiences* because the term suggests "the persons within hearing" and a certain immediacy in the experience of being a member of an audience.[44] Simple audiences benefit from direct communication. Today we think of audiences as people who plan, attend, and enjoy live-action performances such as concerts, plays, films, festivals, political meetings, public celebrations, carnivals, funerals, legal trials, religious events, and sports matches. These events deliver ceremonial or sacred qualities that attendees cannot obtain elsewhere. For instance, elements of contemporary ceremony involved in attending a theater performance include making reservations, dressing up, socializing during intermission, applauding after each act, and buying a souvenir program.

Communication between theatrical performers and audience is direct. The physical and social distance between them is characteristic of what goes on in concerts, courtrooms, football games, and political meetings. This social separation is reinforced by the contrast between the status of performers and the aura of performance—the stars and fans syndrome. Early researchers thought such social separation would produce passivity in live audiences similar to what we see from mass media audiences who become mesmerized by television commercials. Such an outcome was not forthcoming, mainly because of the exchange and engagement of meaning making that occurs between audience and performers during live forms of entertainment.

An audience is made up of unique individuals. Yet live audiences often behave as a single entity—arriving, sitting, clapping, laughing, and exiting together. Unlike mediated audiences, who view, watch, or listen by themselves, live audiences depend upon social interaction for a substantial portion of the entertainment experience. Live audiences also occupy localized or specialized spaces dedicated to an activity, such as stadiums and theaters, which are reserved for the activity and sit vacant at other times. We call such venues *performance spaces*. They are most often public spaces, even when performances are by invitation only. The use of public space reduces audience-audience and audience-performer distances and enables a wide range of socioeconomic groups to attend performances together.

MASS-MEDIATED AUDIENCES

Today, mass media audiences do not interact with one another or with the performers and are thus hidden from view. *Mass audiences,* then, are detached individuals, anonymous to each other but with their attention converging on something of interest outside their personal environment.[45] Mass audiences have been studied seriously for only the past 100 years, primarily since the advent of radio. These audiences are studied for the effects media have on them. Large media audiences, studied in conjunction with mass communication theory and research, are thought to be in control of their mediated experiences[46] as explained by *expectancy-value theory*. This theory suggests that people have certain expectations from media that determine their media usage. According to one study,[47] expected value is expressed in media satisfactions that are determined by the interactions between the media and their users. Four types of satisfactions are identified:

☆ *Diversionary satisfaction* is achieved when a viewer becomes so involved in the medium that he or she temporarily escapes from other problems and enjoys an emotional release.

☆ *Companionship satisfaction* is derived when media are viewed with friends and companions.

☆ *Personal identity satisfaction* occurs when viewers are able to enhance their self-esteem or feelings about themselves through a mediated experience.

☆ *Surveillance satisfaction* results when audiences gather information by surfing the net or survey news and nature programming.

Media effects theories help us to understand how media influence behavior. Effects are particularly important to psychologists concerned about television violence and programming aimed at children. Media affect both groups and individuals as they engage in mediated entertainment. Research on individuals can be generalized to larger populations.

Understanding an audience member's motives for media choices and charting his or her behavior is called the *uses and gratifications approach*. Gratifications research is concerned with how individuals use the media as resources to "satisfy their needs and achieve their goals."[48] This approach involves a shift of focus from the purpose of the communicator to the purpose of the receiver. It is important for entertainment because it stresses the notion of an individual's potential for self-realization. Studying radio soap opera listeners, we learned that some found emotional release from their own problems while listening. Others listened to escape reality, and still others sought solutions to their own problems in the soap opera plots.[49] Uses and gratifications theory provides several ways of classifying audience needs and gratifications. The theory relates to entertainment using *fantasist* vs. *escapist*[50] classifications; this dichotomy is sometimes also referred to as immediate vs. deferred or informational vs. educational. With this approach, attention is concentrated on making choices and the meaningful encounters with cultural products (entertainment).[51] For audiences, choice relies on psychological concepts, such as need, that are shaped by societal systems. The main point of this theory is that people use media and entertainment for many purposes and choose the ones that provide the gratifications they seek.

Today, scholars believe that messages contained in mass media have multiple meanings and are open to the interpretation of the individual viewer, listener, and reader. This approach is known as *reader response theory*. When two people watch a film and have different views from each other and from reviewers, differences are expected. The film does not have a meaning of its own, only the meaning given to it by viewers and reviewers, regardless of how diverse or oppositional they might be.

Media audiences are sometimes referred to as *markets* because of their usefulness for economic analysis. Researchers use information about mediated audiences to measure sales, determine advertising reach, assess market opportunities, test products, and evaluate performance. Audience demographics are valuable for advertisers, who must match audiences with brands and programming. Because advertising is the primary revenue source for mass-mediated entertainment, attracting large audiences is a very competitive business. In addition to audience size, audience satisfaction and trust are also measured and evaluated for use in program planning. Used with television, radio, newspaper, magazines, and the Internet, audience measurement is important for determining advertising rates.

Mass Media Audience Types

Researchers also study the collective response to media. Some audience groups are studied as *interpretive communities*[52] that bring meaning through the environment in which messages are seen, read, or heard. Mystery novel readers, soap opera viewers, and talk show listeners are examples of audiences who are interpretive communities. Interactive media have created virtual communities that function in much the same way as their interpretive counterparts. Audience participants of such communities take an active role in the mediated experience.

By considering mediated audiences in different ways, we are able to make some distinctions for entertainment considerations.[53] One researcher distinguishes between four types of audiences:

☆ Audience as a *group* or a *public*. Listeners of news radio are one such public.

☆ Audience as a *gratification set,* which refers to audiences that form and re-form because of a particular preference, such as rock concerts. People with a particular need seek out media to satisfy that need—for example, reading tabloids to obtain gossip about celebrities. Gratification sets are driven by social status or by cultural categories and, as such, are of primary interest to entertainment programmers.

☆ *Media audience* includes TV/film viewers, magazine/newspaper readers, and radio listeners. Because rates are determined by these audiences, they are particularly important for advertisers. Audiences defined by *channel* (media delivery format, such as television) or *content* (genre, such as mystery). Viewing audiences—as products of the media channel or media content—have immediate practical significance and clear market value.

Active and Passive Media Audiences

The degree of audience activity or passivity is of interest to the mediated entertainment businesses. Mass audiences, such as viewers of advertising commercials, are thought to be passive because they are incapable of collective action. However, we know that viewers have the power to zap commercials and select programming, making them individually active. Audience actions provide feedback for media communicators, and interactive technology has enhanced the activity potential of mediated audiences.

Today we attribute varying levels of activity to all types of mediated audiences, casting aside the notion that people sit and take in information without the power to act for or against content. In fact, the fact that the influence of concerned parents caused television viewer rating levels to be developed is a vivid indication of mass-mediated audience activity. By understanding audiences as active, we acknowledge their power of choice in the competitive world of media entertainment programming.

In the time of Roman Emperor Claudius, audience applause levels told him what the people liked and disliked, and he catered combative entertainment to their wishes. Today, Nielsen ratings measure television audience levels, but they do not necessarily tell us what components of the media experience satisfy viewers. The entertainment business's dilemma is knowing what satisfies whom and how to provide just the right mix of that which is most desired. For without audiences, it doesn't matter if your entertainment is live or mediated—all forms of entertainment fail under those conditions.

DIFFUSED AUDIENCES

The mediatisation of developed societies disperses the theatrical by inserting performance into everyday life.

—Ben Kershaw

The essential feature of the audience experience as we see it in the 21st century is that everyone has become an audience all the time—it is constitutive to everyday life. This new audience concept is called *diffused audience*. The proliferation of entertainment in our lives has, for all intents and purposes, merged mass and live audience functions into a continuum of message reception: all messages all the time. We will refer to everyone who receives entertainment messages as active makers of meaning who engage in watching or listening for pleasure. To be well received, messages must entertain. The level of pleasure audiences derive from media, performance, sports, and other leisure activities is an indication of entertainment's social and psychological value. We need entertainment to maintain our feeling of belonging and our feeling of well-being.

Entertainment is everywhere we want to be! According to one researcher,[54] entertainment is present in almost every sphere of human activity of Western-developed societies. We can look to the travel industry for an example. In tourist industries, costume drama—as retro-dressing or contemporary couture of slick uniforms—is increasingly the norm. It can be detected as easily in the associated industry of catering, where the waiter and the attendants are encouraged to add a flick of "performative spice" to the dining experience. Have you ever been on a flight where attendants use humor and spontaneity to amuse passengers? Or been served by waiters who sing arias at a cafe? What other examples can you think of where performative spice is added to bring entertainment to customers?

As audiences of everyday performance, we constantly engage in a variety of activities that are akin to entertainment. The notion of performance in everyday life conceptualizes all of society as theater in four ways:[55]

☆ Life is performance because illusion and delusion are issues intrinsic to society. We all pretend or role play. In all our social activities, a particular illusion is created that is difficult to sustain outside that activity.

☆ We all play separate roles, and our roles change with the nature of the performance.

☆ Images of people in everyday life reveal performance as pervasive. We see people enjoying themselves in every aspect of their lives.

Table 3.1   Performances in Everyday Life

Audience	Activities
Activists	Supporting political causes
Constituents	Voting
Consumers	Shopping
Diners	Eating out
Enthusiasts	Being members in club sports and being involved in activism
Fans	Worshiping film stars, rock stars, or celebrities
Jurors	Determining guilt or innocence
Listeners	Enjoying radio shows and music
Members	Communing with a spiritual congregation
Mourners	Attending a funeral
Participants	Being movers and shakers
Patients	Seeking medical help
Patrons	Supporting the arts
Players	Gaming and gambling
Readers	Enjoying mystery and romance novels
Shoppers	Browsing, buying
Students	Learning, studying
Surfers	Using the Internet, switching channels
Tourists	Sight-seeing, buying souvenirs
Travelers	Flying, riding
Viewers	Watching TV or film
Visitors	Frequenting theme parks, zoos, museums
Voyeurs	Viewing pornography
Worshipers	Praying, praising

☆ Performance is specific to contemporary society rather than being characteristic of human society in general because media provide an important resource for everyday performance. Before leisure time and prior to mediated entertainment, performance was an occasional event. Today, performance prevails at all times and is present in every aspect of our lives.

Table 3.1 provides a partial list of audience and activity types found in everyday performance. Can you think of any audience groups that are missing from this list?

It may be obvious from this list that most of our social and personal roles fall into a diffused audience category of some sort. Given the nature of capitalism, we all are audience members all the time because we are constantly consuming some form of entertainment activity. And as we engage in a variety of spectacles, we are simultaneously performers and audiences. For instance, as tourists, we perform consumption roles, buying souvenirs and taking photographs of our travel experiences. At the same time, we are audiences for the entertainment provided by our hosts, such as theme parks, tours, and so forth.

A new trend in *audience characterization* that is suitable for entertainment application is dependent upon the relationship between source and receiver of communication messages and assumes a differentiation of audience and purpose. Three models describe this relationship:[56]

1. In the *transmission model,* audiences are seen as receivers of messages from communicators who wish to influence them. Here, the audience is a target for meaning transfer typical of what takes place through education, public information, and advertising messages. Entertainers use this model to promote specific events.

2. In the *ritual model,* communication is shared, increasing the commonality between sender and receiver.[57] In this model, audience members are essentially participants. Audiences are playful or morally committed. Sports and travel are examples of this model.

3. With the *attention model,* the source does not seek to transmit information, but simply to capture the attention of an audience. In this capacity, audience members are spectators, measured by ratings and box office receipts. In this model, no meaning transfer takes place, but objects of attention can attain fame and celebrity status. The entertainment business prefers these audiences over all others.

Audiences can be differentiated according to the duration that they are involved with an entertainment activity and the degree of engagement they have with that activity. Both elements are determinants of financial success or failure of entertainment events.

Spectacle and Narcissism

Spectacle, the aim of which is to see and be seen, pervades life. Spectacle has come to dominate leisure activities at work, home, and elsewhere. Because capitalism has made everything into a commodity, whole areas of free time, private life, leisure, and personal expression are restructured around activities of consumption.[58] Our society is a consumer society; we gaze upon objects and services for sale, longing to possess much of what we see and viewing much of the world and its contents as if they can be owned. We are consumers of images. Our world is constantly becoming more aesthetic, more like a cultural object that invites our gazes. Everything performs for a diffused audience; we are all involved in a symbolic world of spectacle. We are all looking at one another and, as such, are conscious of people looking at us.

Narcissism is the notion that people act as if they are being looked at, as if they are at center stage for some audience. The word *narcissistic* originated in the Greek myth of Narcissus, who falls in love with his own reflection. Today, narcissism describes a personality type characteristic of people in Western societies, especially those in positions of influence. With a self-image constructed only by images others have, a narcissist cannot easily separate himself or herself from others. Some of the attributes ascribed to a narcissistic personality type include the following:[59]

Figure 3.1	The Word *Narcissistic* Originated in the Greek Myth of Narcissus, Who Falls in Love With His Own Reflection

☆ The tendency to live in the present with no sense of past or future

☆ Dependence on others combined with a fear of such dependence

☆ Worship of celebrity

☆ An inner emptiness

☆ A pseudo self-insight related to personal therapies and self-helps

☆ Nervous, self-deprecatory humor

☆ Fiercely competitive yet fearful of competition

☆ Decline of the spirit of play

☆ Intensely acquisitive and demanding immediate gratification

How many of these characteristics do you recognize in people you know? In yourself?

Some critics write of a narcissistic society[60] with a dedication to self-gratification that results in a projection of self into the world. Here, the self is central to a diffused audience. There is no boundary between self and the world of people and things; what stands outside self is merely a reflection of self. Narcissism requires an active audience that reflects the self. The self is connected to an imagined performance, and self becomes a performer under continual scrutiny. The importance of appearance and style links narcissism to performance. This phenomenon is evident in New Age contemporary spirituality that is founded on self-development and getting in touch with our feelings. How many of us would rather look good than feel good?

The technology of *immersive theaters* and virtual reality now places audiences in a life-like representation of the three-dimensional world, which is modeled after our narcissistic desires. Using the powers of ego, we are building a universe of simulation where imagination is in control. This technology is a place where human narcissism meets metaphysics—where our inflated selves, unable to reconcile ourselves to the real world, create imitation worlds that are better suited to our desires.[61] Tricks of art and technology enable audiences to participate in stories that result in "absolute fakes"[62] that are intended to be better than what they imitate. One visitor to Epcot Center suggests that it's more fun to experience different cultures in one safe location than to travel around the world in fear. The real danger is that audiences may come to prefer interaction with images to interaction with their real surroundings, which would interfere with people's relationship to reality or which could even become sources of addiction.

Diffused audiences, then, are constructed around the relationship of spectacle and narcissism. People, objects, and events are perceived as performances that command audiences. Mutually reinforcing, spectacle and narcissism both demand and produce performances where people are seen as—and see themselves as—performers. We are constantly cast in the role of audience member in some form of entertainment (defined here as *any activity in which people participate for pleasure or amusement*). Often our roles shift, transforming us from audience member to actor, host, producer, artist, and so forth. The activity created by shifting between audience member and performer occupies most of our time. The importance of the active audience to entertainment's success is precisely why we study audiences and why we need to understand the needs and motivations of ourselves and of others as we assume the role of audience member. The most important member roles in today's entertainment economy, in terms of their impact on society, are discussed in the following sections.

Shoppers as Audience Members

We think of shoppers as people who are looking to buy something for a good price. But since the advent of malls and mega-stores, shopping has become recreational. Its offshoot—browsing—is an activity that enhances purchase satisfaction. Shopping is often a social activity, offering a break from routine, sensory stimulation, exercise, amusement, and fantasy. People with time on their hands shop to relieve boredom and loneliness, to explore new products, and to meet friends. For many, the act of buying becomes a means of self-realization. The browsing and buying shopper becomes both audience and performer in the consumption spectacle.

Malls make browsing enjoyable and buying easy. Prices are firm and transactions are usually made with credit cards. Unlike shopping in malls and department stores, bargaining at swap meets or in bazaars involves negotiating prices, and most of the challenge for shoppers lies in obtaining an item for below the asking price. Most of us have experienced the triumphant feeling of bartering for bargains at a fair or garage sale. In countries such as Mexico, India, Indonesia, and Turkey, shoppers can still enjoy the thrill of bartering for many of the goods for sale. One of the authors had the ultimate test during her encounter with Turkey's skilled rug salesmen, and she came away feeling satisfied with her negotiated price. Most Americans don't challenge the tagged or computerized price rung up on digital cash registers—we pay the asking price. Yet the act of looking for bargains (also known as *comparative shopping*) has become this decade's most prolific source of entertainment.

Figure 3.2   Painted Faces of Dedicated Football Fans

© Reuters/Corbis.

Fans and Enthusiasts as Audience Members

Some audience members become emotionally and psychologically attached to certain forms of entertainment or specific entertainers. We call these people *fans.* Extremely devoted followers of a media star, performer, performance, or text are considered *media fans.* Occasionally people form attachments to screen or television stars and carry that relationship beyond the content of the film or show. Known as *parasocial relationships,* these attachments relate to the degree of emotional involvement with a media person. One example is the bond that can be created between a woman and the star of daytime soap opera. Fans of soap operas who form attachments to a specific star may fantasize about the person as if the star were part of the viewer's life. Researchers also measure parasocial interaction to describe the degree of commitment that exists between television viewers and their favorite news persona.[63]

Enthusiasts are also people who engage in a form of audience participation. Certain characteristics distinguish them from fans: Enthusiasts' activities are not based on media images and stars, and their activities are usually more organized.[64] Clubs, sports, and music generate dedication and support from enthusiasts who are productive as members, players, and artists. The distinction is based upon the type of participation rather than the level of support manifested by both fans and enthusiasts. Extreme dedication may evolve from fandom into a cult or subcultural activity typical of the so-called Dead Heads, a group of followers of the '60s musical group Grateful Dead, who could be readily identified by their tie-dyed shirts and hippie-style clothing. The entertainment industry courts fans and enthusiasts because they are the audiences who support every type of leisure activity.

ENTERTAINMENT AUDIENCE RESEARCH

Unless we know what people want, what they'll support, and how loyal they are, we cannot deliver the best sources of entertainment. Sociologists, anthropologists, and humanistic marketplace researchers[65] are currently involved in trying to understand audience members as entertainment consumers. Watching people as they enjoy media and as they browse store aisles are primary activities for consumer researchers. Some current trends are outlined here.

Watching People Watch

Researchers who study entertainment audiences attempt to get inside the heads of viewers by watching them as they interact with media and with performance. Called *ethnographic research,* this type of study investigates how people in a natural viewing environment watch and listen to entertainment.[66] Watching people's television viewing habits over an extended period of time in the homes of 200 families in Wisconsin and California, one researcher[67] found that people use television as both an informational resource and to enhance communication in personal relationships. Some families talked about programs and often interacted during shared viewing times. Others watched in isolation, each watching his or her own set of programs in a separate viewing space. As a result of such studies, we know quite a bit about the effects of television on viewers, particularly the impact TV violence has on children.

The results of audience research tell us that performance interactions involve complex symbolic work on the part of watchers, viewers, and listeners themselves. Yet researchers disagree on how best to proceed in investigating the audience. Some are interested in viewing content (violence, sex) itself.[68] Others are concerned with what makes certain entertainment forms popular (habits, motivations).[69] Entertainment media remain a crucial field of study because ordinary members of the public construct a sense of identity and enter into enthusiastic engagements with others through their various interactions with communicative forms. In addition, audience theory helps to assert the rights of people to take part in popular commercial cultures and to uphold their capacity to think against the grain of media texts. Our pleasurable and private engagements are an important component of modern living and have a symbolic rather than informational focus. Entertainment, researchers have found, allows us to participate in a plurality of popular narratives out of which we construct a sense of selfhood and imagined community.[70]

Watching People Spend

As entertainment flourishes, audiences are studied for their ability to generate revenue. Rather than focusing on how people interact with performance, marketers want to understand why people choose a particular type of entertainment for the purposes of audience solicitation. As consumers of popular culture, audiences as *market segments* are sought-after commodities by producers of every type of entertainment available around the world today. Entertainment marketers tend to view audiences as spectators whose attention is captured, measured, and is cashable in the form of subscriptions, box office receipts, and payments from advertisers.[71]

Marketers often define audiences as targets in terms of their lifestyle; in doing so they tend to construct ready-made identities that may or may not reflect reality. Under conditions of intense competition for audiences, marketers may attempt to control their relationships with those audiences using promotional incentives. Film trailers, for instance, are edited to attract specific audiences; those viewers may be disappointed when they find that the actual film content was not accurately portrayed by the trailer.

A market audience is conceived as[72]

☆ a *commodity,* a commercial transaction
☆ *numbers* yielding revenues
☆ *spectators* whose attention-giving or withholding is the key feature of their relationship to content

The current meaning of the concept of audience as market is extended to include buyers and users of entertainment and technology as much as to encompass receivers of messages.[73] And with this shift comes the expansion of *power* to entertainment consumers. Audience as market segment is a powerful influence on entertainment content because of its ability to make or break specific entertainment entities. Entertainment users today have no particular loyalty to their entertainment suppliers, who are just agencies for making connections personally chosen by individual consumers. Given the number of messages about entertainment options that marketers send to consumers daily, audiences have more chance to choose those messages that interest them and to escape exposure to unwanted information. Much greater ingenuity is now required to catch attention and to engage an audience than ever before.

Audience Segments

Marketers view audiences in terms of their ability to bring revenue to a performance or venue. The process of classifying audiences is called *segmentation.* Although there are many ways to segment audiences—into demographic, psychographic, geographic, and behavioral segments—marketers prefer to aggregate audiences into three consumer groups: present customers, competitive customers, and emerging customers.[74] For each group, a special combination of messages and incentives about the performance is prepared to attract them to a specific event.

Here is an example of how segmentation works for marketers. A new play by Steven Sontine is opening at the Performing Arts Center. To promote the event, three separate strategies are developed, one for each audience segment. *Present customers*—those who are season ticket holders or regular theatergoers—are sent an informational piece announcing the performance. For *competitive customers*—those who attend other forms of entertainment—promotional trailers are developed and aired on television as advertisements. Incentives (such as group discounts, first-time vouchers, and so forth) are used to entice members of this audience segment to try a performance at the Arts Center. To target new and *emerging customers,* ongoing programs are developed to introduce this audience segment to theater and to develop these people into loyal audience members.

By using informational messages for present customers, incentives for competitive customers, and a combination of messages and incentives for emerging customers, marketers can allocate promotional resources in an efficient way to maximize audience attendance. This planning strategy, called *integrated brand communication,* is successful for promoting products as well as entertainment performances and venues. As a marketing director, would you allocate the biggest budget to retaining current customers or developing new ones? Why?

Because audience expectations are high and because people demand a quality product, performance producers must develop brand equity and establish lasting relationships with consumers in much the same fashion as product manufacturers have had to do to develop loyalty from their consumers. Although the concept of audience has changed, the importance of audiences to the entertainment business continues to increase.

FOCUS ON LIFESTYLE SEGMENTS: CONSUMERS AS MEDIA AUDIENCES

Marketers categorize consumers according to their values and lifestyles using a system developed by Stanford Research Institute in Palo Alto, California. Their VALS (Values and Lifestyles) system, developed for North America, segments consumers by self-orientation and resource dimensions. There are three self-orientations:

☆ *Principle-oriented* consumers are guided in their choices by abstract, idealized criteria rather than by feelings or desire for approval and opinions of others.

☆ *Status-oriented* consumers look for products and services that demonstrate success to their peers.

☆ *Action-oriented* consumers are guided by a desire for social or physical activity, variety, and risk taking.

Each of eight resource dimensions specifies distinct attitudes, behaviors, and decision-making patterns. Those segments and their application for entertainment audiences are presented here:

☆ *Actualizers* are successful, take-charge people with high self-esteem and abundant resources. To these audiences, image is important to express taste, independence, and character, and these people do not conform to any single self-oriented behavior. Actualizers are avid supporters of the performing and fine arts, are active participants in competitive sports such as yachting and golf, and prefer exotic travel experiences.

☆ *Fulfilled* and *Believer* segments are principle-oriented audiences who seek to make their behavior consistent with their views of how the world is or should be. Mature and reflective people who value knowledge and responsibility, fulfilleds are well-educated professionals who follow college sports, ski and mountain bike, and travel for business and pleasure. Believers are conservative, conventional people with concrete beliefs based on tradition codes: family, church, community, and the nation. They watch television, go to the movies, coach little league teams, and participate in craft fairs.

☆ *Achievers* and *strivers* are status-oriented audiences who have or seek a secure place in society. Whereas strivers look to others for personal direction, achievers seek recognition and self-definition through achievements in work and their families. Achievers are career-oriented people who are in control of their lives. They take their families to national parks and zoos, support the popular arts, and take cruises. Image is important for what others think of them, and they like driving expensive cars and going places considered to be "in." Strivers are typically low on income and social and psychological resources, but they seek to emulate people who own impressive possessions. They are fans of car racing, play the lottery, attend boxing matches, take trips by car or camper, visit theme parks, and shop at discount stores.

☆ *Experiencer* and *maker* segments are action-oriented audiences that like to affect their environment in tangible ways—makers at home, experiencers in the outdoor world. Experiencers are young, enthusiastic, and rebellious, continually seeking variety and excitement. They surf, kayak, play rugby, and explore wilderness areas. They see independent films, attend rock concerts, and take flying lessons. Makers are more practical, living to experience life through physical work, such as by fixing a car or canning vegetables. They fish, drive pickup trucks, and take their kids camping.

☆ *Strugglers'* lives are constrained by limited economic, social, and emotional resources, and often poor health. Their main focus is on survival and meeting needs of the present moment. Television provides most of their entertainment.

How can the VALS system help entertainment marketers to reach specific audiences? In which segment do you see yourself? What are the limitations of such a system for reaching audiences?

THE CHANGING NATURE OF AUDIENCES

To understand contemporary audiences, we must understand the importance of spectacle. As discussed previously in this chapter, *spectacle* is the notion that everything in the world is treated as something to be attended.[75] Everything in the world is an event or a performance. As such, every object, event, and person is made to perform for those watching. This spectacle/performance paradigm[76] highlights the dimensions of a diffused audience, as follows:

(a) we spend most of our time consuming media of all types, (b) media constitute everyday life, (c) society is performative, and (d) people are increasingly narcissistic. Acknowledging the importance of diffused audiences for entertainment, we focus on the impact audiences have on paid-for performance.

Entertainment providers are realizing that audiences no longer flock to whatever events are presented to them, regardless of effective advertising or brand name. Evidence the failure of Disney's California Adventure theme park built next to Disneyland in Anaheim, California. The park opened with great fanfare and publicity to a very small crowd, and attendance has continued to falter. Reversing its usual no-discount policy, Disney offered a two-for-one entrance policy during the summer of 2001 just to fill the park. The same people who flocked to Disneyland scorned the mediocre rides and mundane amusement activity they discovered at the park next door. The "build it and they will come" notion is no longer the case. Audiences have a plethora of choices and the power to determine what succeeds and what doesn't.

Let's look at six dominant changes in the ways audiences behave.

☆ The old distinction between sender and receiver of mediated and entertainment messages is no longer considered valid. The most obvious force of change is technology, but globalization and market forces are also serious contributors. The model that characterizes communication as sender-directed messages aimed at an audience that willingly makes meaning of that message no longer applies to communication's new internationalized capabilities. As economic growth produces surplus income and free time, a huge demand for media and entertainment products and services is created. Audiences are now buyers and users of technology as much as receivers of messages. The Internet has caused public communication to be personalized and private communications to become more public.

☆ We also expect a trend toward segmentation and fragmentation that results from the increase in opportunities for audiences to form according to factors that cut across residential patterns, such as lifestyle and taste. Specialization in both media and entertainment offerings and the opportunity for multiple choices will cause audiences to become more segmented. At the same time, the same amount of audience attention is dispersed over more and more choices, fragmenting them into specialized niches.

☆ Power has shifted from entertainment providers to audiences as consumers of media and performance. Unfortunately, segmentation and fragmentation have eliminated a way to collectivize and use that power. Former loyalties of readers, viewers, and listeners that stabilized the system have vanished as audience members take up their own interests. Entertainment providers find it more difficult, more expensive, and more unpredictable to reach any large general public. In a constantly competitive marketplace, audiences will decrease and become less attentive.

☆ Another change phenomenon is the creation of new audiences that are great distances from the place of the original production. Much of the world shares the same media experience regardless of geographic location. News coverage, Hollywood gossip, popular music, and brand advertising, beamed by satellite to most countries of the world, contribute to the homogenizing process of mediated global culture. The decline of communism and infusion of a free market and tourism into China have expanded distribution of Western cultural communication. Reproduction of American theme parks allows Western culture to invade Europe and Asia, two continents where Disney has built. Although audiences will continue to experience a dilution of culturally distinctive mediated products, local and regional performance is benefiting from new technologies of production and distribution.

☆ Audiences are now more active, more resistant to influence, and directed by their own particular social and cultural context. Research on the appeal of interactivity, defined as the "quality of electronically mediated communications with increasing control of the process by both sender and receiver,"[77] has yielded mixed results. With self-control, choice, involvement, rich experiences, and resistance to influence, interactivity has many forms. Video games, virtual reality, home shopping, Internet searches, electronic voting, off-track betting, home learning, game shows, downloading music, and so forth all extend the power of the audience to intervene and talk back.

☆ Diffusion has not replaced simple or mass audiences; it has simply added a new dimension. Technology has instituted quite a change from the notion of passive spectator that defined audiences in the past. However, we shall probably retain the term *audience* in its traditional sense and make use of the different social, cultural, behavioral, and economic definitions described in Table 3.1. As we perform for others and watch others perform, we are at once the audience and the performer. By acknowledging this blurring of roles and by creating appropriate spectacles and illusions, entertainers will be able to amuse us well into the 21st century.

As audience members yourselves, perhaps you notice other audience trends. Can you describe any of these changes and what you think is the reason behind the change?

FADE TO BLACK

Entertainment audiences, then, are groups of people who constantly engage in message exchange and who gain pleasure from using entertainment in a variety of everyday contexts. They have evolved from simple, direct association with the performers into isolated masses of media spectators. As entertainment and media pervade our society, audiences assume different roles and become involved in performance once again. Only this time, audience members have dual roles: that of performer and of audience. The diffusion of roles enables us to be participants of the spectacle of life.

Generally, we may characterize the main dimensions of entertainment audiences by their[78]

☆ degree of activity or passivity,
☆ degree of interactivity,
☆ size and duration (how many and for how long),
☆ location in space (where they encounter an event),

☆ group character or cultural identity,

☆ heterogeneity of composition,

☆ social relations between sender and receiver,

☆ message vs. social/behavioral definition of situation,

☆ degree of social presence

Because we are all audiences of some form of entertainment, we have experienced the joys and disappointments inherent in all of its manifestations. By paying attention to audience needs and wants, we can learn how to provide entertainment experiences that are enriching and satisfying. Through audience study, we can also begin to understand how to attract and keep loyal participants in all types of entertainment spectacle.

 A Closer Look

Enthusiast, Fan, or Fanatic?[79]

Most Americans have experienced a sports spectacle. Although emotional reactions to sports vary, some sports enthusiasts experience hormonal surges and other physiological changes while watching games, much as athletes do. Self-esteem rises and falls with the game's score. Tracing the role of sports for society, scientists say that sports re-create the same emotions as tribal warfare did for our ancestors. Sports heroes have been cast as warriors and symbols of self. When the team gains respect for winning, the enthusiast who wears the team's shirt or hat shares in that respect.

Research indicates that people who are *highly identified* with their team show extreme arousal compared to the average fan. Men and women who are *diehard fans* are much more optimistic about their own sex appeal after a team victory. Teams love diehard fans for their support, both emotionally and financially.

The role of spectators for sports teams is important because it determines the success or failure of a particular franchise over time. Building loyal enthusiasts (or fans) is an important function for sports marketers. To determine an individual's attachment to a team and how ardently he or she roots for it, the following test is used in studies to determine fan behavior. Survey respondents report their levels of commitment by circling an appropriate number for each of the seven questions. Take the survey to determine your level of sports enthusiasm.

Instructions:

List your favorite sports team _____.

Answer the following questions based on your feelings for this team. Circle the number for each item that best represents you.

1. How important to YOU is it that this team wins?
Not important 1 2 3 4 5 6 7 8 Very important

2. How strongly do YOU see YOURSELF as a fan of this team?
Not at all a fan 1 2 3 4 5 6 7 8 Very much a fan

3. How strongly do your FRIENDS see YOU as a fan of this team?
Not at all a fan 1 2 3 4 5 6 7 8 Very much a fan

4. During the season, how closely do you follow this team via ANY of the following ways?
a) in person or on TV, b) on the radio, and/or c) TV news or a newspaper
Never 1 2 3 4 5 6 7 8 Almost every day

5. How important is being a fan of this team to YOU?
Not important 1 2 3 4 5 6 7 8 Very important

6. How much do you dislike the greatest rivals of this team?
Do not dislike 1 2 3 4 5 6 7 8 Dislike very much

7. How often do YOU display this team's name or insignia at your place of work, where you live, or on your clothing?
Never 1 2 3 4 5 6 7 8 Always

Where did you score?

Add up the numbers you circled. A score below 18 is considered to be a low identification. Between 18 and 35 is moderate. Above 35 is considered highly identified. From 49 to 56 is the diehard fan level.

DISCUSSION AND REVIEW

1. Explain the difference between the audience of a commercial for Pepsi and the audience attending a circus in terms of active vs. passive participation. Are both activities sources of entertainment? Why or why not?

2. Compare and contrast audiences of rock concerts with those who probably attend an operatic performance using the following dimensions: degree of activity or passivity, event location, group character, social relations between audience and performer, and performance message. In which dimension is the most distinctive difference between the two groups?

3. In what major ways do football fans and football enthusiasts differ? Which group poses a potential threat to other audience members? Why?

4. As an entertainment marketer, how would you promote an event to a passive audience? To a competitive audience?

EXERCISES

1. Record the number of audience participation activities, as listed in Table 3.1, in which you engage during a 48-hour time period. From your record, develop a description of the term *audience* as it applies to your activities. How well does your definition fit into the chapter discussion of entertainment audiences?

2. The Internet is a new form of entertainment with a different type of audience. After going online for one hour doing any activity that entertains you, write a definition of an Internet audience. How well does your definition fit into the chapter discussion of entertainment audiences?

3. Discuss the problems with lifestyle surveys for determining segments. How might the Japanese VALS differ from the American VALS?

RECOMMENDED READINGS

Abercrombie, N., & Longhurst, B. (1998). *Audiences: A sociological theory of performance and imagination.* London: Sage.

Lull, J. (1990). *Inside family viewing: Ethnographic research on television's audiences.* London: Routledge.

McQuail, D. (1997). *Audience analysis.* Thousand Oaks, CA: Sage.

Moores, S. (1993). *Interpreting audiences: The ethnography of media consumption.* London: Sage.

4

Theoretical Foundations

Drama Is Queen

The office of drama is to exercise, possibly to exhaust, human emotions. The purpose of comedy is to tickle those emotions into an expression of light relief; of tragedy, to wound them and bring the relief of tears. Disgust and terror are the other points of the compass.

—Laurence Olivier[80]

DRAMA

The Pleasure Principle

Sigmund Freud maintained that humankind's mental life began in fantasy; the oldest primary mental process was the pleasure-pain principle described as the "waking tendency to shut out painful experiences."[81] The *pleasure principle* dictates that we strive to seek pleasure and to avoid pain. It seems reasonable to assume, then, that an important criterion for entertainment is to bring pleasure. Many forms of entertainment bring direct pleasure; going to a movie, a ballgame, or an amusement park might all result in pleasure. Yet many people seem to be entertained by experiences that, at least at first glance, would seem far from pleasurable—long, painful sports workouts, or movies that bring tears of sadness or screams of terror. What is it about these experiences that makes them entertaining?

Consider another approach. What makes something entertaining rather than just simply interesting? Compare a television sitcom or drama to a documentary or a classroom lecture. Often (we hope) you might find a lecture interesting, but is it entertaining? Have you ever heard a lecture or speech that was not just interesting, but also entertaining? If so, think of what made it entertaining. You may recall a lecture that was really inspirational, shocking, or funny—one that made you feel like your head, heart, or gut was going to burst. The key word here is *feel*. We feel happy when we win a game, perhaps angry or upset when we lose one. We may feel scared when we see a horror film and sad when we hear "that song." Interesting experiences or information are often designed to make us *think* but, with entertaining experiences, a more significant emphasis seems to be placed on making us *feel*. And, to make us feel, entertainers create drama.

Dramatic Formula

Drama is the driving force of many forms of entertainment. Genres such as suspense, tragedy, comedy, and mystery are typically considered to be specialized forms of drama. Although dramatic genres are traditionally associated with books, films, television programs, and live performances, elements of drama can be found in most forms of entertainment, from video games and sporting events to music and dancing. Thus, it might be argued that good entertainment hinges on good drama.

According to Webster's dictionary, drama creates "a state, situation, or series of events involving . . . intense conflict of forces."[82] These events enable audiences to experience the entire range of human emotions. Drama produces conflict and its resolution by depicting events that affect the welfare of dramatic characters: the protagonists (good guys) and antagonists (bad guys). The events that are depicted create a narrative or story in which good and/or bad things happen to the characters involved. As audiences witness these events, they form judgments about the characters and events that transpire. They may love some characters and events and hate others.

According to the *disposition theory of drama,* our reactions to dramatic events depend on our opinions about the characters involved.[83] We feel good when good things happen to characters we like and when bad things happen to characters we dislike. Conversely, we experience negative emotions when bad things happen to characters we like and when good things happen to those we dislike. A drama must include both "lovable" and "hateable" characters, and audiences may feel amused, sad, terrified, angry, excited, or triumphant depending upon what happens to whom. Thus, a winning dramatic formula relies on the strategic use of character and story development to manipulate audience emotions. This basic formula has proven to be successful throughout the ages. In Roman and Greek drama, for example, masks were used for the portrayal of characters. Each mask had its own shape and color to denote the character or emotion being depicted. The most well-known of these are the masks of Comedy and Tragedy, which still symbolize the theater today (see Figure 4.1). One measure of the quality of a dramatic presentation, then, is its ability to evoke desired emotional reactions from its audiences.

Figure 4.1 Entertainment is driven by drama and, according to disposition theory, our reaction to drama, whether it makes us happy or sad, is largely determined by what happens to whom as the drama unfolds.

© Corbis.

One common emotional reaction to drama—whether found in a book, comedy sketch, or ballgame—is suspense. *Suspense* is the emotional experience of anticipation and uncertainty about upcoming events. Thus, suspense occurs before the audience is certain about the final outcome. As the outcome is revealed, the audience's emotional state changes to feelings such as joy or sorrow. Therefore, suspense is an emotion that evolves during the uncertainty and anticipation of that crucial outcome.[84] Uncertainty will trigger suspense, however, only if the audience cares about the fate of the characters involved.

This necessity begs an interesting question. Why do audiences care about the welfare of dramatic characters, particularly fictional characters? Dolf Zillmann proposed two mechanisms by which audiences relate to dramatic characters.[85] The first mechanism is *identification*. Audiences begin to identify with protagonists so that they feel what the protagonist feels to the point where they almost believe they are the protagonists. The notion of identification is often criticized, however, because cues often prevent the audience from feeling as the protagonist does. For example, the protagonist walking through the forest may feel peaceful, but the audience who sees the monster lurking behind the tree and hears the scary music feels afraid.

Another proposed mechanism is *empathy*. Audiences are thought to feel for, rather than with, dramatic characters. Onlookers feel happy and triumphant for the protagonist when things go well, and they feel scared, sad, or angry when things are going poorly. Positive feelings for the protagonist trigger hope and happiness for the character's good fortune and distress for the character's misfortune. Conversely, audiences should feel counter-empathy for the antagonist, resulting in distress regarding the character's triumphs and pleasure for the character's demise.

Most audiences are familiar with the standard three-act "boy meets girl; boy loses girl; boy wins girl back" dramatic plot. Story lines can be varied for different genres by substituting "girl" or "boy" with "life-threatening illness," "secret military jet," or "gruesome space alien," but the basic formula remains the same. In the first act, the characters are introduced; in the second act, the major conflict emerges sprinkled with minor conflicts; and in the third act, the conflicts are resolved. It is not difficult to understand why audiences would find empathizing with feelings of love, joy, and triumph entertaining, but what is entertaining about suspense and conflict? Or, in simpler terms, why must the boy lose the girl at all? Imagine a drama in which a boy simply meets a girl and they live happily ever after. Sound entertaining? Probably not. Conflict and uncertainty are the essence of drama. That is what makes drama exciting and interesting. In life, we often find that hard-fought victories are more enjoyable than those that come easily. Our enjoyment of dramatic representations of such victories is no different. There are many theories that attempt to explain exactly why audiences find drama and suspense so appealing.

Drama's Appeal

Excitation transfer theory provides a physiological explanation for why the standard dramatic formula works.[86] According to this theory, emotional reactions are accompanied by physiological excitation or arousal. When we are afraid, happy, or angry, our body reacts. Our blood pressure rises and our heart rate increases. According to this theory, our body reacts in the same way regardless of which emotions we are experiencing. In fact, it has been suggested that the emotions we feel are simply our subjective interpretations of these physiological reactions. Although we are not consciously aware of it, our bodies may react first, and then we may analyze the situation to determine how we are feeling. The theory further postulates that the physiological excitation that accompanies emotional reactions may linger long after the emotions themselves have subsided. This residual excitation may then transfer onto the next events we witness or experience (see Figure 4.2). We misattribute this arousal to the new event and, as a result, our feelings are intensified. In other words, if we hear a joke soon after we receive a scare, we may laugh a little louder and find it a little funnier than we normally would. The standard dramatic formula is said to capitalize on this phenomenon. The more conflict and suspense there is in the drama, the more excitation there should be to transfer, making the happy ending that much more enjoyable. This theory can be used to explain the appeal of most forms of entertainment. Sporting events, books, video games, films, even roller coasters are all made up of series of "scenes" or events. As the events unfold, the excitation generated from one event, whether positive or negative, transfers to the next, enhancing the overall experience.

Figure 4.2   The Excitation Transfer Process

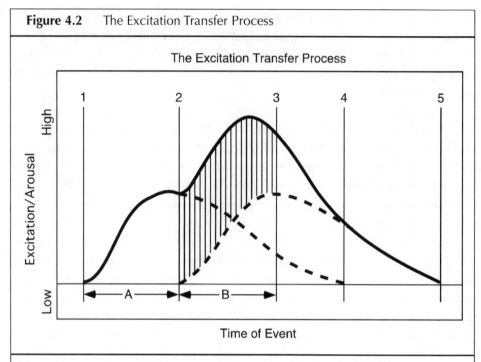

Event A begins at Time 1. By Time 2, the thoughts and emotions associated with Event A may have subsided, but the physiological arousal that is generated takes longer to decay or go away. Thus, arousal is still high from Event A when Event B begins at Time 2. The shaded area indicates the extent to which Event A increases the arousal activity and thus presumably also intensifies the accompanying cognitive and emotional reactions for Event B. The dotted lines show how arousal reactions would have been if each event happened separately.

Excitation transfer theory suggests that the more intensely the audience reacts to threats or conflicts in drama, the more they should ultimately enjoy the happy ending. Some scholars, however, have questioned whether that is the *only* value of the intense, negative emotions that drama can evoke. They question why audiences would tolerate what are often long periods of negative emotional circumstances, only to experience relief through excitation transfer in the last few minutes or seconds, if at all.

One popular theory used to explain the appeal of most forms of entertainment is *escapism*. According to this notion, entertainment can serve as an escape or diversion from the worries and shortcomings of everyday life. If the enjoyment of drama primarily hinges on its ability to distract audience members from real-world problems, it may not matter what emotions the drama creates—fear, anger, sadness, joy, amusement—as long as it makes them forget their own concerns. Another suggestion is that drama serves an *informative and self-reflective function*. In almost direct opposition to escapism, this theory suggests that some audiences may enjoy drama because it allows them to reflect on their own feelings and experiences.[87] This notion suggests that individuals enjoy drama that parallels their own lives because it allows them to replay events they have experienced, evaluate their actions, and get ideas for how to act and react in the future. For drama to serve this function, it needs to be realistic; indeed, some might argue that if real life appears to include a great deal of conflict and suffering, so should drama.

Mood management theory similarly suggests that audiences often seek out media (and presumably other forms of entertainment) that will enhance their moods. This theory rests on the premise of *selective exposure*—namely, that audiences will seek information and experiences consistent with their feelings and beliefs and will avoid those that are inconsistent. This theory is a popular explanation for the appeal of tragedy. Indeed, there is evidence that people, particularly women, are more likely to select sad songs or movies when they are sad, and to avoid them when they are happy. Note, however, that the basic theory is not called mood enhancement, but mood management, reflecting the notion that people may sometimes seek to change rather than enhance their moods. Thus, although some individuals may prefer sad music or stories when they are upset, others may search for something more upbeat to cheer themselves up.

GENRES

Although the general theories discussed in the previous section are applicable to most forms of drama, certain dramatic genres also possess unique appeals (see Table 4.1). Here we review some of the unique qualities of major genres, including tragedy, mystery, comedy, and action/horror.

Tragedy

As with all drama, tragedy depends on the audience's dispositions toward the dramatic characters. In contrast to traditional drama, however, where good usually triumphs, the essence of tragedy is bad things happening to good people. If audiences do not perceive a character as noble or good, they will not interpret the character's misfortune as tragic. Thus, the formula for good tragedy is to create very good, noble characters who meet terrible fates. A common theme in tragedy, as found in many of Shakespeare's plays and sonnets, is love lost. Lost love is also a popular theme in contemporary tragedy, including films such as *Titanic*. Tragic elements are also found in many award-winning television dramas (such as *ER* and *The West Wing*), in popular novels (such as Anne Rice's vampire books), and, of course, in countless love songs.

Similar to how individuals enjoy other forms of drama, they may welcome tragedy as an escape from their own problems or, as mood management theory suggests, individuals may prefer tragedy when they are upset because it matches their mood. Following the old adage that misery loves company, it may be that those who are sad or upset find dramatic tragedy comforting because it makes them feel that others share and understand their pain and despair. Several other explanations have also been offered. Dating back to Aristotle, the

Table 4.1   A Review of Major Genres

Dramatic genres each have their own unique characteristics and formulas. This chart provides descriptions and examples for a few select genres.

Genre	Formulas and Characteristics	Examples (from film, television, etc.)
Tragedy	Features a tragic ending, where bad things happen to good people.	*Romeo and Juliet, Titanic,* many country songs
Mystery	Begins with what happened and traces back to "whodunit." Introduces numerous possibilities.	*The Usual Suspects, LA Confidential, Clue* (board game and movie), Mary Higgins Clark novels
Comedy	Disparagement and putdowns with light-hearted cues. Irony, incongruities, and resolutions.	*Meet the Parents,* the *Three Stooges, The Simpsons,* Jay Leno's monologue on *The Tonight Show*
Action/ Horror	Aggressive battles between good guys and bad guys—good guys usually win in the end.	*Star Wars,* war films, *Dracula, Jaws,* Stephen King novels and films

catharsis doctrine provides one of the oldest explanations for the appeal of tragedy and dramatic distress. *Catharsis* is described as the therapeutic release of emotions that cause tension or anxiety. It is argued that, instead of acting on their emotions, individuals who harbor fears or anger resulting from certain life experiences may be relieved of their feelings by vicariously living through similar experiences found in games or depicted in drama. Thus, this theory suggests that audiences may enjoy conflict and tragedy because it provides them with an opportunity to purge rather than enhance any negative feelings that they have been experiencing. *Social comparison* theory offers a related explanation. This theory states that people feel better when they can make favorable comparisons between themselves and others. According to this theory, people may feel better about their lives when they can compare themselves to individuals who "have it worse." Thus, another reason individuals may enjoy conflict and tragedy drama is because it provides them with ample opportunities to make favorable life comparisons.

Although good characters often die, in many cases one or more protagonists remain to cope with the aftermath of the tragedy. Thus, tragedy may also provide a particularly valuable *informative function* by demonstrating successful coping strategies for people facing similar personal tragedies. Finally, another thought is that people simply enjoy experiencing the range of human emotions. We tend to assume that emotions such as anger, sadness, and fear are unpleasant, but the success of such genres as tragedy and horror suggest that some individuals may actually enjoy these emotions. Of course, experiencing these emotions through drama allows a certain amount of safety or detachment. Audience members are free to feel sorrow or fear without actually having to cope with the situations that created those emotions. The feelings drama creates have been called *meta-emotions,* suggesting that it may not be the emotions themselves that audiences enjoy as much as it is that they appreciate drama's ability to "safely" but effectively simulate such intense emotions.

Mystery

In standard suspense stories, there are typically only two major outcomes. The protagonist either defeats the opponent or does not. The heroine either defuses the bomb, or the building explodes. Suspense is enhanced by the magnitude of the potential consequences and by the intensity of the audience's preference for one outcome over the other. In a mystery, however, uncertainty is enhanced by introducing numerous possibilities. Mysteries are often retrospective. The outcome may be known (something is stolen or someone is killed). The suspense revolves around the uncertainty of who did it and/or how it happened. Thus a good, suspenseful mystery is one in which several equally viable possibilities are presented. It is argued, however, that the involvement of too many suspects and situations may overwhelm audiences to the point where they lose interest. Mystery can be found not only in books, plays, and films, but also in board games, video games, and promotional contests. Magic acts are shrouded in mystery, and themed dinner theaters that put on live mysteries, where guests can actively solve and even participate in a mystery, are gaining in popularity.

Some mysteries are designed so that, although the solution is not overly obvious, audience members should be able to solve the mystery as they go, ultimately having their suspicions *confirmed* at the end when all is revealed. Other mysteries keep the audience guessing the entire time, maximizing *uncertainty*. Still others lead the audience on, making them feel they know who did what and how, only to *surprise* them in the end. Audiences are thought to vary in terms of the types of mystery outcomes they enjoy.[88] Although some individuals might prefer having their suspicions confirmed, others may prefer mysteries that surprise them or keep them guessing. Researchers speculate that thrill and sensation seekers, who value confronting problems more than they value solving them, might prefer uncertainty-maximizing mysteries because solutions terminate the thrill of the unknown. In contrast, the surprise model should be favored by individuals who love to take on a challenge and who are not disturbed when they are outwitted. And finally, the confirmation model might prove more satisfying to persons of low self–esteem because they may feel better about themselves when their hunches are validated. It is also possible that individuals may prefer different types of mysteries at different times, depending upon their moods.

Humor and Comedy

Comedy abounds as a source for entertainment. In fact, comedy accounts for almost one half of the top movies and television programs of all time (see Figures 4.3 and 4.4). In addition to the standard dramatic outlets of film, television, and print media, comedy is also popular in radio shows and in live performances. Comedy is typically considered to be a form

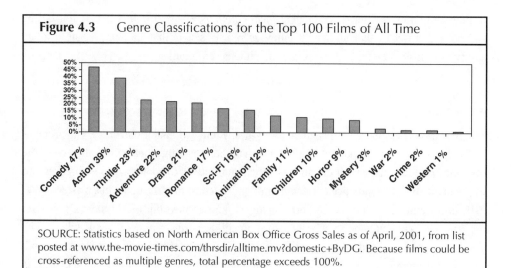

Figure 4.3 Genre Classifications for the Top 100 Films of All Time

SOURCE: Statistics based on North American Box Office Gross Sales as of April, 2001, from list posted at www.the-movie-times.com/thrsdir/alltime.mv?domestic+ByDG. Because films could be cross-referenced as multiple genres, total percentage exceeds 100%.

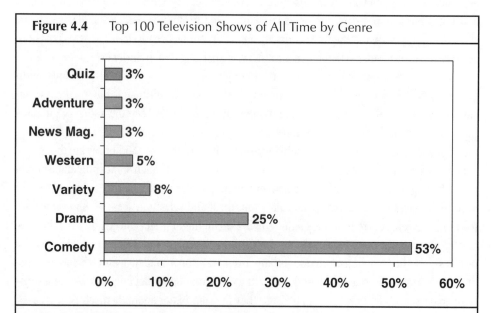

Figure 4.4 Top 100 Television Shows of All Time by Genre

SOURCE: The list of shows and their genre assignments were taken from Brooks and Marsh (1999). The shows are all prime-time network television series. For the graph, genres were collapsed so that comedy also includes shows categorized as situation comedy, comedy/variety, humor, and comedy adventure. Drama also includes police drama, drama anthology, detective drama, legal drama, medical drama, and fantasy. Variety also includes musical variety, music, anthology, talent, and talk, and adventure also includes adventure drama.

of drama. Serious drama, such as mystery and tragedy, is said to differ from other forms of entertainment because of the importance it attaches to an overarching plot. By contrast, genres such as situation comedy, erotica, and horror may derive their appeal more from discrete scenes. Enjoyment of these stories may not require detailed background and plot development. Nonetheless, the events and dialogue in individual scenes still typically reflect basic principles of drama. Comedy includes conflict and its resolution as well as character and plot development; however, whereas most drama takes time to develop, a comic skit can be developed more quickly, making it popular for venues such as radio programs and live performances.

Comedy, by its nature, is lighthearted and not serious. Freud argued that audiences rely on cues that signal the play context of humor and comedy, and he outlined features of joke-work that can serve as these cues.[89] Freud differentiated between nontendentious and tendentious humor. *Nontendentious* humor relies on jokework, including innocuous plays on words, irony, and exaggeration that does not victimize, humiliate, or disparage. This is the humor of innocent "Knock, Knock" jokes and "Why did the chicken cross the road?" riddles. In contrast, *tendentious* humor emphasizes the victimization of one party by another. Humor that pokes fun at others is often called *disparagement humor*. Like other forms of drama, disparagement humor has been explained by disposition theory. If the audience is positively disposed toward an individual, they are more likely to laugh at his or her jokes. In other words, the more a comedian or comic character is liked, the funnier the audience will find the humor. It is argued that people find it funny when a joke is targeted at someone that is disliked. People are not as amused, possibly even insulted by jokes that target liked individuals. According to Freud, although nontendentious jokes and riddles may produce a few smiles and polite giggles, they are rarely capable of producing the intense amusement that tendentious humor elicits with ease. He further maintained that very little of what we label as humor is truly innocent. Instead, much of even the most simple wordplay and jokework includes tendentious undercurrents of hostility and taboo topics.

Nonetheless, it is argued that even tendentious humor relies on nontendentious elements—jokework such as plays on words, irony, and exaggeration—to serve as the cues for audiences to laugh. It was Freud's contention that audiences do not truly understand exactly what it is about tendentious humor that makes them laugh. He argued that although audiences may believe that they laugh at the jokework and wordplay, the fact that innocent jokework does not create the same level of mirth suggests it is the tendentious elements—the hostility and taboo topics—that truly inspire amusement. These speculations inspired the formulation of a *misattribution theory of humor*.[90] As the name suggests, this theory postulates that individuals misattribute their enjoyment of hostile humor to the innocent, nontendentious humorous cues. The logic is that it is not considered socially acceptable to laugh at others' misfortune. Thus, even though deep down audiences might be intrigued, even amused, by blatant hostility, they are not free to admit or express that enjoyment due to fear of social censure. In comedy, however, the nontendentious humorous cues that accompany hostility may unconsciously provide audiences with the justification they need to laugh openly.

Thus, it would seem that it is these lighthearted cues that differentiate drama from comedy. Although both drama and comedy are governed by disposition theory, the victimization and demise of a villain in a dramatic presentation might produce feelings of exhilaration, even triumph, but laughter would be inappropriate. Comedy, however, includes humorous cues that create a lighthearted context for this victimization, informing audiences that laughter is not only tolerated, but encouraged. Tendentious and disparaging humor are prevalent in commercial entertainment. Slapstick comedy found in movies and cartoons, for example, tends to focus on physical humor, such as people slipping and hitting each other. This tendentious form of humor can actually be quite violent, yet it includes cues such as music and facial expressions that let the audience know it isn't serious. For example, Leslie Nielsen is famous for his parodies of popular action films such as *Wrongfully Accused* (1998), a spoof on *The Fugitive* (1993) film and television series (1963-1967) and *Spy Hard* (1996), which mocks James Bond films. These action/comedies often follow a similar story line of characters and events as their dramatic counterparts; however, there is additional jokework and exaggeration that signal to audiences that they should not take these events too seriously. Thus, although audiences may have held their breath in suspense and sighed in relief in the original thriller, in the parody, the same story line may have audiences holding their sides and hooting with laughter.

Although disposition theory may explain why we laugh at some forms of humor, *incongruity-resolution* provides another rationale.[91] Riddles and other forms of humor often pose a question or some confusion (incongruity) that is then explained by the punch line (the resolution). Some humor of this type may be tendentious or disparaging, but often it is innocent and victimless. Consider the verbal joke "What is black and white and red all over?" "A newspaper." The incongruity of how something can be black and white and red all over simultaneously is resolved when the punch line "A newspaper" triggers recognition of the wordplay on red and read. Similar to mystery, the belief is that if a joke or riddle is too easy or obvious, audiences will not find it very amusing; however, if it is too difficult to figure out, they may not get it at all. Thus, in true Goldilocks fashion, the goal is to create a riddle that poses just the right amount of challenge. The irony found in many comedies reflects the notion of incongruity-resolution. Many comedies contain ironic elements—an immigration department for "illegal aliens" from outer space run by *Men in Black* (1997, 2002) or a *Wedding Planner* (2001) who can't find a groom—and it is these incongruities that form the basis for the humor.

One thought is that the incongruity creates tension and uncertainty. When the punch line or resolution is provided, this tension is released in the form of laughter. Theory also suggests that laughter reflects triumph and feelings of *mastery* and *superiority*. Laughter has been equated with the roar of triumph over one's enemies in battle. Therefore it has also been speculated that individuals who understand a joke laugh in triumph, feeling superior to those who don't get it. Feelings of superiority have also been tied to disparagement humor, which is thought to stimulate feelings of superiority over the individuals who serve as the butt of the joke.

New technology is providing new media and new challenges that are creating an environment in which comedy thrives. Many new media (such as the Internet) and handheld devices (such as cellular phones and palm organizers) are thought to be better suited to shorter, less complex entertainment content.[92] Although many other dramatic genres require time for character and story development, comedy can be developed quickly and easily. Consider cartoons in which a single still image, often without any text, can convey an entire comic plot. Thus, comedy becomes a natural choice for new media.

People need only check their own e-mail inboxes to recognize the proliferation of humor and comedy on the Internet. And it is reported that organizations such as Shockwave.com are enjoying success with so-called performance animation, including Flash-generated cartoons, often lasting just a few seconds, that can be downloaded and e-mailed to friends. These animations often feature recurring characters—such as a disco-dancing alien, jiggling to the song *I Will Survive,* who gets flattened by a falling disco ball.[93] According to Errol Gerson, a senior agent in the new media department of the Los Angeles-based agency Creative Artists Association (CAA), "This interactive programming is going to be a new entertainment format. It fits the Web audience profile, giving people a short laugh every now and then."[94] Other prevalent Web formats include short films spoofing TV shows or movies.

Although current technology restricts the length and complexity of the material that can be transmitted through new media devices, it is thought that even if and when these obstacles are overcome, brevity will still rule the day for many of these new media. It is reasoned that when individuals have time for more involved entertainment, they would prefer viewing a big screen from a couch or a theater seat than sitting at a desk squinting at their computer or PalmPilot. Thus, it would appear that humor and comedy are well-positioned to continue their reign in the media entertainment kingdom.

Although comedy is a popular genre, humor is also often incorporated into more serious drama as *comic relief. Oxford's Companion to the English Language* (1992) defines comic relief as "an amusing scene, incident, or speech introduced into serious, tragic, or suspenseful drama to provide temporary relief from tension."[95] One theater historian notes that "an audience may concentrate better on crises if it has relaxed at moments in between. Anyone who has watched a chick struggling out of its shell realizes how often Nature's way is 'strain—rest—strain—rest'."[96] Thus, comic relief may serve as a break in serious drama, providing audiences an opportunity to mentally and physically relax and settle down after tense or tragic scenes. Comic relief has been used to varying degrees by most dramatists, including Shakespeare. Today, the prevalence of humor in more serious drama is evidenced by the number of popular films of various genres that are cross-listed under comedy. Indeed, of the 47 top-grossing films of all time listed as comedy, 40% (19) were cross-listed with more serious or suspenseful genres, including action, adventure, drama, crime, thriller, mystery, and/or horror.[97]

Action and Horror

Action and horror are also found in traditional forms of entertainment, including books, films, and even music, and they are equally popular in video games and amusement park rides and attractions. Action and horror genres are both typically characterized by high levels of violence. This type of drama typically follows the standard dramatic principles, including exciting conflict between good and evil. Not surprisingly, disposition and excitation transfer theories offer reasonable explanations of the appeal of these dramas. It has been suggested that these genres also provide catharsis, allowing audience members to purge their own anger and fear.[98] Horror and other threatening drama are thought to give individuals an opportunity to face and master their fears by forcing them to confront and vicariously conquer their "demons." Evidence suggests that audience reactions to violent drama may also reflect socialized gender roles. Violent drama, particularly horror, is thought to provide adolescent males the opportunity to demonstrate their manhood by acting fearless. At the same time, young female viewers can display the appropriate fear response to gain "protection" from their male companion. Indeed, research indicates that females find males more attractive when they appear brave and fearless while watching horror, whereas males find females more attractive when they appear afraid and turn to the males for comfort.[99]

The Watchers

Perhaps not surprisingly, adolescent males are the dominant audience for graphic violence, particularly horror. Studies find that males enjoy horror films more than females do, and females are more distressed by horror films than males are. Research also suggests personality differences in preferences for violence and horror.[100] The personality variable that has been researched most often in association with exposure to horror and thrillers is *sensation seeking,* the desire to seek out experiences that produce "sensation" and arousal. Sensation seekers, in particular, seem to enjoy the thrill caused by the fear that scary films create. Differences in *empathy,* the degree to which individuals relate to and feel for others, may also play an important role in determining the appeal of graphic horror. Research has found that nonempathic individuals find horror more appealing. The reasoning here is that highly empathic individuals relate closely to the victims and, thus, may become too distressed to enjoy the films. Low levels of wandering imagination (daydreaming about unreal situations), fictional involvement (transferring one's feelings into the actions and feelings of movie characters), and emotional contagion (becoming emotionally caught up in the film) are good predictors of the appeal of horror. Again, the logic is that an individual who does not daydream or let his or her imagination wander never forgets that the horror isn't real, and therefore does not get upset by these events, whereas an individual who gets very emotionally involved in drama may find horror and graphic violence too upsetting.

Individuals who enjoy violence and horror appear to do so for different reasons. Johnston identified four motivations that adolescents report for viewing graphic horror films:[101]

☆ The *gore-watcher* personality is characterized by low empathy, low fearfulness, and high adventure seeking. This combination of personality traits makes gore-watchers seek high arousal originating from graphic portrayals of blood, death, and even physical torture. Gore-watching motivations may reflect a curiosity about physical violence (the ways that people are killed), a vindictive interest in killing (victims get what they "deserve"), and an attraction to the grotesque (viewing blood and guts). Gore-watchers, particularly males, tend to identify more with the killer than the victims.

☆ *Thrill watchers* enjoy the thrill of being startled and scared. Unlike the gore watcher, who focuses on blood and mutilation, the thrill watcher focuses more on the suspense. The personality of the thrill-watcher is characterized by high levels of empathy and high levels of adventure seeking.

☆ *Independent watchers* view horror films to test their maturity and bravery. They have low levels of dispositional empathy, show no preference for either violence or suspense, and report positive feelings both before and after viewing horror films.

☆ *Problem watchers* report being angry and lonely. The personality of the problem watcher is characterized by sensation seeking, which can take the form of substance abuse and low dispositional empathy. Problem watchers' identification with the victim may be a reflection of their own perceived helplessness. Unlike the other three viewing motivations, only problem watchers reported feeling bad both before and after viewing graphic horror.

From classic 18th-century gothic horror to 20th-century "shoot-em-ups," most violent action and horror films followed standard dramatic principles, concluding with good ultimately triumphing over evil; however, evil has had more success in recent tales of violence and horror. Gone are the serious and silent, but inevitably doomed, killers of traditional action and horror. Originally, horror and other violent thrillers followed a traditional formula where, at the end of the story, the evil is unequivocally destroyed. Various film critics, however, argue that many films no longer follow this tradition. Starting in the early 1970s with the success of *Rosemary's Baby* and *The Exorcist*, a new thriller formula emerged that portrayed defenseless victims in terrifying no-win situations where the evil/antagonist triumphed over the forces of reason and rationalism.[102] Typically, these films contain teaser endings in which, although at first it may appear that the villain or monster has been destroyed, a final scene reveals that the evil has survived. Many popular film series—such as *Halloween*, *Friday the 13th*, *A Nightmare on Elm Street*, and the Hannibal Lecter films— contain teaser endings. Not only do the villains and demons of contemporary violent action and horror films often survive for the sequel, today characters such as Hannibal Lecter (from *Silence of the Lambs, Hannibal*, and *Red Dragon*, and Freddy Kruger (from the *Nightmare on Elm Street* films) are quite sophisticated and witty. Although these developments suggest alternative character and plot options for those who seek to create entertainment, there is also concern about the impact that these trends may have on audience members. These possibilities will be explored in the next chapter.

CONTEMPORARY TRENDS

Entertainment providers are always experimenting and looking for new ways to attract and maintain audiences' attention. They introduce new ideas, try new twists on old genres or story lines, combine genres in different ways, and add new elements in an effort to keep drama fresh and engaging. Such ideas may be born of nothing more than one individual's creativity and ability to think outside the box and uncover new possibilities. In many cases, however, these ideas are inspired or facilitated by larger societal trends or technological advances.

The Blender Effect

Many forms of contemporary entertainment introduce novelty by violating our expectations or established traditions. As suggested earlier, drama and dramatic genres tend to reflect certain norms that audiences come to expect—for example, good guys usually win, bullies never prosper in the end, romantic comedies end happily ever after. Indeed, norms can be found in most forms of entertainment—video game characters can come back to life, plays have intermissions, bars and clubs have music playing, and so on. However, many entertainers and audiences thrive on breaking the rules and violating established norms. Such manipulations reflect the postmodern nature of contemporary entertainment, as discussed in Chapter 15.

Time Manipulation

One way in which entertainers have experimented with drama is to play with the time order in which a story is told. Instead of starting at a single point in time and continuing forward in a direct, linear order, a story may begin at the middle or the end and progress backward and forward from there. As mentioned earlier, mysteries often contain elements of retrospection. Stories involving time travel also often move forward and backward in time. Traditionally, however, distinctions were made so that the audience knew where they were in the time sequence—flashbacks in time might be signaled by a verbal cue (I remember when . . .), auditory cue (echo or distant quality to voices and sounds), or a visual cue (rippling or cloudy effect to the scene). Increasingly, however, a drama may progress forward or backward in time without offering any cues, so the audience may not be able to accurately piece the sequence of events together until the end, if then. This technique is reflected in many popular films, such as *Pulp Fiction*, *Sliding Doors,* and *Vanilla Sky.*

Technology has also allowed audiences the ability to manipulate the time order of entertainment. On the Internet, hyperlinks allow individuals to sift through content, moving forward or back at their own pace, and TiVo, DVD, and better VCR technology have made it easier for audiences to move forward and back within a program or film. Video games also often allow players to shift to different times, scenes, or universes. Many forms of entertainment have also manipulated time by blending history and culture from different centuries within a single scene. Movies such as *Shrek* and *A Knight's Tale*, for example, told stories reminiscent of the Renaissance era, but they also included elements of popular culture, such as music, dance, hairstyles, and some fashion influences from the late 20th and early 21st centuries. Similarly, television shows such as *Hercules* and *Xena* often blend together references from different eras.

Genre Blending

Many new entertainment offerings reflect a blending of genres. Comedy, for example, has been blended with horror in films such as the *Scream* and *Scary Movie* series, and it has been combined with action in films such as *Rush Hour.* Genre blending is not limited to drama; it is also found in music, where artists experiment with blending different styles together—rock and jazz, techno and hip hop, pop and classical music—and even in cuisine, with "fusion" blends of different ethnic foods, such as Thai pizza or Mexican sushi. Although not all genres, styles, or tastes may mix well together, genre blending is a popular strategy because it introduces a bit of novelty while still relying on elements that have proven successful in the past.

Manipulations of time and genre often force audiences to confront ideas about reality. By violating our norms and expectations, such entertainment often begs the question of what is real and what isn't. Is there an objective reality out there, or is it all in our heads—just a matter of perspective? Many audiences are fascinated by such questions.

The Reality Principle

To Freud, the pleasure principle may explain much of our motivation for entertainment; however, fantasy and make-believe cannot produce real gratifications. Although the world of make-believe might be pleasant, our pleasure is tempered because we know it is not real. The land of make believe cannot sustain us. In the real world, we must work and struggle to survive. Nonetheless, real experiences, although imperfect and often unpleasant, are valued because they are genuine. Thus, the individual is forced to strive not only for what is pleasant, but for what is real even if unpleasant. This is the *reality principle*.

Stephenson[103] distinguishes play and leisure as separate from reality and work: "Leisure time is our free time, time for recreation, hobbies, or self-cultivation. Work deals with reality, with earning a living, with production. Play, on the contrary, is largely unproductive except for the self-satisfaction it provides." Stephenson also outlines characteristics of play, as follows:

> Playing is pretending, stepping outside the world of duty and responsibility. Play is an interlude in the day. It is not ordinary or real. It is voluntary and not a task or moral duty. It is in some sense disinterested, providing a temporary satisfaction. Though attended to with seriousness, it is not really important. . . . Play is secluded, taking place in a particular place set for the purpose in time and space: it has a beginning and end.[104]

The qualities that Stephenson outlines characterize entertainment as "pretend" in that it doesn't have any real impact on us, that it is somehow separated from everything else in our lives. But therein lies the dilemma. Although we may use entertainment to escape the turmoil of our lives, we seem to find it difficult to truly enjoy experiences that seem "pretend" and unrealistic. It is perhaps this tension that has led the lines between drama and reality to become increasingly blurred. Although individuals do enjoy fictional drama, audiences appear to increasingly demand more "real" entertainment. Analysts contend that "the tastes of the younger generation of viewers, a group more interested in visceral "realistic" programming than artificial jokes from fictional characters in ersatz living rooms, seem to be taking command of an industry that is more than ever driven by the need to cater to the tastes of young adults."[105]

Figure 4.5   TV Talk Show Cartoon

"We really need to talk about our relationship, so I've booked us on a TV show."

Reality Programming

Although most drama is at least loosely based on reality, typically the stories are scripted rather than spontaneous and, even in impromptu performances, actors are given characters and basic scenarios to act out. More recent reality programming involves real people and real events. Television programs such as *Real World* and *Survivor* follow so-called "regular" people and just let the cameras roll. The early popularity of these shows was astounding, including popular subgenres such as game shows (*Who Wants to Be a Millionaire* and *Weakest Link*), shock/stunt shows (MTV's *Jackass*), tell-all talk shows (*Maury, Sally,* and *Jerry*), and slice-of-life programs that follow people presumably just living their lives (*Real World* and *Big Brother*). Many programs include elements of more than one of these subgenres. Consistent with the principles of the attention economy detailed in Chapter 2, some people enjoy broadcasting their personal dramas to the world as much as other people enjoy viewing them. Humanity's love affair with attention is what makes reality programming work.

Summer 2001 saw the introduction of *Fear Factor* and *Spy TV*. *Fear Factor* centered on stunts, such as contestants being forced to eat sheep eyes (while surrounded by sheep wearing eye patches), and *Spy TV* featured hidden camera stunts, such as staging a fake surgical procedure in a motel room and then ordering a pizza to scare the willies out of the delivery man. Following season program lineups included a new *Big Brother,* another *Mole,* more titillation on *Temptation Island,* at least three new shows about contestants getting lost and trying to win a race, a pseudo murder mystery with real people being eliminated (symbolically) by a serial killer (*Murder in Small Town X*), more young singles experimenting with on-screen coupling on cruise ships (*Love Cruise, Shipmates*), more programs about young singing hopefuls trying to form pop groups (*American Idol, Popstar*), and even a show about sexy young women trying to become Playboy playmates (*Girl Next Door: Search for a Playboy Centerfold*).

Reality programming, however, is really not new. Radio broadcasts have always relied on real people and events for much of their entertainment, and game shows were among some of the first television programs ever produced. Television and movie producers have also experimented with other reality programming over the years in TV shows such as *Candid Camera* and *Cops* and films such as *Faces of Death*.

The formula of reality programming is, in essence, the same as it is for all drama. There are "good" and "bad" characters that audiences root for and against. Drama, of course, is driven by conflict, so program producers usually create situations in which conflict is likely to occur. Individuals with strong personalities are forced to live together or compete against each other. Audiences appear to enjoy these programs even in cases where they suspect events might be staged. In fact, even though these shows continue to be more spontaneous than most programming, the term *assisted reality* has recently emerged, acknowledging the fact that "reality" often needs the help of writers, producers, and editors to enhance its dramatic appeal.[106] Even scripted programming, however, has shifted to reflect a more "realistic" feel and look. Television programs such as *ER* and films such as *The Blair Witch Project* and *Traffic* use camera angles, panning, and sound quality that make scenes appear as if they were recorded with home video cameras. Programs such as *The West Wing* incorporate current events and real public figures into their story lines, again blurring the line between fact and fiction.

In some cases the "realistic" nature of these programs may make them perhaps more believable, and thus more entertaining, but in other cases, the events are so extreme and unusual, it is difficult to believe that is their main appeal. One factor that may increase their interest is their spontaneity. In theory, even the program producers do not know what will happen next. When you watch *Survivor* in any given episode, for example, you don't know whether you will get comedy, tragedy, or action/adventure. This uncertainty may enhance suspense and thus enhance program enjoyment. Some analysts believe that audiences are attracted to the voyeuristic nature of these programs. Consistent with the notion that drama serves an informative and self-reflective function, audiences may look to these programs for ideas on how to act or behave. Or, in cases of some of the more extreme programming, they may provide a sort of catharsis where people can vicariously live out experiences they would not dare to attempt themselves.

Brian Graden, the president of programming for MTV, thinks he knows why the trend in spontaneous reality programming originally exploded:

> For these young people, the odd artifice of a layer of writers and actors is the abnormal thing. These shows are being watched by young audiences who grew up watching O.J. and Monica as entertainment. They have had a much different video access than any previous generation.[107]

Graden observes that many in today's 25-and-under generation have actually grown up as videotaped subjects, endlessly filmed by parents who have wielded video cameras at every major (and often minor) event in their children's lives. For young viewers, reality shows on network television are out of the same tradition that produced *Jackass, The Man Show,* and other outrageous fare on cable television. According to Jeff Zucker, the president of entertainment for NBC, the shift in taste is not unlike what happened in television comedy in the mid-1970s when Lorne Michaels brought *Saturday Night Live* to NBC—to the dismay of older fans of Bob Hope and Jack Benny and to the delight of comedy fans under 30. "The young viewers are looking for high-octane television, stuff that is full of adrenaline," said David Goldberg, the president of the American branch of Endemol, the Dutch company responsible for reality formats such as *Big Brother* and *Fear Factor*.[108]

And if young people are hooked on these programs, whatever else is said about them does not matter. More than ever, network television is steered by youth culture. Advertisers prefer young viewers, and networks will do anything to deliver them. "We have to start reaching this next generation of viewers," Zucker said. "Our economic future depends on it."[109]

Will Survivor *Survive?*

Producers of the reality program *Survivor* used many techniques to maximize and sustain the program's dramatic appeal, including staging postcompetition events, such as reunions and interviews, which furthered character and plot development, and generated the potential for more spontaneous conflict and controversy (see Figure 4.6). *Survivor* was still receiving top 10 program ratings in early 2002, but many producers were already beginning to question how long people would remain hooked. Although the novelty of reality programs seems to appeal to viewers, in many cases, once the novelty wears off, the audience loses interest, and the shows are quickly canceled. Some predicted that, in the wake of the events of September 11, the entire genre of reality programming would lose its appeal. Assuming that reality shows' appeal lay in their "authenticity" and shock value, producers and critics speculated that these shows would seem tame and possibly even insulting in comparison to the truly authentic and shocking television coverage of the attack on the World Trade Center. Although the ratings of some reality programs did drop somewhat late in 2001, it is unclear whether such drops were influenced by September 11. The continued popularity of radio talk shows, televised sports broadcasts, and television and film dramas infused with "reality" content and cinematography, however, suggests that audiences have not lost their taste for reality-infused entertainment. It may simply be that reality programs tend to have shorter life cycles, possibly as a result of limited concepts and formats. However, attention may turn away from *Survivor* only to turn toward similar reality competitions like *American Idol,* or toward other reality concepts, such as *The Osbournes*, which documents the domestic life of aging rock star Ozzy Osbourne. The generation of reality programming that brought in the new millennium may die out, but, as do many entertainment trends, it may continue to influence generations of entertainment to come.

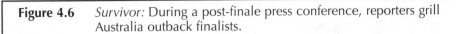

Figure 4.6   *Survivor:* During a post-finale press conference, reporters grill
Australia outback finalists.

© AFP/Corbis.

Interactivity

Spontaneity such as that found in reality programming can be further enhanced through
audience interaction. For many forms of entertainment, particularly media entertainment,
the audience is passive. Audience members are simply observers who have no impact or influence on the entertainment they experience. Stories, for example, whether in books or movies,
usually follow a predetermined progression of events that plays out oblivious to audience reactions. Other forms of entertainment, however, allow audiences to actively participate, interact,
and influence the events as they unfold. Technically, any form of entertainment in which audiences participate rather than merely observe could be classified as interactive entertainment.
Activities such as sports, games, and dancing can serve as both passive entertainment for
audiences and interactive entertainment for participants.

The concept of interactivity, however, is often used in reference to those forms of entertainment in which audiences can interact and influence events while remaining spectators
rather than participants. To create this interactivity, audiences must have some way of communicating their wishes to the "entertainers." For example, musical performances in which
audience members shout out requests can be considered interactivity, as can radio shows
where individuals call in to make requests or to participate in talk show discussions. Such
interactivity is not new. In fact, interactive entertainment might be traced back to the days of

Showtime Goes Interactive[111]

The cable station Showtime has taken an aggressive approach to interactive television that utilizes the Internet on the TV set. Each month, 60,000 people log on to Stargate-SG1.com to become part of an online version of the hit Showtime series. Players assemble themselves into 16 teams and play for points that advance their rank and allow them access to classified areas of the site. They are expected to "report for duty" regularly but, while on the site, they can also chat, catch up on the show's episodes, get information, and download photos. An elaborate fantasy filled with information about the universe as it's depicted in the series, Stargate-SG1.com started out as a Web site created by a fan. "It was getting a lot of activity, so we checked it out and liked it so much we hired the guy who'd created it," explains Mark Greenberg, Showtime executive vice president of corporate strategy and communications.

On the TV set, there's Showtime Interactive 24.7, which allows subscribers with access to Wink technology to check network schedules and pick up information about a movie, series, or event. The enhanced material for each show or movie also includes a Spotlight section that offers original, behind-the-scenes branded content about the program. Interactive 24/7 content is displayed along the bottom of the screen, so viewers can continue watching a show while delving deeper into related information.

Greenberg remembers the day when Showtime executives first realized that their viewers were keenly interested in interactive programming. Showtime Event Television was airing a heavyweight boxing match between Mike Tyson and Frank Bruno and, as an added attraction, the network offered live online scoring. "We were overwhelmed by the number of people participating online," he recalls. "We realized that if you give people a reason to interact, they will."[112]

Since then, Showtime has conducted periodic studies of the phenomenon of viewers watching and being online simultaneously. "On any given night, 25% of the people watching TV are also logged on," Greenberg says. Young people, in particular, are apt to "co-use" the TV and PC. Showtime research last year found that 48% of teens are simultaneous users, whereas about 30% of adults aged 18-49 are.

Those young viewers grew up with cable and are accustomed to paying for their TV, Greenberg says, but they also expect more from their premium services. Hence, options like StargateSG-1.com, which allow fans to delve deeper into the Showtime offerings they like most. "We don't expect every subscriber to watch everything we air," Greenberg says, "but for a service like ours, it's important that we create a culture and a community."[113]

gladiators and court jesters where audiences were often empowered to decide the fate (to live or die) of entertainers following their performances.

Until recently, however, most interactive entertainment was limited to live events where audiences could directly communicate their wishes to the entertainers. Mediated entertainment—including most print, television, and film—was considered passive because the audience could only submissively observe predetermined content. Over the years, however, some authors have dabbled with interactive "choose your own adventure" books that allow readers to make choices as events unfold (should Billy go through the door or turn back?). And now, new technology has enabled most media to be interactive. So much so, in fact, that today "interactivity" is most commonly used in reference to forms of electronic media. In this field, *interactivity* has been defined as "the extent to which users can participate in modifying the form and content of a mediated environment in real time."[110] Such forms of entertainment allow audiences to make choices and shape their own entertainment experiences as they are happening.

Levels of Interactivity

Researchers have developed five criteria to evaluate levels of interactivity in electronic media.[114] First, the *degree of selectivity* ranges from low selectivity, where selection is limited to deciding when exposure starts and ends, to selecting between simultaneously presented offerings, to selecting different dimensions. Examples of highly interactive offerings according to this criterion are video games, which often allow the user to select the level of difficulty, the characters involved, and the environment (such as city, countryside, or space-age landscape). Second, the *degree of modification* is low when possibilities exist only to store or delete information and is high when it is possible to add more information along with the user's intention and interest. A Web site like Yahoo.com, which allows users to add and delete pages as well as modify page color, content, and layout, reflects a high degree of modification. The third criterion, the *quantity of different content* that can be modified or selected, evaluates the sheer number of options (Can you choose from two doors or five? Do you only have one opportunity to choose or several?). Fourth, the *linearity* dimension evaluates whether or not the user has to accept the order of the presentation (as in movies) or may skip around or alternate sequences (as with hypertext functions on Web sites). The fifth criteria considers the *number of different senses* (sight, touch, sound, and so on) that are activated. Simulator rides and games such as Star Wars Pod Racer allow users to see, hear and feel their entertainment experience. Although these dimensions do not offer any guidance regarding how to effectively incorporate interactivity into entertainment, they do provide an idea of the range of opportunities.

Interactivity in Practice

Some of the first forms of electronic interactive entertainment were video games. Even the earliest video games possessed enough interactivity that individuals considered themselves to be participants rather than spectators. Today's video games are so interactive that in many cases individual are not only game players but also game creators, building characters, scenes, rules, and challenges. The Internet has played a large part in the proliferation of interactivity through Web sites where individuals can shape their own entertainment in the form of pictures, stories, games, and music. Actors, musicians, film studios, hotels, theme parks, and so on all have Web sites that provide interactive opportunities.

The technology also exists for films and videos that allow individuals to make choices in the same manner as in the "choose your own adventure" books; however, to date, this technology has been used more for educational tools rather than purely for entertainment. Still, it appears that almost any form of entertainment can be infused with interactivity, even music videos. Digital Hip Hop produced a video for the rapper Ja Rule in which viewers can choose several options throughout the video—for instance, whether the rapper vanquishes demons with swords or a chain saw. Viewers are prompted to make their choices from a series of icons that pop up at the edge of the video moments before the interactive portions appear on screen.

Television has also experimented with interactivity. Programs have tried to encourage audience interaction for decades, but because viewers cannot directly communicate their wishes through the television, program producers must find other ways to interact with their audiences. Television programs have run viewer call-in polls that are posted during broadcasts, and on talk shows viewers can call in and have their comments aired live. Although viewers can write or call in by telephone, the Internet is rapidly becoming the preferred medium for interaction. Using this technology, programs are even allowing viewers to determine the fate of specific characters. For example, each of the three networks has turned to the Internet as a way to get soap opera viewers more involved. On *All My Children,* online responses picked out a character's wedding dress, and another campaign asked viewers if a young character should tell her mother (Susan Lucci's Erica Kane) she was gay. *Passions* bumped off a main character chosen by Web votes, and *Days of Our Lives* fans went online to decide the paternity of Hope's baby.

The sitcom *Just Shoot Me* allowed the audience to choose between three possible endings for one episode. The three endings, involving David Spade's character Finch, were called "Finch sleeps with Nina's sister," "Finch gets dumped by Nina's sister," and "Things get weird." What made this vote unique was that it happened in real time. Rather than conducting the vote weeks before, viewers voted on the Web site during the first half of the broadcast, and the broadcasters were able to tally the vote and cue up the selected ending by the end of the show. Emerging technologies are also enabling television to become more directly interactive. Although viewers cannot yet directly influence and change events in program content, they can control features such as freezing or forwarding programming as well as obtaining program listings and background information. (See the box "Showtime Goes Interactive" earlier in this chapter.)

Do Audiences Want Interactivity?

There is much debate about how much audiences enjoy interactivity. Much like "reality" drama, interactivity allows for spontaneity that might enhance suspense and thus, ultimately, be more entertaining. It is also argued that, by giving audiences a say in how events unfold, they may begin to feel responsible for those events, making them care and feel more deeply about what happens, which should also further enhance suspense and entertainment. By definition, however, interaction requires audiences to be active. They must pay attention and make choices, and thus, some critics argue that interactivity may begin to seem more like work than play. They suggest that audiences might often simply prefer to passively sit back and be entertained.

As with most issues related to entertainment, it seems likely that audience enjoyment of interactivity may be influenced by a number of factors. Some audiences may generally enjoy interactivity more than others do. And some individuals may enjoy certain forms of interactivity but not others, or interactivity at certain times but not others. The degree of selectivity certainly seems to play a role in audience enjoyment. If audiences are allowed too few choices, they might become bored or frustrated, yet if they are given too many choices, they may become overwhelmed and equally frustrated. For game developers, dot.coms, and others eager to capitalize on interactive entertainment, the exploration of these issues is critical. Yet researchers are only now just beginning to explore how audiences engage with and react to interactivity.

FADE TO BLACK

Drama is a driving force in most forms of entertainment. Drama drives the excitement and emotion in entertainment that makes us feel. There are many speculations regarding the appeal of drama. It may distract us from our problems, help us purge negative emotions, make us feel better about ourselves, and give us ideas for our own lives. Different dramatic genres are characterized by their own twists on the standard dramatic formula, and much research has explored who likes these different genres and why.

Genre blending, shifting time order, reality programming, and interactivity are recent trends that have been incorporated into many forms of dramatic entertainment. Technological advances have facilitated the development of many of these trends, allowing entertainment providers to experiment with different types of programming and options. It is not always clear, however, if or for how long audiences will enjoy these new innovations.

 A Closer Look[115]

Stock Characters and Situations

When in Rome . . .

Although dramatic trends may come and go, contemporary entertainment still reflects many classic dramatic elements. Ancient Roman plays, for example, contained many stock characters and situations that can still be found in the drama of today's books, films, songs, and the like. Listed in the following sections are some of those stock characters and situations. See if you can think of any recent books, films, and so on that feature aspects of one or more of them.

Young Loverboy

The young loverboy is a handsome young man, but he is a bit of an airhead. He relies on the help of his parents and friends to survive.

Beautiful Maiden

This character is loved by the young loverboy. Like the loverboy, the maiden is absolutely beautiful but may not be very bright. In modern times we might call her a ditz. However, on occasion, the maiden can be tricky and cunning.

Old Man

In Roman plays, there is almost always an old man. He is sometimes silly or foolish. He can be overprotective of his daughters, often standing in the way of the young loverboy and the beautiful maiden.

Harsh Wife

The harsh wife can be mean and strict. She may be overly critical or suspicious of others—including being distrustful of her husband and suspecting his involvement with other women.

Arrogant Soldier

This character is very egotistical. The arrogant soldier is always chasing after women. He thinks that he is extremely handsome and believes that all women are in love with him. He likes it when people talk about his (usually false) accomplishments.

Tricky Servant

The tricky servant is often the star of the show. He or she is smart and is always coming up with elaborate plots to get more food or to gain freedom. Sometimes the servant is intrinsically good, and his or her plots and schemes are noble; other times, the servant is intrinsically bad, formulating plots and schemes that may be spiteful or criminal in nature. In Roman plays, servants often are seen with very big, open mouths and huge stomachs, to emphasize how much they love food.

Stock Situations

Some of the stock situations found in Roman drama include love, confusion, silly physical humor, twins, role reversal, and happy endings.

Film Examples

Listed here are some films that include many of these elements. In addition to any examples that you can come up with, think about these films or rent them to look for the characters and situations just described.

A Comedy of Errors
A Funny Thing Happened on the Way to the Forum
The Little Mermaid
Meet the Parents
Sleeping Beauty
Trading Places
Twins

DISCUSSION AND REVIEW

1. Review theories regarding the dramatic formula and the appeal of drama. Consider some of your entertainment favorites and see if you can identify any ways that they reflect these theories and principles.

2. Examine examples of songs, films, television programs, and so on that reflect different genres. Identify examples of each genre and use the theories in the text, as well as your own ideas, to pinpoint what differentiates good from bad examples of each genre—i.e., what qualities make a good horror film, comedy, reality program, etc.?

3. Review recent trends such as blending, reality programming, and interactivity. What future, if any, do you think they *will* have? What future, if any, do you think they *could* have? React to and expand on what the chapter says about these trends.

EXERCISES

1. Do an informal poll. Ask as many people as you can what their favorite films and television programs are. Note the genres of those shows (comedy, mystery, etc.) and look for patterns in who likes what including demographic differences such as age and gender and any personality differences you can identify. Compare what you find to the trends explored in the chapter.

2. Look on the Internet to find a listing of the top films for last year. Break them down into the genres listed in Figure 4.3. How do your findings compare with this figure? What conclusions can you draw?

3. Take another look at the genres in Figure 4.3. See if you can come up with general formulas and characteristics for some of the subgenres not specifically discussed in the text.

RECOMMENDED READINGS

Bryant, J., & Zillmann, D. (Eds.). (1991). *Responding to the screen: Reception and reaction processes.* Mahwah, NJ: Lawrence Erlbaum.

Zillmann, D., & Vorderer, P. (Eds.). (2000). *Media entertainment: The psychology of its appeal.* Mahwah, NJ: Lawrence Erlbaum.

5

The Devil
Made Me
Do It

Entertainment Effects

*Even the most conservative estimates indicate that preschool children in America
are spending more than a third of their waking hours watching television. What are
the effects upon the vulnerable and developing human organism of spending such a
significant portion of each day engaged in this particular experience?*

—Marie Winn, *The Plug-in Drug*[116]

The effects of entertainment can be examined in much the same way one might examine
the effects of a prescription drug. Indeed, some critics even contend that entertainment
(such as movies, television, music, and video games) may have drug-like effects. When
researchers are testing a new drug, they examine both its intended effects (how well it does
what it is supposed to do—e.g., relieve a headache, clear up acne, or cure an infection) as well
as potential, unintentional side effects (e.g., nausea, weight gain, sun sensitivity, and so on).
Researchers have examined effects of entertainment, particularly media entertainment, in a
similar manner, often relying on methods and techniques similar to those used in medical
research.

The most obvious intended effect of entertainment, of course, is to entertain. Performers, writers and producers create stories, movies, games, songs, and experiences with the intention of entertaining audiences. And audiences expose themselves to these experiences with the intention of being entertained. Thus, research that focuses on the intended effects of entertainment usually explores how "effective" different forms of entertainment are at entertaining audiences. In Chapter 4, we introduced some of this research, which reveals how drama is used to create emotional, psychological, and even physiological reactions that form the crux of the entertainment experience. As is the case with drugs, not all forms of entertainment have the same effects on all audiences. Research finds that some forms of entertainment "work better" for some audiences than others.

Entertainment also creates a number of other effects, both intentional and unintentional. Chapter 3, for example, relates a variety of the effects or "gratifications" that audiences seek from entertainment, including distraction from life's problems and information about societal norms. As suggested in Chapter 2, entertainment often has other intended effects. A corporate sponsor of a sporting event hopes that the event will not only entertain audiences but also capture attention and ultimately result in an increase in sales of its products. And many books, films, or songs are written not only to entertain but also to educate and persuade audiences about specific topics or issues that are important to the writer. For example, books like *Uncle Tom's Cabin*, movies like *American History X* (1998), and songs like NWA's (Niggaz With Attitude) *Fuck the Police* may entertain audiences, but they also promote certain views about race relations.

Entertainment, like drugs, may also have some unintentional "side effects." If entertainment can intentionally affect our emotions, thoughts, and physical reactions, as suggested in Chapter 4, some argue that these effects may also unintentionally extend beyond the entertainment experience to affect our more general feelings, thoughts, behavior, and physical well-being. Although books, sports, movies, music, and video games are often accused of initiating negative effects such as encouraging violence, drug use, racial stereotyping, and eating disorders, they have also been credited with some positive impacts such as relieving stress, educating children, increasing awareness of social issues, and improving physical health.

EFFECT TYPES

This chapter explores media and entertainment effects, both intentional and unintentional, that extend beyond the effect of being entertained. Most of these effects can be categorized into one or more of the following effect types:

☆ *Psychological effects.* Researchers are interested in many psychological effects of entertainment. Can what we see, hear, and do for entertainment influence our more general thoughts and opinions? For example, can movies like *American History X* and songs like NWA's *Fuck the Police* influence people's opinions about race relations, prejudice, and police action? Much of this psychological research focuses on the impact of entertainment on our knowledge and opinions about societal issues or certain groups of people, including our own self-images.

☆ *Behavioral effects.* Can our entertainment choices affect our more general behavior? Can movies like *American History X* influence not only our opinions, but also our actions toward other people? Can they make us more introverted, more aggressive, or more fashionable? Corporate sponsors of films, sporting events, concerts, and other entertaining activities spend a great deal of money because they believe that pairing their brands with these entertainment options will encourage people to buy and use their products and services. Behavioral effects research focuses on how entertainment such as films, music, video games and sports might influence behaviors ranging from our meal choices to our career choices.

☆ *Physiological effects.* Researchers have even examined physiological effects of entertainment. As discussed in Chapter 4, some research has examined how the suspense found in entertainment can influence our heart rate, breathing, and other physical reactions. Research has also examined other physiological effects. Some research even suggests that humor and other forms of drama may boost our immune systems, increase our pain tolerance, and aid in healing.

THE HISTORY OF MEDIA EFFECTS THEORIES

Given that so much contemporary entertainment is media based, it is perhaps not surprising that much of effects research has focused on the media. Although not all media research focuses on entertainment (some research examines news or informational media), most of the theories and studies can be easily adapted. Furthermore, as the lines between news and entertainment and even between live and mediated communication become more blurred, these distinctions may become even less relevant.

Media effects research has gone through several stages of development or paradigms. As research advances, different ideas or hypotheses are tested, and gradually a uniform theory or paradigm emerges. A *paradigm* serves as an overarching view of a field that summarizes and is consistent with existing research. However, as research continues, new insights are made that may conflict with that view, and often our thinking begins to change. Old ideas are replaced with new ones. Sometimes thinking can change quite radically, resulting in what is often called a *paradigm shift*.[117] Our theories and ideas about what is true are fundamentally altered, and a new paradigm emerges.

Powerful Effects Theories

The idea of *powerful effects* or *mass society theory* reflects what many media scholars consider to be the first media effects paradigm. The first research on the impact of the media emerged when mass media itself emerged, beginning in the second half of the 19th century with the "mass" circulation of newspapers and magazines and continuing through the first half of the 20th century with the invention of silent films, talkies and radio. These times were characterized by the industrialization and urbanization of society in the United States and Western Europe. The fabric of these societies was changed as immigrants traveled and settled in different countries and regions in search of better opportunities and quality of life. In the United States, some leaders saw these changes as threats to the "American" way of life. They felt that the media undermined traditional values by sensationalizing and oversimplifying content to pander to the limited language levels and the perceived low tastes of the immigrants. These fears were reinforced by the successful media propaganda campaigns by totalitarian governments in Europe, such as Adolf Hitler's regime in Nazi Germany. In the United States, demands were made for media control to prevent such abuses.

These ideas—that the media are all powerful and that the average person is defenseless against this influence—served as the overarching view of the powerful effects or mass society paradigm. One prominent proponent of the powerful impact of the media was Walter Lippmann. In his famous book, *Public Opinion,* Lippmann argued that we see the world not as it really is but as "pictures in our heads"—pictures shaped not by our personal experiences, but by the mass media.[118] The views of this era are often summarized by the *hypodermic needle theory* or the *magic bullet theory*. Like a dangerous drug or bullet, media messages were thought to be mindlessly absorbed by audiences, as though injected or shot into their systems.

Limited Effects Theories

The Scientific Perspective

Mass society theory is an example of a *grand theory*—a simple, all-encompassing theory that tried to describe and explain all aspects of a phenomenon (in this case, the effects of the media). However, it became readily apparent that audiences were not becoming brainwashed en masse by subversive media messages. Media effects proved to be too complex for a single grand theory, and eventually the paradigm collapsed.

Paradigm shifts typically do not happen suddenly; rather, they develop over an extended period of time. Nonetheless, these shifts are often sparked by key events or research findings. This was the case in mass media research with the shift from a powerful effects paradigm to a limited effects paradigm. One crystallizing event happened on Halloween in 1938 when Orson Welles broadcast his dramatized version of the H. G. Wells science fiction novel, *War of the Worlds,* over the radio. This radio dramatization portrayed the Earth under Martian attack in docudrama style. Thousands of people fled from their homes in panic, believing the attack to be real. Mass society theorists claimed this phenomenon as proof of their theory. Further research, however, called this conclusion into question. Scientists at Princeton University found that although 1 million people may have been frightened into taking some action, the other 5 million people who heard the show did not. These researchers concluded that different factors led some people to be influenced whereas others were not, calling into question the mindless, universal impacts predicted by mass society and powerful effects theories.[119]

This research reflected a new, emerging *limited effects* paradigm based on a more scientific approach to the study of media effects. Although the theories that developed within this paradigm still suggested that the media can have psychological, physical, and physiological effects on their audiences, these effects were argued to be "limited" by many factors. These theories provided conditional rather than universal explanations of media effects, isolating the impacts of specific media phenomena for specific audiences. Yale psychologist Harold Lasswell, who studied World War II propaganda, outlined a systematic approach to media effects with his model of mass communication: *Who, Says what, In which channel, To whom, With what effect,* and thus, a new era of research was born that focused on isolating and examining each of these facets.

This approach was championed by Paul Lazarsfeld, who argued that mere speculation and anecdotal evidence alone could not explain the complexities of media effects.[120] He and his colleagues advocated the use of well-designed studies based on survey research, polling, and other social scientific methods. Based on Lazarsfeld's work, researchers began to isolate individuals and groups who tended to be more or less susceptible to media influences and identified individual differences (e.g., intelligence, age, education), social categories (e.g., religion, political affiliation) and personal relationships (e.g., friends, family) that accounted for differences in media impact. The collection of theories that came out of this first era of systematic and scientific study of media effects has been labeled limited effects theories.

Two-Step Flow Theory

One popular example of a limited effects theory is Lazarsfeld's own *two-step flow theory* of mass media and personal influence.[121] In their study of the 1940 presidential election, Lazarsfeld and his colleagues found that the media's influence on voting behavior was filtered through *opinion leaders*—that is, people who regularly consumed media content on topics of interest to them, interpreted media content based on their own beliefs and values, and then passed along their thoughts to *opinion followers*, people who have less exposure to the media. Thus, according to this theory, media impact flows through a two-step process: first to opinion leaders and then indirectly through the opinion leaders to everyone else. Opinion leaders are still important today, particularly in influencing trends in entertainment; however, because television and other advances have given people greater exposure to the media firsthand, opinion leaders are not thought to play as critical a role in filtering the media's influence for the rest of society as they once did.

Cumulative and Cultural Effects

Beginning during World War II, the limited effects approach dominated thinking about media for several decades. As this research progressed, however, it reached a level of complexity that led some theorists to argue that yet another new paradigm had developed. They speculated that one reason that research had not revealed more powerful effects of the media was because of the narrow, short-term focus of many of the more scientific media studies. As a result, new approaches began to expand the scope and duration of media studies. Whereas some research continued to follow a more classically scientific, quantitative approach, other investigations began exploring the impact of the media from a more subjective, cultural approach. Investigations of both types began to once again consider potentially more powerful *cumulative* media effects—effects that accumulate gradually from long-term repeated media exposure. Given the diversity of contemporary theories and approaches, many mass media scholars argue that, today, there exists not one but several paradigms of effects research. Many of these theories and research methods have implications not just for media entertainment but for all forms of entertainment.

RESEARCH METHODS

Researchers have studied the impact of media and entertainment in many different ways. In general, quantitative media scholars tend to study media from a detached, objective, and clinical perspective similar to the way biologists, chemists, or medical researchers conduct research in their fields. In comparison, qualitative or cultural theorists tend to study media effects using a more involved, subjective approach, gaining personal insights by immersing themselves in their studies, sometimes as participant observers; such techniques are similar to those of anthropologists or literary scholars. This difference in perspective is reflected in the varying methods that are used to study media and entertainment effects.

Quantitative Measures

In *quantitative analyses,* psychological, behavioral, and physiological effects are *quantified*—counted and statistically analyzed to determine how media and different forms of entertainment may affect people. These studies often look for statistical differences in the thoughts, behaviors, or physical conditions of those who have been exposed to certain forms of entertainment and those who have not. Some quantitative measures are based on *direct observations* whereas others are based on *self-reports.* Observations might be quantified by watching people and counting the number of times or the length of time that they perform a specific action—for example, counting the number of beers fans drink at a ballgame when their team is winning versus when their team is losing. Self-reports can be similarly quantified by asking people (verbally or on a survey) to estimate the number of times or length of time that they perform a specific action, such as asking them how many beers they drank at the ballgame.

Quantitative researchers interested in the effects of video games on a child's behavior toward other children might collect their data through observation or self-reports, or both. They might first observe children playing video games or survey them about their video game playing habits and then either observe how those children interact with other children (whether a child plays well and shares with other children or plays off by oneself) or use reports of behavior obtained either by asking the child questions about his or her interactions with other children or by asking the child's teachers or parents.

Observational and self-report measures each have relative advantages and limitations. Observations are usually preferred, but researchers may be restricted in what they can observe, so studies are often limited to self-report measures. For example, we cannot directly observe opinions and attitudes. Instead, we must rely on estimates usually obtained through self-reports on surveys and questionnaires. We may ask people to rate their opinions on scales from 1 to 5 to reflect their agreement with listed statements. Answers to these questions provide us with quantifiable opinion measures.

Qualitative Measures

Qualitative and ethnographic studies of media effects include observations, self-reports, and historical data. Instead of converting this data into numbers and statistics, qualitative studies analyze the phenomena they study in their natural textual, auditory, and/or visual forms or through narrative descriptions. Behavioral observations, for example, are documented either through videotape, audiotape, or transcribed descriptions. Results of the analysis are presented as excerpts and summaries of these observations.

Two popular qualitative strategies for acquiring self-reports are *in-depth interviews* and *focus groups*. In-depth interviews allow researchers to probe individuals' thoughts, opinions, and self-reports of behavior with less structure but more detail than a written or verbal survey or questionnaire. Researchers begin with very general questions and then adapt their probing based on what the interviewee says. For example, in-depth interviews exploring the influence of video games on children's social behavior might start with asking children what games they like to play and why, and then progress to asking them to talk about what other things they like to do for fun, probing to discover their interest and play interactions with other children. Focus groups are very similar to in-depth interviews, but instead of interviewing people one on one, people are interviewed in a group, which allows the interviewees to interact with each other and respond to each other's comments. Rather than statistically analyzing who says what, qualitative researchers review the entire interview sessions looking for trends and isolating and reporting specific comments that represent key findings for their study.

In historical analyses, researchers may examine the relationship between media and societal trends by documenting historical issues and events and relating them to media offerings of the time. One advantage of qualitative studies is the depth and richness of their analysis, but the subjective nature of this research leads some critics to be skeptical of their findings.

Entertainment Exposure

Laboratory Research

Experimental research most closely follows the clinical, quantitative tradition. In true experiments, researchers select a sample group of participants from a population they are interested in studying (e.g., citizens of a certain city, fifth graders, single women) and bring the participants to a lab or controlled environment and then expose them to different media. For example, in one of Albert Bandura's classic Bobo doll studies,[122] children were selected to be part of a sample group. That group was then divided in two. One group, the *experimental group,* was shown a film that showed someone beating up an inflated Bobo doll, and the other group, the *control* or *placebo group,* saw another version of the film where the same individual played nonviolently with the Bobo doll. After they saw the film, the children were placed in a room with a Bobo doll to see what they would do. Sure enough, the children who had seen the more violent film were more aggressive toward the Bobo doll than the children who had seen the nonviolent film (see Figure 5.1).

Experimental studies are carefully structured to give researchers maximum control over who is exposed to what. Ideally, experimental researchers want *random selection,* meaning that individuals who are picked for the study are selected at random from the larger population, and *random assignment,* meaning that participants are randomly assigned or placed into different groups or conditions (in the Bobo doll experiment, violent or nonviolent film conditions). This randomness is necessary to help assure that the different groups are relatively equal to each other and to the larger population that is being studied before the experiment begins. If, for instance, the experimental group was older than the control group, or tended to generally watch more television than the control group did, then any differences found in the study might be due to those differences rather than the "treatment" they received. Similarly, if everyone who participated in the study was on average older or watched more television than the rest of the population, then the researchers wouldn't know if the impact they found in their sample group would affect children in the general population in the same way. Researchers can try to "match" groups to make sure they are equivalent, but because people can differ in so many ways (age, personality, demographics, and so on), random selection is typically considered to provide the best assurance that these differences are not concentrated in one group more than another.

This need for control makes it very difficult to conduct true experimental media and entertainment research. First, it is difficult to obtain a truly random selection of a population. It is often very difficult to find and persuade people to participate in these studies, so researchers are limited to voluntary and convenient sample groups—people that are willing and readily available to participate. Because most research takes place at universities, studies often focus on college students. This is fine if we are only interested in the effects of media or other forms of entertainment on *college students* who are *willing* to participate (often only those who want extra credit); however, usually researchers are also interested in effects on other populations.

Another challenge is that after you obtain a sample, it is often difficult to create random assignment. We may be able to convince individuals to come to our labs to watch one film, play video games, or listen to an hour or two of music that we select for them. However, just as one dose of a drug may not have much effect, one "dose" of media or other form of entertainment may not be enough to have much effect, either. It is much more difficult to control what people do and see for long periods of time, particularly when it comes to entertainment.

Even perfectly controlled laboratory studies are open to criticism. One concern is the impact of the "laboratory" environment itself. People typically do not watch movies or listen to music for pleasure while seated at desks in college classrooms. That, however, is often the

Figure 5.1   Bobo Doll Study

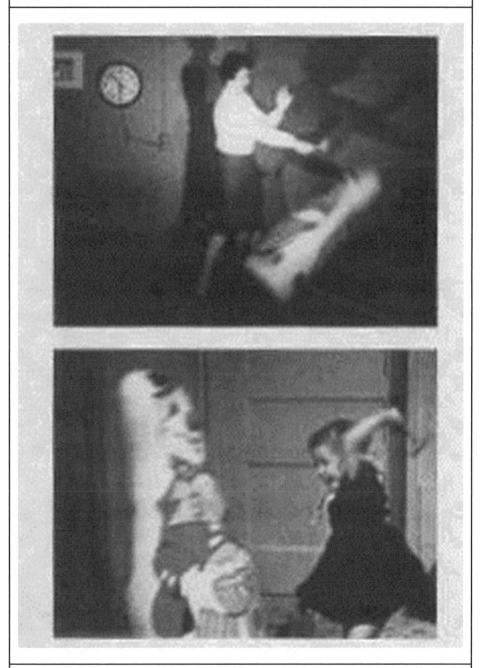

Albert Bandura found that children who saw an adult attack a Bobo doll in a film imitated the violent behavior the film depicted; in spite of extensive research, however, the exact relationship between media violence and real violence is still unclear.

environment in which effects studies are conducted. Thus, there is some question as to whether individuals will act and react the same way in the lab as they would in a more natural environment, particularly when they know they are being watched. To create more natural settings, many modern research facilities include complete theaters and even mini "homes" that simulate or imitate natural environments. Thus, for a study on video games, researchers might create a lab that looks like a living room with a home game system, an office or bedroom set up for computer games, or even a room set up to look like a video arcade. People are then brought into the lab and asked to play video games as they normally would at home, work, or at the arcade. Even in the most realistic labs, however, individuals may still not behave as they normally would, because they usually still know that they are being observed. Thus, although laboratory research allows for control, it is less *ecologically valid* than other forms of research, meaning that the study environment is less representative of the real world.

Field Research

To overcome the artificiality of the laboratory environment, some researchers turn to field studies. In these studies, rather than having the people come to the researchers, the researchers go to the people. Researchers go to theaters, concerts, video arcades, bars, sporting events, and other natural environments to observe how audiences are affected by entertainment experiences. For example, researchers might go to a video arcade and look for trends in what types of children (age, gender, ethnicity, and so on) play which types of video games, and then they might try to determine if playing different games changes the way the children think or their behavior—such as making them more or less assertive, aggressive, or shy with other children. Some of these investigations follow in the quantitative tradition, where researchers document individuals' media and entertainment experiences and the resulting effects, collecting data for systematic, statistical analysis. In other studies, however, individuals take a more qualitative approach, interpreting information obtained through field observations or interviews more subjectively.

Although these studies have the advantage of being better grounded in the real world, typically they are not based on random selection or random assignment. It is natural for people to choose their own entertainment, as well as when and where they will experience it. Assigning people to specific groups in a field study would be difficult and artificial. Even in field studies where more control is established (for example, if individuals were randomly selected to go see specific movies or concerts or play certain video games), people are still usually aware that they are being observed or studied, so there is still no way to be sure that people will react as they normally would. Nonetheless, although field studies usually provide less control than laboratory studies, they are usually more ecologically valid, or more representative of the real world.

Self-Reported Exposure

Rather than controlling the media or entertainment "treatments" that people receive, as is done in a laboratory study or by directly observing individuals' media or entertainment choices, as is done in a field study, researchers often must rely on self-reports of exposure. Increasingly, researchers are interested in studying more long-term, cumulative effects. Because it is difficult if not impossible to control or even observe what people naturally see, hear, and do for weeks, months, or years at a time, researchers often simply ask individuals what they typically watch, see, or do and then look for differences in their attitudes or behaviors based on what they report. Thus, researchers may ask on a survey what kind of video games a child typically plays and how often and then see if children who regularly play certain games think or behave differently than those who do not.

But, of course, in self-report studies, as in many field studies, we cannot control the "treatments" or entertainment that people receive. As a result, any differences we find between people who select different entertainment may not be due to the entertainment itself but to any number of other factors. For example, when a survey study finds a correlation between exposure to violent video games and aggressive tendencies, it may not be that playing these video games makes children become more aggressive, but rather that children who are more aggressive tend to choose more aggressive games. Or, there may be other factors that are involved. We might find that a survey suggests that individuals who attend rock concerts are more likely to develop emphysema than individuals who go to classical concerts. Does this mean that live rock music causes emphysema? Hardly. It might simply be that people who attend live rock concerts smoke more cigarettes than do people who go to classical concerts and that it is the smoking that is causing the emphysema. If researchers also include survey questions about other potential influences (such as smoking, in this case) they can try to statistically separate and identify the effects of each (e.g., the impact of attending live concerts versus the impact of smoking), but it can be difficult if not impossible to ask questions for every possible factor that might influence differences in these effects.

Content and Text Analysis

If we want to truly understand how audiences are affected by media entertainment, we also need to understand the nature of the media themselves. A pharmaceutical researcher would not test the effects of a new drug without knowing the contents of the drug. Similarly, media researchers cannot truly test or explain the effects of different forms of media entertainment without knowing the content or *text* of those media, including words, images, and sounds. Most content analyses include very systematic, quantifiable measures of media content, where researchers actually quantify the amount of different types of content—for example, measuring column inches devoted to certain topics in magazine articles, counting the minutes of violence in movies, or the number of women or minorities that play certain roles in television programs.

It can be difficult, however, to develop objective, quantitative measures of media content. How, for example, do you create a measure of the amount of violence in a film? Does violence include instances when one character pushes another or holds a gun to someone's head but doesn't pull the trigger? Do you measure violence by the length of time that fighting occurs or by the number of people that are killed or injured? The measures that are used in a study usually depend upon what the researchers are specifically interested in studying. Nonetheless, researchers need to be very careful about clearly defining the measures they use because those methods need to be objective and reliable—that is, when different people use the same measure to analyze the same content, such as the violence in a film, they should come up with the same results.

In other research, content or text is analyzed from a qualitative perspective. In these studies, instead of trying to objectively count content, researchers subjectively demonstrate trends by selecting excerpts or examples and interpreting them from a specific theoretical approach or perspective. Different researchers might isolate different examples or trends depending on their own opinions or perspectives. For example, Jean Kilbourne has created a series of documentary movies called *Killing Us Softly* that makes the argument that advertising depicts unrealistic and sexist portrayals of women. She makes her case by showing examples of advertisements and pointing out distortions in those messages.

Researchers have analyzed the content of many forms of media entertainment, including films, television programs, magazines, video games, sporting events, song lyrics, and the images in music videos. Therefore, when individuals self-report high exposure to certain forms of media, researchers gain a better sense of what exactly they have been exposed to. In formal content analyses, however, evaluations are typically limited to objective measures of content. Although this analysis might be combined with surveys or other data for further evaluations, content analyses alone do not attempt to interpret or evaluate the meaning or potential impact of that content. In other words, content analysis can tell us only how often guns are shown in prime-time television programs or how many women in fashion magazines are showing their midriffs; it does not tell us what those depictions mean or what impact they may have on their audiences. Exceptions to these limitations, however, are found in qualitative analyses of media content, such as Jean Kilbourne's studies, which often do include interpretations of the meaning and impact of the trends they find.

Both quantitative and qualitative analyses of media content often serve as a starting point for more media effects research. For instance, a study on how the media influence stereotyping might first analyze content to look for stereotypical depictions. Researchers might analyze the content of films or television programs to see if certain ethnic groups are disproportionately portrayed as criminals or deadbeats. If such stereotyping does appear to exist, then the researchers might do further research to see if individuals who report watching more films or television are more likely to hold the stereotypical views portrayed by the media. Content analyses can thus provide useful insights into understanding the impact of media entertainment. Although content analyses are informative, critics contend that these studies are not sufficiently objective because of the difficulty researchers have in creating clear, informative measures of media content.

A Final Note on Research Methods

Quantitative and qualitative analysis, observational data and self-reports, laboratory and field studies, and content and text analyses—each method and approach has relative strengths and weaknesses for studying media and entertainment effects. Many studies now incorporate a mixture of approaches to take advantage of the strengths of each. But there is no such thing as a perfect study; every investigation is open to criticism. Researchers, however, do not abandon their investigations simply because they cannot design a perfect study. Instead, they recognize that the value of their research lies not in the individual results of a single study but in the cumulative findings of many studies over time. The following section reviews some of these findings and the theories that have been used to explain them.

THEORIES OF MEDIA EFFECTS

Limited Effects

Interested in understanding how to use the media to effectively generate and counter war propaganda, both the United States and Germany provided generous government funding for media research during and following World War II. This era was characterized by the limited effects perspective or paradigm. Many of the emerging theories and the resulting research followed the quantitative, scientific tradition, relying on carefully structured and controlled experiments.

Attitude Change Theory

The United States Army established an Experimental Section inside its Information and Education Division and staffed it with Carl Hovland and other psychologists who were experts in attitude change. In what are commonly called the *Hovland studies,* these researchers developed *attitude change theory,* which sought to explain how people's attitudes were formed, shaped, and changed through communication, and to understand the relationship between attitudes and behavior.[123] This research followed the social scientific tradition; they tested their ideas experimentally, as medical researchers might, by exposing individuals to different media or messages and testing differences in their effectiveness. Typically, these studies were done in laboratories. And, thus, this research is often criticized for being artificial.

Nonetheless, this research, which sought to explain why the media do not affect everyone the same way, made important contributions to our understanding of media effects. One concept that emerged was the notion of *cognitive dissonance.* People are said to experience cognitive dissonance, a kind of mental discomfort, when they are confronted by information or media that conflict with their own experience, ideas, or opinions. Because dissonance is uncomfortable, people are thought to engage in screening processes that can help them avoid or reduce their discomfort. Researchers propose three interrelated selective processes regarding information or media that individuals consume, remember, and interpret.

☆ *Selective exposure (selective attention)* refers to the tendency for people to expose themselves to or to pay attention to only those messages consistent with their preexisting attitudes or beliefs. People tend to read newspapers and magazines, watch television programs and movies, and to listen to music and radio commentators that reflect their own views.

☆ *Selective retention* suggests that people best remember messages that are consistent with their preexisting attitudes and beliefs. Research finds that when individuals are exposed to media that present multiple views on an issue, they better remember the information that is consistent with their own views.

☆ *Selective perception* maintains that people will interpret messages in a manner consistent with their preexisting attitudes and beliefs. For example, if your favorite public figures, politicians, athletes, actors, or musicians change their position or style, they are perceived to be experimenting or responding to the demands of their public, but when those you don't like do the same thing, they are seen as sellouts.

These selective processes were proposed when the limited or minimal effects paradigm dominated media studies. If people filter out information or experiences that are inconsistent with their beliefs, we would not expect to see much attitude or behavioral change. If the only information or experiences audiences expose themselves to, retain, and perceive are those consistent with their existing attitudes and experiences, the most we might expect is reinforcement of those attitudes and experiences.

This concept is supported by Thomas Klapper's *reinforcement* or *phenomenistic theory*.[124] According to Klapper, the media may contribute to changes in attitude and behavior, but these changes are usually instigated by larger societal changes that are only reinforced through the media. Rather than conducting experimental, laboratory studies, Klapper's research relied more on field-based survey studies. Through these surveys, Klapper measured media exposure as well as other influences (such as church, family, and school) and found that these other influences tended to be much stronger predictors of attitudes and behaviors.

Supporters of the reinforcement view argue that critics should not be overly concerned about the impact of the media because people only read, watch, and listen to news and entertainment that is consistent with what they already think and do anyway. Because this research relies on voluntary, self-reported media use rather than experimentally controlled exposure, studies involving this theory are subject to many of the criticisms of field and self-report studies described previously in the research methods section. In addition, because Klapper's reinforcement research was conducted prior to the invention of television, some theorists speculate that Klapper might have found more powerful effects for the impact of television and other new media.

Agenda Setting

Another theory that reflects the limited effects paradigm is *agenda-setting theory*. News research has found that, by focusing more on some issues than others, the media may help set the agenda by influencing how important certain issues are perceived to be.[125] In these studies, measures of actual media content obtained through content analysis were compared to survey measures of media exposure and to other influential factors and opinions on key issues. These studies have found that the more media exposure people report, the more their rankings of issue importance reflect the amount of coverage those issues get in the media. When more news stories focus on health care, we think health care is a more important issue, and when more stories focus on education or the death penalty, we think those are more important issues. However, perhaps due to the selective processes described previously or perhaps simply because it is extremely difficult to change opinions, this research suggests that the media may influence the relative importance we ascribe to issues, but they do not necessarily influence our specific attitudes toward those issues. Thus, if the media start focusing more on the death penalty, people may begin to rank the issue as more important, but their opinions (either for or against the death penalty) are likely to remain the same, even if the media coverage appears to be biased one way or the other. Thus, the crux of agenda-setting theory is embodied by this paraphrase of Barnard Cohen's statement:[126] *The media may not tell us what to think, but they are stunningly successful at telling us what to think about.*

Although the research on agenda-setting has focused on news media, we might expect the same effects for entertainment media. Like news, entertainment media often go through different trends, where certain topics or genres proliferate the media. Often these trends reflect or respond to trends in the news media. For example, shortly after the September 11, 2001, attack on the World Trade Center in New York City, fantasy and heroic themes dominated film, television, and even music. It is reasonable to think that these offerings might similarly affect people's perceptions of the relative importance of different issues. As with all survey-based effects studies, however, agenda-setting research can reveal only correlations or similarities between media or entertainment and perceptions of issues; it cannot prove that the media or entertainment directly creates or influences those perceptions.

Social Cognitive Theory

Another approach to media effects that reflects the scientific tradition is supported by social cognitive theory. Albert Bandura proposed *social learning theory,* later revised to *social cognitive theory,* which applied popular psychological theories of observational learning to mass media.[127] He proposed that people model the behaviors they see in the mass media. Bandura and his colleagues maintain that observers can acquire or learn new behaviors from the media in the same manner that that they can learn from observation in any other context. In other words, you can learn to dance, flirt, smoke, and so on from watching someone else do it in a movie just as easily as you could learn from watching your cousin do the same things in your own backyard. Many of us may never have actually shot a gun, but we have a general idea how to do it from watching others, typically in television programs or in the movies.

Modeling may occur either through direct *imitation,* where individuals directly replicate behavior they observe in the media, or through *identification,* where individuals do not directly replicate behavior, but they behave in ways that reflect related, generalized responses. For example, a child who sees the cartoon Road Runner character hit Wile E. Coyote over the head with a frying pan might directly imitate the behavior by hitting a sibling over the head with a frying pan or indirectly imitate or identify with the aggressive action by kicking or punching the other child instead. People, however, obviously do not replicate *all* behavior that they see in the media. Consistent with a limited or conditional effects approach, social cognitive theory outlines key conditions that are necessary for effects to be modeled:

☆ *Attention.* To acquire new attitudes or behaviors, an individual must first take notice of (or attend to) what the role model says or does. If people aren't paying attention to behavior that is being modeled on television or in some other form of entertainment, they cannot replicate it.

☆ *Retention.* An individual must symbolically encode and retain the modeled behavior. If we do not remember what we have seen, we cannot replicate what was shown.

☆ *Physical reproduction.* The individual must be capable of performing the behavior. If we do not have the necessary resources (strength, money, gun, time, and so on), we cannot replicate it.

☆ *Reinforcement.* The individual must be reinforced for the behavior, either directly or vicariously (by watching others be rewarded).

The need for reinforcement results in two modeling effects that the media may have: inhibitory and disinhibitory effects. *Inhibitory effects* occur when the media inhibit or decrease the likelihood of imitating a behavior we otherwise might have engaged in. When we see a model, such as a movie character, punished for a behavior, we are less likely to imitate that behavior. For example, our natural inclination may be to help a stranger who has fallen on the street. However, this reaction may become inhibited and we may become less willing to help if we watch movies that show people being sued or shot when they try to help a stranger. *Disinhibitory effects* occur when the media disinhibit or increase the likelihood of imitating a behavior. When we see models rewarded for their behavior, we are more likely to imitate that behavior. Thus, if we see behaviors that might not normally seem that appealing, such as smoking or starving oneself, reinforced or rewarded in the media, we may be more inclined to imitate them.

Such effects are not necessarily negative. Media models might inhibit a child's natural aggressive tendencies if aggressive models are punished. Likewise, media models might encourage positive behavior, such as modeling and rewarding outgoing sociable behavior to help individuals overcome shyness. Nonetheless, the potential for modeling effects forms the basis for complaints against media depictions that appear to glorify undesirable behavior (such as drug use and criminal activity) and to discount desirable behavior (such as doing well in school).

Social cognitive theory is one of the most common theories used to understand the impact of entertainment media. Many studies have applied social cognitive theory to television programs, feature films, and video games, typically in laboratory-like settings, making this theory one of the few in the scientific tradition to focus more on entertainment than news media. Some of these studies will be addressed more specifically later in the chapter. One reason this theory is so popular is because it intuitively makes sense. The idea that people may imitate their favorite television or film characters, athletes, or musicians is readily accepted. Typically, when we think of this form of learning, we think of children who run around karate kicking like Power Rangers or wearing lightning bolts on their foreheads and casting spells like Harry Potter. Most of us, however, can also think of our own anecdotal examples of adults who have imitated the dress, talk, or actions from a movie or music video.

Priming and Association Theories

Leonard Berkowitz and his colleagues proposed a theory that focused on extremely short-term, temporary media effects.[128] *Priming theory* holds that witnessing, reading, or hearing of an event or idea through the mass media can *prime* or stimulate related thoughts or ideas. These thoughts are believed to stay with us for a short time after our media experience and influence our reactions and behaviors in consistent ways. Thus, according to this theory, if someone hits our car as we are driving out of the movie theater parking lot, our reaction may vary considerably depending on the movie we have just seen. If we have seen a violent action film, we might react more aggressively than we normally would, because the film has made aggressive thoughts and ideas more salient or prominent in our minds. Many studies on priming have examined the role of media violence on subsequent violent behavior. If we have just seen a romantic comedy, however, we might be more understanding than we normally would be because the film may have made warm and lighthearted ideas more salient or prominent. In another example of priming theory, a study found that participants who read a "boy meets girl" story smiled more, talked more, and leaned forward more when talking to a female after reading the story than did those who read a control story.

Research has examined priming effects of many forms of entertainment, including film, television, radio, video games, and sporting events. In most cases, research suggests that ideas or concepts from the entertainment can influence later thoughts and behaviors. These effects, however, tend to be extremely short lived. The primed ideas and thoughts quickly begin to fade as we become preoccupied with other ideas and activities. Research suggests that priming can occur automatically without us even knowing about it. One study found that when participants were unknowingly exposed to hostile words (flashed so quickly on a screen that individuals didn't consciously register them), they made more hostile and negative evaluations of a person than did those not exposed to the hostile words. This subconscious priming provides one explanation for the effectiveness of music, lighting, and other cues in films, plays, and other forms of entertainment. For example, certain melodies, tones, or music tempos have come to be associated with fear, excitement, joy, and so on. Thus, playing a certain type of music may trigger related thoughts and feelings, priming audiences' reactions for the events that follow. If we concentrate on the music itself, we may recognize how our reactions are being manipulated, but often, when we are absorbed in the entertainment experience, we become less aware of the specific cues that are being used to prime our reactions.

Like social learning, the priming function of entertainment has intuitive appeal. We have all had the experience of having a sudden craving for something we just saw in a film, perhaps a sudden desire to eat a burger or go swimming. An athletic coach, for example, might find that the team plays better after watching an inspirational sports film or listening to energetic, aggressive, or triumphant music. Although priming is typically considered a short-term effect, other *association theories*, such as classical conditioning, suggest effects of entertainment cues that may last longer. The reasoning is that by repeatedly pairing certain cues with certain concepts or events, the two become associated or connected in people's minds, and we become conditioned to the point where merely witnessing the cue will trigger thoughts about the primed concepts or events.

Celebrity endorsements and product placements in films are often made on the premise of association. Companies hope that by pairing their products with popular celebrities or films, the positive thoughts people have about the celebrities or the films will become associated with their products to the point where, when we see these products, we will have the same positive thoughts even without the presence of the celebrity or the film. Critics, however, condemn entertainment for some of the associations they believe may be formed. Certain rock music videos are criticized, for example, because repetitiously pairing degrading and aggressive lyrics with images of women in some videos is feared to create a lasting association in viewers' heads, so that any women or images of women that these individuals later encounter begin to cue degrading and aggressive thoughts and behaviors.

Physiological Effects

Physical forms of entertainment, such as dancing, sports, and games like tag or hide and seek, can have obvious short-term physiological impacts, such as increased heart and breathing rates and muscle strains or bone breaks, as well as long-term impacts, such as weight loss, lowered blood pressure, arthritis, and tendonitis. As we discussed in Chapter 4, research suggests that relatively passive forms of entertainment, such as watching a movie or listening to music, can also have short-term physiological impacts. When a film or song excites us, our hearts may start to beat faster, and our breathing may become irregular. Some research also suggests possible short- and long-term health benefits for such forms of entertainment, particularly for humor and comedy.

Folk wisdom suggests that humor can relieve pain as well as stress, ward off illness, and aid in healing. These speculations have led to a growing body of scientific, experimental research on the health benefits associated with humor and comedy.[129] Humor and comedy have been found to increase feelings of relaxation and decrease levels of stress-linked hormones. Research suggests that laughter can increase the flow of oxygen and nutrients to tissues and promote the movement of immune elements throughout the system to help fight infection. Exposure to comedy and upbeat drama was also found to increase pain tolerance. Some studies, for example, have found that patients in hospitals or senior homes who watch more comedies ask for less pain medication than patients who watch serious dramas. Interestingly, increased pain tolerance has also been observed after exposure to tragic films.

It is unclear why some forms of media entertainment, including comedy, appear to increase pain thresholds, although several explanations have been offered. One thought is that the positive emotions stimulated by media entertainment simply serve to counteract the negative perceptions of the pain. A similar notion, based on the distraction principle, is that any engaging film serves to distract individuals from their pain to the point where they may even continue to cognitively reflect on the film even after the film has ended, and thus remain distracted from the pain. Others postulate that the physiological arousal—whether positive or negative—generated by entertainment such as a film serves to increase one's pain threshold directly or through the release of special hormones, although research has failed to confirm this relationship.

Inconsistencies in methodology and findings make it difficult to draw any firm conclusions about the health impacts of comedy and other forms of entertainment. Nonetheless, given the overwhelming concerns about negative media effects, it is encouraging to see even limited evidence for positive effects of comedy and other forms of media entertainment.

Cumulative and Cultural Effects

The distinction between *scientific* and *cultural and critical* theories is not clear cut. Contemporary theories in both traditions acknowledge the potential for more powerful but conditional media effects, and both reflect a shift in focus from limited, short-term effects to cumulative, long-term influences. Today, most researchers in both traditions recognize that meaning is subjective; thus, there is no objective Truth (with a capital T) of the media's impact. Different audiences will interpret and thus react differently to the media. For the social scientist, this is an important qualification, one that makes research difficult. However, ultimately, most social scientists are relatively comfortable with the idea that some level of objectivity can and should be obtained for understanding how audiences are differently affected.

Cultural and critical media studies, however, typically embrace the subjective nature of the media's influence. Cultural researchers maintain that the media and other experiences have more global, profound influences, not only on individual perceptions and behavior but on our society and culture. They believe that these effects cannot be easily isolated or quantified. They question the need and advisability of "quantifying" subjective concepts like media content or individuals' opinions. From the cultural perspective, an objective, detached approach to media or entertainment research is unnecessary if not impossible. This difference in perspective leads many scholars to suggest that cultural studies of effects reflect a distinct paradigm. As researchers in both traditions increasingly share ideas and methodologies, scientific and cultural perspectives exist perhaps more as a continuum than as separate approaches, with different theories and theorists falling more to one side than another yet still reflecting aspects of each.

Dependency Theory

Many limited effects theories, such as agenda-setting and social cognitive theory studies, suggest that the effects of the media and entertainment, although limited to specific effects or conditions, tend to build over time. Melvin DeFleur and Sandra Ball-Rokeach argued for more powerful, cumulative media effects with the introduction of *dependency theory*. Introduced in 1975, this theory argued that people were becoming increasingly dependent on the media to understand their world, to be told how to behave, and as a means for escape when that world became too overwhelming. According to this theory, we rely more heavily on the media for some situations and issues than others. In the case of a crisis or a national disaster, we turn to the media. Again, consider the events of September 11. For most of the world, including even most of those in New York City, our knowledge and experience of the event was largely limited to what we saw and heard from the media. We turned to the media not only for information about what had happened but also for comfort and companionship—to share our grief. We even used the media to escape, turning to videos, games, or music to distract ourselves from what had happened.

Simple logic would dictate that, if our only exposure to an issue or event comes from the media, any resulting thoughts, attitudes, and behavior would necessarily be shaped by the media. Most of us do not know, however, if our perceptions or actions are any different than they might have been if we had received information from sources other than the mass media, such as direct experience or personal accounts. Nonetheless, according to dependency theory's conditional effects model, although the media have only limited effects when they are only one of many sources for our information and experiences, the media may have quite powerful, although not necessarily unique, effects when they are a primary or sole source of information and experience.

The researchers that proposed dependency theory come from a social scientific tradition of structured, empirical testing, but the spontaneity and magnitude of the types of issues and situations that are media dominated, such as crisis and national disasters, make it difficult to control and isolate the effects of the media and compare them to societal influences. For example, it would be difficult to empirically test the impact of media coverage for September 11 because it would be virtually impossible to maintain a control group of people who were not exposed to the media coverage. Interestingly, and perhaps not surprisingly, however, the rationale behind dependency theory is also reflected in some of the cultural theories whose research methods depart from the strict social scientific tradition.

Diffusion of Innovation

Studies examining the diffusion of innovation examine how the media and other forms of communication, including entertainment, introduce us to information about new discoveries in technology and culture, including products to make our lives easier, inventions, and other innovations.[130] The term *diffusion* refers to the idea that information about new ideas and other innovations slowly spreads throughout society propelled by the media and word of mouth. This theory proposes that media can play an important role in triggering awareness, interest, and ultimately adoption of new ideas, trends, inventions, and innovations. This process is said to be guided by four steps: interest, evaluation, trial, and acquisition.

Imagine that you are considering buying a new mobile phone. While flipping through a magazine, you might come across an advertisement for a new, small, sleek phone. You glance at the ad briefly and recognize the phone as one used by Tom Cruise in a movie you recently saw. Later, you see a television advertisement for the phone. Now, you are really becoming *interested*. You then begin *evaluating* the phone. You might look up information about the phone on the Internet and talk with some of your friends who have bought similar ones. You might go to a dealer to look at the phone. A friend who has just purchased the phone might let you make a *trial* phone call to test the reception quality. Finally, after you discover there is a sizable mail-in rebate, your mind is made up, and you *acquire* the phone by purchasing it. Evidence for diffusion is found not only for technological advances, but also for fashion trends. For example, Ray-Ban claims that sales of the Predator 2 sunglasses worn by Will Smith and Tommy Lee Jones in *Men in Black* tripled to almost $5 million after the release of the movie in 1997.

Symbolic Interaction(ism)

Another theory that focuses on more cumulative and cultural effects is symbolic interactionism. *Symbolic interaction* or *symbolic interactionism,* also borrowed from psychology, maintains that symbols are learned through interaction and that, once learned, these symbols mediate and influence further interaction. For example, we designate the color red to represent danger and, once designated, this meaning guides our interactions, how we react and behave—whether it's the red of a traffic signal or the red of a cocktail dress. According to communication scholars Don Faules and Dennis Alexander, communication is "symbolic behavior which results in various degrees of shared meaning and values between participants."[131]

Symbolic interaction is a cultural study because the theory dictates that different experiences and interactions create different symbolic meanings, and these differences both create and reflect cultural differences. The word *cultural* is not used here to merely reflect ethnic or socioeconomic differences, but any factors that work to create shared symbols—workplaces, sporting events, restaurants, concerts. Any environment that facilitates interaction creates the opportunity for the development of shared meanings and subcultures of employees, fans, patrons, or audiences. Researchers have thus examined how different factors, such as the media and other experiences, shape and reflect shared meanings and cultures. Rather than relying on quantitative, structured surveys and behavioral measures, symbolic interaction is usually documented through less structured, qualitative data collection through text analyses, artifacts, and in-depth interviews and focus groups.

Symbolic interaction theory has interesting implications for the study of entertainment because entertainment itself is rich with symbolism. Almost all forms of entertainment rely on shared symbols to connect with audiences. In a live play, audiences recognize that an actor wearing a leotard and mask is a lion, and a white glowing globe hanging from the ceiling is the moon. Music relies heavily on symbolism and shared meanings. Even without words, the tone and beat of a melody can convey emotions—fear, anger, sadness, excitement, or joy—to audiences. Research that examines the symbolic interaction of media and entertainment

Figure 5.2 *Tomb Raider*

Diffusion of Ericsson: Focus on *Tomb Raider*

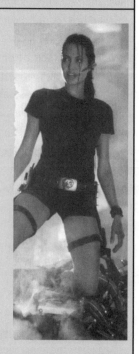

To help Lara Croft save the world from evil domination, Paramount Pictures teamed up with Ericsson, one of the world's leading mobile communications companies. For *Tomb Raider* (2001), Ericsson equipped Lara Croft (played by Angelina Jolie) with products on her car dashboard, her head, and even in a holster on her hip. Many of the products she uses are actually available for consumer purchase, such as the Ericsson Bluetooth Headset seen hooked over her ear.

Croft's home base boasts an Ericsson Cordless Web Screen, which offers voice communication, Internet access, email, voicemail, and her own top-secret address in one easy-access, virtual-touch screen device. Ericsson launched the Web Screen later in the year of the movie's release. The bright-orange R310 phone mounted to the dashboard of her Land Rover was developed in real life for professional adventurers and extreme sports enthusiasts.

Reflecting the diffusion of innovation process, the rugged R310s were even used behind the scenes by the crew throughout filming. Therefore, they were exposed to varying climates, from the heat of Angkor Wat, Cambodia, to the frozen Siberian tundra. Ericsson, of course, generously supplied the filmmakers with these products in the hopes of encouraging diffusion to film audiences.

Ericsson and other manufacturers outfit Lara Croft with the latest gizmos and gadgets to pique audience interest and demand for these new products.

focuses not only on the shared meanings that develop within these experiences (while watching a movie or play, listening to music, or playing a video game) but also on how these experiences influence interactions in our everyday lives.

Social Construction of Reality

A related perspective on the influence of the mass media is borrowed from sociologists Peter Berger and Thomas Luckmann's social construction of reality theory.[132] This theory argues that people who share a culture also share an "ongoing correspondence" of meaning. Some things have direct, objective meanings that almost everyone shares, such as the meaning of a stop sign. Things that possess objective meanings are called *symbols*. Other meanings, although more or less commonly shared, are more subjective. Things with more subjective meanings are called *signs*. For example, a car may be a symbol of transportation, but a BMW or a Ferrari is a sign of wealth or success. The meanings of both symbols and signs are negotiated. People learn them through experiences and interactions but, for signs, the development of meaning is more complex.

Over time, people collect what they have learned about different symbols and signs to form *typification schemes*—collections of meanings assigned to some phenomenon or situation. Typification schemes form the basis for people's interactions and interpretations in their everyday lives. For example, when you enter a library, you automatically recall the cultural meaning of various elements. You recognize this facility as a library as opposed to a restaurant, nightclub, or even a bookstore by the arrangement of the rows of books, posted signs, furniture, and so on. This recognition causes you to invoke your "library typification scheme." You know to study quietly and speak in whispers. You may know not to bring in food or drink. You may expect to wait longer for assistance or request help more politely and formally than you might at a bookstore. Many of these rules may not be published on the wall. You applied them because they were appropriate to the reality of the setting, or at least to your "social construction" of that reality. In other cultures, even quite similar subcultures, behaviors in this setting might be quite different. Indeed, on some college campuses, libraries can be loud, sociable, informal environments.

Social construction of reality can be applied to the study of media and entertainment effects in much the same way that symbolic interaction can be applied. They both explore how our entertainment experiences can shape our everyday perceptions. As is the case with symbolic interactionism, research on the social construction of reality tends to rely on qualitative data analysis, where media content or entertainment experiences are subjectively analyzed and compared with societal trends and perceptions. For example, what do politicians mean when they say they are going to "get tough on crime"? The meaning of this statement is shaped for both the politicians and the voters by their previous experiences. For many people, crime signifies (is a sign for) gangs, drugs, and violence. This is their socially constructed reality, even though there is 10 times more white-collar crime in the United States than there is violent crime. For many people, direct experience with crime is relatively limited. Most of what people know about crime comes from what we have read or seen in news media or on television programs or in the movies.

Thus our "construction of reality" is thought to be based on these mediated experiences. And, because both news and entertainment media tend to focus more on violent crime than on white collar, nonviolent crime, that is the "reality" that shapes our understanding of the concept of crime. Our understanding of getting "tough" is similarly socially construed. Thus, for those raised on a Hollywood diet of action films, getting tough on crime might signify more heavily armed police forces and the use of lethal force and vigilante justice. To the politician, however, "tough" might only mean longer jail sentences. Even though, realistically, voters may know that a politician would not support more radical, vigilante responses to crime, the politician's statement may still appear "tougher" thanks to the lingering images perpetuated by the entertainment media.

Cultivation Analysis

Dependency theory, symbolic interaction, and social construction of reality are all consistent with *cultivation analysis,* which maintains that television cultivates or constructs a reality of the world that, although potentially inaccurate, becomes culturally accepted because we believe it to be true. George Gerbner and his associates developed cultivation analysis as an explanation for the impact of television violence on perceptions of crime, and this analysis has since been applied to television's cultivated effects on perceptions of beauty, sex roles, religion, the judicial process, marriage, and other concerns. In every case, the premise is the same—that repeated, heavy exposure to television cultivates a distorted perception of the world we live in, making the world seem more the way television portrays it than it is in real life. One of the popular conclusions from this research is *mean world syndrome*—the idea that because television portrays unrealistically high levels of violence, people who engage in heavy television viewing perceive the world as a much meaner, more dangerous place than it really is. Like agenda-setting research, cultivation analysis relies on quantitative analysis of television content combined with self-reports of media use and resulting perceptions. Thus, in the mean world study, researchers analyzed television content, found that television portrayed an inordinate amount of "mean" violence, and surveyed people; they found that those who watched a lot of television (and thus a lot of violence) perceived the world to be a meaner place.

The term *cultivation* reflected Gerbner's perspective that television did not influence views by directly offering facts and figures about societal trends; instead, it influenced indirectly through the accumulation or cultivation of consistent images. Television never directly says, "There is lots of violent crime committed by people of color, so you should be afraid of these people." However, because television tends to show a bias toward portraying minorities as violent criminals, we form our own conclusions that reflect this bias. Cultivation theory does not suggest that television can radically alter societal views; rather, it suggests that television serves to stabilize social patterns by reinforcing existing power relationships and societal beliefs. The term *mainstreaming* is used to describe the process in which television helps move people toward a shared understanding of how things are.

Cultivation analysis has typically been limited to studying the influence of television. Gerbner felt that television was fundamentally different from other mass media because it is so pervasive. However, much has changed since the early days of this research. In the past, television offerings were more limited and homogeneous. Today, offerings are more diverse. Thus, some scholars question whether television images are universal or consistent enough to influence perceptions in predictable, "mainstream" ways. Other scholars have more fundamental criticisms of cultivation analysis, arguing that the correlational, survey-based, methodological approach provides no control over media exposure. Again, because the research relies on self-reports of media use, a popular counterexplanation for mean world syndrome and other cultivation effects argues for reverse effects. In other words, it is not that watching television makes people afraid of the mean world, it is that people who think the world is a mean place stay home and watch television because they are afraid to go outside. Nonetheless, Gerbner and cultivation research are among the most widely cited references with regard to media effects. Cultivation theory provides a valuable theoretical and methodological approach for studying entertainment effects—not only for television programs, but also for other pervasive forms of entertainment, such as music videos or content on the Internet.

Narcotizing Effect

Still other theorists propose yet other potential effects of long-term, cumulative, heavy media or entertainment exposure. Rather than changing opinions or mobilizing people to act, some theorists claim that, over time, the media can lull people into passivity. This *narcotizing effect,* sometimes called *narcoticizing disfunction,* is supported by studies finding that when people become overloaded with information, they begin to withdraw. One thought is that when people obtain an abundance of information on a subject—for example by watching several movies, reading several books, or surfing the Internet—they become lulled into feeling as though they have actually done something about the issue. They may begin to use passive news or entertainment offerings as substitutes for active involvement. So people may continue to watch films about racial injustice—like *Mississippi Burning* (1988), *Do the Right Thing* (1989), *Malcolm X* (1992), *Amistad* (1997), or *American History X* (1998)—that make them feel involved instead of actively becoming involved in civil rights groups, writing letters, signing petitions, or attending rallies. Another thought is that people simply begin to feel overwhelmed by the ominous or conflicting views that the media present. Feeling confused and helpless, people become paralyzed and do nothing.

Critical Cultural Theory

A major influence on modern media and entertainment theory comes from *critical cultural theory,* which echoes some of Gerber's cultivation sentiments, maintaining that the media operate primarily to justify and support the status quo, supporting certain groups or elites at the expense of ordinary people or select groups of people. Modern neo-Marxist theorists believe that people are oppressed by those who control the culture, the superstructure—in other words, the mass media. In the opinion of traditional Marxists, these oppressors are right-wing political elites who use the news and entertainment media not only to convey their own ideologies but also to keep the masses pacified and distracted. It is reasoned that elites try to keep people happy and entertained so that they are less likely to protest or challenge the existing power structure.

Critical scholars approach their studies from a variety of perspectives. Feminist critiques examine ways in which the media and entertainment reinforce patriarchy and male domination in society. Gay and lesbian critiques examine the ways in which the media marginalize lesbians and gay men. African American critiques focus on ways in which the media subjugate African Americans, and so on. Critical scholars approach their studies qualitatively, relying on subjective analyses of media content and its impact. Modern critical theorists possess a number of different conceptions of the relationship between media and culture, but all share several identifying characteristics:[133]

☆ They tend to be macroscopic in scope, examining broad, culture-wide media effects.

☆ The are openly and avowedly political. Based in neo-Marxism, their orientation is typically from the political left.

☆ Their goal is minimally to instigate change in government media policies, at the most to effect wholesale change in media and cultural systems. Critical cultural theories assume that the superstructure, which favors those in power, must be altered.

☆ They investigate and explain how elites use media to maintain their positions of privilege and power. Issues such as media ownership, government-media relations, and corporate media representations of labor and disenfranchised groups are typical topics of study for critical cultural theory because they center on the exercise of power.

This section has reviewed many different theories that have been offered to explain how entertainment—particularly media entertainment—affects its audiences. Although there is some overlap, many of these theories suggest very different effects. For review, take a look at Figure 5.3 and see if you can match the theory to its predicted impact for the image shown. The next section will detail some of these impacts more specifically.

Figure 5.3   Match the Theory to the Effect

Match the Theory to the Effect	Effects
What perceptions or impacts might media news and entertainment images like the one pictured here have on audiences?  Undercover officers arresting a sniper suspect. © David Turnley/Corbis.	1. Reinforces criminal stereotypes. 2. Inhibits/reduces criminal behavior. 3. Makes crime seem like a serious issue. 4. Marginalizes minorities and strips their power. 5. Temporarily triggers violent thoughts and actions. 6. Lying down conveys subservience and submission; weapon conveys dominance. *Theories* A. Agenda-setting theory B. Critical theory C. Cultivation theory D. Priming theory E. Social learning theory F. Symbolic Interaction/Social Construction of Reality

Answers. 1C. Repeated depictions of certain groups create and reinforce stereotypes. **2E.** Crime is punished, not positively reinforced or rewarded. **3A.** Media tell us what issues are important. **4B.** Images perpetuate the power of the elites over the rest of society. **5D.** Images stimulate related violent behaviors and thoughts. **6F.** Images create and reinforce signs and symbolic meaning.

ENTERTAINMENT EFFECTS: THE IMPACT

I wish there was a knob on the TV to turn up the intelligence. There's a knob called "brightness," but it doesn't work.

—Gallagher, comedian

Socialization

Stereotyping

The media are often accused of encouraging *stereotyping,* or the application of a standardized image or concept to members of a certain group, usually based on limited information. The media, particularly entertainment media, present only a slice of life, but that slice is not necessarily representative of real life. Mundane, normal, everyday people and events typically are just not all that interesting or entertaining. Instead, entertainment often focuses on unusual or exceptional individuals and situations. Content analyses conducted over the last 40 years have demonstrated that people of color are depicted as perpetrators of crime and aggression more often than is the case in the real world and that women and people of color are more likely to be depicted as victims of aggression than they are in the real world. Other portrayals also encourage stereotyping, such as the dumb blonde, the jolly fat guy, and feeble-minded old folks.

Many of the theories discussed in this chapter, especially dependency theory, cultivation analysis, symbolic interaction, and social construction of reality, might predict that the repeated, regular exposure to media and entertainment containing distorted representations might lead to stereotyping people in the real world. The fear is that the media influence our perceptions and that these perceptions then influence our behavior toward stereotyped groups.

Should a lone female feel safer walking alone in Oklahoma City or New York City? Or in Rapid City, South Dakota, or Washington, D.C.? Consider how you develop your stereotypes of the people who live in these places. Where did you get the images and ideas that form the basis for constructing your understanding of these places and the people who live there? What theories might explain how these stereotypes develop? Then consider the actual statistics. The FBI reports that in Oklahoma City, the incidence of forcible rape is 73.9 per 100,000 females, three times the levels of New York City and Washington DC, and the city with the highest rate of forcible rape in the United States is Rapid City.

Issues and Trends

Many theories suggest that media and other forms of entertainment can also shape our perceptions of societal issues and trends. For example, movies such as *Dead Man Walking* or *The Green Mile* might influence our thoughts and opinions about the death penalty, whereas songs such as Ani DiFranco's *Lost Woman Song*, Ben Fold Five's *Brick,* or Everlast's *What It's Like* might influence our thoughts about social issues like abortion, homelessness, and drug use. Theories like agenda setting hypothesize that, with repetition, these messages might affect how important these issues are to us, whereas attitude change, social learning, dependency, and cultivation theories might suggest that they may help shape and perhaps even change our opinions on these topics.

As suggested by diffusion of innovations and other theories, media and entertainment can also shape societal trends, influencing what we buy and wear, where we go, and what we eat. Consider recent fashion trends, the latest hairstyles, or the newest "must have" toy or gadget. Think about where you first saw or heard of these concepts. Perhaps in a magazine or in a movie or on a television program? Or, perhaps from a friend . . . who may have gotten the idea from a magazine, a movie, or television (see the "Diffusion of Ericsson: Focus on *Tomb Raider*" box earlier in this chapter).

Role Models

Entertainment also provides us with role models. Audiences pay close attention to the behavior of actors, musicians, and athletes whether they are in their roles as entertainers in films, music video, or a sports contest or out of their roles in their everyday lives. Chapter 3 discusses the parasocial relationships that audiences develop with entertainers. Audiences become attached to their favorite actors, recording artists, and athletes, feeling a special bond to them. They often carefully follow their favorite entertainers' careers and personal lives from their performances and from the news and gossip media.

Social learning theory suggests that people may adopt or reject behaviors that they see modeled by entertainers based on whether those behaviors are rewarded or punished. Entertainers usually possess many desirable traits—they are talented, successful, good looking, and well liked. These qualities or the desire to possess these qualities provide even further incentive for people to view entertainers as role models for their own values and behavior. There is concern, of course, about what sort of roles these entertainers are modeling given the sexual scandals, drug use, deceit, or violent altercations they portray in movies, music videos, and even sports events, not to mention similar highly publicized activities in their personal lives. Concerns about the impact of violence, sex, and drugs in media and entertainment are explored further in the next section.

Causes and Effects: The Media and Terrorism

Many people have speculated about the relationship between Western media and entertainment and the September 11, 2001, terrorist attacks on the World Trade Center in New York City. There is consideration of both how media entertainment may have played a role in precipitating the attack as well as how it may have influenced how people reacted to the attack.

First, there are concerns about the images of Western culture that are portrayed by news and entertainment programs—sensationalized images of crime, violence, sex, and lifestyles of the rich and famous. Americans seem to have so much, and yet many Westerners portrayed in the news and entertainment media appear to be ungrateful, godless criminals who do not care about anyone but themselves. Meanwhile, even before September 11, U.S. books and films also portrayed Middle Easterners in very negative ways, often as the enemy, as villains and terrorists. Given these images, some argue it is no wonder that individuals from other cultures might view Westerners, particularly Americans, as violent, unscrupulous hedonists who hate Middle Easterners. Indeed, such views reflect the very accusations that Al Qaeda and other terrorist groups have made against the Western world—accusations that they have used to rally support for their causes and to justify their attacks.

Books, films, and other forms of entertainment have also been accused of aiding terrorists by giving them ideas for attack strategies. People have noted parallels, for example, between Tom Clancy's book *Debt of Honor* (published the year after the failed bombing of the World Trade Center in 1993) and the September 11 attacks. In the book, the antagonist flies an airplane into the Capitol building during a joint session of Congress and into other targets, similar to the actual 2001 attacks on both towers of the World Trade Center and the Pentagon (as well as an attack probably planned for the Capitol or the White House but that was prevented when the fourth plane crashed in a Pennsylvania field).

Video games have been similarly accused of providing ideas and perhaps even practice for would-be terrorists. Following the attacks, Microsoft announced the elimination of the World Trade Center from the skyline of its upcoming *Microsoft Flight Simulator 2002*—a game said to be so realistic that some student pilots use it for training. Other video game makers also planned to purge images of destruction involving New York from new releases following the terrorist attacks at the World Trade Center. Activision indefinitely postponed release of its PlayStation game *Spider-Man 2—Enter: Electro* a day before it was to hit stores because the superhero battles villains atop skyscrapers resembling the World Trade Center.

Shortly after the attack, Hollywood executives met with Karl Rove, a senior advisor to U.S. President George W. Bush, and unanimously endorsed the government's request for film and television projects promoting America and "American values." Rove had, in fact, enumerated seven specific themes, from tolerance to volunteerism, that he hoped the entertainment industry would address. Thus, the events of September 11 show us not only how the media and entertainment may influence our society but also how societal events influence media and entertainment offerings.[134]

Terrorists, of course, are not the only ones who may be affected by entertainment images. Even the most law-abiding citizens may inadvertently begin to adopt stereotypical views, such as suspecting all Middle Easterners of being terrorists because that is how they are depicted in books, games, programs, and movies. Our experience with entertainment media may also influence our perception of news coverage of events such as those that occurred on September 11. Many people were unable to resist the coverage of the U.S. terrorist attack. As horrific as it was to watch on television or read about in the newspaper and in magazines, many people found it nearly impossible to turn away. Some people say that they watched hoping for information or because they felt fearful of a future attack and wanted to be prepared; others say that they were watching in an effort to digest and process the event.

Some critics, however, contend that the media intentionally created seductive and addictive images almost like an action movie. Whether that was the intention or not, some say that viewers did seem to view the news coverage as if it were a movie—a self-contained story that would include a beginning and an ending. However, news coverage is not the same as a movie. In a movie, audiences expect and typically are given all the information they need to understand the story—all of the characters are introduced, background and details are provided. It is difficult if not impossible, however, to gain the same depth of information from a news report. In real life, stories are much more complicated. When did the battle between the United States and terrorists like Osama bin Laden and his followers really begin, and will it ever really end? In real life, it is difficult to pinpoint a beginning and an ending, and to collect all of the information necessary to truly understand events as they unfold.

Although this may seem obvious once you stop to think about it, years of entertainment (watching movies and television, playing games, reading books) combined with the recent trend of making news more entertainment-like, may train people to interpret news as if it were entertainment. As a result, viewers may watch more passively and less critically, assuming that watching a couple of hours of CNN will tell us the complete and accurate "story" of what is happening in our world.

The events of September 11 offer almost limitless opportunities to explore the relationship between the media, entertainment, and the real life they portray and imitate. As with all media effects, however, we will probably never completely understand the impact of Western media and entertainment on the terrorist attack and its aftermath.

What do you think? Do you think entertainment such as movies, books, television programs, and video games in any way influenced the terrorist attack? If so, how? What theories might explain these effects? What role, if any, do you think entertainment may have had in how people reacted to the attack? What do you think about the entertainment industry leaders' reactions to the terrorist attack? Should they have done anything differently? Should they do anything differently in the future?

Violence, Sex, and Drugs

Violence

No entertainment effect has received more public, legislative, or industry attention than the impact of media violence on societal aggression. Violent entertainment has been accused of increasing juvenile delinquency and violent crime rates (including instances of spousal abuse, rape, and murder) and of scaring people to the point that they are afraid to go outside their homes. Studies have analyzed the impact of violence in films, television programs, live sporting events, music, and video games, yet research on the subject is far from conclusive. Although some studies have found a relationship between media violence and aggressive behavior, others have not. And results each way are almost always questioned and criticized by other researchers. Thus, the question of whether or not media and entertainment violence can encourage violent behavior cannot be clearly answered. Nonetheless, several theories suggest that such a relationship may exist.

Some theories suggest short-term impacts of media violence. As mentioned earlier in this chapter, *priming theory* suggests that media violence may prime aggressive ideas or thoughts, which might make people tend to react more aggressively for a period of time after viewing the media violence. Similarly, *excitation transfer theory,* discussed in Chapter 4, suggests that the excitement and adrenaline generated by media violence, such as in an action film or at a sporting event, may keep people in an agitated state so that, for a brief time afterwards, they may react more intensely and aggressively than they would otherwise if provoked. *Catharsis theory,* however, suggests the exact opposite: that witnessing aggression in a film, game, or other form of media allows us to vent our aggression vicariously along with the characters or players, thereby purging our hostility so that we may actually become less aggressive for a short time afterward.

Other theories suggest more lasting impacts. For example, *social cognitive theory* suggests that we might learn from the media or other forms of entertainment to behave aggressively if such behavior is rewarded. Conversely, however, we should learn to be *less* aggressive, if such behavior is punished. *Cultural and cumulative theories* suggest that the nature of the violence displayed (by whom, against whom) can have significant societal influences on the status and power of certain groups.

Thus, the exact relationship between media violence and real violence is still unclear. At one extreme is the view that media violence can actually decrease violent tendencies and reduce real aggression. At the other extreme is the view that media violence significantly increases real-life violence. Most researchers, however, tend to take a middle-ground perspective that certain depictions of violence under certain conditions may prompt violence in certain persons.

Sex and Drugs

Critics have similar concerns about the impact of media portrayals of sex, drugs, and alcohol use. Content and textual analyses reveal how these activities are portrayed in media and entertainment. The primary accusation is that the media glorify behaviors such as smoking, drinking, drug use, and sexual promiscuity. Consistent with *social cognitive theory*, it is feared that glorified, rewarded depictions of these activities will lead people, particularly youths, to imitate what they see. Again, research results are mixed. Some studies find evidence that media portrayals can influence sexual behavior and drug use, whereas others do not. Of course, not all media portrayals glorify sex and drugs. Studies have also examined whether drama that includes negative portrayals and consequences of drugs (e.g., TV programs such as *NYPD Blue* and *ER* and movies such as *Trainspotting* and *Boyz N the Hood*) can decrease drug use. Again, results vary.

Limitations

Research on media effects on behavior such as aggression, sex, and drug use face the same methodological limitations as all effects research. From a classic scientific perspective, to accurately evaluate the impact of the media on behavior, you must have complete control over exposure to the media in question and valid, reliable measures of aggression and violent behavior. As mentioned earlier in this chapter, this is extremely difficult to do. Researchers usually have only very limited control of people's media exposure. They may be able to control a single movie, sporting event, or concert they see, or even a series of films or events, but they cannot control all of the other media people are exposed to. Thus, it is difficult to establish a control comparison group that has not already been repeatedly exposed to media depictions of violence, drugs, and so on. And, any group that has managed to avoid exposure has probably done so intentionally because they do not want to see media violence or sex or drug use. As a result, even if they would be willing to participate in a study, they would probably not be representative of the type of people the researchers would want to study.

Researchers also have difficulties measuring impacts on aggressive and sexual behavior and drug use. Such behaviors are typically not ones that participants or research review boards are readily willing to let you observe. Most research review boards will not allow researchers to place participants in hostile, health-threatening, or legally questionable situations and, even if they would, if people know they are being observed, they might behave differently than they would otherwise. As a result, researchers are often limited to pencil and paper, asking questions such as "What do you typically do . . .?" or "What would you do if . . .?" These measures ask people to self-report their behavior, which may not accurately reflect what they would actually do. Nonetheless, each additional study can potentially add to our understanding of the relationship between media and entertainment portrayals and audience behavior. And the significance of these issues encourages researchers to continue their efforts to understand these effects.

Prosocial Effects

Although many critics warn of potential negative impacts of media and entertainment, there are also many potential positive impacts. Not all of the messages that are conveyed are bad. Television, movies, music, sports, and video games often convey positive messages about tolerance and diversity, about honesty, cooperation, and friendship, about healthy habits,

Figure 5.4 *Sesame Street* Original Cast

One of the pioneer television programs created to both entertain and educate its young watchers; evidence from decades of research suggests that the program was successful on both counts.
© Bettmann/Corbis.

responsibility, and consequences. And if audiences are influenced by media and entertainment messages, they should be influenced by these positive messages (see the "A Closer Look" section later in this chapter). Although sports such as football and hockey can be very aggressive, they also often demonstrate positive values, such as teamwork and perseverance. Although video games may prevent some children from getting exercise or interacting with their peers, they may also sharpen reasoning skills and reflexes.

Indeed, research has found that the media can influence people, particularly children, in very positive ways.[135] A sizable body of research demonstrates that people, especially children, can and will model the good or social behaviors they see in the media. Research also suggests that media portrayals can encourage cooperation and constructive problem solving. Children's programs (such as the classic *Sesame Street*, produced by Children's Television Workshop, and Nickelodeon's *Blue's Clues*) are designed to educate and socialize children as well as to entertain them. And research suggests that these programs can be very effective. Furthermore, although the media and entertainment may shape our world, they are also reflective of that world. The media teach us about our society, values, customs, and concerns.

The media show us parts of our world we might never see—African wildlife preserves, the top of Mt. Everest, hurricanes, snowstorms, the birth of a child. Not all of the stories and images are good; many do reflect the bad and the ugly of our society, but sometimes these stories and images can help us better cope with some of these less pleasant realities.

Edutainment

Combining entertainment with education is not new. In countries with rich oral histories, entertaining folktales with mores and larger-than-life heroes have been part of a child's informal education for thousands of years. Music, drama, dance, and other folk traditions have also been used for centuries in many countries for recreation, devotion, reformation, and instructional purposes. However, the concept of entertainment-education or "edutainment" in contemporary entertainment (such as radio, television, comic books, and rock music) is relatively new, emerging only in the last 25 years in forms of entertainment that have existed at least twice as long or longer.

In radio, the first well-known example of edutainment began in 1951 when the British Broadcasting Corporation (BBC) began broadcasting The Archers, a radio soap opera that conveyed educational messages about agricultural development. In the late 1950s, a writer-producer trained at the BBC began experimenting with edutainment in Jamaican radio serials to promote family planning and other development issues. Edutainment for television was discovered almost by accident in Peru in 1969 through a television soap opera called *Simplemente María.* The program featured a single mother who worked and took adult literacy courses at night. As the program increased in popularity, the number of young women enrolling in adult literacy courses began to rise. Similar results were found when the program was broadcast in other Latin American countries. Among poor, working-class women, María became a role model for upward social mobility.

Inspired by this success, Miguel Sabido, a television writer-producer in Mexico, developed a methodology for entertainment-education soap operas. Between 1952 and 1982, Sabido produced seven entertainment-education soap operas for social change that encouraged enrollment in adult literacy classes, consideration of family planning strategies, and acceptance of gender equality and other concepts. These shows were strong commercial hits, demonstrating that educational messages do not have to detract from the entertainment value of the programs. Since that time, this strategy has spread to many other countries, including India, Kenya, and Tanzania, promoting the same social messages and others, such as HIV/AIDS education.

The edutainment strategy has been used in a variety of ways, not only in television and radio but also in films, print, and the theater. In India, Bangladesh, and Zimbabwe, films have been produced that contain social messages. Dr. Seuss in the United States and others around the world have produced books, comics, and cartoons to educate children and adults about social issues. Groups in India and other countries have used street theater and pantomime to promote educational messages. Edutainment has also been infused into rock music for promoting sexual responsibility among adolescents in Latin America and the Philippines, for promoting responsible parenthood in Nigeria, and in more than 60 other projects in more than 30 countries.

FADE TO BLACK

Many theories and methods have been invoked to study media and entertainment effects, and each possesses various strengths and weaknesses. Content and text analyses may be best for identifying cultural themes and images that might have significant impacts. Experiments and limited effects theories may be best for demonstrating whether media and entertainment are capable of producing specific, isolated effects and for ruling out possible effects. Field studies may be best for assessing the presence and extent of these effects in the environment. Cultural, qualitative, and ethnographic studies may be best for examining the complexity of these effects and for understanding how the media's impact fits within our larger social fabric.

Theories variously suggest that media and entertainment may influence our thoughts, behavior, and even our health. The movies we watch, the music we listen to, and the games we play and observe may all serve in different ways to reinforce or discourage stereotypes, destructive behavior, the value of education, and other perceptions and behaviors. Debate continues, yet together these theories and methods have provided researchers, industry professionals, and audience members with a comprehensive array of tools and perspectives for understanding how, when, why, and to what extent media and entertainment effects may occur.

 A Closer Look

Intentional Effects: Using Entertainment to Effect Social Change[136]

Writers and producers often incorporate specific messages or views into entertainment fare. In a book, film, or song, an artist might include a story line that makes a subtle or not-so-subtle statement about sexual harassment in the workplace or spousal abuse, hoping that, in addition to entertaining audiences, the story might influence people's attitudes or behaviors about these societal issues. However, the entertainment industries have also embarked upon large-scale, collective efforts to change attitudes and behaviors about serious, social issues.

U.S. Television and Designated Drivers

In 1988, Harvard professor Jay Winsten launched a campaign to get the television networks to push his novel "designated driver" concept. Today, most people are familiar with the term; a "designated driver" is the person in a group who abstains from drinking alcohol during an occasion and serves as the sober driver for everyone else in the group. Neither the concept nor the term existed until Professor Winsten, with the help of CBS executive Frank Stanton, contacted the chairman of NBC, Grant Tinker, and pitched his plan to use television programming to develop a new social norm. Tinker was intrigued by Winsten's plan and helped him enlist the cooperation of the heads of the 13 companies that did most of the production for the major television networks.

As a result, designated drivers were part of the story lines of 160 different prime-time shows in the following four network television seasons. Winsten's designated driver message was viewed by hundreds of millions of viewers, and research suggests that these efforts did make a difference. Within one year of the introduction of the designated driver concept, 67% of adults said that they were aware of the concept. By 1991, 52% of adults under 30 years of age said that they had served as designated drivers. From the first year of the campaign in 1988 until 1997, the number of drunk driving fatalities dropped by 32% in the United States. Professor Winsten recognized that embedding such messages in prime-time television wasn't a "magic bullet" that single-handedly injected the designated driver concept into viewers' thoughts and actions. But his work suggests that such messages can work as part of a larger strategy to make real cultural differences.

Figure 5.5   Drunk driving prevention messages, including frequent references to the use of designated drivers, were incorporated into the scripts of top-rated TV shows such as *The Cosby Show*, pictured here.

© Jacques M. Chenet/Corbis.

DISCUSSION AND REVIEW

1. Review the different types of effects that entertainment may have on audiences and give specific examples of each.

2. Explain the different paradigms of effects research, including examples of theories and studies from each of them. Speculate on how these paradigms might continue to evolve.

3. Explain and compare and contrast each of the following pairs: quantitative vs. qualitative research, self-report vs. observation, laboratory vs. field research, content and text analysis. Which methods do you like best and why?

4. Consider your own (or others') images of different groups—women, African Americans, Asians, Hispanics, Middle Easterners, blondes, the elderly, lawyers, people who work on computers. How do you envision "typical" individuals of these groups? What do they look like? How do they behave? What images or stereotypes immediately come to mind? Use theories from the chapter to explain how these images may form.

5. What do you think about the relationship between media violence and aggressive behavior? Do you think that watching media violence can make people more or less aggressive? Why or why not? What theories, if any, do you think best explain this relationship? Why?

EXERCISES

1. Consider each of the following: smoking in movies, hip-hop music, and *Harry Potter* or *Lord of the Rings* books. What kind of effects might each of these have on people? How might they affect attitudes and behavior? Now design research strategies to study these effects.

2. Pay attention to new trends you see in fashion, hairstyles, toys, gadgets, catch phrases, and so on and see how many you can trace back to entertainment—from movies, music videos, magazines, and so on, or actors, musicians, athletes, and so on. Use theories from the chapter to explain how these trends form.

3. Search through a database of social science research (Expanded Academic, PsychAbstracts, and so on) for effects studies. Try using the word "effect" or "effects" and other keywords you are interested in, such as "media violence," "video games," "heavy metal music," "horror films," and so on. Read through a few articles and see if you can find any of the theories and methods discussed in this chapter. Comment on what you find.

4. Researchers have noted some interesting trends in entertainment media. One trend is lighthearted but still very violent movies, including action films such as the *Rush Hour*

movies and horror films such as the *Scream* and *Scary Movie* series. Another trend is reality programs like *Survivor* and *Big Brother*. List any other trends you notice (consider not only television and film, but music, video games, books, and so on). Speculate about what effects these trends might have on audiences.

RECOMMENDED READINGS

Bryant, J., & Zillmann, D. (1994). *Media Effects: Advances in Theory and Research*. Hillsdale, NJ: Lawrence Erlbaum.

Fischoff, S. (1999). Psychology's Quixotic Quest For the Media-Violence Connection. *Journal of Media Psychology, 4*(4). Available online at www.calstatela.edu/faculty/sfischo/

Jeffries, L. W., & Perloff, R. M. (1997). *Mass Media Effects* (2nd ed.). Prospect Heights, IL: Waveland Press.

Lowery, S. A., & DeFleur, M. L. (1995). *Milestones in mass communication research*. White Plains, NY: Longman.

6

The Power of the Press

*Print and the
Publishing Industry*

A good book is the best of friends, the same today and forever.

—Martin Tupper, 1871

Publishing is a complex commercial activity during which words and illustrations are selected, edited, and designed. Publishers sell information in the form of books, newspapers, and periodicals that are copyrighted. Stimulated by the growth of professional authors, the spread of literacy, modernization of retailing, and the use of computers, publishing is the business of mass marketing printed forms of entertainment. Most publishing houses have their origins in printing, book selling, or both. Although mergers and acquisitions have created huge publishing conglomerates, electronic publishing houses continue to emerge. With electronic publishing, data are communicated online to a customer's computer or transferred to a portable medium, such as a disk or CD-ROM.

Unlike their electronic counterparts, printed documents are portable, user friendly, and present content in a variety of ways. The recent experience of one of the authors of this book with Frank McCourt's novel, *Angela's Ashes,* is an example of how print messages can be delivered and received. Excerpts of the book first appeared in a *magazine,* where it came to her attention. Then she read a review of the novel in the *newspaper,* listened to an abridged form on *audiotape,* and finally read the story in its entirety in a *hard-bound volume.* After finishing the book, she heard the author read a chapter on the *radio* and saw him interviewed on *television.* Then she attended a *book signing* for his autograph and, finally, she enjoyed the *movie* version when it appeared on screen. She gave the *paperback* edition to a friend for airplane reading.

The versatility of mediated fiction and nonfiction allows content to be presented in forms that are convenient and affordable. Books go to the beach, magazines are available in flight, and newspapers keeps us company as we commute to work. Nothing stimulates theater of the mind quite like the descriptions we read about faraway places, fascinating people, and suspenseful situations. Key to print's endurance is its ability to integrate content into our busy lives, keeping us informed, challenged, and entertained. Some of the possible disadvantages of print are its required focused attention and time consumption. Print's lack of sensory input, however, may serve as a welcome diversion from media overload.

We hope that by reading this chapter on the forms and content of print, you will develop a reply to the question posed in an editorial in the *Los Angeles Times Book Review* in June, 2001: "Is publishing dead?" Book sensations, newspaper revelations, and magazine delights are covered in this chapter for their contribution to the world of entertainment.

THE HISTORY OF PUBLISHING

The history of publishing is characterized by the interplay of technical innovation and social change, each promoting the other. Publishing as it is known today depends on a series of three major inventions—writing, paper, and printing—and one crucial social development—the spread of literacy. Before the invention of writing, information could be spread only by word of mouth. Writing was originally regarded as a way to fix religious formulations or to record codes of law. Scripts of various kinds came to be used throughout most of the ancient world for proclamations, correspondence, transactions, and records, but book production was confined largely to religious centers. Publishing in the modern sense—i.e., a copying industry serving a public readership—began in nonreligious societies such as Greece, Rome, and China. The power of the printed word, as the saying goes, cannot be underestimated, even when challenged by electronic forms of content delivery. Print has a long history, but many see the printing press as the origin of mass media. The oldest form of transferring ink to paper was accomplished using wooden printing presses as well as movable clay type and blocks. A surviving text from 594 indicates that printing originated in 6th century China and was probably stimulated by a need to examine Buddhist texts. Chinese innovations fed the technological push toward expanding the written word's range of influence. Wang Jie's *Diamond Sutru,* printed in 868, is the world's oldest known printed book. Between 932 and 953, 130 volumes of the Confucian classics were printed using a very labor-intensive arrangement of movable type to present an alphabet that uses thousands of visually specific ideograms.

Metal plates were used for printing by the 11th century; movable metal type appeared in 1040. Learning block printing from Egyptian hieroglyphics, Europeans began using the process in 1375. In the early 1450s, rapid cultural change in Europe fueled a growing need for the quick and cheap production of written documents. Johannes Gutenberg, a businessman from Mainz, Germany, developed a technology to address the economic bottleneck. His first printing job was the Bible. In 1476, England's first press printed Chaucer's *Canterbury Tales,* which was then distributed by William Caxton. Caxton's contributions as an editor and printer won him a good portion of credit for standardizing the English language.

The church, the state, universities, reformers, and radicals were all quick to use the press. Not surprisingly, every kind of attempt was made to control and regulate such a new mode of communication that many considered dangerous. Freedom of the press was pursued and attacked for the next three centuries but, by the end of the 18th century, a large measure of freedom had been won in western Europe and North America, and a wide range of printed matter was in circulation. The mechanization of printing in the 19th century and its further development in the 20th, which went hand in hand with increasing literacy and rising standards of education, finally brought the printed word to its powerful position as a means of influencing minds and, hence, societies.

PORTABLE PRINT: SOFT AND HARD BOOKS

Books, although varied in form and content, are designed to serve as an instrument of communication. The Babylonian clay tablet, the Egyptian papyrus roll, the medieval vellum codex, the printed paper volume, the microfilm, and various other combinations have all served as books.

Pessimists say books are anachronisms, things of the past, dying a slow death from competition such as Web-based novels and books on tape. Our observation of the publishing industry, however, shows healthy growth in specific genres that continue to be popular in spite of technology, such as mystery novels, children's books, limited editions, and tabletop compendiums. In case you think all books are just airport reading material, consider the other major categories available for public consumption today:

- ☆ *Trade books* include adult, juvenile, fiction and nonfiction, hardcover and paperback. The largest market share in dollars and units is held by trade books. Cooking and craft books occupy 11% of all adult books purchased. The best source of trade book titles is the *New York Times Book Review.*
- ☆ *Religious titles* are classified as nonfiction and are available in both hard and paper covers. Bibles make up the largest segment; religious biographies, histories, and inspirational works continue to be a growing market.
- ☆ *Professional books* in business, law, science, technology, and medical nonfiction are printed in both hardbound and paperback versions. English-language books on these topics sold globally are a growing market for publishers.
- ☆ *University press and college texts* continue to sell in cloth, although paper is the preferred format for economic-minded students. This segment shows a growing electronic market.

☆ *ELHI (elementary and high school)* consists of school textbooks of all genres and formats. A big business for publishers, ELHI accounts for 14% of national dollar sales. The market for electronic products is also growing in this category.

Just writing or publishing a book doesn't mean anyone will buy it. To be successful, books of all types must be promoted. To that end, books are marketed in the following ways:

1. As *mass-market paperbacks* sold in the airports, discount stores, warehouse clubs, food/drug stores, and supermarkets; this channel accounts for 20% of all units sold for a 6.7% market share.

2. By *book clubs,* which are a growing source of sales of fiction and nonfiction in both hard and paper formats and account for 18% of sales.

3. In *chain bookstores* such as Borders (26% of adult books are bought here) and in small independent shops usually specializing in out-of-print, used (4%), or niche market (20%) books.

4. By *mail order,* which is declining in popularity (down to 5%) as a way to acquire titles.

5. *Over the Internet* on sites such as amazon.com and barnes&noble.com (www.barnes-andnoble.com), a growing market with no available statistics at this time.

And in the case of this book, through publishing representatives who sell directly to professors. More than half the books sold are distributed by nonbookstore retailers. Campus bookstores, libraries, schools, and wholesalers also distribute books to consumers. New titles, called *frontlist titles,* are the mainstay of most bookstores. *Backlist* titles, such as dictionaries and the Bible, remain in print and continue to sell long after publication.

Marlboro Magic[137]

A Canadian author who could not get his book into the hands of its intended audience through a publisher came up with a unique distribution system—old cigarette machines. The author retrofitted them into coin-operated delivery devices for art, literature, and music. He calls them "Distroboto." In operation since January 2001 in a Montreal bar, Distroboto are refilled weekly with new product. His plan is to expand to local bus and train stations. A key attraction is price: For two Canadian dollars, customers are usually willing to take a gamble (because no browsing is possible) on an intriguing title or cover illustration. Distroboto contain small books of poetry, short stories, history, and comics as well as cassettes, greeting cards, paintings, and fridge magnets—all squeezed into recycled cigarette packs (Canadian packs are larger than those made in the United States). Do you see a future for the Distroboto? Under what circumstances would you be motivated to get a product from such a machine?

The trick to getting books to readers is *niche marketing*—the identification and location of a book's audience. Aggressive news coverage and advertising campaigns account for the industry's increasing sales. Books written from the plot of a hit movie, for instance, benefit from the title's exposure. Titles become brands and are marketed as such by increasing awareness of a title's availability to its genre readers. Results of good marketing are bestsellers, which have trends of their own that are discussed in the next section.

Airport Fare: Bestsellers

Trends are best characterized through the bestseller charts for fiction and nonfiction offerings. What follows is an overview of the fiction and nonfiction books that caught the imagination of consumers during the final decade of the 20th century with sales that landed them on an annual top 10 list according to *Publishers Weekly*.[138] Calculations for the annual bestseller lists are based on shipped and billed figures supplied by publishers for domestic sales of new books.

Popular fiction accounts for half of the books purchased in the United States. Back in 1990, the top-selling fiction title was Jean M. Auel's *The Plains of Passage*, which sold more than 1.6 million copies. That year, four novels sold 1 million or more copies. The novelists that placed in the top 10 were Stephen King, Scott Turow, Sidney Sheldon, Danielle Steel, Robert Ludlum, Jackie Collins, Anne Rice, Rosamunde Pilcher, Judith Krantz, and Dean Koontz. Skip to 1995, and certain elements change radically. John Grisham led with *The Rainmaker*'s sales of 2.3 million. Six other novels sold 1 million or more copies in the course of that year. The authors on the top 10 list were Michael Crichton, Danielle Steel, Richard Paul Evans, James Redfield, Stephen King, Mary Higgins Clark, and James Finn Garner.

In 2000, John Grisham led the pack again, this time with *The Brethren*, selling more than 2.8 million copies. Grisham held the lead position on these annual charts each year from 1994 to 2000. Two other novels in 2000 went over 2 million: *The Mark* by Jerry B. Jenkins and Tim LaHaye, and Tom Clancy's *The Bear and the Dragon*. Patricia Cornwell and Danielle Steel boasted bestsellers with sales of more than 1 million; Steel has placed between one and three books on these top 10 annual charts since 1983. The other authors in the top 10 that year were James Patterson (a regular on these lists since 1997), Nicholas Sparks, and Mary Higgins Clark. Robert Morgan was a beneficiary of an Oprah promotion that began in November, 1996, when she launched her on-air book club. Before Oprah promoted his book in 2000, Morgan had sold fewer than 12,000 copies of his book; in the 5 months following her recommendation, he sold about 638,000.

The opening sales performance of the top players grew considerably during the '90s. The big change over the decade was a result of publishers' newly acquired skill of publication scheduling and the development of one-day *laydown* tactics, which feature massive distribution nationwide. Laydown distribution enables retailers to begin selling a book simultaneously using strong point-of-purchase displays and aggressive print and broadcast advertising campaigns.

Think about the books you read at the beach, in the mountains, on vacation, on an airplane, or before you go to sleep. What kinds of pleasures do books provide you as reader that are not available from other forms of entertainment? How well does your imagination transform words into images? Is our electronic society keeping too many of us from enjoying a so-called theater of the mind?

In addition to providing us with mental movies in the form of fiction, reading gives us in-depth information we cannot obtain from other sources in the form of nonfiction. Nonfiction's popularity changes more often than fiction's popularity because politics, economics, and social issues have a more immediate impact on this group of bestsellers. What's hot and what's not depends on which entertainment and sports personalities are in the news and which Hollywood star has written his or her memoirs. Unlike the public's preference for veteran best-selling novelists, the public taste in this arena is more fickle, and the 15 minutes of fame often goes to new authors.

By looking at titles over the past decade, we can glimpse the trends in popular non-fiction titles. In 1990, CBS News broadcaster Charles Kuralt led the nonfiction charts with *A Life on the Road*, selling 602,000 copies. Three top 10 titles—*The Civil War, The Frugal Gourmet on Our Immigrant Heritage,* and *Homecoming*—all benefited from PBS program-ming. Political top sellers included Ronald Reagan's autobiography and dog Millie's musing about life in the White House. International politics were represented by a book on Israel's Mossad. Sports and celebrity bestsellers included athlete Bo Jackson, country-western singer Barbara Mandrell, and a book on baseball by *Newsweek* columnist George Will. Economics titles encompassed *Financial Self Defense* by Charles Givens and John Naisbitt's *Megatrends 2000.* Cleveland Amory's *The Cat and the Curmudgeon* sold almost 290,000 copies that year.

The authors of the 1995 top 10 nonfiction titles were almost all personalities of celebrity status. In the lead was John Gray with *Men Are from Mars, Women Are from Venus,* which sold 2.1 million copies after 3 years on the bestseller list. Colin Powell, Howard Stern, and Deepak Chopra all had million-copy-plus bestsellers. Bill Gates, Charles Kuralt, Newt Gingrich, Ellen DeGeneres, Oprah chef Rosie Daly, and O.J. Simpson all made it to the top.

The 2000 group of most popular nonfiction books shows to what degree we have become a nation of brevity and sound bites. Four of the top 10 titles were short books of 100 to 125 pages in miniature form. Spencer Johnson's business parable *Who Moved My Cheese?* was number one. Maria Shriver, religious leader Bruce Wilkinson, and Anna Quindlen succeeded with their inspirational and/or religion advice in smaller-format bindings. *Tuesdays With Morrie* (by Mitch Albom) sold more than 5.2 million copies in 3 years. *Body for Life, Relationship Rescue,* and *Eating Well for Optimum Health* represented the popular self-help category. Fiction mega-seller Stephen King's memoir on his life as a writer and Paul McCartney's *The Beatles Anthology* scored impressively. Continuing to sell very well were the annual *Guinness World Records* books and histories, including a World War II memoir on the building of the transcontinental railroad, *Flags of Our Fathers* by James Bradley.

How we dream and how we learn are often dependent upon our exposure to fiction and nonfiction books as we grow up. Depriving children of interaction with the printed word often stifles creativity and postpones their understanding of the world in which we live. By keeping popular print culture alive and well, we facilitate curiosity and develop an informed generation of citizens. Books are an inexpensive source of user-friendly entertainment—portable, poignant, and pleasing. Compare your bestseller experiences with those of a friend. What role do books play in your leisure time?

Whodunit? Mystery Novels

As evidenced by the sales of Clancy and Grisham books, detective fiction is the most popular genre selling today. It all began with Edgar Allan Poe's *Murder in the Rue Morgue* (1841), considered the first true detective story. The first unresolved mystery story—*The Mystery of Edwin Drood*—came about unintentionally when author Charles Dickens died, leaving readers with only clues as to who killed Drood. Detective fiction is usually divided into two schools: the classical school, which features the intellectual detective (e.g., Sherlock Holmes or Poirot), and the American school, which features the hard-boiled detective, best represented by the writings of Dashiell Hammett. The genre also includes such subgenres as the spy story (James Bond), the enforcer story (*Day of the Jackal*), the anti-thriller (books that begin with the end) (Le Carré novels), and the police procedural (McBain novels).

Phillip Marlowe, the first world-weary detective who chased slinky femme fatales, was created by Raymond Chandler in a '40s mystery, *The Big Sleep*. Portrayals of the criminal world and stories about how crime changes people originated with Jim Thompson's *After Dark, My Sweet*. Borrowing from Greek tragedy, Donna Tartt's *The Secret History* (1992) introduced the reverse mystery, where the reader knows "whodunit" from the beginning. Alfred Hitchcock embraced this format for his suspense/thriller films.

Charming, old-fashioned puzzle mysteries like Agatha Christie's *And Then There Were None* have been around for years. But in 1977 when Marcia Muller wrote *Edwin of the Iron Shows*, the first tough female private eye (Sharon McCone) began solving crimes. Female dicks? Yes. Sleuths such as Sara Paretsky's V. I. Warshawski and Edna Buchanan's Britt Montero help travelers kill time waiting for planes, trains, and tickets. These days, whodunits authored by women are enjoying special popularity among female travelers.[139] Airport bookstores stock stacks of mysteries for passengers with a passion for private eyes. Novels, such as those in Sue Grafton's Kinsey Millhone series *("A" is for Alibi* to *"O" is for Outlaw)* begin with strong plot lines on the first page and carry readers easily through various twists and turns to the mystery's conclusion.

With their strong sense of place, mysteries can take readers to Paris as described by Georges Simenon and to Los Angeles as portrayed by Raymond Chandler. Mysteries not only introduce readers to the major tourist sites, they also make them feel the ambience of the place from a local's perspective. Gutsy female detectives contribute a sense of adventure and companionship for women travelers who thrive on these mass-marketed, portable novels. Women detectives, as the antithesis of their smoking, drinking, and womanizing male counterparts, bring humanity to mysteries.

Readers of both sexes enjoy following their heroes and heroines as they solve intricate crimes. Whodunits continue to be popular as travel companions and late-night diversions among people who like suspense enriched with their own visions of action/adventure, which isn't always available on a neighborhood movie screen.

Attracting Kids: The Wow Factor

How can print compete with flashy media? Libraries are trying to attract young readers with children's sections that feature bright colors, tepees, and faux forests. In libraries such as the one in Huntington Beach, California, the children's section contains floating bubbles, a sailboat full of books, and a 600-gallon saltwater aquarium. Storytelling rooms with kid-friendly architecture are designed to welcome children and send a message that reading is a pleasure.[140] So why are such theme-park-like attractions so necessary to promote reading? Because television and the Internet have snatched children away from books, experts say. By putting up reading tepees and forest settings, adults hope their kids will buy into the whole experience of books.

And if that doesn't work, parents turn to pop-up books, which often provide an emotional quality unavailable from flat books. One illustrator and paper engineer, David Carter, designed a kinetic book of iridescent paper sculptures that shift from a whirling tornado on one page, to a floating hot-air balloon on another, to a byzantine Emerald City castle of towers and cupolas that spreads across two pages. Maurice Sendak, author and illustrator of *Where the Wild Things Are*, designed the cover of a pop-up book for a special exhibition of more than 100 pop-up books at the Brooklyn Public Library. Dominating the field in production of pop-up books is Carvajal Caragraphics, a Colombian company that prints in 32 languages for more than 100 countries. Believing that readers are interested in handmade books as a counterreaction to Web books, pop-up book publishers provide a tactile experience with a certain retro quality that dazzles adults and children alike.[141]

The example of J. K. Rowling's *Harry Potter* books suggests that interesting subjects generate interest in reading. First appearing in Britain in 1997 as a juvenile fiction title and in the United States in 1998, *Harry Potter and the Sorcerer's Stone* shot to the top of the adult bestseller list in the United States. *Harry Potter and the Chamber of Secrets* was equally as successful, with sales of more than 2 million copies in Britain and 5 million in the United States for the Harry Potter pair. One year later, they were both still on the children's bestseller list. When *Harry Potter and the Prisoner of Azkaban* went on sale, readers swamped bookstores nationwide, and first-day sales of the title were among the highest for any book to date.[142] At year's end 2000, Rowling had four Potter books on the *Wall Street Journal*'s best-selling books list: *Harry Potter and the Goblet of Fire* (# 2), *Prisoner of Azkaban* (# 3), *Sorcerer's Stone* (# 5), and *Chamber of Secrets* (# 7). Translated into 28 languages, the novels even appear in Icelandic and Serbo-Croatian versions. For the first time in history, children's novels have appeared on adult bestseller lists—four at a time.

By placing appealing characters in interesting but perilous situations with the outcome in doubt well into the story, Harry Potter books feed readers' hunger for enchantment. The illusions set forth in the fictional world of Harry Potter, a skinny kid with glasses, green eyes, and an unruly shock of black hair, have captured readers both young and old who want to believe the unbelievable. The boy, who discovers that he's a wizard who survived an attack by Lord Voldemort and has a lightning-bolt shaped scar on his forehead to prove it, is the center of an epic that bears certain resemblance to the *Star Wars* films, with Luke Skywalker being the parallel to Harry—is goodness or evil the hero's most powerful weapon?

Rowling takes some liberties with classical fantasy literature, allowing Harry easy access to the wizard world in a consistently funny and genuinely scary way. She ably relives her life as an 11-year-old, the age at which we meet Harry for the first time. Harry and his friends grow older with each book, taking them into adolescence with its promising array of new adventures. So if you're a Muggle (nonwizard person), we urge you to open the latest installment to experience Harry's magical world, full of fun surprises like every flavor beans, the candy that can taste like everything from chocolate to tripe. For adults who believe that reading is a lost art among the young and that books have been rendered obsolete in our electronic, hot-wired age, watch out for kids with purple lightning bolt paste-on tattoos as they stampede to bookstores to buy the latest installment of the Harry Potter series even after the films were released.

Focus on Limited Editions: Restricted to the Rich?

To combat the rising interest in electronic books and to create new markets for themselves, publishers are producing *limited edition* books that command astronomical prices like never before. Normally limited to distributions of a few hundred copies, these editions epitomize the essence of elite culture. Probably the most notorious limited edition in recent times is Stephen King's *The Dark Tower: The Gunslinger* published in 1982. Advertised before publication in a few select magazines, the work was originally available for purchase only by ordering directly from the publisher or through one of several specialty book dealers. By 1988, mint condition copies of this limited edition were sold for prices approaching $1,000. *Dark Tower II: The Drawing of the Three* was published in 1987 for a preordered price of $35, but sold consistently for $100 early in 1988.

Capitalizing on the *Dark Tower* mania that occurred around these books, a special slipcased edition of both books (with press runs of 1,200 each) was only available for purchase if you were one of the lucky few whose names were drawn in a lottery. Current market value for these limited, limited editions is now determined by auction houses like Sotheby's. Publishers vie for the right to produce special editions written by King, whose success lies not with his storytelling ability but rather with the stuff of illusion and flourish in the pseudo-realistic world of moneyed collectors.[143]

How do special editions inflate or restrict marketplace demand? Do you think publishers manipulate and control what the marketplace considers to be collectible books?

Reacting to pressure from authors of adult fiction, several bestseller lists have transplanted Potter from adult fiction to the children's fiction category. Adult and adolescent fans alike react against this categorization, insisting that Harry appeals to children of all ages and should be listed with other adult books. As the debate rages, author Rowling seems not to care where her books are listed, just so the sales remain strong. What do you think are the implications of bestseller categories for new authors aspiring to create fiction that may be interpreted as children's literature because of its general appeal?

Out for Show: Coffee Table Books

A philosopher once said that "we are what we read." But some books are not meant to be read. Skimming appreciably is a more suitable term for perusing stylishly photographed volumes of oversized images. Gift books with price tags that show you care enough to send the very best cover subjects from art to cooking. One handsome object popular with the haute Hollywood crowd is *Vanity Fair's Hollywood,* which provides a glimpse into an alternate universe. This book is basically a huge fan magazine as devoid of critical or historical sensibility as a bound volume of *Modern Screen* magazine.[144] Here, stars are presented in their purely glamorous essences. Featuring photographs by Annie Leibovitz, *Vanity Fair's* book includes Madonna with child, Harrison Ford shaving in his underwear, and Kristin Scott Thomas without her shirt. As readers, we become voyeurs of the rich and famous, peeking into their private spaces and wondering how the photographer persuaded them to strike such poses.

You might also peek at *Hollywood Candid*, 150 of photographer Murray Garrett's favorite black and white images of the '50s, when stars welcomed at-home photo shoots. Humorous, often revealing shots include Joan Crawford without makeup, Ava Gardner laughing with the kind of naturalness she never showed on screen, and Marlon Brando at home with his cat. This *Time, Life,* and *Look* photographer shows stars at their most compelling—when they are most candid.

Or you can stylize your surroundings with books on fashion. *Giorgio Armani* is a lavish volume that features Richard Gere and countless supermodels in the designer's minimalist creations. And *China Chic* is a crimson-themed style guide that engagingly melds the history of cutting-edge Eastern culture with designer Vivienne Tam's own life journey. Travel journeys are also popular as books. *Jungles* brings you close-ups of rubbery, fluorescent orange frogs frozen in air to stunning vistas of a sun-splashed lake at dawn in such places as Hawaii, Madagascar, and Costa Rica. *Brazil Incarnate* presents a hedonistic essence in each scene in the land of coffee, *carnivale,* and catwalkers. In black and white shots of everyone from cruising teens to primping cross-dressers, the Argentinean-born photographer illuminates this locale.

Take an historical journey through *The Postcard Century: 2000 Cards and Their Messages,* a book featuring every imaginable image from Lindbergh's Spirit of St. Louis (1927) to brightly thonged beach-goers (1990). Or get in touch with the '60s through *Linda McCartney's Sixties,* which provides photographs and commentary on the beginnings of rock

Figure 6.1 Popular as both books and movies, the Harry Potter products are enjoyed by children of all ages.

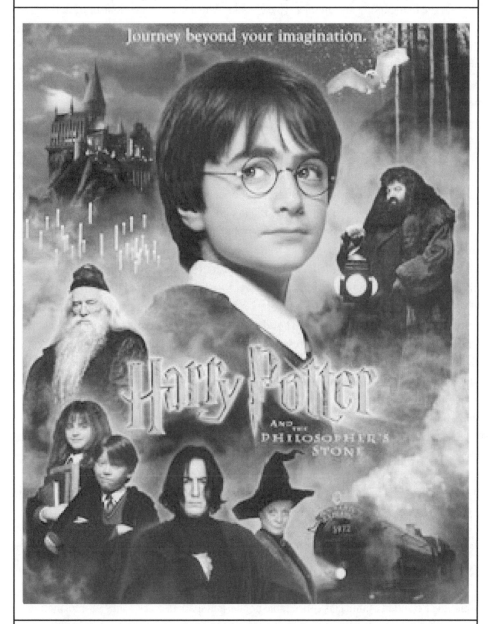

Harry Potter characters, names, and all related indicia are trademarks of Warner Bros. © 2001.

'n' roll and the music of the times. With 221 duo-tone and 32 color illustrations, the book's most interesting aspect is its inside look at the Beatles, particularly the author's husband, Paul.

Big sellers for publishers, books for display and giving often become markdown items within a few years of publication. Price reductions do not diminish their popularity nor their place in the living rooms of America. These books, which act as reflections of both the giver and the receiver, often rate prominent places atop tables and podiums. People may define themselves through their collection of table tableaus. In an era of visualization, elegantly photographed compilations serve as illustrated histories and treasuries of all that is desirable. Next time you visit a friend's home, check out the coffee table books on display. What do these books say about their owner?

Effects of Books on Society

The most significant effect of books has been the spread of education and literacy. The great increase in available reading matter after about 1650 promoted the spread of education to the middle classes, especially to women. The middle classes became readers of the prose novel in the 18th century, when the less affluent bought almanacs and chapbooks containing stories or ballads.

Growth in the book trade led naturally to growth in libraries. Sir Thomas Bodley opened his famous library at Oxford in 1602. Later, Acts of Parliament required the delivery of copies of every book to a varying number of libraries, the most important being the library of the British Museum, founded in 1759. The idea of a definitive collection was adopted in the United States as the Library of Congress, where the Librarian of Congress was appointed copyright officer in 1870. Next, commercial lending libraries and free public libraries emerged, providing access to citizens from all walks of life. To the surprise of many booksellers who feared that free access would curb their sales, the existence of libraries has increased rather than diminished the sale of books, and they are a market in themselves.

Content censorship by government and religious authorities declined in Europe and was abolished completely by the mid-19th century. In the United States, despite the right of free speech, censorship has always been exercised through the courts under the law of libel. Efforts to suppress printed matter have centered on questions of libel, obscenity, or national security.

BLACK AND WHITE AND READ ALL OVER: NEWSPAPERS

Weighing a fraction as much as coffee table books, newspapers carry reams of information in a portable format. A British author once said that "a community needs news for the same reason that a man needs eyes. It has to see where it is going."[145] For William Randolph Hearst, one of America's most important newspaper publishers, news was "what someone wants to stop you printing: all the rest is ads."[146] Both motives have contributed to the development of modern newspapers, which continue to attract millions of regular readers throughout the world despite stern competition from radio, television, and the Internet.

Newspapers can be published daily or weekly, in the morning or in the afternoon; they may be published for the few hundred residents of a small town, for a whole country, or even for an international market. Newspapers differ from other types of publication because of their *immediacy, headlines,* and *coverage* of a miscellany of topical issues and events. Newspapers shape opinions in the "global village," where international concerns and issues are reported and debated.

Technology, Politics, Unions, and Progress

New technology influenced newspapers both directly, through the revolution in printing techniques, and indirectly, through the rapid developments in transport and communications. Electricity, introduced in 1884, was also a stimulus to the printing industry, as were machines that could also cut, fold, and bind together newspapers of any size. Newspaper production was transformed by the speeding up of communication, which allowed news to be gathered instantly from distant cities or even foreign countries (via seabed cables) by telephone. The railroad and the telegraph revolutionized the reporter's conception of time and space. The rail networks not only moved reporters rapidly to and from their destinations but also helped to distribute newspapers, thus making them a more urgent and attractive commodity. Rapid and widespread delivery gave the large newspapers based in capital cities a national status.

In 1835 the *New York Herald* was founded as the first American newspaper to proclaim and to maintain complete political independence. The *New York Times* (1851) exposed an attempted bribe of the *Times'* editor by a politician, thus certifying its independence from city bosses. In New York City the newspaper business was shaken up by the arrival of Joseph Pulitzer, an immigrant from Hungary, who bought the failing *New York World* and in 3 years raised its circulation from 15,000 to 250,000, the highest figure achieved by any newspaper in the world. Pulitzer used sensationalism and idealism to revitalize his newspaper. But press baron William Randolph Hearst also had new ideas to sell newspapers, including presenting rumors and fabrications as news.

The introduction of new technology brought forth strong resistance from the unions of printing workers, which were traditionally among the most powerful labor unions. To combat union power, conglomerates were formed. *The Times* was bought by a Canadian conglomerate and then by News International, an Australian-based media company run by Rupert Murdoch, a businessman with a reputation for toughness. In a major attempt to break the power of the print unions, Murdoch moved *The Times* away from its headquarters, where he started to produce and print it using new technology. Today, Murdoch operates News Corporation, one of the largest media conglomerates in the world.

Today's serious newspapers have broken ties with politicians and unions, and have moved toward providing in-depth detail, analysis, and opinion on many current events. The quality of newspaper coverage of business affairs, the arts, and social issues is increasingly important as publishers deal with more sophisticated readers. The newspaper can still be a forum for thoughtful debate, a medium for creative expression, and a safeguard of the written language.

Newspaper Formats and Trends

Newspapers account for more than $45 billion in sales and revenue activity each year. More than 60 million newspaper copies are purchased every day, and 55 million copies of paid and free circulation weekly newspapers circulate each week.[147] Of the 10,000 newspapers published in the United States, fewer than 15% are dailies. The ramification of this statistic on the industry is profound. To understand how the popularity of daily papers has diminished, we must look at the other types of newspapers available. Nine general categories characterize newspapers; with examples, they are the following:

1. International and national daily (*USA Today, Wall St. Journal*)
2. Metropolitan and/or regional dailies (*Boston Globe*)
3. Local dailies (*Orange County Register*)
4. Nondaily, general audience (*San Francisco Bay Guardian*)
5. Minority (*American Arab Message*)
6. Secondary language (*Chinese Times*)
7. Religious (*Christian Science Monitor*)
8. Military (*Hawaii Navy News*)
9. Specialty (*Women's Wear Daily, Law Bulletin*)

The rising costs of paper and delivery have caused metropolitan dailies such as the *Los Angeles Times* to provide readers with diminishing editorial in exchange for pervasive advertising. Operated from advertising sales, newspapers receive 52% of their revenues from *retail* advertising and 36% from *classified ads; national ads* account for only 12% of advertising receipts. Advertising rates are based on circulation and readership, which are declining steadily. As a result, most metropolitan cities can support only one daily newspaper. In their continuing struggle to retain readers, metropolitan dailies have added sections on lifestyle, international business, health, and local news.

Trends indicate that, although daily circulation is down, Sunday editions and community weeklies are growing in popularity. As more people turn to magazines for national news and television for local news, newspapers concentrate on features about local personalities, school team sports, and community events. They include calendar sections to provide entertainment reviews, information on performing arts, and movie listings. And they attract shoppers with classified ads and coupons.

Newspapers have served as our source of news since the invention of the printing press, and some of us still prefer the daily print version to television. And although newspapers may not be the most entertaining medium, they are the gateway to entertainment news. Calendar sections provide readers with current events, reviews, and trends in the arts and film industries. When it's time to go to the movies, we turn to the newspaper for listings and locations. Reading about the stars and perusing the attraction ads precede most forays into entertainment activities.

In addition to giving us information about the latest local and global happenings, newspapers provide us with commentary and opinion. The editorial page provides views on issues of economic and political importance, but what people generally enjoy most are the humorous takes on daily routines that run the gamut from the mundane to the profound. Columnists often give us reports on what's happening socially—a kind of gossip column. A handful of star columnists is responsible for entertaining readers with humor and parody, serving to draw subscribers and Sunday readers. Commentary also comes to us as political cartoons. These satiric caricatures of notables and dignitaries poke fun at government and military figures so that readers can see the whimsical side of newsworthy events.

Most national dailies provide online editions; some even send headlines and preferred information to subscribers by e-mail. For those of us who enjoy breakfast with the morning news or who like the utility of a folding medium for travel to work, no other medium rivals the newspaper for currency and convenience.

MAGAZINE MANIA

Most media have trends, fads, and new innovations. With magazines, all three can be summed up in a single word: MORE. More magazines, more advertising, more pages, more topics, and more readers. We visited a local Borders bookstore to watch browsers as they scanned, felt, flipped through, and purchased both consumer and trade magazines. Much more flipping-through activity took place than actual purchases, but some readers pulled subscription cards to take away, indicating interest in a potential purchase. With newsstand prices hovering around $5 per issue, subscriptions save readers up to 70% of the single copy price.

To give you an idea of just how many magazine categories exist, Table 6.1 lists Borders's 35 categories and numerous subcategories. Of course, these may vary by outlet and city, but the list provides an approximation of your magazine choices.

Magazines are created to circulate relevant editorial content to subscribers who read product advertising that's related to the content. Published primarily in New York, Pennsylvania, Illinois, and California, national and regional magazines are owned by conglomerates. Publishers of most titles are Conde Nast, Hearst, Meredith, Hachette Fillipacchi, and Time Warner.

What distinguishes magazines from other printed material are their defined audience and the fact that they can be issued in any frequency. Unlike newspapers, magazines cater to niche audiences who read them for specific editorial and advertising information. Also, they can be self-supporting from circulation revenues. *Consumer Reports* is one such magazine that does not accept advertising. Subscribers determine rates for advertising, which are calculated either by paid subscription or by the numbers distributed free of charge. Many

Table 6.1   Magazine Categories and Subcategories

Category	Subcategories
1. Animals	
2. Architecture	
3. Art and Design	
4. Audio and Video	
5. Business	Trade publications
6. City/Region	
7. Computer	General, office, desktop, technical applications, Internet, comparative guides
8. Collectibles and Hobbies	
9. Crafts	
10. Culture and Science	
11. Eastern Spirituality	
12. Erotica and Adult	
13. Environment and Nature	
14. Fashion	
15. Film and TV	
16. Food and Wine	
17. Foreign	
18. Gardening	
19. Gay and Lesbian	
20. Health and Fitness	
21. Hunting, Fishing and Guns	
22. Interior Design	
23. Journals	
24. Literature and Poetry	
25. Men's Interest	
26. Newsweeklies	
27. Music	Rock 'n' roll, pop, hip-hop, instruments and production, jazz-blues-folk, fine arts
28. Parenting and Kids	
29. Photography	
30. Political Commentary	
31. Science Fiction and Mystery	
32. Sports	Boxing, martial arts, climbing, hiking, cycling, running, walking, skiing, skating, surfing, scuba, tennis, golf, team, seasonal
33. Transportation	Automobiles, boats, sailing, motorcycles, planes, trains
34. Travel	Domestic, world
35. Weddings	

community magazines, mailed to subscribers without charge, are supported by local retail and restaurant advertising.

Most magazines have Web sites and hefty subscriber lists, which is why you see so many pages dedicated to advertising. Graphics and paper quality seem to be the most significant visual differentiation. Editorial content, of course, ranges in sophistication from simple

Table 6.2	A New Generation of Feminist Magazines		
Title	*Bitch*	*Bust*	*Moxie*
Subtitle	Feminist response to pop culture	For women with something to get off their chests	For the woman who dares
Founded	1997	1997	1998
Circulation	15,000	100,000	20,000
Mission	To debunk myths about women in popular culture and offer feminist-friendly advice	To bring a funky edge to feminism	To provide an alternative to *Cosmopolitan*

SOURCE: Kuczynski, A. (2001, September 10.) The new feminist mystique. *New York Times,* p. 8.

single-sentence descriptions to lengthy academic and professional discussions. We find most magazines entertaining in some form, especially those with unique photography and unusual advertising. Taken as a whole, the page proliferation staggers the mind and makes one wonder what more can possibly be written? Next month's issues must struggle with that dilemma. If Borders's racks are any indication of what's to read, none of us should ever be without more and more pages to turn.

A recognizable trend is the infusion of magazines trying to define feminism for women in their twenties and early thirties. Started as a backlash against the *Cosmos,* and *Glamours* of the world, titles such as *Bitch, Moxie, Bamboo Girl, Hip Mama, Bust,* and *Rockrgrl* have sprung up around the country. In contrast to their activist foremothers, these publishers discuss lipstick and liberation in the same breath. Table 6.2 overviews three of these magazines. Debby Stoller, editor of *Bust,* said, "We're going to take our place right up there with the big girls."[148]

Taking a closer look, you might notice that some of what's on the stands is there to promote products. Skate manufacturers, for instance, publish skating magazines that advertise their brand through interviews and editorial content. What better place to present the best of what your company offers than a magazine directed right at its users? If you fish and read fishing magazines, chances are those publications will tell you about the best fishing gear, and you might be tempted to purchase some. If you check the affiliation between the publisher and the manufacturer, don't be surprised if they are one in the same. Is such a hidden affiliation ethical? Should publishers disclose their product ownership? Anyone *can* publish a magazine, but *should* anyone?

WHAM! POW! SHAZAM! CARTOON CAPERS

Visual narratives (pictures and illustrations) appear in many print genres. Cartoons bring to mind one-panel illustrations that you might cut out and tape to your refrigerator or office door. Comics are a series of drawings that read as a narrative and are usually found arranged horizontally in newspapers, magazines, or books. Comic strips are multiple panels in a gag-delivery system, and comic books are stories about superheroes. Whereas graphic novels often explicitly describe violence, comics imply violence, which is more viewer friendly.

The first cartoon appeared in 1734, but cartoons did not become prevalent until the mid 1800s, when the first issues of *Punch Magazine* in London and *Puck Magazine* in America were printed featuring cartoon covers. Early in 1900, comic strips ("Buster Brown," "Mutt and Jeff") appeared in New York and San Francisco newspapers. By 1920, "Captain and the Kids," the "Katzenjammer Kids," and "Felix the Cat" appeared as strips, and "Buck Rogers" was presented in the *Amazing Stories* comic book August issue. By the end of the decade, "Tarzan" and "Popeye" were born, and the '30s gave us "Blondie," "Mickey Mouse," "Dick Tracy," "Alley Oop," "Li'l Abner," "Flash Gordon," and "Secret Agent X-9." By 1936 comic syndicates were established, and detective and action comics (*Superman*) made their debut. Marvel comics' "Batman" and "Donald Duck" emerged 2 years later. By the '40s we had "Wonder Woman," "Pogo," and western comics to choose from. "Dennis the Menace," "Miss Peach," and "Andy Capp" hit newspapers; Jules Feiffer began his syndicate in the '50s. The first comic book convention was held in New York in 1963 and, in 1966, the first museum of cartoon art was established in Omiya, Japan. By the '70s we had "Wizard of Id," Marvel superheroes, "Hagar the Horrible," "Scooby-Doo," "Flintstones," "Yogi Bear," and "Bullwinkle and Rocky."

Comic strips are popular among newspaper readers. In fact, some people get the paper just to read the funnies. Comic strips fall into 10 main categories:[149]

1. *Gag strip*—Depends upon an anecdote that ends with a bang in the last panel; continuity comes from the cast of characters (e.g., "Peanuts").

2. *Single protagonist strip*—Includes minor characters and a story line with changing scenes (e.g., "Orphan Annie").

3. *Fixed-cast strips*—Includes a story line and guest characters who live out long or short episodes (e.g., "Dick Tracy" and its villains).

4. *Cartoon situation*—Has no story line (e.g., "Blondie").

5. *Passage-of-time strip*—Characters grow up and age realistically (e.g., "Gasoline Alley").

6. *Special-milieu strip*—Has one theme ("Joe Palooka" and boxing, "Steve Canyon" and flying).

7. *Adventure strip*—Is characterized by a heroic-adversity nature ("Superman").

8. *Fantasy strip*—Is usually based on anthropomorphized animals (e.g., "Donald Duck").

9. *Chain-of-subjects strip*—Uses a variety of settings and topics (fun of golf, joys of childhood).

10. *Serious strip*—Continuous story of the past ("Prince Valiant") or an uplifting chronicle ("Mary Worth").

Sensing the popularity of comic strips, artist/authors began publishing so-called feature-length stories in book form. Comic books became popular during World War II among soldiers away from home who needed relaxation. But the reach and gratification of comic books go way beyond relaxation for displaced Americans. Once described as "movies on paper,"[150] comics influence the fantasy lives of children, giving them superpowers to defeat the monsters of their dreams. Soon, monsters became warmongers armed with savage weapons. When comic violence became prevalent, the industry established self-censorship against violence and promoted domestic drama, gag strips, political satire, parody, and adult comics instead.

Superman, a gentle savior, is the purest example of the American superhero.[151] Motivated by an abstract concern for justice and fair play, Superman transcends nationalistic and religious boundaries. He hides his powers in the guise of journalist Clark Kent; both sides of Superman view the world objectively from the perspective of an outsider. Fighting for truth, justice, and the American way, Superman was the embodiment of all the values that Americans cherished in the 1930s, the decade when he was conceived to shore up the sagging spirits of a country that had lost its innocence in the Great Depression. His mission was not to punish the wicked but to save the innocent. In his comic strips, he helped victims in the Tennessee flood valleys and the Oklahoma dust bowl, and he rebuilt slums for the poor.

The presence of Superman dictated a change in the concept from hero to superhero, transcending reality into magnificence. Superheroes had few personal relationships, no sexual contact with mortals, a sense of objectivity, and nothing could distract them from saving the world. Serialization enabled the superhero to move from adventure to adventure without restrictions, which became the basic plot pattern for comic heroes. Superheroes continue to exist to the present day, mostly because of the intervention of the editor of Marvel Comics, Stan Lee. Lee made superheroes flexible by giving them more human personalities.

One of the most prolific cartoonists ever, Lee is now in his eighties and still producing out of his Encino, California, based offices. Creator of Spider-Man, the Incredible Hulk, the Thing, and the X-Men, Lee has seen his X-Men and Spider-Man creations featured in big-budget movies. And he is even writing stories for Marvel's competition, DC Comics (Superman, Batman, Green Lantern).

What makes Lee unique is that his heroes are more interesting than invincible, defined as much by their weaknesses as their strengths. Lee's characters face real-life dilemmas and mundane problems, such as family fights—similar to issues readers experience themselves. Spider-Man, for instance, is neurotically obsessed with status and worldly success, and he hates to fight. The members of the Fantastic Four, a nontraditional family unit, spend almost as much time fighting among themselves as they do confronting bad guys. The Incredible Hulk was really Bruce Banner, a meek nuclear scientist transformed into a brutal behemoth by a gamma ray bomb who retains his humility to defend street justice.

Figure 6.2   Spider-Man went from comic books to the big screen.

All of Lee's characters are the kind of heroes America seems to need and identify with. Spider-Man's motto is "With great power comes great responsibility." Lee's superheroes have influenced artists, writers, and filmmakers who prefer action to violence. Lee says he doesn't like too much violence, choosing instead action-packed stories that parents want their children to read.[152] Because Lee writes in the present tense, his superheroes possess an immediacy that allows them to live on in popular imagination.

Although superheroes are still part of our popular culture, they have been updated for film, TV, and video games. Clark Kent, although still a wimp, is now a TV anchorman instead of a newspaper reporter. The Fantastic Four still fly off from their apartment to fight Dr. Doom, even though they are distracted by mundane tasks like tenant meetings. Our superheroes sew themselves into new costumes (Spider-Man), pin traveler's checks inside their pants' waistband (Hulk's Bruce Banner), and get new human parents (Superman) to make the fantasies more palatable to today's sophisticated audiences. Distinctions between right and wrong are not as clear cut for our more trendy versions of superheroes, but the bad guy usually still gets punched out in the end. Readers no longer rely on all-purpose superheroes, preferring instead multiple characters that possess both vulnerable and heroic qualities. What does this shift from superhero to more humanistic "everyperson" say about today's popular culture?

Satan Made Me Do It

One comic hero is a crusading Christian who fights the Devil in a unique comic innovation, the cartoon gospel. The cartoon's plot is a proletarian message targeted to the suffering masses in small, 24-page illustrated booklets called *tracts*. Individuals, ministries, churches, bookstores, and prisons have purchased 450 million copies at 13 cents each for the past 40 years. Tracts are the core products of the 35-employee Chick Publications company that also pushes full-size, full-color comics. The most popular is a Crusaders series featuring two butt-kicking Christians who do things like smuggle a microfilm Bible into Bucharest in their fight against the Devil's minions. A sampling from the Jack Chick catalog includes: *The Sissy,* showing Jesus as a guy with guts, which is designed to appeal to truckers and bikers, and *Party Girl,* where the woman of the title learns that Satan is planning her eternal damnation. When carrying the damnation message to its extreme, Chick's tracts use humor to bring home the point. The characters never behave quite like real people, and the dialogue is stilted. A recurring exclamation ("Haw Haw") has become a Chick trademark along with his slang: "When Jesus Christ was born in Bethlehem, Satan freaked out."[153] Chick is unpopular with Catholics because of his stance against them, but Chick's only concern is saving the souls of his audience of loners who have lost their way.

Do you think the comic medium is appropriate for religious messages? Should comics be used as vehicles to spread doctrine to less-educated audiences?

A variety of human and superhuman heroes can be found in Japanese comics. The decline of serious literature in that country is attributed to the boom in *manga,* the hefty comic books whose readership exploded in the 1970s and '80s, spawning their own unique and intensely popular subculture. During the '80s, the most popular *manga* titles averaged weekly sales of more than 2 million copies. At the peak of the trend, up to one third of all published material in Japan consisted of comics directed at audiences from businessmen to schoolgirls.[154] With over 3 billion copies printed per year, paper for comics outsells paper used as toilet tissue. According to one expert, the formula for *manga*'s success is that its major theme is the harmony of three elements: perseverance, friendship, and victory.[155]

Adolescent boys are the prime audience for these 350-page comic sagas, which are illustrated sagas of male response to his removal from infant paradise and his assignment to a journey of adult conflicts and demands. From a Freudian perspective,[156] these comics present distinct themes of oral, anal, and Oedipal stages of male maturation. Oral themes are presented as constant eating and reference to food in plots of oral delights, orally oriented monsters, oral aggressions, and oral eroticism. Anal aggressions are overly apparent in these comics in portrayals of mooning, farting, and defecation. Issues revolving around toilet training strike responsive notes in young readers of these comics. The Oedipal stage is evidenced by allusions to phallic sexuality and phallic tales in locker room type humor. Male transition into adulthood is shown in stories about boys who excel in individual sports, such as boxing and wrestling, in contrast to adult conformity with group desires. Because the transition from infancy to adulthood is a journey of ever-increasing social pressures filled with conflict for Japanese males, young men devour and idolize *manga* heroes, who protest the transition and rebel against it.

In contrast, adult readers are the preferred audience for alternative comics, which are almost exclusively written for and by men. The genre's roots are traced to books by Robert Crumb, the man whose "Zap Comix" defined underground comics in the '60s. Currently, successful alternative artist Daniel Clowes writes and draws "Eightball," a series of comics aimed at adults. Influenced by everything from "Peanuts" to punk rock and magic realism, Clowes's memoir-like narratives have raised the medium to a new art form.[157] He is sponsored by the largest publisher of alternative comics, Fantagraphic Books, which features many of the country's best artists. Clowes's stories are dreamlike and disturbing, set in Hopperesque bars and motels where lonely men are haunted by nightmares, rumors of the apocalypse, and sexual drives. What distinguishes Clowes is his gem cutter's touch with language. His best-known work is *Ghost World,* a 1998 graphic novel about Enid and Becky, two disaffected high-school graduates who mock everyone as "pseudo-Bohemian" losers. This affecting portrayal of adolescence was made into a film of the same name. He also sells framed comics as pieces of art.

A recent exception to this male genre is the supple medium of confessional comics that tell traumatic, picaresque stories of female adolescence. These comics explore the power a girl feels in her emerging sexuality as well as the damage inflicted by those who prey upon it. Author Phoebe Gloeckner is one of this cadre of cartoonists creating unsettling stories about the dark side of growing up female. In *Diary of a Teenage Girl* (see Figure 6.3), text periodically bursts into comics the way a musical bursts into song—without notice. The author uses words rather than images to explore raunchier themes. In *Diary,* character Minnie describes her excitement at provoking desire in adult men in a bar and her revulsion when they

---

Figure 6.3   From Gloeckner's *Diary of a Teenage Girl*

Courtesy of Phoebe Gloeckner.

---

respond. The most explicit images threaten to implicate the reader, transforming a sympathetic eye into a voyeuristic one. Some bookstores refuse to carry the work, fearing its potentially offensive nature. Defending her art, Gloeckner said, "Drawing things as either black or white is a lie. Because that titillation is in you. I'm not saying it's good, but it's there."[158] Gloeckner is also published by Fantagraphic Books, which is creating some of the edgiest work about young women's lives in any medium.

Today, the cross-pollination between cartoonists and artists produces work that appears in galleries and coffee table publications. Cartoonist Chuck Jones's galleries exhibit individual frames of his cartoon characters that are sold for thousands of dollars. In work such as these, where art and words are conceived and fused into a single medium, comics become the mutant sister of fiction in that they do everything fiction can, and often more. What are your experiences with comic books? What role did cartoon heroes play in your childhood?

READABLE RENDEZVOUS

Have you ever taken a date to or met a friend at a bookstore for coffee or a book signing? If not, you're in the minority. Providing coffee cafes, reading areas, listening areas, and even discussion venues, bookstores have made reading a fashion statement. One of the author's first visits to Borders was in San Francisco, when she wandered by chance into a multistory venue populated by hundreds of browsers and buyers all spending their Saturday evening with print.

With multiple outlets in metropolitan areas, Borders and Barnes & Noble have put "occasion" back into book browsing. They have become quasi-libraries, complete with comfortable chairs, tables for doing research, and the absence of a hands-off policy for reading anything on the shelves regardless of your intention to buy. More traditional booksellers that restrict their offerings to more high-end titles (such as Rizzoli) may have started this trend, but bigger has become better.

Discovering specialty bookshops (such as City Lights in San Francisco) and rare book emporiums is certainly more interesting, but their spaces often lack the social opportunities available at the larger retailers. Mega-bookstores offer popular events to stimulate traffic and host authors, critics, musicians, and scholars for intimate gatherings that conclude with opportunities to purchase. The phenomenon of collective book browsing provides a counteractivity to individual Web browsing and seems to be gathering momentum, if our experience with Borders is any indication of this trend's popularity. And by integrating popular brand coffeehouses into their venues, bookstores have combined an ideal purchase environment for reading and socializing.

PRINT MEDIA AND TERRORIST TIMES

Since the events of September 11, 2001, response time has been a key issue for the print genre. Although newspapers can stop the presses or produce a late edition to report breaking news, magazines are particularly hard pressed to stay relevant with 4- to 6-week lead times. Responding to the possibility of continuing post-terrorist attacks and anthrax threats, as well as rapid changes in the economy, magazine publishers had to take a close look at lead time policy and content appropriateness.

Atlantic Monthly was caught with an October 2001 issue cover detailing the struggles of the U.S. military in peace time; in the midst of disaster, a "Peace Is Hell" headline screamed across its cover. Even publications near deadlines had some fast shuffling to do to modify covers and lead-story content. *Esquire* editor David Granger was able to replace a cover photo of actress Cameron Diaz and her eight-page profile with more timely content—photos of the World Trade Center burning outside the photographer's Battery Park apartment window, first-person articles by former war correspondents, and an essay about the imminent war by a policy expert. As a measure to avoid being cut short in the future, both publications cut their lead times from 4 to 2 and 3 weeks respectively.[159]

After the immediate terrorist news was covered, a dilemma about what to print for coming issues loomed large for big media corporations. Hearst's editors were forced to re-examine their vision of hard news to consider juxtaposing news with lighter fare. *Good Housekeeping* editor Ellen Levine said she was "not used to editing in the age of anthrax," where uncertainty kept her from knowing whether readers would want "something totally escapist or totally relevant."[160] Granger, who said, "An equally important part of my mission is to entertain and delight,"[161] decided to mix articles shaped by September 11 with lighter pieces.

Selecting content and changing lead times were not the most serious problems encountered by the magazine industry. Steep revenue declines in the wake of those events forced magazines to reduce staffs and pages, cut back salaries, merge, or even disappear. Ad pages for all monthlies were down by 13.45% from the previous year for the November 2001 issue, and ad pages for weeklies fell 15.3% for the same time period.[162]

FADE TO BLACK

Once threatened by the challenge of electronic media, publishers worldwide now recognize the continuing need for print. Content is currently available to us in multiple languages and physical forms. We can get books on tape, CD, and even download books on our computers and palm devices. The fact that most newspapers and magazines provide Web sites where much of their editorial content is available online indicates publishers' acceptance of complementary—not competitive—modes of presentation. Books and films are often released to promote the other format; hardback often initiates movie renditions, and films often trigger printing of a paperback version.

The point is that in spite of rumors to the contrary, publishing is alive and well. In fact, it's enjoying a very prolific and prosperous period. If you have any doubts, log on to www.amazon.com and browse the plethora of reading matter. Or visit your local mega-bookstore to check out the endless aisles of global newspapers, magazines, fiction, and nonfiction offerings. With its new infusion of product, publishing is undoubtedly thriving in your neighborhood and in your college bookstore.

 A Closer Look

Political Satire and Cartoon Commentary

Satire has been a popular feature of newspapers since they began publishing editorial comment. With a quick wit and a skillful pen, political cartoon artists critique current issues, ideas, and events. Editorial cartoons are often controversial; cartoonists may take a stand that shocks or dismays the targets of their commentary. For example, before and after the presidential election in November 2000—a time of campaigning, voting, awaiting the results, and finding out about the flawed vote-counting system—cartoonists had a field day chiding the candidates and the courts for their parts in the drama that captured world attention for months.

Profiles of some of the most renowned cartoonists and their views are presented here for your enjoyment.

Pat Oliphant, a Pulitzer Prize winner, is the most widely syndicated political cartoonist in the world. He began his cartooning career in 1964 at the *Denver Post,* was an influential cartoonist for the *New York Times,* and has been internationally syndicated for 35 years.

Figure 6.4

© Pat Oliphant. Reproduced with permission of Universal Press Syndicate.

Paul Conrad has been syndicated internationally by the *Los Angeles Times* for decades. His Impolitic "Gallery of Opinionated Art" can be viewed at www.conradprojects.com.

Figure 6.5

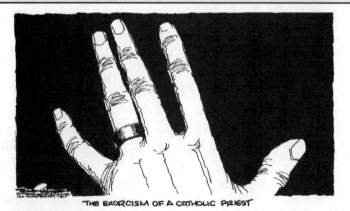

© Paul Conrad. Reproduced with permission.

Tony Auth began his career as a medical illustrator and first cartooned for college newspapers before being hired by the *Philadelphia Inquirer* in 1971. Also a Pulitzer Prize winner, Auth's editorial cartoons appear daily in the *Inquirer*.

Figure 6.6

© Tony Auth. Reproduced with permission of Universal Press Syndicate.

Stuart Carlson joined the *Milwaukee Sentinel* in 1983 as a cartoonist and by 1991 was considered the nation's best cartoonist by the National Press Association. His work has appeared in the *New York Times, Newsweek, The Washington Post, Barron's, Playboy Magazine,* and on ABC News' *Nightline.*

Figure 6.7

© Stuart Carlson. Reproduced with permission.

Ann Telnaes is one of the few nationally syndicated women cartoonists. She was awarded the Pulitzer Prize for Editorial Cartoons in 2001, one of which is featured here. Her *Los Angeles Times* cartoons appear weekly through the Tribune Media Service.

Figure 6.8

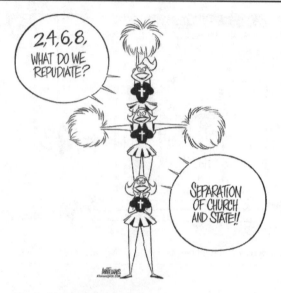

© Ann Telnaes. Used with permission.

Jules Feiffer, one of our favorite cartoonists, has had his drawings in the *Village Voice*, a weekly newspaper published in Manhattan, for 40 years. And he drew for the *London Observer* for over 20 years. He appeared regularly in the *New Republic, Playboy, New Yorker, Esquire,* and *The Nation.* His nationally syndicated weekly cartoon ended in 2000 when Feiffer returned to writing books and teaching at Southampton College.

Figure 6.9

© Jules Feiffer. Reproduced with permission of Universal Press Syndicate.

Cartoonist **Herb Block**, who died at 91 in 2001, was the subject of an exhibition by the Library of Congress in 2000. A *Washington Post* political cartoonist since 1949, "Herblock" (as he was often called) promoted a liberal perspective without being a Democrat. His 50 years of political cartooning took place during the era when daily newspapers dominated American media and the shaping of public opinion. Today, according to show curator Harry Katz, "cartoonists do a lot more 'plucking'—developing imagery from popular culture in a witty way but not necessarily in a bold way."[163]

Figure 6.10

© Courtesy of the Library of Congress Archives.

Because newspapers are now owned by conglomerates, some cartoonists find it difficult to be independent of advertising and are unwilling to put strong opinions into print for fear of reprisal. Many of today's satires are simple jokes that attract occasional reader-fans. Most are much more whimsical than the serious commentary with die-hard followers typical of Herblock's era.

DISCUSSION AND REVIEW

1. As the competition for advertisers increases, what may be the outcome of the current trend of the proliferation of magazine titles? Why?

2. Are novels and nonfiction books likely to disappear with the expansion of Internet information? Why or why not?

3. What is the role of comic strips and cartoons for social criticism? How effective are they in changing reader opinions? In changing reader behavior?

4. How has the newspaper's role in society changed? What is the relationship between metropolitan and community newspapers? Which one plays the more important role in your life? Why?

EXERCISES

1. Using the comics page from a daily or Sunday newspaper, classify five of your favorite comic strips according to the distinctions made in this chapter and give a rationale for your classification choices.

2. Visit a Barnes & Noble or Borders bookstore and check out this month's events calendar. Peruse the list of authors selected to talk on the Internet and determine their potential draw for audiences of their respective genres. Which genres are most prominent? Which are absent? What can you determine about genre popularity from the calendar of events?

3. Take an inventory of a magazine stand and count how many magazines of each type (sports, news, and so on) are available to readers. From your tally, which audience is targeted most? Least? What does your research tell you about advertising potential or drawbacks for magazines?

4. Read an issue of the *New York Times*. Then go online and look over the same issue. Which experience was most entertaining? Why? What does your experience say about the future of newspapers in print?

RECOMMENDED READINGS AND WEB SITES

Grecco, A. N. (Ed.). (2000). *The media and entertainment industries*, Chapters 1 and 2. Boston: Allyn & Bacon.

McCloud, S. (2000). *Re-inventing comics*. New York: Paradox Press.

www.comic-art.com and www.marvel.com provide inside looks at your favorite comic superheroes.

www.fanfiction.net is an anthology of stories; readers can contribute their own versions of favorite books and comics.

www.salon.com is a reader's guide to 225 contemporary authors with illustrations and author profiles, reviews, and bibliographies.

7

And the Beat Goes On

The Rapidly Changing World of Music and Radio

Music is perhaps the most important artistic creation in the history of human invention. No form of art has been more instrumental in shaping the way we think, feel, and live. Throughout history, music has been cherished, exalted, and at the same time condemned and despised. No matter how one may think of it, music shapes the way we live our daily lives.

—Anonymous[164]

MUSIC TRENDS

The true origin of music is unknown. Records and artifacts suggest that even the most ancient civilizations had flourishing musical cultures. Some scholars speculate that music originated as a primitive form of communication to facilitate cooperation and communal labor necessary for survival. Primitive percussion, wind, or other instruments can project farther than can the human voice alone, and information and instructions may be better remembered when incorporated into a melody. Others speculate that music originated as a sacred part of religious ceremonies.

The Dawn of Music

Historical and cultural research shows that music in different parts of the world developed with a very complex interaction among peoples of various races and cultures. Although prehistoric musical artifacts have been found in central Europe, Western music is typically traced to the eastern end of the Mediterranean Sea. In that region, the Mesopotamian, Egyptian, and Hebrew nations, among others, evolved political, social cultures that were later absorbed by the conquering Greeks. The Greeks, in turn, were conquered by the Romans, who ultimately transported a relatively sophisticated form of music back to Western Europe.

The inhabitants of the Mesopotamian region around the Tigris and Euphrates rivers (the Sumerians, the Babylonians, and the Assyrians) flourished from 3500 to 500 B.C. Drawings and the few surviving artifacts indicate that they had instruments of every basic type—*idiophones,* whose sound is made by resonating the whole instrument (striking rocks, pieces of wood or, in later times, metal as with xylophones); *aerophones,* which resonate a column of blown air (wind instruments); *chordophones,* with strings to be plucked or struck (string instruments); and *membranophones,* made of stretched skins over a resonating body (drums). There is even evidence of a primitive system of musical notation found in an undecipherable hymn engraved in stone, dating from circa 800 B.C. It is thought that the Egyptians, who entered historical times about 500 years later than the Mesopotamians, enjoyed all of the same types of activities and instruments. This belief is based on their numerous written references to music and the existence of other musical artifacts, particularly pictures with musical motifs that are preserved on pottery utensils.

Music plays a vital role in shaping societies. In all early cultures, the social functions of music are thought to have been essentially the same because their climate, geographic location, cultural pace, and mutual influences produced many more social similarities than differences. The primary function of music was apparently religious, ranging from heightening the effect of magic to praising deities. In some societies, such as Greece, music played a fundamental role in the school curriculum to address both the body and mind. Plato was of the opinion that music affects the very roots of social order. Other musical occasions depicted in both pictorial and written accounts were equally functional: to rally patriotism and inspire and incite soldiers for battle, to serve as rhythmic accompaniments to communal or solitary labor, to heighten reactions to drama for storytelling and early theater, and to enliven social gatherings. In most cases, musical sounds were accompanied by bodily movement (dance, march, game, or work) or song. Although individuals in early societies may have enjoyed music, it does not appear that they perceived music as a form of entertainment in and of itself.

In the West, music emerged around 500 A.D., when the Roman Empire was overrun by the Huns, Vandals, and Visigoths. The newly emerging Christian Church dominated Europe and generally dictated the destiny of music, art, and literature. During this time, Pope Gregory I is believed to have collected and codified the approved music of the Church, known as Gregorian chant.

Music of the 20th and 21st Centuries

Over the centuries, music has changed and evolved—often radically—sometimes following rigid rules and structures and, at other times, flowing more randomly and freely. The era of the 20th and 21st centuries is hard to define in terms of musical style. As with previous eras, *nationalism* was an important musical device used during the first half of the 20th century. Composers used folk songs and other sounds and rhythms to reflect and reinforce national pride and solidarity. Examples can be found in the music of Ralph Vaughan Williams (England), Béla Bartok (Hungary), Heitor Villaó-Lobos (Brazil), and Aaron Copland (USA).

Music of the 20th century has been described as being more refined, vague in form, delicate, and having a more mysterious atmosphere than music that preceded it. And because of its unique expression and orchestral technique, it does not fit into any other category but its own. Whereas some early 20th century music can be seen as an extension of music from previous eras, much of the music of the 21st century can be seen as a rebellion. Composers did not look to build on what was standard; instead, they created music freely and used sounds that went against the previous grain.

Jazz

Jazz and popular musical styles influenced composers from both the United States and Europe. *Jazz,* a musical movement that dominated the 1900s, remains popular as a mainly American musical form to this day. Jazz can be defined as anything from popular music of the 20th century to the improvised sounds of a dance band. Some prominent forms of jazz throughout the century have been ragtime, blues, swing, Dixieland, bop, and boogie-woogie. Since the second half of the 1900s, new jazz forms and techniques have emerged. These include funky hard bop regression, cool jazz, progressive jazz, and rock and roll. In general, these newer styles have a greater range in harmony, rhythm, and melody, and are less oriented to dance music. In addition, they sometimes borrow techniques and forms from classical music—and vice versa, in that modern classical music often also contains jazz elements.

Electronics

In 20th century musical styles, traditional forms and structures were broken up and re-created or composed using non-Western musical techniques and abstract ideas. Technology also became an extremely important factor in the making of music during this time period. Recording equipment made it possible for different musical performances to be replayed and combined with other musical elements in an unlimited number of ways. Electronically created sounds began to be used in combination with other electronic sounds or played together with traditional music instruments. Computers have radically influenced music production, allowing sounds to be manipulated during live and recorded performances, creating new sounds, improving sound quality, and decreasing production costs.

Current Trends

Talk About Pop Music

What is "pop" music? In the strictest sense of the term, *pop* refers to *popular*. A 1996 study examined the popularity of various forms of music in the United States.[165] Although rock and country continued to reign, as they had for most of the decade, both categories had experienced a drop in market share from the previous year (rock dropped from 33.5% to 32.6%, and country dropped from 16.7% to 14.7%). At the same time, a range of other genres—most notably gospel, jazz, and classical—grew in consumer popularity. In the case of gospel music, which increased its market share from 3.1% to 4.3%, higher popularity was attributed to a strong commitment on the part of a number of major record companies to market and merchandize gospel—and particularly contemporary Christian music—more aggressively, increasing awareness of the range and depth of the genre. Rap music also did well in 1996, increasing its market share from 6.7% to 8.9%. Interest in other music genres remained small but steady, including ethnic, standards, big band, swing, Spanish, electronic, instrumental, comedy, humor, spoken word, exercise, language, folk, and holiday music.

The term *pop music,* however, is also commonly used to refer to a specific subset of music commonly played on "Top 40" radio stations. In the 1990s top 40 pop music flourished with a parade of boy bands and teen queens—led by the Backstreet Boys, 'N Sync, and Britney Spears. Music from Latin stars such as Marc Anthony, Ricky Martin, Jennifer Lopez, and Christina Aguilera also enjoyed pop success at this time. Boy bands and teen artists continued to dominate pop music into the new century, topping the charts for album and concert sales. Radio play for teen pop, however, began to decrease. For example, Britney Spears's song *Stronger* was one of the best-selling singles in the United States for several weeks and reached the top spot in January 2001. On *Billboard Magazine*'s airplay chart only 2 weeks later, it was not found among the 100 top songs playing on pop radio.

Analysts found this trend puzzling. Sky Daniels, general manager of *Radio & Records,* an industry trade publication, says,

> It's as if there's a sense by a lot of radio programmers that now is the time that they're supposed to end the cycle. . . . [Programmers are saying,] "At any moment this is going to go, and I want to be the first one to proclaim it." They want to be trendsetting. They don't want to be the last one to pull out. . . . Sometimes the cycles change because there is a backlash from the fans, but you have to ask yourself: Do you see any backlash from the fans right now toward Britney Spears? The answer is no.[166]

Some analysts, however, question whether teen pop even needs top 40 radio now that live music venues, television, film, the Internet, and other advances have multiplied the outlets for artist and music exposure. Although her songs were receiving a decreasing amount of airplay, in 2000 Britney Spears was the most-searched-for music star on the Internet, and in 2001 she was on the cover of *Time* magazine and began work on the film *Crossroads*. Spears, 'N Sync, and the Backstreet Boys were still staples on youth-embracing Disney Radio and Nickelodeon,

Figure 7.1 Britney Spears managed to maintain high music sales and visibility in spite of receiving a decreasing amount of radio airplay.

© Rune Hellestad/Corbis.

and all three acts had a global stage as part of Super Bowl XXXV. Nonetheless, music trends are just that—trends that tend to come and go. The question isn't usually *if* a trend will die out or come back into style again, but *when* it will happen. Teen pop has come in and out of popularity for decades and will likely continue to do so for years to come.

Has Techno Killed the Rock 'n' Roll Song?

Disc jockey (DJ) Allen Freed coined the term *rock and roll* to describe a new wild sound, emerging in the late 1940s, that mixed country western music, gospel, blues, rockabilly, and rhythm and blues. As technology continued to evolve, the melody and rhythms of electronic guitars, basses, and synthesizers accompanied by drum percussion became the mainstay of the rock and roll sound—a sound that dominated popular music in the western world for the remainder of the 20th century.

Writer Michael Dunaway argues, however, that in the 1990s, the creative, cutting-edge, great music came not from rock and roll but from two upstarts: techno and hip hop. He identified bands such as Public Enemy (hip hop), Prodigy (techno), and Beck (hip hop—especially when you look at the underlying structure of his music) as those that were setting a new direction for music. It is difficult to trace the evolution of techno. Some sources claim it emerged from Chicago's mid-'80s house music explosion, caught the ear of London club DJs, and infused Europe's dance scene. Columnist Edna Gundersen characterized techno as "an aggressive, electronic revival of disco, concocted by synthesizer-savvy computer freaks with a do-it-yourself punk attitude and shoestring budgets."[167] Rapidly evolving into an icy, hyper-kinetic (up to 140 beats per minute) sound seasoned with elements of psychedelia, punk, hard-core thrash, world beat, reggae, and funk, techno returned to the United States as a hot import.

Fueled by techno's popularity at underground dance clubs, in 1992 *James Brown Is Dead* by Belgium's L.A. Style became the first techno single to hit the *Billboard* chart. According to Dunaway, while most of the fans "in the clubs cared only that the beat was good and that the lyric had a suitably vague, detached, cynical feel, those words [James Brown Is Dead] stood as a kind of manifesto for many on the vanguard of the burgeoning techno scene—namely, that rock and roll has had its day, but now we're taking over. Techno is the wave of the future; rock and roll is a museum piece. James Brown is dead."[168] Major labels began signing techno acts, and the fan base grew. Hip hop—another new, influential genre—is discussed in the next section.

Music and American Culture: Country and Hip Hop

Music is an integral component of a region's culture. Music unifies and identifies cultures and subcultures in much the same way languages, dialects, clothing, foods, and other traditions do. The types of instruments used as well as the tone, tempo, melody, and lyrics convey the nature and values of a culture. Popular music and radio are thought to both shape and reflect popular culture. The conceptualization of music as culture can be seen through a comparison of two distinctly different styles of American-born music: country and rap or hip hop.

Country music, said to have roots in the Southern Appalachians, has a slower, often melancholy sound that perhaps reflects the slower pace of rural life in the early Deep South. It relies heavily on string instruments like fiddles, banjos, and guitars—instruments that were relatively inexpensive and easily portable for singers peddling their music across the Southland. As the name suggests, country songs speak of the hard work and hard luck, heartache and homecomings of country life.

Some historical accounts[169] suggest that American country music was inspired by the ballads and songs of the British Isles, which were brought over by early British settlers. The British songs often focused on the supernatural, avenging spirits, love stories, and violent tales. Yet they tended to be very objective, often relating gruesome stories in a very matter-of-fact style. In America, the songs became more subjective and personal. They downplayed the supernatural, and songs about crime emphasized the evil acts while minimizing the gore. When the songs had to do with love gone wrong, the Americanized ballad usually removed the violence and vulgarity altogether. These changes may have been due to the rise of the Victorian Age, but they also seemed better suited to the philosophy of the Southern lifestyle. American country ballads also tended to add moral statements at the ends of songs, reflecting the Puritan belief that art must be functional or else it is frivolous. Ballads throughout the centuries were often written to share news and happenings from around the world, but with the invention of the printing press this trend declined in many places in Europe. In the vast, rural American Southlands, however, these ballads continued to serve as a fairly accurate way for the more isolated townsfolk to get news of current events. To this day, the instruments, sounds, tempo, and lyrics of country music continue to reflect the stories, people, and culture of country life.

By contrast, rap and hip hop were born in the crime-ridden neighborhoods of the Bronx, where, according to rapper Kurtis Blow,

> Gifted teenagers with plenty of imagination but little cash began to forge a new style from spare parts. Hip hop, as it was then known, was a product of pure streetwise ingenuity; extracting rhythms and melodies from existing records and mixing them up with searing poetry chronicling life in the 'hood, hip hop spilled out of the ghetto.[170]

Faster and often angrier than other types of music, hip hop reflects the culture of the young urban teens who created it. Early rap, often viewed as a subset of hip hop, frequently consisted of nothing more than talking in rhyme to a rhythmic beat—music that could be performed without expensive instruments. The term *hip hop* typically refers to the broader genre of music and culture. According to musical artist and social activist Afrika Bambaataa,

> Hip Hop means the whole culture of the movement... when you talk about rap.... Rap is part of the hip hop culture.... The emceeing[,] ... [t]he djaying is part of the hip hop culture. The dressing[,] the languages are all part of the hip hop culture. The break dancing[,] the b-boys, b-girls ... how you act, walk, look, talk are

Figure 7.2 Hip hop artists Ice Cube (left) and Dr. Dre accept lifetime achievement awards at the 2000 Hip Hop Awards.

© Reuters, Inc./Corbis.

all part of hip hop culture . . . and the music is colorless. . . . Hip Hop music is made from Black, brown, yellow, red, white . . . whatever music that gives you the grunt . . . that funk . . . that groove or that beat. . . . It's all part of hip hop.[171]

Hip hop has evolved to reflect not only different sounds but also different perspectives. Even the work of individual artists has changed and evolved over the years. For example, the early rap of Dr. Dre (starting in the early 1980s) reflected hardcore but cautionary tales of the criminal mind, but his records with Ice Cube in NWA (Niggaz With Attitude) in the late 80s and early 90s celebrated the hedonistic, amoralistic side of gang life. After he left NWA in 1992 and began producing on his own again for himself and others, his music progressed further into G-Funk, a slow-rolling variation that relied more on sound than content.[172] In recognition of their role in the progression of hip hop, Dr. Dre and Ice Cube received lifetime achievement awards at the 2000 Source Hip Hop Awards (see Figure 7.2). Today, of course, both country music and rap and hip hop have evolved and mixed with other genres, just as the cultures that shape them continue to evolve and mix.

Recorded Music

In 1877, Thomas Edison applied for a patent for his talking machine which he called *a phonograph,* taken from the Greek words meaning "to write sound." His invention consisted of a cylinder wrapped in tin foil. Sound was recorded or "written" on the foil with a stylus or needle that cut a groove in the foil that varied with the sound vibrations. To hear the recording, you would put the cylinder on a player and run a needle through the groove, thereby feeding the resulting sound vibrations through a horn. In 1878, Alexander Graham Bell developed a better cylinder and player, and Columbia offered cylinders for coin-operated players. Neither Edison's nor Bell's recordings, however, could be duplicated.

In 1887, Emile Berliner overcame this hurdle by replacing the flimsy foil used for recording with a sturdy metal disc. From the disc, Berliner made a mold that could be used to make near-perfect copies of the original disc onto a thermoplastic material. Berliner's *gramophone* system led to mass production of sound recordings, including music. By 1901, the Victor Talking Machine Company was formed and began offering Berliner's disc players and recordings. In the 1920s, The Columbia and Victor record companies began producing records based on an electrical system perfected by Joseph Maxwell of Bell Laboratories, which introduced the use of microphones to magnify sound electromagnetically. Magnetic tape, developed in Germany, was used to broadcast propaganda during World War II. Longer-playing records made of plastic vinyl and advances in magnetic recording shortly followed.

In 1978, a technological revolution began with *digital recording.* No longer were sound waves inscribed physically on a disc. Instead, sound waves were sampled at millisecond intervals, and each sample was registered in computer language as a specific on-off binary number. When discs were played, the numbers were translated back to sound at the same millisecond intervals. Because the intervals are played so quickly, the sound seems continuous, just as the individual frames on motion picture film become a blur that appears continuous when viewed on a screen. By 1983 digital recordings were available to consumers in the form of compact discs read by CD players that track the digital recordings by laser light and convert the numbers back to sound. These advances were quickly followed by the introduction of devices that could play digital music files downloaded directly from the Internet or other sources. Some critics, however, felt that digital sound was too perfect. Some listeners prefer the imperfections and realism of live performances (or at least recordings of live performances) over digitally sterilized and perfected sounds produced in the recording studio.

The Recording Industry

The Big Five

Apart from a brief stint in the 1950s, the recording industry has existed as a tight *oligopoly* dominated by a few large companies. Today, five large international conglomerates own and control an estimated 86% of the recording industry in the world.[173] The ownership of these five companies reflects their international scope (see Table 7.1).

Table 7.1   Who Owns the Music?

THE BIG FIVE (As of December 2002)

BMG. Owned by Germany's Bertelsmann; releases music on labels such as RCA and Arista.

EMI. Began with the merger of three labels in the United Kingdom and remained primarily European until it acquired Capital Records in the United States. EMI carries labels such as Capitol, EMI-Chrysalis, and Virgin Records.

Sony. Japanese-owned electronics conglomerate; releases music on labels such as Columbia and Epic.

Universal Music Group. Owned by French conglomerate Vivendi; controls labels such as MCA (however, Vivendi announced plans to de-merge their U.S. entertainment holdings as this book was going to press).

Warner Music Group. Owned by U.S. media giant AOL Time Warner; includes labels such as Atlantic, Electra, and Warner Brothers.

Artistic Autonomy

Critics argue that this concentrated ownership allows commercialism to undercut artists' musical freedom and creativity. Profit-driven record labels are said to favor familiar formulaic music from established artists rather than taking risks on new and different sounds from unproven newcomers. As far back as the 1950s there is evidence that the major labels would refuse to record music they felt violated existing norms and would insist that artists modify songs to make them more mainstream. Because of the integral role that music is said to play in cultural development, sociologists and cultural historians worry that this mainstreaming creates *cultural homogenization,* resulting in bland sameness instead of rich cultural diversity. To them, killing artists' autonomy and authenticity is tantamount to killing their cultures.

Demassification

Although industry-dictated commercialism and homogenization may continue to be a concern, they are perhaps less of a problem today than they were in previous decades. Record label executives may try to dictate everything from artists' music to their hairstyles and wardrobes, but many performers today will not just meekly accept such commands. Technology has made high-quality, low-cost recording and mixing equipment affordable for many start-up or garage bands. The number of home recording studios has risen to more than 10,000 while commercial studios have dwindled from 10,000 to 1,000 in less than 20 years. Thanks to the Internet, start-up bands are also rapidly gaining a high-quality, low cost alternative for distribution. And some of these self-made musicians have made significant cultural impacts. Rap/hip hop and early Seattle grunge, two styles of music that have each significantly influenced distinct American subcultures, were homegrown. However, the high costs for marketing and publicity and industry control over traditional distribution and concert venues still make it difficult for independent bands to reach large audiences and make large profits.

I Want My MP3: Dubbing and Piracy

In the 1970s, instead of buying records and tapes, people began dubbing music from shared records or live concerts onto inexpensive blank tapes. Radio stations would often even announce when they would be playing uninterrupted albums so dubbers could tape off the radio. The Internet and organizations like Napster and MP3 revolutionized dubbing by enabling listeners to post, find, listen to, and download music from the Web.

Of course, if people dub instead of buy their music, the recording industry and artists lose that potential revenue. Some people, however, claim that music sharing on the Internet has actually led them to increase their legal music purchases by making them more aware of new and different music. Nonetheless, the Recording Industry of America estimates that the industry loses $1.5 billion a year—the equivalent of about one fifth of its sales—as the result of illegal dubbing. Figure 7.3 shows Hong Kong customs officials sorting through music and video compact discs after they seized 600,000 discs in 1998 worth $1.3 million. The discs were being smuggled from the nearby Portuguese enclave of Macau, which, with Hong Kong, saw an explosion of copyright piracy after a clamp down in mainland China. The industry has taken several steps to try to compensate for losses like these. First, in 1992, the U.S. Congress approved a "taping tax"—a 1% fee on blank tape sales that is passed along to songwriters, music publishers, and others who lose royalty income from home dubbing. The tax was later extended to blank CD purchases. The industry has also engaged in lengthy legal battles to shut down illegal dubbing operations, including Internet sites that facilitate online dubbing.

However, following an "if you can't beat them, join them" philosophy, the five major recording companies have also begun to explore relationships with Web sites and Internet music sharing software companies. Their goal is to create mechanisms that will allow them to collect royalties for music that is played and downloaded from the Internet. For example, in January 2002, Ecast, Inc. announced that it has entered into nonexclusive licensing agreements with all of the major record companies—BMG, EMI Recorded Music, Sony Music Entertainment, Universal Music Group, and Warner Music Group. These companies will offer their music in Ecast's Internet-enabled digital jukeboxes located in public venues. Under the terms of the agreements, the labels would each license their titles to Ecast, which provides a software platform for the delivery and management of entertainment content to Internet-connected jukeboxes.

ON THE RADIO

Historical records document that the first radio or wireless transmission happened in 1897 using spark-coil transmitters to communicate Morse code from a land station to a ship at sea up to 18 miles away. By 1901, the letter "S" was successfully transmitted across the Atlantic

Figure 7.3 Hong Kong customs officials sort through 600,000 smuggled music and video compact discs.

Ocean. Although the priority use of early radio was for maritime safety, its potential for entertainment was recognized from its inception. As early as 1906, experimenter Reginald Fessenden successfully transmitted voice and music programs on Christmas Eve and New Year's Eve short distances and from land to sea.

Since the sign-on of the first commercial radio station, KDKA Pittsburgh, in 1920, the radio industry has enjoyed tremendous popularity, providing listeners with endless hours of entertainment and information. A January 4, 1930, headline reported on radio's growing influence as an entertainment medium: "Radio Seen As One Of The Biggest Branches Of The Show Business." According to the *Billboard* article,

> Against its wishes, in some respects, the amusement industry is being forced, more and more, to recognize the radio field as one of its most important and powerful branches. . . . Five years ago a hybrid form of entertainment and frowned on by show business in general, the radio infant has grown within record time to the point where today it is second only to motion pictures as a gigantic industry in the entertainment business. And it is growing bigger all the time.[174]

Soon, radio stations' regular on-air personalities became almost as popular as the visiting entertainers. As early as 1930, radio announcers were receiving fan mail and gifts from listeners.

When radio broadcasts first began, they were seen as a threat to other entertainment industries. The vaudeville community actually ordered its acts to stay off the air under penalty of contract cancellation. Musical, concert, and operatic managers similarly feared radio, concerned that "songs plugged too strongly over the air would lose their sales value."[175] Eventually, however, vaudeville and the rest of the industry came to recognize radio as a way of stimulating sales and generating additional revenue streams. By 1930 *Billboard* was reporting that "sheet music and record dealers now consider radio a boon to their business, rather than a detriment."[176] Today, U.S. music radio stations pay more than $300 million annually to songwriters and composers (generally through collection associations ASCAP, BMI, and SESAC, discussed later in this chapter) for the right to perform their compositions.

Revenues and Regulation

Early commercial radio stations quickly adopted an *advertising-based revenue model.* Unlike print media, radio stations could not supplement their earnings with subscriber or purchase fees because their broadcast signals could be picked up by anyone with a radio receiver. Fortunately for them, radio has proven to be a very cost-effective medium for advertisers. Not only are radio spots usually less expensive to produce, radio's cost to reach every 1,000 listeners is among the lowest of all mass media. Advertisers also gain speed and flexibility because radio spots can be quickly developed or modified. And because radio station programming is typically localized and narrowly niched, advertisers can target their audiences with a great degree of precision. Radio also has a high level of acceptance among consumers. Localized programming and on-air personalities create a personal feel for listeners, making them more open to and accepting of radio messages, including advertisements.

Radio, however, does have its limitations. Because radio is an audio-only medium, audiences are often easily distracted. Listeners often divide their attention between radio and activities such as driving, working, or talking. Advertisers cannot use charts, graphics demonstrations, or attractive models to sell their products. They must rely on only music, sound effects, and dialogue to create messages that are simple and engaging.

Like other forms of media, the radio industry has been heavily regulated. In the United States, the government limited the number of broadcast outlets in a single market that could be owned by one entity and the total number of broadcast outlets that could be owned by one entity nationwide. As discussed in Chapter 2, freedom of expression is considered essential to democratic society; as radio became a predominant form of public communication, it was feared that *concentrated ownership* (where only a few companies or individuals own all of the outlets) might limit free expression, not to mention limit entertainment choices.

However, throughout the 1980s and 1990s, the Federal Communications Commission (FCC) relaxed its rules, believing that more bandwidth as well as a growing number of other communication outlets (television, magazines, the Internet) provided ample opportunities for competing views and preferences to be heard. In spite of these advances, some critics still feel that ownership is too concentrated. Another view, however, suggests that concentrated ownership might actually increase listener choices. Whereas different owners might try to compete by offering the same programming, it would seem counterintuitive for stations sharing an owner to want to compete with each other. Thus, the logic is that rather than duplicating programming, owners of multiple stations would be motivated to offer different programming on different stations to appeal to different audiences.

The Big Payola

Payola, a contraction of the words "pay" and "Victrola" (LP—long-playing—record player), refers to the practice where recording companies pay cash or gifts in exchange for airplay. Although payola schemes have probably existed from the advent of recorded music, such practices were not scrutinized or condemned until the late '50s, when several independent labels recording rock began beating the majors—in particular, Columbia, RCA, and Decca—in sales and airplay of popular records. This troubled not only the older labels, but also the American Society of Composers, Authors and Publishers (ASCAP). In the '30s and '40s, ASCAP had profited from the sales of sheet music, piano rolls, and recordings of Tin Pan Alley songs, but radio formats changed in the early '40s when recorded music was introduced. Following a battle between radio stations and ASCAP over royalty payments, the stations decided to boycott recordings registered with ASCAP, and they began operating their own publishing corporation, Broadcast Music Incorporated (BMI). Because ASCAP tended to ignore music composed by blacks and those they perceived to be hillbillies, BMI ended up with a virtual monopoly on songs in those fields. And as rock 'n' roll—at first the music of blacks and hillbillies—emerged as a musical force, so did BMI.

As a result, it was hardly surprising when ASCAP, in 1959, urged a House Legislative Oversight subcommittee chaired by Representative Oren Harris to broaden its investigation of corrupt broadcasting practices, which had been centered on rigged TV quiz shows, to include the practice of payola in radio. When Representative Harris announced that his subcommittee would probe payola, *Variety* reported that ASCAP songsmiths took credit for switching the spotlight from TV quiz rigging to disc jockey payola. The assumption was that songs copyrighted with BMI would be revealed as having become hits fraudulently, thanks to payola.

These accusations were further fueled by critics who believed that rock 'n' roll was responsible for a breakdown of morals among youth, that it encouraged misogyny, and that it was a subversive tool of "godless communism." It was commonly believed that teenagers were tricked into listening to this terrible music by greedy DJs who pocketed payola and then played a record so often it was imprinted on listeners' impressionable young minds.

In 1960, Congress, the FCC, and the Federal Trade Commission initiated an exhaustive probe of the entire music industry, from small publishing houses to major radio networks, covering 27 cities and digging for evidence of payola, including misuse of "freebies" (gifts), chart rigging, and kickbacks. In one of the first and most famous cases, the reputation and career of WINS New York disc jockey Alan Freed were destroyed when he was indicted on commercial bribery charges and accused of taking money to play records. Although rock 'n' roll may no longer be feared to be a communist plot and restrictions have eased considerably, the U.S. government continues to limit and investigate payola schemes under the auspices of ensuring fair business practices.

Radio Programming

Early radio was divided into independent and network-affiliated stations, and most programs aired in 15-minute blocks. Unlike today's focused, niche programming, a typical station's programming in 1932 averaged 62.9% music, 21.3% educational, 11.8% literature, 2.5% religion, and 1.5% "novelties" or special programming.[177] Radio also broadcast dramatic programs or stories such as mysteries, action adventures, and comedy sketches with sound effects and "actors" who would read different parts. By 1933, however, radio was starting to fear competition for dramatic programming from yet another new medium: television.

In the '50s, radio formats began to look more like they do today, under the direction of programmers like Todd Storz, who is credited with inventing the top 40 format, and Gordon McLendon. In 1955, programmers Chuck Dunaway and Kent Burkhart initiated what is believed to be the very first radio station playlist at KXOL Fort Worth, Texas. These pioneering programmers and others who followed began to coax radio stations to shift away from a "something for everyone" philosophy (playing a wide variety of music, often based on the personal preferences of the disc jockeys themselves), and toward today's tightly programmed, niche formats and carefully researched playlists targeted at specific demographics. Not everyone, however, supports this shift toward more tightly controlled programming. Some groups, including many of the DJs themselves, argue that radio play should be viewed more as an art than a science, thus allowing DJs greater freedom in music selection (see the box that follows).

Radio Play: Art or Science?

As popular music has grown into a billion-dollar industry, the competition between radio stations for listener attention has become fierce. Today's corporate-owned and -controlled radio stations tend to view radio play as a science. They employ marketing consultants who use formal research methods such as surveys and focus groups to determine audience preferences and to strategically develop formatted playlists of music for disc jockeys to follow. Such an approach, however, is still relatively new. Traditionally, disc jockeys viewed their craft as an art, relying on their own artistic expertise and inspiration from listener suggestions to determine musical selections.

No one is more aware of the tension between creativity and commercialism in radio than Los Angeles disc jockey Jim Ladd. Since the mid-1960s, Ladd has been a popular member of the L.A. radio scene. More recently, he has become an outspoken advocate of what he refers to as *free-form radio*. Ladd refuses to work within the confines of formats and playlists; instead, he insists on controlling the music played on his show himself. "In my definition, free-form radio means that the person on the air gets to play whatever they want," he says, although he does regularly take listener requests as well. In this way, he maintains the unique listener–disc jockey relationship that once characterized rock radio.

Ladd regards music as a creative medium that can be used as a tool for social impact. His show commonly features music with a message, celebrating such ideals as peace, human kindness, and brotherhood. Often, he weaves songs together into thematic sets that segue neatly from one song to the next. "I try to use whole songs as [a rock musician] would use a note or a chord," he says, describing an approach for selecting songs that is clearly artistic.

Ladd refers to marketing consultants as "the suits," and he argues that their approach to meeting audience preferences results in little more than an endless repetition of selected songs. Ladd's refusal to bow to corporate pressure has, at times, kept him out of work. But he has a strong following, and currently his fans form a powerful audience.

Station revenues, of course, are dependent upon being able to deliver a large number of listeners for their advertisers. Marketing consultants argue that the problem with viewing radio play as an art is that not everyone appreciates the same "art." Thus, stations view free-form radio as a high-stakes gamble, and they are hesitant to rely on the creative hunches of individual disc jockeys regarding what listeners will like.

The consultants maintain that formalized research and structured playlists simply serve as a more efficient means of ensuring that radio stations are satisfying their audiences. Indeed, both the consultants and the disc jockeys pay close attention to listeners' opinions when choosing the music to be aired. But disc jockeys like Ladd argue that the consultant-controlled model prevents them from being able to interact meaningfully with listeners. They maintain that free-form radio allows them to introduce their audiences to new music and to new ways of looking at the music they love.

Ultimately, whether free form or "suit-motivated," radio programming is based on listeners' preferences. In the end, it is the listener who votes by turning the dial. What do you think? Should radio play be approached more as an art or a science? Consider your answer from several perspectives—that of a radio listener, a station manager, a disc jockey, and an advertiser—and see if your answer begins to change or if it remains the same.

Radio's *niche formats* both reflect and shape changing music trends. By 1975, the once-popular nostalgia format was being quickly replaced with disco, reflecting the music played at a growing number of discotheques around the country. Country, MOR (middle of the road), and progressive rock stations, which first emerged during the 1960s, had also become prominent by the late '70s. In 1982, black-oriented stations across the United States developed an urban contemporary format that blended black music with rock and pop. Although the format was popular, some programmers of black stations felt that it diluted black music to make it more acceptable for nonblacks. During the '80s radio became big business as stations began trading for unprecedented dollar figures. Top programmers and talent began earning equally unprecedented sums, full-time satellite programming networks emerged, and radio took on a much more professional, corporate style. The growing radio industry has established a proven growth rate over the last 2 decades, remaining financially healthy even when other industries were struggling to remain competitive. Today, there are almost 12,000 radio stations in the United States, representing approximately 80 distinct formats.

Talk Radio, FM Zoo, and Shock Jocks

In addition to music, two popular entertainment radio formats are political talk and FM Zoo. On political talk shows, a host will often introduce a topic and then invite discussion from one or more guest experts. Call-in shows where listeners are invited to share their opinions are a particularly popular format for these shows. Many political talkers are syndicated, but local shows are also popular. An Annenberg national poll found that 18% of adults listen to at least one call-in political talk radio program a week. Typically conservative shows (with hosts such as Rush Limbaugh and Gordon Liddy) tend to fare better than more liberal-leaning programs. Not surprisingly, those who listen to such shows tend to be males who are older, more conservative, predominately white, and who are very interested in politics, are politically active, and hold anti-Washington attitudes.

The *FM Zoo* refers to the morning drive format that dominates contemporary FM stations. During the rest of the day, these stations typically play some genre of popular music (contemporary hit radio, adult contemporary, hot country, oldies, and so forth). During the

Figure 7.4   Disc Jockey Jim Ladd is a leading advocate pushing for radio stations to allow DJs more creative freedom in selecting their own playlists.

© Courtesy of Jim Ladd and KLOS radio/Los Angeles.

morning drive, some of this music is played, but much of the time is spent in informal banter (often of a sexual nature) among the hosts, a traffic reporter, a sports reporter, and a news anchor.

Shock jocks might be seen as an outgrowth of both political talk and zoo genres. Shock DJs tend to push the limits of societal norms by using inflammatory language and issuing views so controversial that some critics consider them to be sociopathic. Howard Stern might be seen as the poster boy for shock jocks. On his syndicated radio show, Stern prays for cancer to kill public officials he does not like, jokes about bodily functions, and finds a way to insult virtually every societal group. Shock jocks like Stern and the radio stations that broadcast them defend these programs as an exercise of their First Amendment right to free expression. Nonetheless, the FCC has issued fines in excess of $1 million to stations that carry Stern's show.

Although critics are loud in their protests, shock jocks exist and even prosper because people listen to them. In fact, some supporters contend that Stern and others like him play an important cultural role, providing a safe place where issues can be discussed, facilitating cultural evolution that might otherwise be stunted by oppressive social censure. For many critics, however, such sentiments only reinforce their concerns as they contemplate the culture that might evolve from this programming.

Digital Technology

Record companies are not the only ones who have been affected by the digital revolution. Radio is also experiencing new opportunities and threats introduced by rapidly advancing technologies.

Digital Radio

Several digital technologies now exist for the broadcast of traditional terrestrial radio stations, but stations were hesitant to make the conversion from analog because a standard had not been set by the FCC. However, as of the beginning of 2002, iBiquity Digital was the sole developer and licenser of digital AM and FM broadcast technology in the United States. The company's investors include 14 of the nation's top radio broadcasters, including ABC, Clear Channel, and Viacom; technology companies Harris, Lucent, Texas Instruments, and Visteon; and leading financial institutions such as J. P. Morgan Partners, Pequot Capital, and J&W Seligman. iBiquity's in-brand-on channel (IBOC) technology was also endorsed by the Geneva-based International Telecommunication Union (ITU). IBOC technology relies on digital compression to shrink digital and analog signals, allowing stations to broadcast both digital and analog formats simultaneously on a single channel without requiring additional spectrum.

Satellite Radio

Another outgrowth of digital technology is satellite radio. Although the potential for this medium remains to be seen, satellite radio providers boast better signal and sound quality and more stations with more diverse offerings. The first two U.S. coast-to-coast satellite radio providers, Sirius and XM, each launched with the promise of 100 stations. Satellite radio delivers some commercial radio broadcasts, but most stations developed by the satellite providers and their partners offer commercial-free music and news talk and/or information, narrowly focused to suit specific style and interest niches. The tradeoff, however, is that listeners must pay for these satellite radio services (much like premium cable and satellite television services) whereas traditional, broadcast radio remains free. Thus, the question becomes whether audiences will find satellite offerings and sound quality worth the price.

Internet Radio

There are two basic models for Internet radio: *radio simulcasts,* where over-the-air broadcasts are streamed simultaneously on the Internet, or *Web-only radio,* which can be accessed only over the Internet. In 2001 there were about 5,000 traditional and 500 Internet-only broadcasters streaming news, sports, and some of the most eclectic music programming imaginable, according to BRS Media.

By the end of 2001, however, traditional radio simulcast broadcasters had been virtually swept from the Web. Many of the industry's largest broadcasters had ordered their stations to cease live streaming. Several factors contributed to this abandonment. First, an act advanced by the Recording Industry Association of America (RIAA), required stations to pay royalty fees to the artists for Internet streaming. Emerging court cases also threatened other fees. These costs were in addition to what radio stations across the nation already paid through licensing arrangements with SESAC (the Society of European Stage Authors and Composers), BMI, and ASCAP for traditional radio broadcasts of the same music. Beyond these costs, the American Federation of Television and Radio Artists (AFTRA) drew attention to a little-known provision of the Recorded Commercials Contract instituted in October 2000 that requires advertisers to pay union talent *300%* of the normal session fee if a spot originally recorded for radio is used on the Internet. Thus, rather than welcoming the added bonus of reaching audiences via Internet streaming, advertisers began protesting and threatening to pass along the added costs to the radio stations. Broadcasters like Clear Channel Communications, Emmis, Radio One, ABC/Disney, and others, started closing down station live streams nationwide because they were fearful that future court rulings might involve retroactive fees to be paid to AFTRA members.

Music and Radio: A Rocky Marriage

Radio and the recording industry have a history of interdependence. Radio depends on the recording industry for a continuous flow of new material to broadcast, and the recording manufacturers depend on radio for the exposure of their product to potential consumers. Despite their close affiliation through the years, the music and radio industries have often clashed over issues. But considering that radio accounts for about 80% of record sales in America, the major record labels have almost always compromised on any conflicting issue, judiciously opting not to bite the hand that feeds them—until recently.

Digital and satellite technologies are transforming the entire music entertainment industry. With the potential of wireless Internet and high-speed digital connectivity, the music industry could be in a position for the first time to break free of its alliance with radio as its primary source of introducing new music to consumers. The music industry has not openly admitted to waging battle with radio. Critics, however, suggest that the additional licensing and performance fees and higher fees for advertising talent and commercial content that have been levied against radio stations to make room for the major record labels to get into the Internet game. By developing their own Internet radio sites and utilizing music download technology, recording companies might be able to bypass the retail industry and the radio industry, and instead promote and sell their music directly to consumers.

Under such a plan, the role of traditional radio would be reduced. The day could come when labels no longer send stations free music to promote but instead charge a subscription fee to them if they want to get the music first and fresh. To regain leverage before it is too late, some radio broadcasters have considered several strategies, ranging from simple blackouts of traditional advertisements from their Internet feeds to more radical changes, such as charging a promotion fee for airtime dedicated to specific songs or artists. The future of the music entertainment industry is uncertain. Nonetheless, the market for music will likely remain strong, regardless of who delivers the product.

MUSIC LIVES

Before recordings and radio, music videos and televised performances, the only way to experience music was through live performances. Although technology now provides myriad ways to enjoy music, live musical performances continue to be a popular form of entertainment.

Live Music

Audiences watch live performances in venues ranging from small bars and clubs to forums and amphitheaters seating tens of thousands of fans. These concerts generate serious revenues. In North America, ticket sales for live concerts reached $1.5 billion dollars in 1999, breaking a $1.4 billion record set in 1994. Promoters began raising their prices in 1994 to reduce the gap between a ticket's face value and the prices charged by scalpers and ticket brokers. By 1999, the average ticket price of the top 50 tours in North America reached $43.63, according to Gary Bongiovanni, editor-in-chief of Pollstar Inc., a music industry trade magazine and online service in Fresno, California. That is an increase of more than $10 per ticket from 1998—a 30% jump in one year. Ticket prices are also linked to audience demographics, he adds. Elton John tickets carry higher prices than Blink 182 tickets because John's audience represents a higher income level.[178]

Critics, however, have accused ticketing agencies of inflating ticket prices. This criticism centers on exclusive arrangements ticketing agencies often make with venues. If a band or other act wants to book a venue, they must do their ticketing with a specific agency. The concern is that these arrangements create monopolies eliminating competition that would keep ticket prices lower. Others, however, argue that centralized ticketing actually keeps prices lower (see "A Closer Look" later in this chapter).

This dispute, however, has not appeared to dampen audiences' enthusiasm for live music. Like other live performances, live music creates a different experience than mediated entertainment. Audiences enjoy the immediacy of live music, the physical closeness to the musicians, and the communal experience with other audience members. People also enjoy the spontaneity of live concerts. Live events are unpredictable. No two performances of even the most carefully planned and choreographed productions are exactly alike.

Festivals

An increasingly popular live music format is the multi-act concert festival. One such festival was Ozzfest 2000, which featured Ozzy Osbourne, Godsmack, and Ministry, with Ticketmaster Online tickets ranging from $35.25 to nearly $60. Another 2000 festival was The Vans Warped Tour, which showcased Green Day and the Mighty Mighty Bosstones. These types of festivals can be traced as far back as the 3-day Woodstock festival held in 1969, which featured an impressive collection of artists, including Janis Joplin, Jimi Hendrix, the Grateful Dead, and numerous others. Since then, music festivals have become increasingly popular, likely due in large part to their efficiency. Audiences can see several bands in a compact period of time, usually for less money than if they saw each one separately. And, in addition to music, these concerts, which may last for days, typically draw a range of vendors peddling food, drink, clothing, and other novelties to round out the festival experience.

Trade industry magazine editor Gary Bongiovanni speculates that the uniqueness of these events may be usurped by the increasing number of radio station shows.[179] Radio's influence on music trends gives stations an advantage in brokering concert deals. It can be hard for the festivals to compete when radio stations are putting on multiband concerts for as little as $10 or $20 a ticket—even if the artists sing only one or two songs in short 20-minute sets instead of performing full 90-minute sets.

Rave Culture

The most recent trend to hit the music scene is the rave, a type of event that originated in London during the late 1980s. The term *rave* generally refers to a gathering or party, usually lasting all night, where people (mostly teenagers and twenty-somethings, but with an increasing number of thirty-to-forty-somethings) come together to listen to and dance to music. Raves can range from small "underground" warehouse parties of 50 people to large fairground festivals catering to thousands. Although raves are live events, as is the case with many traditional club or bar scenes, the music itself is not directly performed live.

The predominant type of music heard at these parties is techno or house, each of which has many evolving sounds, such as garage, jungle, drum 'n' bass, house, happy core, and trance. DJs use turntables to spin records and a mixer to manipulate this electronic music.

The music is usually accompanied by light shows that might include strobe lights, lasers, and visuals projected on screens. DJs play a critical role at raves, controlling the tempo, mood, and energy of the entire party by their selection and manipulation of the music they play. Skilled DJs often produce their own signature sounds and mixes, establishing loyal followings. Thus, although rave music is not directly performed live, these DJs, in a sense, become performers creating the spontaneous, audience-driven feel of a live music experience.

As has been the case with many music scenes throughout the years, raves are often associated with drug use. The most popular drugs are methylenedioxymethamphetamine (MDMA), commonly known as ecstasy, and crystal methamphetamine, commonly known as crystal meth or speed. Although drugs popularized by beatniks and hippies in the 1950s and 60s—such as lysergic acid diethylamide (LSD, also called acid) and marijuana—are still common, newcomers like gamma hydroxybutyric acid (GHB), ketamine, and 4-bromo-2,5-dimethoxyphenethylamine (2C-B) have also emerged onto the scene. Although many rave-goers do use drugs, many others enjoy these parties sober, enjoying the music and the atmosphere at face value.

Raves are typically organized by promoters who spread word of these parties by phone voicemail, e-mail, Web pages, rave calendars, and flyers. Many early raves were held in abandoned warehouses or fields without proper licenses or permits. The underground nature of these parties combined with the noted drug use gave the rave something of an illicit reputation. Today some raves continue to be private, homegrown affairs, but others have become sponsor-driven commercial extravaganzas. Because of the fear of growing trendiness as well as the stigma and stereotypes of drug use and illegal activity associated with the label *raves*, many people prefer to use the more generic term *parties* when referring to these events.

Although raves may have introduced new sounds, sights, and drugs to a new generation of music lovers, these parties reflect traditions that can be traced back to tribal times. In fact, ravers and those who study rave culture draw many parallels between raves and ancient religious rituals. DJs are often said to serve the role of spiritual priests or guides that help elevate ravers into an altered psychological or spiritual state. Raver Janne Leino from Helsinki, Finland, defines raves as "a modern high-tech form of an ancient tribal ritual where shamans gather to dance themselves into deep trance or self-hypnosis. Raving is a very deep spiritual experience like the enlightenment states in many religions."[180]

People at raves are usually racially diverse and are from different backgrounds. Nonetheless, ravers, like other music fans, form their own subcultures. The rave community prides itself on being very accepting of anyone—young, old, black, white, and so on. Many ravers believe in PLUR, which stands for peace, love, unity, and respect. They also believe in the positive vibe the music and atmosphere at a rave create. Ravers claim that the only true way to understand this feeling is to experience it for yourself, standing on the dance floor surrounded by hundreds of people as the music builds to a crescendo.

Over the years, individuals who have shared values and a common interest in music and rave experiences have organized themselves into community-based groups, often called *collectives* or *tribes*. In addition to throwing parties and other music-based events, these collectives usually function as extended families for their members. Many collectives become very involved with social and often political issues in their communities. Proceeds of the events and parties they organize are often donated to local charities. Each collective has a unique culture and focus. Many groups are very environmentally conscious, often organizing and participating in clean-up and recycling efforts as well as promoting ballot initiatives that are consistent with the collective's focus.

Music and Video

Music Videos Give Music a Face

The Music Television Channel (MTV), introduced by the Warner media conglomerate in 1981, is commonly credited with popularizing music videos, but the actual introduction of music videos can be traced back to Europe during the 1970s. Because state-regulated radio avoided pop music, European record companies, seeking new publicity vehicles, created videos that featured recording artists acting out their music. The videos were played in dance clubs, and record sales began to rise. Seeing their success, record makers in the United States soon began making videos as well. When MTV was first launched, skeptics questioned whether a full-time music video cable channel would attract enough viewers to interest advertisers, make money, and stimulate record sales. Those skeptics were silenced, however, by 1984, when MTV claimed 24 million viewers, more than any other cable channel. MTV appealed to the teenagers and young adults that tend to buy the most music. MTV programming, however, is no longer limited to music videos. More than 20 years since its introduction, MTV is now transmitted via satellite worldwide, reaching more than 353 million households in about 140 countries.[181] The 1990s introduced a number of new music video channels to the American market, including VH-1, M2, CMT (County Music Television), TNN (The Nashville Network), and BET (Black Entertainment Television). MTV itself has changed over the years; currently, it airs music videos from a variety of genres and shows nonmusic, youth-oriented programming, including launching one of the first and most popular reality programs, *The Real World*.

Music Video's Impact on the Industry

Music videos in general and MTV in particular are thought to have changed the face of the rock music tour. Before the advent of music videos, recording artists could simply appear before microphones and play their music. Today, concerts are spectacular visual and audio productions, complete with mega-screen videos, light shows, and backup orchestras and dance troupes. Although some artists (such as Pearl Jam) have shunned music videos, most songs do not make top sales charts without video accompaniment. Introducing video to music opened the floodgates of cross-platforming and marketing music with other media. Today's top hits often involve major tie-ins with motion pictures, television programs, and sometimes even advertising campaigns.

Critics, however, warn that the growing emphasis on visual elements has overshadowed the music. Today's artists must sound good AND look good if they want to sign with a major recording label. A&R scouts look for artists that are charismatic and fun to watch. As a result, many of today's successful artists have been created by promoters based on casting call searches for individuals that fit a desired image, such as the Backstreet Boys, En Vogue, and the Spice Girls.

The impact of MTV and music videos on the entertainment industry may also extend beyond music. MTV is often credited with popularizing the montage, quick-cutting cinematic style now often used in film and television cinematography. And, as previously mentioned, MTV also helped trigger the reality television craze with its original program *The Real World,* which followed the lives of a group of roommates. The formula was quite simple; the producers simply threw a handful of (strategically selected) young people with strong personalities under one roof for a year and let the tapes roll. Soon, all the networks were boasting similar low-budget, voyeuristic programs.

Other Visuals

Over the years, other visual accompaniments have also been added to music. In the 1960s, rock music lovers created psychedelic "light circuses" by squishing around colored oil globs on overhead projector lenses. The '70s brought strobe lights and disco balls. Most recently, in the era of techno music and raves, sophisticated argon lasers have become the craze. Now cheap, powerful computers are inspiring a new generation of eye-candy musical visualizations. These graphical creations can magically morph, changing colors and effects that correspond directly to the beat and sound of the music booming from loudspeakers.

Let the Music Play: Appeal and Impact[182]

Young people around the globe, particularly in Westernized societies, report music as one of their most preferred leisure activities. Music's popularity has been attributed to several factors. Research suggests that music produces pleasurable mood states and physiological arousal. Music can evoke a wide range of emotions, making us feel happy, sad, excited, even angry. Research has found that listening to favorite music can reduce unpleasant feelings of anxiety, lift the spirits, and pump people up. If, as suggested in Chapter 4, a primary function of entertainment is to make us feel, then it is no wonder that music is such a popular form of entertainment.

Music and Emotions

Music and radio also enjoy another advantage over other forms of entertainment: Audiences can enjoy music without exerting a great deal of energy or attention. Individuals may choose to devote a significant amount of their energy and attention to music, dancing and singing along to tunes cranked up full blast, but they do not have to. People can also enjoy music even if their attention is focused elsewhere—for example, on working, driving, or dozing. To truly enjoy a book, film, or video game typically requires much more energy and attention. One reason for this difference is that music alone is predominantly an auditory experience, whereas other forms of entertainment engage multiple senses. Video games, for example, often engage sight, sound, and touch. Video games and other forms of entertainment (such as films, books, and other drama-based entertainment) also require more cognitive effort if they are to be interpreted or appreciated. Although song lyrics may be interpreted cognitively, the beat and the tone of music can also have a more direct visceral effect on our emotions.

Music's single sensory input (sound) and effortless emotional connection make it a popular supplement to other forms of entertainment. Films include soundtracks to cue audiences' emotional reactions—playing scary music to stimulate fear, melancholy songs to evoke sadness, and so on. At sporting events, music is played to rally the players and fans. Music is also played in restaurants, bars, retail stores, theme parks, and other leisure settings to facilitate and enhance patrons' enjoyment without detracting from the social activities and interactions that take place in these environments.

Socialization

As suggested earlier in the chapter, music is an important component of culture, particularly for teens. The content of popular music can act as an agent of *socialization,* providing young people with information about society, social and gender roles, and behavioral norms. Furthermore, adolescents learn to define themselves by their music, imitating the speech, dress, and even actions of their favorite artists. Music videos, with their powerful visual imagery, can be especially influential sources of information about social roles, consumerism, and culture.

Listening to music may help shape adolescents' *self-identity* and *group-identity*. Popular music creates shared meanings that may ease peer-group identification and facilitate social communication among peer subgroups. Teens' musical preferences both shape and reflect the friendships they develop, the clothes they wear, and other lifestyle choices they make. Shared music preferences can bring young people from different social strata into the same cultural subgroup. Being part of a shared subculture can ease the transition away from parents and toward peers.

That's the Way (Uh Huh, Uh Huh) I Like It: Music Preferences

Music preferences established in young adulthood tend to predominate throughout a person's life. Given that music is integrally tied to our social identities, it is not surprising that individuals who share music preferences also tend to share other characteristics. For

Table 7.2	Personality Characteristics of Music Fans by Genre
Hard Rock and Heavy Metal	*Punk Rock*
High in machiavellianism	Less accepting of authority
High in machismo	Say that family was not close while
Low in need for cognition	growing up
High in toughmindedness	Feel misunderstood by parents
High in excitement seeking	Report high estimates of young
High in sensation seeking	people who:
High in recklessness	own weapons
High in risk taking	have vandalized something
High in delinquency	have committed a crime
Greater use of tobacco, alcohol,	have gone to jail
and marijuana	
Reports higher estimates of young	*Rap*
people who:	
have premarital sex	May be misunderstood
use cocaine and marijuana	Low in need for cognition
have satanic beliefs	
have stolen parent's car	*Pop*
Report lower estimates of young	
people who:	High in empathy for characters in books
have been involved in date rape	and movies ("fantasy")

SOURCE: Reprinted with permission of Lawrence Erlbaum from Hansen, C. & Hansen, R. (2000). Music and music videos. In D. Zillmann & P. Vorderer (Eds)., *Media entertainment: The psychology of its appeal (p. 186)*. Mahwah, NJ: Lawrence Erlbaum.

example, when fans of late 1980s punk rock music were compared with nonfans, several interesting differences were observed. Punk fans were significantly more likely to have engaged in vandalism and antiauthority behavior, owned weapons, committed a crime, and gone to jail. Research has found that hard rock and heavy metal fans tend to score high on traits such as machiavellianism, machismo, toughmindedness, excitement seeking, and drug use. Although there has been less research examining rap and pop music, findings suggest shared fan traits for these genres as well. Table 7.2 provides a summary of some of the characteristics associated with fans of different music genres based on the research obtained from these and other studies.

What's That You Say? Music and Video Content

Song Lyrics

Although music styles change over the years, research suggests that lyrical themes remain fairly constant. Love is, perhaps, the most common lyrical theme. In the 1940s and

1950s, lyrics centered on romantic love. During the 1960s, lyrics began to focus more on physical love and, reflective of the era, themes such as drug use and war protests also emerged. In the 1970s, romance and fun reemerged in disco lyrics. Violence and occult themes began to appear in the lyrics of 1980s punk rock and heavy metal genres. Lyrics of the 1990s became increasingly more explicit with violent, sexual, and misogynistic themes reflected in rock music and newly emerging genres like gangsta rap.

An analysis of song lyrics over four decades (the 1940s through the 1970s) revealed interesting patterns. References to women's physical characteristics rose significantly each decade, with mentions in 6.4% of songs sampled in 1946, 11.7% of songs sampled in 1956, 13.6% in 1966, and 30.4% in 1976. From the 1960s to the 1970s, characterizations of women as "child-like" with terms such as *baby* or *girl* increased from about 25% to 50% of songs sampled; however, references to women as sex objects remained steady at about 20%.

Censorship

Certain music genres, themes, and lyrics have become a focal point for public controversy. In the 1920s, some people viewed jazz as morally loose, whereas many white racists of the 1950s had unkind words for the early rock they associated with the "Negro" community. Others were angered by the war protest and drug-glorifying songs of the 1960s. Although the government rarely responds with direct efforts to censor music, the FCC has worked indirectly to keep some music off the market by pressuring radio stations to restrict the airplay of offensive songs. FCC broadcasting regulations include a mandate that radio stations that are dedicated to serving the public interest should know the content of lyrics they play. The implication? Police the songs you play, or risk losing your broadcast license. The logic is that record labels, recognizing their dependence on airplay, become equally hesitant to produce offensive music.

In the 1980s, groups such as the Parents' Music Resource Center (PMRC) came out strongly against popular music lyrical themes focusing on sex, violence, Satanism, and drug or alcohol use, claiming links between explicit lyrics and social ills such as teen suicide, teen pregnancy, physical abuse, broken homes, and criminal activity. Some of the songs singled out for opposition included Prince's song *Sister,* thought to glorify incest; Motley Crue's *Live Wire,* for its fascination with strangulation; and Guns N' Roses songs, accused of expressing racism. Music labels responded to the pressure exerted by these groups with voluntary labeling schemes to warn consumers about songs containing explicit lyrics. Although some groups lauded these efforts, many felt they did not go far enough. Some critics advocated censorship and age-restricted sales policies, arguing that voluntary labeling only increased the music's appeal to curious and rebellious young listeners. In the highly publicized case of Ice-T's song, *Cop Killer,* Time Warner did eventually pull the music from the market (see the box that follows).

Time-Warner "Cop Killer" Protest[183]

In 1992, Time-Warner rap music recording artist Ice-T (a.k.a. Tracey Marrow) and his new band, Body Count, released their first album. Included on the album was a song called *Cop Killer,* in which the lyrics openly advocate the killing of police officers as a form of social protest.

Police officers from across the nation, as well as many others, were outraged by the release of this song. Time-Warner defended the album as a free speech issue protected by the Constitution.

Police associations called for citizens to boycott Time-Warner and all of its subsidiaries, including its publications, cable companies, and amusement parks. One form of protest included taking subscription cards from Time-Warner magazines and mailing them back with a written protest. Not only did Time-Warner have to pay the postage for the returned cards, it had to pay their employees to sort through them. Literally thousands of these cards were mailed to Time-Warner from across the country.

In July 1992 Time-Warner's annual shareholders meeting was held in Beverly Hills, California. CLEAT (Combined Law Enforcement Associations of Texas), along with major police associations from across the nation, planned a protest for the day of the shareholders meeting. Hundreds of police officers flew to California for this protest, which attracted national media attention. Even Ice-T showed up and showed his opinion of the protesters with a well-recognized hand gesture.

Time-Warner eventually pulled the album from the market, a move that Ice-T attributed in a later interview to the pressure the police put on Time-Warner during the entire controversy.

Music Videos

The content of music videos, particularly violent and sexual content, has also faced strong public criticism, and it has been the subject of much research.[184] One analysis found sexual imagery in between 40% and 75% of music videos. Almost half of all women in music videos were found to be dressed provocatively compared to only 10% of the men. Women were much more likely than men to be treated as sex objects. One study reported that women were "put down" by or dominated by men in approximately three quarters of the music videos that were sampled. Women and men tend to be portrayed at the polar ends of their stereotypes, with women portrayed as affectionate, nurturing, and fearful, whereas men are portrayed as adventuresome, aggressive, and domineering. Occupational roles depicted in videos also reflected sex-role stereotypes, with women frequently portrayed as waitresses, hairstylists, dancers, or fashion models, and men shown in roles of police officers, scientists, athletes, and business executives. In addition, in the videos studied, white characters tended to be older and of higher social status than nonwhites.

Violence is another prominent theme in music videos; in fact, many studies have found violent imagery in more than half of the videos sampled. A similar percentage of videos has been found to contain antisocial content, including rebellious and socially unacceptable behavior. And drug, alcohol, and tobacco use have been noted in from 20% to 27% of videos.

Music Effects

Sex Sells

Perhaps the most obvious and uncontested effect of sexual themes is that audiences like them. Research finds that individuals report liking the music and the visuals better in sexy videos. However, studies have found that violent video content, particularly when combined with sexual content, may actually decrease the appeal of the visuals and the music.

Critics of lyric and video content, of course, are concerned that such content encourages immoral, antisocial, stereotypical, and criminal attitudes and behaviors, particularly among impressionable adolescents. Countering these accusations, some researchers argue that adolescents do not seem to perceive song lyrics in the same way that the critics do. Some studies have found that young listeners do not know or understand all of the words in popular songs and that what they do comprehend, they may interpret differently. For example, Led Zeppelin's *Stairway to Heaven* song has been condemned for glorifying drug use or sexual experiences. When teenagers were asked what the song meant, however, they interpreted it quite literally, stating that the song was about climbing steps into the sky.[185]

There is a growing body of evidence that listeners can be affected by even brief exposures to popular music and music videos. These studies often find that the effects of rock music and videos reflect their thematic content.[186] Although many of the theories discussed in Chapter 5 might help explain the potential effects of music and music videos, much of the existing research tends to support a *priming model*. It is theorized that thematic content such as sex and violence "primes" viewers' cognitive schemas, which, in turn, influences subsequent impressions and social judgments in ways that reflect those themes. Take, for example, a rap music fan. Rap songs and videos are likely to trigger positive feelings for most fans (which is the reason they are fans). Many rap songs and videos, however, portray women as sex objects. Listening to these songs and watching these videos are thought to trigger fans' "women as sex object" schemas. And because the fans associate positive feelings with the music, they may also begin to associate positive feelings with these schemas. As a result, fans may begin to consider women as sex objects. In support of this theory, many studies have found that subjects are more likely to endorse violent, anti social and sexually permissive attitudes and behaviors after watching rock videos with those themes than after watching neutral videos. Research has also found greater endorsement of sex-role stereotyping after watching videos with stereotypical portrayals.[187] Practical constraints on research (see Chapter 5 for discussion) make it difficult to know if such effects are only short-lived or if they have more lasting impacts, but it is reasoned that these attitudes may become more stable personality traits.

Excitation transfer theory suggests another possible explanation for the short-term impacts of music and music videos. Physiological arousal is thought to be an important component of music appreciation. As previously discussed, music, like many other forms of entertainment, makes us feel. The reactions inspired by music are thought to be particularly powerful. Music arouses us both physically (increasing our heart rate, blood pressure, and breathing) and emotionally. As explained in Chapter 4, research has found that arousal from one experience can unconsciously influence our reactions to subsequent arousing experiences. Thus, listening to arousing music or watching arousing music videos may influence how we react to other people or events we encounter while we are listening or watching, or immediately afterwards. Say, for example, you are listening to your favorite CD on the way to work. If someone suddenly cuts you off on the freeway or if your boss yells at you for being late, you might react differently than you normally would, perhaps responding more intensely without knowing it. Thus, according to this theory, listening to music or watching music videos may lead people to react in more stereotypical, violent, or sexist ways simply because they are more aroused. If this theory is correct, then any form of arousing music might have the same effect, regardless of whether or not the songs or videos contain stereotypical, violent, or sexist content.

Clearly, there are many questions regarding the impact of music and music videos that have yet to be answered. Some experts speculate, however, that with the growing global popularity of contemporary rock music and other genres that some consider questionable, we may witness a similar growth and interest in research that addresses these questions.

FADE TO BLACK

Music possesses perhaps the longest and richest history of any form of entertainment. It has chronicled our sagas, inspired our citizens, shaped our cultures, and socialized our youth. Music is a dynamic form of entertainment capable of stimulating powerful emotions, thoughts, and behaviors. People often define themselves and those around them by their musical preferences. In a very real sense, music is the soundtrack of our society, reflecting the issues, trends, and customs of distinct peoples and eras.

As the 21st century dawns, it is difficult to predict what the future holds for music and radio and their influence on society. The landscape of these industries is changing almost daily as technological advances and legal rulings alternately expand and restrict opportunities for music production, reproduction, duplication, and distribution. Although the future is unclear, it is safe to predict that tomorrow's music will both inspire and be inspired by the issues, trends, customs, and cultures of tomorrow's societies.

 A Closer Look

Is More Always Better?
The Case of Pearl Jam vs. Ticketmaster[188]

The Accusation

In the spring of 1994 the rock band Pearl Jam brought an antitrust suit against Ticketmaster. In a memorandum filed with the Antitrust Division of the U.S. Department of Justice on May 6, 1994, Pearl Jam argued that Ticketmaster has a "virtually absolute monopoly on the distribution of tickets to concerts." *Time* magazine called the legal battle "Rock 'n' Roll's Holy War." According to Pearl Jam and other Ticketmaster critics, the company keeps ticket sales organized and revenue high, but often at the expense of fans. The service charges that Ticketmaster adds to tickets range from $3 to $6 and can add more than 30% to a ticket's face value.

Ticketmaster and its supporters defend these fees as a lower-cost alternative, suggesting that these fees are reasonable compared to the time and transportation expenses that would accrue if people went to the box office. Indeed, although people may grumble, if they really felt that purchasing tickets from the box office was the best option, that is what they would do. And, if that were the case, then Ticketmaster would be out of business. Critics, however, maintain that if Ticketmaster were competing not just with the box office, but also with other ticket agencies, these fees would be lower.

One reason these surcharges are purported to be so high is that Ticketmaster pays a small fee to venues or promoters for every ticket sold in order to maintain exclusive contracts that give Ticketmaster sole control over those sales. Ticketmaster was said to have even loaned promoters money to meet the guarantees of stadium acts and to have given money to venues for promotion and marketing. Several lawsuits called Ticketmaster dividends to venues "kickbacks." Critics argue that these exclusive arrangements unfairly limit competition, leaving musical artists, venues, and music fans completely at Ticketmaster's mercy. They contend that fans would be better served if more ticket agencies were allowed to compete for their business.

Is Ticketmaster a Monopoly?

The question of whether or not Ticketmaster maintains a "virtually absolute" monopoly is open to debate. Patent law creates monopolies (single seller positions) in inventions and innovations; copyright confers monopolies in literary and artistic works. Pearl Jam has a legal monopoly on any songs and performances the band creates, meaning that no one else can legally try to sell Pearl Jam's work without permission. The question, then, is whether or not Ticketmaster has a monopoly on tickets. On the macro level, other companies can try to compete with Ticketmaster. Indeed, others have tried, but most have failed. Ticketron, the largest competing ticket service, sold out to Ticketmaster in 1991 after losing millions of dollars a year since 1988.

Pearl Jam and others, however, charge that Ticketmaster engages in anti-competitive practices, such as exclusive venue contracts, that give it monopolistic power. Defenders counter that the money Ticketmaster loans or gives to arenas or promoters actually benefits both venues and fans by serving as a guarantee that the show will be performed. Some even speculate that Ticketmaster started these loans and promotion subsidies in response to people who complained after shows were canceled. The concern, however, is that such policies are anti-competitive because small-scale ticket services are often unable to duplicate them. They do not have the resources to loan or give money to venues as guarantees, particularly if they are trying to gain a competitive advantage by charging less for their tickets. Another question then becomes whether concert-goers would rather spend more money or pay less and risk a show cancellation because the venue couldn't meet its guarantees. Ticketmaster's policy is predicated on the belief that people would rather pay more. The company's success would seem to support that preference. Still, critics maintain that Ticketmaster simply leaves people no other choice.

Would Competition Lower Ticket Prices?

Would more competition lead to lower prices? Many Ticketmaster critics believe that it would. Ticketmaster supporters, however, claim that it would not. They maintain that other ticketing agencies *were* given an opportunity to compete, but they folded because Ticketmaster beat them out with better pricing and value. The thinking is that Ticketmaster can offer better pricing because of its high volume of sales. To let smaller agencies compete, it is argued, Ticketmaster would have to raise its fees to match the higher costs of the smaller agencies and risk being sued for price fixing for keeping ticket prices artificially high. Critics, however, counter that if Ticketmaster is so confident that it can offer the best pricing and value, it should be able to maintain high-volume sales without relying on exclusive arrangements with venues that eliminate the possibility of even small-scale competition. Ticketmaster again emphasizes that exclusive arrangements are the only way it can offer venues guarantees . . . and the argument continues back and forth in similar fashion.

Who Will Win The War?

The justice department eventually ruled in favor of Ticketmaster, ending the 2-year dispute between Pearl Jam and the ticketing agency. Ticketmaster also won a second legal battle against charges of monopolistic control brought against the company in a class action suit launched by consumers who had purchased tickets from Ticketmaster in 1998. This case was appealed all the way to the Supreme Court, which ruled in January 1999 that the consumers did not have proper legal standing to launch the suit. However, some critics contend that Ticketmaster's victories to date are more the result of legal technicalities than any ultimate verdict on current ticketing practices, and debate continues regarding whether or not Ticketmaster maintains monopolistic control of the event ticketing market.[189]

What do you think? Is Ticketmaster a monopoly? Does Ticketmaster provide the best value for concert-goers, or would music fans be better served by having more ticket agencies competing for their business?

DISCUSSION AND REVIEW

1. Pick examples of today's music and explain the ways you think they shape or reflect certain subcultures or society at large. What is your favorite type of music? Your favorite radio station? What appeals to you about this music/radio station? Do you think the music and radio programming you like shapes or reflects your own identity and subculture? Explain.

2. How much recorded music do you personally own? How much of it was obtained legally? Trace the development of technology for music reproduction and distribution. Do you think that the Internet has increased or decreased business for the recording industry? What do you think should be done, if anything, about dubbing and piracy? Given the types of technology that are developing, how do you think the recording industry should handle music distribution in the future?

3. Trace the historical relationship between the recording industry and radio stations. What do you think of this relationship? Is it fair? How much influence do you think they have over each other? Explain. Has this relationship changed with the introduction of the Internet? Explain.

4. What sort of societal impacts, if any, do you think music videos may have? Review both impacts on the recording and entertainment industries as well as effects on viewers. Use your own examples (based on what you have seen, read, and perhaps personally experienced) to argue for and/or against the different impacts of music videos discussed in the readings as well as any other impacts you can think of.

EXERCISES

1. How has broadcast radio programming changed over the years? Do an Internet search and explore Internet radio offerings. How do Internet offerings compare to broadcast radio offerings? How do you feel about current music and programming offerings on broadcast radio? Do you think radio programming should be viewed as a science or an art? Explain.

2. Listen to three different morning show radio broadcasts. Compare and contrast these programs. Speculate about any differences you think there may be between the audiences they cater to.

RECOMMENDED READINGS AND WEB SITES

Hansen, C., & Hansen, R. (2000). Music and music videos. In D. Zillmann & P. Vorderer (Eds)., *Media entertainment: The psychology of its appeal* (pp. 175-196). Mahwah, NJ: Lawrence Erlbaum.

Hull, G. (2002). *The recording industry: readings in mass communication*. Boston: Allyn & Bacon. For current news and trends, check out the following Web sites:

- ☆ *Billboard:* www.billboard.com/billboard/index.jsp
- ☆ Recording Industry Association of America: www.riaa.org
- ☆ *Radio Magazine:* http://beradio.com/

8

Two Thumbs Up

What's at the Movies?

A good movie can take you out of your dull funk . . . a good movie makes you care, makes you believe in possibilities again.

—Pauline Kael

One of the most popular forms of entertainment—movies—has fascinated audiences for decades. Produced on film stock rather than videotape, movies bring large-screen action and romance to audiences worldwide. An industry that was once dominated by Hollywood studios now consists of anyone with a story, a camera, and a distribution outlet. Film festivals, held annually throughout the world, provide a venue for independent and amateur filmmakers to present their films in the hopes of selling the rights to an entertainment company. With more than 500 releases each year, movies come to us in the form of blockbuster, independent, foreign language, and avant-garde films. And although we have to leave home to watch a movie, fans are willing to pay for wide screens, Dolby sound, and fresh popcorn.

Before we look at specific content, let's see how the film industry makes its money by using television and video to take movies from the theater and deliver them to your home.

HOW IT WORKS: INDUSTRY STRUCTURE

Movie success or failure is determined during the first weekend of its run. After the promotion bubble bursts, audiences may stay away from the box office. Although poor attendance minimizes box office receipts, it does not necessarily determine the film's overall revenue generation. When films have exhausted their theatrical potential, a series of exhibition *windows*—for example, VCR, pay-per-view, and fiber-optic video-on-demand—are used to maximize profits.

Windowing Theory

Windowing, a second-degree price discrimination model, is the economic theory that underlies the film industry. According to windowing, profits can be maximized by segmenting consumers into clearly distinct groupings and charging them their "reservation prices."[190] To extract the highest prices, classes of customers must be clearly identified and must correspond to various exhibition windows and the profit objectives. After theatrical release, the sequential order for a film is VCR, pay-per-view, pay cable, network TV, and syndication. Video-on-demand, where consumers can order a film or video program directly from a computer and download it for play whenever they choose, is expected to move to the front of the line as a primary exhibition window for films. Profits are maximized by keeping short the elapsed time between theatrical release and sequential exhibitions. Because films have the most value immediately after release, viewers are willing to pay the highest prices for the newest films.

Because consumers have various demographic and psychographic makeups, movies experience different levels of popularity as they move through the windows. Less popular films have shorter windows, and low-budget movies may even bypass theaters completely by going directly to VCR or cable. Windowing also provides opportunities for TV stars and personalities from other media to appear in movies. Each subsidiary window is important to a film's overall success.

For years, film studios worried that television would take audiences away from the theater. Then, during the 1960s, the television network market used movies to fill up to 40% of regularly scheduled prime-time programs, to the delight of the studios, which prized this distribution window. In the late '60s, networks attempted to produce their own films with little success. The attempt was quashed when, in 1980, the Prime-Time Access Rules of the Federal Communications Commission (FCC) limited the ability of the networks to produce in-house television movies. Thereafter, reliance on theatrical movies was reduced, and today made-for-TV movies are preferred to televised theatrical releases for their first-run exclusiveness to the producing network.

Restricted by the FCC rules from producing their own films, pay television markets such as HBO were able to get those limitations declared null and void for pay cable networks. The decree enabled these markets to compete directly with the commercial networks, and the cable revolution was on. The major movie-driven networks (such as The Movie Channel,

Showtime, and Cinemax) have been joined by specialty networks (like Disney, American Movie Classics, and Bravo) that offer specific film genres. New technologies such as home satellites and LCD (liquid crystal display) widen the exhibition market for pay TV networks and should translate into higher license prices for theatrical movies. In spite of their dominance of the pay cable market, these networks have diminished in importance with the strength of the VCR market, where consumers can directly select movies they prefer. The most powerful technological advance is video-on-demand; in spite of its relative expense, its use is becoming widespread.

The videocassette and DVD markets have become the viewing preferences of choice by consumers because of their versatility and the freedom they provide from programming time constraints of network and local channels. And although the theatrical motion picture industry still has a larger than 70% share of sales, VCRs can act as major distributors for themselves. The distribution process works much as it does for magazines, paperback books, and records. Disney, Warner, CBS/Fox, and MCA/Universal lead domestic revenues of home videocassette suppliers received from sales, not rentals, of videos and DVDs. Although rentals account for most consumer transactions, first sale copyright provisions permit distributors to collect payments only the first time the cassette or DVD is sold. Sales prices to retailers are high but, because retailers receive rental revenues, they pass along the high prices to encourage consumers to rent rather than purchase. Consumers can pick up titles with their groceries and their prescriptions, making the rental business a lucrative market for many retailers.

The international market is the second most important subsidiary, with more than 80 trading partners. The size and power of the American market cause it to dominate world distribution. To combat some of the competition, many countries restrict production to local companies or provide them with tax breaks and favorable loan rates. Some American producers circumvent governmental tactics by establishing their own companies abroad to escape the penalties levied at foreign production. Foreign coproductions have become commonplace, and the export market continues to grow.

Social Impact

As the costs to produce films soar above the 100 million dollar mark, the film industry endeavors to gain revenues from various windows and world markets. But with promotion comes problems, a few of which are discussed here. Accusations of artistic imperialism against American filmmakers continue from countries where VCR rentals are illegal. Outcries from governments in the Middle East are strong, and citizens of many of the countries in that region are still arrested for possession of foreign videocassettes. However, American filmmakers are continuing to invest in production companies throughout the world to encourage filmmaking in countries where facilities and capital have traditionally been scarce.

Copyright infringement is another problem those in this industry encounter. Chinese entrepreneurs duplicate cassettes, often distributing first-run films before they hit theaters in the United States. And although steps are being taken to curtail illegal duplication, artists are not receiving royalties because of the copying businesses that still thrive in many countries.

At home, rating systems continue to be manipulated to retain the largest audience segment possible for a single release. Marketers striving for the youth market often add or subtract restricted elements from films to attract this audience. Parents claim the ratings have a reverse impact on teenagers, causing them to sneak into films they perceive to be aimed at adults. For example, an R rating may lure teens who would ignore the same film if it was rated G.

As Hollywood continues to be a dominant force in global entertainment, film stars and content are important because of their impact and influence on our culture. Technology's contribution to film content is explored next as we enter the movie theater for a peek at the progression of animation and action films as well as current trends in both genres.

TECHNOLOGY'S PROGENY: ANIMATION AND ACTION FILMS

W-W-W-What's Up, Doc?

Audiences have always loved the make-believe and humor of cartoons. As technology revolutionizes animated films, we get further and further from the Flip the Frog cartoons that predate Mickey Mouse. Cartoon films are, in fact, cash cows—as evidenced by *The Lion King*'s $300 million in domestic box office revenues. The appeal of cartoon characters is that talent on both sides of the camera comes cheap—animation stars work without agents or unions, and the characters don't get old. Animators (until DreamWorks entered the picture) received small salaries and received no royalties.

Animation greats Chuck Jones (Road Runner, Wile E. Coyote) and Tex Avery (Droopy, Frito Bandito) pioneered the cartoon genre. Jones's films for Warner Brothers were about barnyard critters with humanity—Porky, Daffy, and Bugs Bunny—who approached life's pitfalls with amazing grace and wit. Avery's movies, on the other hand, used motion to explode into violent emotion. In one cartoon, when a wolf spies Red Hot Riding Hood, his tongue springs out zig-zaggy and his eyes pop out in sections like a dozen contact lenses.[191] About the same time, Bill Hanna and Joe Barbera were making *Tom and Jerry* cartoons for MGM, and Walt Disney gave us his famous creatures. It was only a matter of time before cartoons graduated into full-length motion pictures. In one of Disney's first animated feature films, a more fragile animal than some of those previously mentioned pulled audience heartstrings: *Bambi*.

Today, studios are battling for prominence in the blossoming world of animated feature films. The first challenger to Disney was DreamWorks, a studio built by producers Jeffrey Katzenberg, Steven Spielberg, and David Geffen. Using Pacific Data Images for computer animation, DreamWorks released *Antz* ahead of schedule to pre-empt Disney's forthcoming insect feature. *Antz*, enhanced with the voices of Woody Allen, Sharon Stone, and Gene Hackman, appealed to older audiences than Disney's kid-friendly film with a Randy Newman music score. *Shrek,* a feature starring an ogre whose swamp was overrun by annoying fairy-tale creatures, and *Tasker,* the adventures of a small team of elephants escaping poachers across South Seas Asia, are two of DreamWorks's efforts in production that feature animated creatures.

Although both *A Bug's Life* and *Antz* revolved around bugs and ants, Disney's rendition took the task of perspective more seriously than its competitor did. Steve Jobs, Pixar Animation Studio CEO, said *Bug's Life* stars were created using a Bug Cam that was used to examine real bugs. By looking at life from a bug's perspective, animators were able to craft a totally different world.[192] In a cartoon first, Disney featured dozens of product tie-ins to snuggle up with the film's adorable, candy-colored bugs. Part of Disney's overall merchandising efforts uses film to sell products. By cross-marketing toys and movies, Disney is able to convince parents that movies are not harmful for their kids while persuading kids to ask for spinoff items and toys.[193]

Other studios are also producing their own versions of the cartoon genre. Nickelodeon, for instance, jumped from 20 years of TV into making successful feature-length cartoons. Before making *Rugrats in Paris*, the studio quizzed *Rugrats* fans about what they wanted in a sequel. Fans responded to the queries in Nick's magazine, on its Web site, and in a focus group with three requests: a family vacation, new characters, and more of Chuckie, the TV show's hero. Following these suggestions, the studio created a film in which the characters go to France and Chuckie gets top billing as he picks up a new mom and stepsister.[194] During its opening weekend, *Rugrats in Paris* clobbered Disney's Thanksgiving offering, *102 Dalmatians,* confirming the wisdom of conducting research.

Global animators are also successful with animated cartoons. Britain's Aardman Studios used stop-motion animation for *Chicken Run,* a comedy adventure film about Ginger and the other chickens of Tweedy's Farm who try to escape. Mel Gibson's voice inhabits a character created from a plasticine puppet in a mini set that was adjusted 24 times for every second of film. Made for $42 million in Bristol, *Chicken*'s animal accents add a humorous English flair to this *Animal Farm* parody. Another example of popular foreign animation is *Pokémon,* a Japanese battle-oriented cartoon in which combat is the prime focus of entertainment.

Although cartoons are not the only uses for animation (special effects like photo-realism, morphing, and digital technology are incorporated into action adventures such as George Lucas's *Phantom Menace* of the *Star Wars* trilogy), our purpose here is to understand why animated cartoons successfully entertain kids of all ages. Part of their allure is the dominance of fantasy. Fantasy, by its very nature, frees audiences from the mundane, allows us to acknowledge our own frailties, and gives us permission to laugh at ourselves. The animals, bugs, and humanized characters presented through animation techniques dramatize our subconscious reality without the pain of conscious recognition. More simply put, animated cartoon films are nonthreatening.

And cartoons fill fantasy with humor. Most of the literature on humor is grounded chiefly upon introspection[195] and can be explained with three theories:[196]

☆ The *incongruity-resolution theory* says that humor results from unexpected solutions to conceptual challenges. (When Wile E. Coyote schemes to drop an anvil on Road Runner's head, the problem of what's for dinner seems solved.)

Figure 8.1   Action Animation Character from
Ice Age in 3D

© 2002 Fox.

☆ The basis of *tension-relief theory* is that comic moments in cartoons are often accompanied by a sense of powerful emotional release. (We are relieved when Road Runner escapes the anvil's fall.)

☆ *Superiority theory* holds that humor, because it is relatively nonviolent, is a socially acceptable form of aggression toward others. (We won't drop an anvil, but we can do it vicariously through Wile E. Coyote.) And because laughter and smiling are socially motivating behaviors, we can enjoy the pleasures of animated humor with other people.

One trend is to produce feature-length films of animated video games like *Tomb Raider* and to use real actors. *Final Fantasy: The Spirits Within* bucked this trend; it is the first film with human leads played by noncharacters—that is, they are all created with computer software. Aki Ross, the computer-generated heroine, has very realistic hair and is almost sexy. One reviewer[197] complains that the "lip movements of animated figures are slightly slow so you feel as if you're watching a badly dubbed Japanese creature feature from the '60s" and says that the aliens' consumption of the crackling blue souls of human prey may be the best reason to sit through the film. Technology will certainly compensate for these shortcomings within the next few years, taking computer games to the screen with animation excellence. The most recent step toward excellence is *Ice Age* (see Figure 8.1), the first animated film to use 3D, taking viewers directly into the action.

Unlike their video game counterparts, cartoon characters are androgynous, revealing their sex only through voice pitch and/or the audience's recognition of a certain actor's voice. Live-action or computer-generated movies can foster gender stereotypes, especially in action films. One exception to the traditional female stereotype is a new breed of action woman, explained in the next section.

Take That, You Fiend!

Female warriors are invading Hollywood. Tradition has held that men are the tough ones and women are present to tell them just how tough they are. Only since the James Bond films have women been allowed to show their muscles as well as their legs—and then only as co-stars. Pioneers like Sigourney Weaver (*Aliens*) and Linda Hamilton (*The Terminator*) were the first women to take starring roles in action films. Women action figures occupy roles comparable to those of their male counterparts. These muscular action heroines disrupt the traditional binary oppositions that have differentiated masculine and feminine bodies.[198] Female "tough guys" appear in increasing doses as "body genre" films (where muscle and power prevail) gain popularity.

A director who favors the underdog in the world of prize fighting, Karyn Kusoma, put a woman in the ring for *Girlfight*. This story of a teen Latina from Brooklyn profiles a girl who learns to stand up to an abusive father and fight as an equal with her boyfriend. In this teenage right of passage genre film, star Michelle Rodriguez's "female masculinity" won favor from her male trainers, who were skeptical about a woman in the ring.[199] According to the Sony film Web site dedicated to *Girlfight* (www.sonypictures.com/movies/girlfight), women can maximize their potential and gain greater respect from men, who are socialized to value forceful physicality, "heralding new femininity for a new century."

A more civilized form of female combat comes to the screen from Eastern cultures. The first martial arts film with a female lead, *Come Drink With Me* starring Cheng Pei Pei, was released in 1965. By 1992, three female action-film stars, Anita Mui, Michelle Yeoh, and Maggie Cheung, portrayed crime fighters in the *Heroic Trio*. Seven years later, Eastern arts joined Western films as Carrie-Anne Moss appeared with Keanu Reeves in the futuristic film *The Matrix* and, in 2000, Lucy Liu starred with Drew Barrymore and Cameron Diaz in *Charlie's Angels*. In these and other martial arts films, women scale walls, leap buildings, and duel with 40-pound swords.

Women kicking butt are in vogue. Although sexy bodies help, the true female warrior must be fear-inspiring. Their cinematic appearance coincides with the popularity of female athletes such as Olympic track stars Florence Joyner and Marion Jones. The acting counterparts to these athletes bring a similar graceful, balletic force to defense. But only with lots of training. In preparation for *Charlie's Angels*, actors trained for 6 hours a day doing kicks, leaps, somersaults, and wire work for months before filming began.[200]

In the 2000 film *Crouching Tiger, Hidden Dragon*, Michelle Yeoh and Asian film idol Chow Yun Fat play warriors who contend for a sword, twisting, leaping, spinning, and flying in encounters as meticulously choreographed as Balanchine ballets.[201] Against panoramic backgrounds of deserts, mountains, and bamboo forests, Yeoh reveals herself as an equal match for her male counterpart. Because director Ang Lee believes that "a good fight should be like a good dance work,"[202] actors in this film studied ballet techniques for balance, posture, and timing. To accomplish airborne scenes, actors were suspended in harnesses from wires in a technique borrowed from the circus.

Tomb Raider, a video game brought to life on screen with Angelina Jolie, features a sexy heroine as an archeologist who overcomes evil in all of its ghastly forms. By combining humor with grace and agility, female warriors of all types bring a new dimension to action thrillers: defense without death. True to the code, females never kill unless in self-defense—unlike their male counterparts, who tend to wipe out enemies for good. In fact, during fight scenes between the two female leads in *Dragon,* the victor continually spares her opponent's life. Audiences of warrior films are still predominantly male. However, with the appearance of kinder, gentler warriors, films of this genre may soon appeal to women as well. Why? Retribution, perhaps. By watching agile women of strength overpower and outperform men, women may experience an emotional satisfaction unavailable in their own lives. Men may cheer for a victor, but when physical agility is executed without excessive violence, female audiences can appreciate the skill and beauty of the performance itself regardless of who emerges as the winner.

CONSUMING IMAGES: WHY AUDIENCES WATCH

Driven by economic factors, media businesses strive to provide their audiences with what they want to see and hear. Two factors important for understanding why we watch television and film deserve our attention as well as further investigation: *violence,* said to foster our societal ills, and *stardom,* said to be the focus of our aspirations.

Hands up or I'll Shoot

Why are film and television audiences so attracted to violence as entertainment? Some directors think they know the answer. Sam Peckinpah's trend-setting piece *The Wild Bunch* makes us see the beauty of a massacre and other atrocities. "Audiences are alternately horrified by the butchery and exhilarated by the orgiastic energy his balletic spectacles stir up," said one critic of this film.[203] Editing and special effects also determine an audience's attraction to violence, as we saw during the shower scene in Hitchcock's *Psycho.*

To put the appeal of violence into perspective, we must remember that violent entertainment is not as popular as comedies and sitcoms among most audiences. Often it's not the violence per se but other forms of gratification that attract audiences. Violence may be a means to an end that is enjoyed not for what it is but for what it does for the viewer. The thrill of fantasy and challenge stimulates players of violent video games, for example.

The appeal of violence can be experienced in three distinct ways.[204] First, we may enjoy violent films for the violent images that evoke pleasure. Or we might have overall enjoyment for the movie but find the violent scenes unpleasant. Finally, we might enjoy a violent movie for the gratifications that are indirectly related to the images but are experienced after viewing them. A theory of sensation-seeking, which hypothesizes that a combination of delight in the visuals and the novelty of violence,[205] is another way to explain the appeal of violence.

We know that images of violence are jolting, and they provide fodder for discussion and social posturing. But because audience segments differ in their reasons for enjoying violent portrayals, no one theory addresses all our motivations for watching. Taken together, several theories provide an integrated approach to understanding the attractions of violence that are relevant to entertainment.

All children find most displays of excess exciting.[206] Boys like to watch violence more than girls, and adolescent boys like violent entertainment more than any other group,[207] as evidenced by their preference for toy guns and combative video games. Cartoon violence is more joyful for children than watching realistic physical violence as portrayed on the news.[208] Research shows that children who enjoy violent entertainment have high levels of aggression, but no evidence exists to suggest that violence produces aggressive behavior.[209] In other words, aggressive kids may enjoy watching violence, but violence does not create aggression in kids who watch it.

Some researchers believe that we enjoy violence because of our notion of fair play and retribution. When someone has been wronged, we enjoy seeing the "eye for an eye" notion played out. Violence in the name of getting even is not only tolerated, it's justified and enjoyed. We all love to see the good guy win over the bad guy. The degree of predictability present in films containing violence may contribute to the level of entertainment value.

One of the most attractive features of violent entertainment media is their ability to take us into fantasyland. Suspension of disbelief may enhance a tolerance for violence for media consumers. But to maximize enjoyment, audiences must feel safe in their viewing environment. They must be able to detach from the film (or book or program) far enough to feel the security of space existing between themselves and what is taking place in the narrative or images they experience.

According to a compendium of authors, violence is attractive when a variety of subject characteristics, appealing image characteristics, and context conditions are met.[210] And although those conditions are known, questions remain about the "why" and the cultural implications of those conditions. Regardless of their reasons for watching, audiences make the final determination of what displays of violence are acceptable and unacceptable. In other words, we can choose to watch or not to watch. Of course, as long as lines form at theaters showing *Terminator* genre films, as long as we tune into video footage of police beatings, and as long as we buy Stephen King novels, violence will remain a prominent fixture of our media landscape.

Stardom

Audiences love celebrities. Some of the best evidence we have that film has radically changed society's values lies in the growing phenomenon of the celebrity. Folklore characters (Paul Bunyan) and renowned individuals (scientists, artists, politicians, and so on) once served as our heroes and our role models. Actors were mostly anonymous, known only on stage in their character roles. However, after 1912, actors were liberated from anonymity by the appearance of fan magazines. Today, actors and their fictional characters have fused to become stars, who have a unique relationship with their publics. In contrast to *celebrities,* who are well-known people appearing as themselves, *stars* are extraordinary psychological models of a type that never existed before.[211] A star is created by a group of people because of an admired quality that star possesses.

According to a *New Yorker* columnist,[212] *stardom* is the name for a discrete and recognizable episode in the life of a star. Stardom means you are what people want; stardom is the intersection of personality with history, a perfect congruence of the way the world happens to be and the way the star is. But every episode of stardom, he cautions, carries within it the seeds of its own negation, for it can last only 3 years.

Stardom can be a phenomenon of production (what filmmakers provide) or of consumption (what the audience wants). Fashion is a function of star production—a star serves to fix a type of beauty that defines norms of attractiveness. Because of the economic importance of stars, image building and character typing suggest the power of the forces of cinematic production. However, audiences and other consumption factors also play a dominant role in star building. Four categories of star/audience relationship have emerged:[213]

- ☆ *Emotional affinity*—Audience members feel a loose attachment to a star that extends from the personality of the viewer.
- ☆ *Self-identification*—The audience member becomes so involved with the star that she or he lives the part being played.
- ☆ *Imitation*—The star acts as a role model for the viewer.
- ☆ *Projection*—An extreme form of imitation that develops into the viewer being starstruck.

Stardom is also an image of the way stars live. They are a combination of the spectacular and the everyday, the special and the ordinary that articulate basic American/Western values. With the impact of consumerism on media, both film stars and TV celebrities adopt *personality personae*—that is, we judge them through their appearance and the significance of their

---

Kinder, Gentler Men?

Hollywood "star cinema" creates a strong identification between hero and audience. Two powerful male personas—the tough guy and the urbane sophisticate—dominated movies until 1950. The soft-spoken rebel of the '50s was epitomized by Marlon Brando and James Dean. Both stars enjoyed popularity that amounted to fan hysteria (in Dean's case, from adolescents who mourned his death). Other star types based on social aspects[215] are The Good Joe (Tom Hanks), The Tough Guy (Clint Eastwood), and The Pinup (Marilyn Monroe). Recently, the Girl Next Door (Meg Ryan) and the Bad Girl (Angelina Jolie) have become prominent star types. What other female personas can you identify?

lifestyle.[214] Star lifestyles are elements of the "fabulousness" of Hollywood. Large houses and limousines, parties, expensive clothing, svelte bodies, and glamorous leisure activities indicate star fashion.

Audience fascination with film stars continues to be fueled by paparazzi, entertainment TV, fashion magazines, and commercials. Film tie-ins and trailers promote stars; stars also sell products, politics, and philanthropy. Michael Jordan became a shoe style for Nike. In fact, stars themselves have become brands by creating a strong identity between the star and a film style—a "hyper-personification." Woody Allen films are a mere extension of the person himself—a Woody Allen–brand film. One example of branding of a star's image is Jack Nicholson's performance as the Joker in *Batman*. Here, we saw his demonic form (shown in such films as *The Shining* and *The Witches of Eastwick*) turned into comic hysteria with an excessive display of Nicholson-ness.[216] We expect a film with Nicholson in it to feature that brand, and we are disappointed if the film is not consistent with our expectations.

Cinema audiences have been conceptualized as spectators[217] in instances when the moviegoer is an identity targeted by image producers. One example of *spectatorship theory* is the framework of narrative cinema that centers on the woman as an object of spectacle or gaze. Advocates of this theory believe that the audience perspective is directed toward the pleasures of male heterosexual desire. A problem with spectatorship theory is that we really don't know whether or not audiences actually do view women as spectacles. In fact, some women imagine female stars as their ideal other, a relationship called *cinematic identifactory fantasy.*[218] All versions of spectator theory render the audience inactive and prey to the whims of producers, a position we do not share. However, we can continue to examine and understand the role stars play for audiences by charting the ways in which identity and reality are created in, through, and by stars.

The role of celebrities in a global society also includes their ability to raise funds for philanthropic causes. Willie Nelson began the trend by presenting concerts for Farm Aid during the '70s, when farmers lost their land to foreclosure. Stars rally behind diseases such as Jerry Lewis's annual muscular dystrophy telethon. More recently, hundreds of film and television stars sponsored a telethon for victims of the terrorist attacks in New York and Washington, DC. Hours of performances yielded call-in donations to phone banks staffed by stars, who raised $22 million for families of firefighters and police who lost their lives helping others.

With new forms of entertainment also come new audiences. Teens of yesterday, attracted to the "gross-out" movie genre of *Scary Movie* and *Joe Dirt,* walked away from nasty teen flicks in 2001. According to a MarketCast study,[219] a new generation is rising: the Millennial Generation. As of 2002, half of all college students were Millennials, the cutting edge of new consumers for the film business. Growing up protected, treasured, and prodded to achieve, these kids like action-packed adventure with bushels of slapstick fun and uplifting finales (*Shrek*) or heroic, positive depictions of young people (*Spy Kids*). The laughs and gasps they want (as found in *Harry Potter* and *The Matrix*) are hardly the nudity pics released by studios a few years ago. Millennials demand big productions, elaborate sets, and synchronized choreography, with epic stories and real people. The task of the movie makers of tomorrow will be to produce a generation-defining film that will do for Millennials what *The Graduate* did for boomers and *The Breakfast Club* did for Generation Xers.

New technology also delivers editing power to audiences, who are striking back at the tyranny of the artist. First, professional editors get their shot at cutting and pasting: Movies first appear as ads for themselves (trailers), are re-edited before release from results of test screenings, and are reformatted for airplanes, colorized for TV, expurgated for theaters or video outlets, and even reconfigured for foreign consumption. At the same time, old movies are being reworked or rereleased in versions made for special events. In retaliation to studio edits and director's cuts, fans are making their own cuts. These fan cuts, called "special corrector's editions"[220] are created on Web sites dedicated to films that allow fans to individualize movies for themselves (such as was developed with *The Phantom Menace* during its run in theaters). Technology will continue to allow moviegoers to put themselves into Internet-customized versions of films using a form similar to the morphing technique pioneered in *Forrest Gump*. We predict that a Hollywood version of "power to the people" is only the first sign of the audience's attempt to control movie content.

FADE TO BLACK

With ticket prices for the movies hovering just under $10, audiences are demanding more for their money than just a nice story. But sometimes better quality means an improvement in the quality of the story rather than showing off the power of technology. Oscar winners for 2002 exemplify this trend. Winner for best picture, *A Beautiful Mind,* is a simple story about a genius schizophrenic, and Oscar nominee *In the Bedroom* is a family drama. The 2002 Oscars also were important because diversity was realized, with African American recipients taking top honors. Denzel Washington won best actor, and Halle Berry, the first woman of color to win best actress, captured the hearts of viewers with her role in *Monster's Ball.*

An increase in quality is also shown in the popularity of independent films, which are often handicapped by limited distribution. The phrase "I'll wait for the video" is heard more often today, yet producers continue to make films that are not small-screen friendly. The Cohen brothers produced *The Man Who Wasn't There* in black and white, preferring techniques that emphasize plot and characterization over visual tricks. Ultimately, product of all types is coming to a screen near you, then coming again to your home screen. Where you choose to watch does not affect the bottom line of movie revenue, but it may affect how much money you have left over for popcorn.

Figure 8.2 *Monster's Ball Film* Poster

© 2002 Lion's Gate Entertainment.

🔍 A Closer Look

Advertising as Product Placement

Your last encounter with the movies probably included an interaction with products and brands. If you saw *Other People's Money*, you heard Danny DeVito say, "If I can't count on Dunkin' Donuts, who can I count on?" in front of the shop's logo. Voice mentions (called *impressions*) and visual brand placements like these mean $60 million annually for the film business. Placements usually take one of three forms:

☆ *Visual or script placement*—The product is mentioned or talked about in a conversation.

☆ *Verbal or screen placement*—Incorporates the brand into scenes or it is used or talked about on the set.

☆ *Plot placement*—The product takes a major role in the story line or in building the persona of a character.

Such placements often combine verbal and visual aspects from a brand's mere mention or a brief appearance to make sure the product is solely identified with a single star. In one James Bond film, the star's tie-in with BMW is an example of such a high-intensity placement.

Audience's processing works through perceptual encoding that involves our memory codes. A coding redundancy hypothesis[221] suggests that our memory increases directly with the number of alternative memory codes available for an item. For instance, plot placements that rely on both visual and verbal information produce higher levels of brand recall than just one or the other. Second, individual differences in style of processing moderate the effectiveness of different types of placement.

Also known as "embedded advertising," product and brand placements have been significant since 1982, when Reese's Pieces increased their sales by 300% after appearing in the film *ET*. Soon Tom Cruise was drinking Coke and wearing Ray-Ban sunglasses in *Top Gun*, and the placement rush was on. Companies were lining up to bid for their products to appear in major motion pictures.

Huggies, for instance, paid $100,000 to be the diaper of choice in *Baby Boom* (1987). In *It Could Happen to You* (1994), Bridget Fonda engages in a dialogue about Miracle Whip. *Reality Bites* (1994) is the epitome of brand advertising. One of the biggest advertising feature films, *Menace II Society* (1993) features 10 drink brands for a total of 340 images and mentions, eight car brands (20 impressions), three types of tobacco/drugs (15 impressions) to say nothing of clothing, shoes, candy, magazine, and condom brand impressions. Even if the film flops at the box office, revenues from product placements often significantly help mitigate the cost of production.

The reason for placement frenzy is simple. Films offer outlets for products such as cigarettes and alcohol that are otherwise banned or prohibited from traditional outlets. Promotions can be tailored to fit theater and home videos in several forms, including trailers, teasers, billboards, and video jackets. But not all placements are smooth transactions. Some companies have landed in court over problems with their branding choices. Philip Morris, for instance, sued to have its name deleted from *Harley Davidson and the Marlboro Man* (1991). Orkin forced a change in the language of a pest control man wearing an Orkin uniform in *Pacific Heights* (1990). And when a Black & Decker placement was cut from an edited scene in *Die Hard II* (1990), the company settled out of court for $150,000.

Children's films also contain subliminal product messages. *Teenage Mutant Ninja Turtles* (1990) and *Gremlins* (1992) used merchandising to hype attendance and to sell products that doubled profits in sequels. To illustrate the extent to which advertising is tied into plot line, we take a look at *The Mighty Ducks* (1992), *Ducks 2* (1994), and *Ducks 3* (1996).

Prior to filming the hockey team adventure story, Disney Studios signed more than 100 cross-promotional and licensing agreements. The films were made to incorporate ads and to serve as public relations for the hockey team headquartered in Anaheim, California, that is owned by Disney. Hockey equipment makers and skates were the focus of all close-up shots and camera angles. Ads around the skating rink for fast food outlets and Coke were prominently featured in the films, and the Ducks were placed on the cover of Wheaties cereal boxes following the film's release.

Advertising that relies on emotion rather than reason is called transformational. Product placement in conjunction with pleasure renders the experience of seeing the brand as enjoyable. Transformational ads placed on television and in film can be analyzed on four dimensions:

☆ *Personal relevance*—The degree to which the viewer connects himself or herself with the film.
☆ *Experimental*—Emotional identification of the audience with the film; this is the most important dimension for effective placement.
☆ *Informational*—Relevant brands that become part of the story bring symbolic imagery to the experience. For instance, Humphrey Bogart's use of cigarettes associates smoking with masculinity, elegance, and sensuality. This affective process allows viewers to become directly involved in the brand's symbolic meaning.
☆ *Executional*—a good match must be made among the product, the film, and its stars.

In successful placements, the viewer's own experience with the products will reflect the experience portrayed in the film or video. Several theories account for the success or failure of a placement. According to *learning theory*, product placement relies on classical conditioning for its effectiveness. Product transformations occur unconsciously for viewers who pair unlike things in their minds. Celebrity endorsements, for instance, allow viewers to match a product with a star so that when they see one, they also see the other. *Modeling theory* suggests that we tend to imitate behavior of others, so we use products associated with our favorite stars. Television and film stars often serve as role models for consumers. Finally, the more familiar viewers are with the product, and the more connected they are with the show, the stronger the placement becomes.

Product placements have several implications for audiences and content production. First, scripts may be tailored around products rather than using products to add realism. Second, place-based ads may limit the diversity of film content as requirements from sponsors become increasingly strict. Third, concerns about artistic control have caused some alarm among film directors who feel compromised by advertisers' demands. To address those concerns, Hollywood executives have established a trade association to self-regulate the placement industry (Entertainment Resources and Marketing Association, www.erma.org) with a code of ethics that addresses client-agent relations.

DISCUSSION AND REVIEW

1. Discuss the relationship between film stars and film popularity. How might producers use stars to promote an otherwise routine movie to entice audiences? What is the role of movie star fans for film success?

2. Explain the role of technology in film production and audience enjoyment. How do special effects change the viewing experience? Will technological enhancements provide motivation for attending a movie rather than plot or story line?

3. Describe the role of windowing for generating revenue for the film industry. What impact will DVD and LCD have on the home viewing experience? Will home viewing help or hinder windowing philosophy?

EXERCISES

1. Select a film star for whom you have an emotional affinity and discuss what media you use to keep up to date on the star's social and professional life. What role(s) does that star play in your life? Which star qualities reflect your self-image?

2. Next time you go to the movies, take a close look at the film marketing posters. What elements dominate the poster? How is text used? Critique a poster for a film you have seen according to its ability to reflect the film and to market the film. Which condition prevails, reflection or marketing?

3. During your next visit to the movies, count the products placed and the conditions under which they appear. How did these placements correspond to the conditions and theories described in the "A Closer Look" section of this chapter? How did the placements contribute to or detract from the film's plot? Its enjoyment?

RECOMMENDED READINGS AND WEB SITES

Dyer, R. (1998). *Stars*. London: British Film Institute.

Hirschman, E. (2000). *Heroes, monsters, & messiahs: Movies and television shows as the mythology of American culture*. Kansas City: Andrew McMeel.

Monaco, J. (2000). *How to read a film: Movies, media and multimedia*. New York: Oxford University Press.

www.imdb.com, a film resource that contains voluminous details on virtually every movie made.

www.rottentomatoes.com for current film reviews and page links.

9

Talking Pictures

The Power of Television Images

The White man's names are not good. They don't give pictures to your mind.

— Anonymous Apache

Volumes have been written analyzing and critiquing television and film content and their effects on audiences. Although we discuss these two forms of media in two separate chapters, we think of the images produced for and delivered by both television and the movies as a single entertainment content.

Rather than revisiting critical theory, our discussion here focuses on recent entertainment content and its historical counterparts in television and film to understand its impact on contemporary society. Although children can never be excluded from visual programming, this discussion focuses on television entertainment intended for adults.

Theories relevant to the genres of mass entertainment are presented in discussions of audiences for each television genre we discuss, including reality TV, soaps, infotainment, and religious television. We also take a glimpse at television sponsors, who often drive the medium's content, and the product placements that force us to associate a brand with a star.

America loves live-action TV, and with action comes violence, an ever-popular form of entertainment. Such all-consuming images play an important role in why we watch film and television fiction and nonfiction. We also discuss television trends, such as the emerging need for TV writers and producers to explore alternate plot lines and formats to retain viewer interest.

STRUCTURE OF THE TELEVISION INDUSTRY

Unlike early television's configuration of stations and single owners, today's cable and satellite providers are giant conglomerates. During the 1990s, mergers, acquisitions, and joint ventures proliferated among cable companies and programmers, and between cable companies, programmers, and a host of interested parties from various fields (e.g., telephone, computer, film, and electric utility industries). A decade before, *convergence* became an industry watchword. A foundation concept for the National Information Infrastructure and the Information Superhighway, convergence accurately describes what is taking place today with mediated technology. We expect that, in the near future, cable and telephone industries may merge or synthesize into an entirely new system.

Deregulation and technical innovation that have delivered programming and services are challenged by distribution platforms now capable of providing customers with a similar set of programs and services. Collapsing consumer markets that previously were separate businesses results in a redefinition of relevant markets for these industries. Lower prices and better service render consumers the benefactors of converging markets.

The players in this area can be categorized, as 1) companies (such as your local cable system) that distribute content to homes, and 2) networks (such as CNN and HBO) that create or provide content and services. Although the lines between the two types are becoming increasingly blurred, we will use these categories to distinguish between the hardware or distribution technology, and the software or programming services. Table 9.1 characterizes the structure according to distribution technology and programs and services.

Wireless Industries

Proliferation of mom-and-pop dominated cable companies has given way to ownership by large conglomerates. According to numbers of subscribers, the top two companies are Turner Communications International (owned by American Telephone & Telegraph) and Time Warner. TCI has full or partial ownership of many leading cable networks (including Encore, Discovery Channel, BET, QVC) and the Turner channels (including CNN and TNT). It also owns broadcast properties, clothing stores, and a major interest in McNeil-Lehrer Productions. Time Warner has large holdings in publishing, recording, and film. Following the acquisition of Turner Broadcasting in 2000, Time Warner became the world's largest media conglomerate.

Table 9.1 Industry Organization Matrix

Distribution Technology	*Programs and Services*

Wireline
Cable TV
Telephone
Utilities
	Video
	Programming networks and services
	  Basic networks
	  Pay-per-view
	  Video-on-demand

Broadcast: Terrestrial
Traditional VHF/UHF
Emerging multichannel VHF/UHF
Multipoint, multichannel
  distribution (MMDS)
Local multipoint distribution (LMDS)
	Broadcast Retransmission
	Local stations
	Regional imported stations
	Superstations
	
	Local Cable
	Local cable origination
	Cable access channels: leased, public,
	  educational & government

Satellite Satellite carriers Fixed service satellites (FSS) Direct to home satellites (DTH) Direct broadcast satellites (DBS) Television receive only (TRVO) Satellite master antenna (SMATV)	**Telephone** Plain old telephone service Competitive access providers Personal communication services **Data** Internet and WWW access (e-mail, shopping, banking, games) Telemetry—fire and burglar alarms Distance education Telecommuting Paging and positioning

SOURCE: From Parsons, P., & Frieden, R. (2000). The structure of the cable and satellite industries. In Greco, A. N. (Ed.), *The media entertainment industries* (p. 176). Boston: Allyn & Bacon.

Through deregulation, cable lost much of its legal market protection, and the doors opened to new players. One of the most important communication business developments of the '90s was the entry of the telephone industry into television. The size of competitors such as AT&T, MCI, GTE, and Sprint now dwarfs cable operators. Even utility companies are becoming contenders for wireline television customers, although the likelihood of their becoming major players in video and data services is uncertain.

Broadcasting

Since the Telecommunications Act of 1996 loosened restrictions on ownership, most of the 1,190 commercial broadcast TV stations in the United States are owned by groups or major networks such as CBS, ABC, and NBC. Most of the stations that run network programming are affiliates with contractual arrangements to carry their schedules and to run national advertising that pays for the programs. Independent stations, without such advertising clout, rely on local advertising to provide their schedule of network reruns, old movies, talk shows, and game shows.

Broadcast licenses are assigned by the Federal Communications Commission (FCC) according to the size of the market. The larger the market, the more licenses are allotted. However, as cable infrastructures grow, so do their *ratings* (percentage of viewers watching TV) and *share* (percentage of viewers watching a particular program or network) of overall viewership. Each year, networks lose more viewers to cable and independent stations and the Fox network, and the trend shows no signs of reversing itself. Networks, however, will continue to supply the bulk of original programming for the broadcast industry. With the advent of digital technology, local multipoint distribution systems (LMDS) can provide several hundred channels of programming. Digital and interactive video's narrowband wireless option offers the biggest challenge to traditional broadcasters.

Satellites

Satellite manufacturing, begun as a government contracted project, is proliferating with new, smaller models that are both affordable and user friendly. General Motors is the principal owner of one of the two dominant digital broadcast system (DBS) satellite services, DirecTV, a subsidiary of Hughes Space Communications. The other major provider, Lockheed Martin, runs second in sales. Satellites now provide links for distribution of digital signals. Service packages are priced competitively with cable, and most have more channel offerings than cable companies. As consumer choices expand with the deployment of digitally compressed programming services, consolidation of companies that provide multichannel television will continue, and those companies will press to develop bundled services of video, voice, and data to the home.

Viewer Choice

Technology has changed the way we think about and watch television. Early television presented network-sponsored programming with three viewing options. Today, viewers may choose from hundreds of program options, with or without advertising. As a result, program content is being tailored to very specific target segments. Channels may offer programming on a single topic (e.g., animals, food, nature, and so on) or in a single format (e.g., movies, television reruns, news, and so on). No longer confined to networks, viewers vote with their remotes. Subscription programming is replacing advertising sponsorship, and networks are forced to consider the impact of lower revenues. Networks have downsized their reporting staffs, used second-tier stars in their sitcoms, and are rethinking late-night options to reduce operating expenses. To appreciate the significance of technological change, let's take a look at the evolution of programming content.

LIBERATING COUCH POTATOES: TELEVISION CONTENT

Television came into America's homes during the 1950s, changing the dynamic of family communication forever. This window to the outside world brought information, amusement, and stories that fascinated young and old alike. Meals were eaten in front of the television, and family members fought to watch their favorite programs. Early television was all free of charge and live—live audiences watched live action that was televised live to viewers on three major networks. Commercials were performed by the show's stars in the program's context. Live audiences applauded and booed, laughed, and cried at the staged performance. Audiences delighted when performers made mistakes or improvised when the unscripted or unexpected occurred. Programs such as Sid Caesar's *Show of Shows* came into the nation's living rooms each week, bringing 30 minutes of *comedic sketches* written by Carl Reiner, Mel Brooks, Neil Simon, and Woody Allen. Jackie Gleason's *The Honeymooners* pioneered *situation comedy*. Stars of these shows were performers in the true sense, mesmerizing studio audiences and viewers alike.

As technology became more sophisticated, editors carefully removed mistakes and added canned laughter, which is typical of situation comedies like *M*A*S*H*. Here, actors read scripted lines in documentary-style video. Using color, one-line jokes, and stars in the situation comedy mix, *Three's Company* and *The Cosby Show* were broadcast on networks and then syndicated to cable stations. Television drama presented the *realism* of life in evening sitcoms and daytime soaps. Their realism attempted to make sense of the actions of regular people in the context of their everyday lives. Show discourse followed the basic laws of cause and effect (he acts, she responds), and every element existed to help the activity make sense to viewers.

Both then and now, television content generally fits into one of two broad categories: fiction and nonfiction. Basically *fictional* in nature, action and adventure shows (e.g., *ER, NYPD Blue*) and drama (e.g., miniseries, family sagas, soap operas) are based around common plots and story lines. Essentially *nonfictional* offerings include sports, news, and documentaries. Game shows, talk shows, and how-to programs are less dependent on story narrative than their fictional counterparts. Combining aspects of both fiction and reality, *infotainment* takes news and information content to another dimension. Religious television also features blended content. "Reality-based" television, presented as stand-up comedy, music, and variety shows, blurs the distinction even further.

Today, television has come full circle from where it began—from live action to its antithesis and back to live action. And it's no longer free. Cable and satellite dishes bring us programming for a price, and in some cases we still get the advertising. Rejecting formulaic production, viewers now clamor for the real stuff—live game, quiz, talk, and cooking shows that make up the genre of *reality TV*. Today's *reality* has replaced yesterday's realism. Reality TV is unscripted and enjoyed because it's not supposed to make sense in the traditional fashion. A program's reality-based entertainment relies on the impromptu actions of participants that yield elements of surprise and suspense.

Different forms of reality are presented on television. We begin with the game shows, contests, and quiz shows that keep us glued to our chairs. Next, we discuss broadcasts with a particular take on reality, as presented in a combination of news and information. Finally, we look at religious television, which takes us out of reality and into the comfort of entertainment as spiritual enlightenment. Because of reality-based programs' recent impact on contemporary values, we also include a section that focuses on reality-based programs, the audiences who watch them, and a brief word about the companies that sponsor them.

Screen Creeper[222]

TV has become a print medium. You've probably noticed the continuous stream of yellow or white news copy at the bottom of your screen. News people call this the *crawl*. Since the terrorist attacks of September 11, 2001, Fox, CNN, and MSNBC have all switched to the crawl and, as of this writing, have not switched it off. The rationale? News has become impossible to channel through a single televised human. Crawl is multimedia's best alternative to Babel. Networks like the crawl because they can run stories they haven't confirmed, with attribution to a wire service like Reuters. People naturally drawn to text find themselves distracted by the crawl. Other viewers misread headlines when distracted by the video. What do you see as the value of the crawl to viewers? Should it be maintained on news programs as a permanent fixture?

Sneaking and Peeking

First-generation reality entertainment was nothing more than edited highlights of unstaged events in the style of a show called *Candid Camera*. Hidden cameras captured unrehearsed reactions to manipulated events. A typical segment showed a wallet presumably lost on the sidewalk. When a passerby bent down to pick it up, the wallet was snatched away by an attached string. The reactions of multiple passersby, accompanied by a laugh track, made up an episode of the show.

Our fascination with gawking at other people arose with America's love of the camcorder and grew into vicarious experience shows with titles like *America's Most Dangerous Rescues, America's Funniest Home Videos,* and so forth. Then we witnessed rocket explosions, air show crashes, and countless other disasters as presented on prime-time UPN's *Maximum Exposure*. The show's 60 accident-packed minutes contained commentary as astounding as the content. For instance, as a jet plows into stands loaded with spectators, the narrator explains, "The bad news is it's a crash; the good news is that it's only a Russian plane." And after their commentary on a rocket launch—"The freaking rocket exploded"—they replayed the spectacle of falling debris 12 more times.

Today, viewers have graduated from gawking at real-time disaster to peeping at real life. A pioneer of the *reality genre,* MTV's *The Real World* has used videotaped surveillance of roommates as a program format since 1991. What began as part social experiment, part real life, and part competition pitched voyeurism to a new level, and the location of the series changed every year. Nine years after the debut of *The Real World, Big Brother* launched with the same premise; the show presented nine strangers as they lived together as houseguests for 100 days with 24 cameras and 59 microphones.[223] Nightly broadcasts and 24-hour Internet feeds were televised to viewers, who thrilled to the joy of peeking into others' private lives. As *Big Brother 4* begins recruiting houseguests for its next season in the United States, clones also appear in Germany and Spain.

An outgrowth of spontaneous responses in shows like *The Newlywed Game,* the most recent breed of *reality game shows* carries the surveillance concept way beyond "day in the life of" programming. The first season of CBS's *Survivor* showed a group of contestants pitted against one another on an island; group participants voted each week to evict one member until only one—the winner—remained. The series became wildly popular, attracting millions of viewers who speculated on who would win. Such game shows are based not on contestants' knowledge but on their endurance, popularity, and ability to outmaneuver the other contestants. The series was aired only after the contest was over, but the contestants were sworn to secrecy. During filming for *Survivor II* in Australia, reporters seeking to discover the upcoming series' intended winner used aerial photography to spy on the Goshen cattle station where CBS was filming. Confident that tens of millions of *Survivor* fans would lash out at anyone selfish enough to ruin the program by announcing the details of its conclusion, the network became steadfast in its belief that the outcome would remain a secret, which it did.[224] Interviewed while planning for *Survivor III,* set in Kenya, creator Mark Burnett said he'd be insane to change the formula of the show, which ended up number one in television.[225] *Survivor IV* was set in the China Sea; and *Survivor V* was filmed in Thailand.

NBC's summer success with reality shows such as *Fear Factor* and *Spy TV* did not faze Fox's alternative-programming chief, Mike Darnell, who rebounded with *Temptation Island,* a saga of couples testing their relationships against the lure of sexy singles. His new formats include programs like *Murder in Small Town X,* a mix of reality and a movie plot about a serial killer, and *Love Cruise,* an R-rated reality series featuring 16 seaworthy singles battling it out for the best mates and a cash prize. At the signal from the host of *Love Cruise,* ladies claim the male of their choice for the journey's first two days of companionship. The rest is up to fate. Cabins, wired for sight and sound, reveal what alcohol and close companionship can do for prime-time TV.[226] Darnell also developed two other shows with plots he won't reveal that he hopes to air in the future.

Television producers know that viewers need the element of secrecy to stay interested in game shows. Audiences want the assurance that there is something left to discover. Like finding a folded bill inside an old jacket pocket, uncertainty is as necessary as comfort and security. Secrets make the world seem bigger, provide affordable glamour, and suggest danger without presenting an actual threat.[227] Maintaining secrecy at all costs is not only network policy, it's a necessity in keeping the audience's faith that television provides what other media cannot.

Combining the style of *NYPD Blue* and the reality base of *Big Brother*, *Brooklyn North Homicide Squad* was produced by Court TV as a three-part reality series using cameras to follow homicide detectives for seven months. Brilliantly edited and paced, the series is slick and compelling. Thumping music and dramatic techniques rival the show's fictional counterparts in storytelling engagement. What is disturbing about this series is the blurring of the lines between public and private, putting viewers in the role of voyeur. This show goes further than other genres in turning real-life tragedy into sheer entertainment.[228] *Brooklyn North* carries a hint of the forbidden, reminding us that we have no right to be looking. Murder as entertainment has reached prime time—we can't get more real than that.

Competition that combines ingenuity and teamwork was presented live on The Learning Channel on Thanksgiving Day for 15 consecutive hours. Billed as "Junkyard Wars," the event featured teams competing to put together land yachts and underwater chariots from parts found in the local scrap heap. This and similar productions are designed to attract niche audiences who might not otherwise be willing to stay with one channel over an extended period of time. In such contests, everyday knowledge rather than academic knowledge is required, and winners are rewarded with status rather than prizes.

Nearly 20 reality shows crowded their way onto all four broadcast networks for the fall season in 2001, revealing just how dramatically audience tastes have changed. The fall 2002 season introduced *The Bachelor* (ABC), which took viewers on a man's dates with female contestants who vie for his choice, and CBS paired up teams for a global scavenger hunt in *Amazing Race 3*. Viewers tired of artificial jokes and applause meters are more interested in visceral, realistic programming. Steered by a youth culture, reality programming delivers these prized consumers to advertisers who have embraced the emerging audience's preference. Believing that *Who Wants to Be a Millionaire* and *Survivor* have changed television for the next 20 years, the shows' producer, Michael Davis,[229] admits that reality shows are being overhyped and overmarketed. He hopes a shakeout will send the low end of the genre off the reality island for good.

Reality Show Audiences

People who enjoy watching reality television often are just as enthusiastic about participating in the program. In the American version of *Big Brother*, the contestant who neither cracks under the scrutiny nor is vetoed by the fans receives a $500,000 prize. This format is so popular that audience contestants flocked to CBS interviews located in 16 cities at their own expense. The desire to relinquish privacy and endure ruthless scrutiny drives many men and women to want to surrender themselves to viewing audiences. Human knowledge (what we learn from being on the planet), not factual data, is required of these contestants.

Such kwik-gloss (instant glitz) facets of pop culture give participants more than just their 15 minutes of fame[230]—many contestants are featured in magazines and receive product endorsements. As contestants get rich, viewers get to watch everyday life as entertainment.

Actually, the audience gets fooled into thinking it's everyday life. This is a deception; as much planning goes into reality TV as any other kind. And there is nothing ordinary about the "ordinary people" featured; they have been carefully selected, edited, and packaged. As one critic put it, we're actually watching "rats trapped in a very public maze."[231]

Now that there have been five renditions of *Survivor* and three of *Big Brother*, viewers understand that reality-TV shows are just another kind of game show. Still, some viewers will do just about anything to get on television. One group of 50 people who thought they were trying out for a reality show called *Cannibals* signed waivers taking responsibility for their possible beheading, and three out of four actually ate pieces of what they were told was human flesh (it was pork).[232] For viewers unwilling to risk all for the sake of reality, quiz shows provide a safer and more manageable opportunity for on-screen participation.

Wheeling and Dealing

All television shows where participants play games according to predetermined rules under the direction of a host or master of ceremonies can be considered to belong to the game-show genre. Subgenres can be categorized according to game type, such as *competitive games* (e.g., *Family Feud*), *guessing shows* (e.g., *The Big Prize*), *prize games* (e.g., *Wheel of Fortune*), and *interactive games* (e.g., *Blind Date*). The popularity of game shows is derived from the intersituative relationship to the participants' and spectators' reality of everyday life in their social contexts and lifeworld.[233]

Descendants of *The $64,000 Question*, *quiz shows* are part of the subgenre of competitive game shows that give audiences a chance to participate in the dreams of contestants, who probe the far reaches of their memories for answers to trivia questions about every aspect of life. Quiz show contestants have equal chances at winning; those with a greater ability to respond correctly amass winnings. Positioning contestants as different but equal in opportunity is reminiscent of capitalist ideology, where winners and losers are separated and classified by individual or natural (intellectual) differences. Quiz shows are dependent upon contestants' knowledge and are not chance based; luck plays a minor role in their outcome. The luck factor differentiates quiz shows from game shows, which are much more chance oriented. Networks love the quiz format, where sponsors provide the funding for giveaway incentives (soaring to 1 million dollars on *Who Wants to Be a Millionaire*) that lure millions to their sets and thousands to the studio for a try at winning.

The quiz show cast of characters usually features a mild-mannered male host who introduces contestants and facilitates the show's dialogue; sometimes, a female assistant helps him. Sponsors and advertisers appear between the show's three segments. Contestants, usually selected from a contingent of applicants for their knowledge and/or special skills, are both real people and surrogates for the viewers at home who play against them. Winners represent the hopes and dreams of audience members who vicariously delight in the victory of their on-stage counterparts.

The latest quiz show host is not, however, your traditional mild-mannered personality. Anne Robinson, host of *The Weakest Link*, is famous for humiliating contestants. A veteran

Table 9.2	Typology of Television Competition Shows		
Show Type	*Knowledge Base*	*Knowledge Type*	*Show Name*
Quiz	Factual	Academic	*Jeopardy!, Who Wants to Be a Millionaire*
Contest	Factual	Everyday	"Junkyard Wars"
Game	Human	People	*Survivor, Big Brother*
Game	Human	Individual person	*Newlywed Game*

SOURCE: Adapted from a typology developed by Fiske, J. (1990). *Television culture* (p. 269, Figure! 14.1). London: Routledge.

journalist of 30 years, Robinson is a feisty redhead who roots out the bogus and the phony with the curt dismissal: "You are the weakest link. Goodbye." Occasionally, the ousting brings contestants to tears. Fans love it. This British BBC import to NBC is the newest entry in the network clamor for original and innovative ways to stump quiz show contestants and their viewing audience counterparts.

Tennis bad boy John McEnroe hosted *The Chair,* a game designed to test contestants' stress levels by monitoring their heart rate as stress-inducing events transpire—for example, the stage catches fire, or the host puts pressure on a contestant to respond to a question within a diminishing heart rate range. In an almost last-ditch attempt to continue the game-show craze, networks are going to great lengths to bring innovative formats to prime time. But with fickle viewers, who could have forecast the demise of this series before the end of its first 13-week segment?

Quiz show games can be categorized by the type of knowledge contestants must possess to answer the questions or to successfully complete the tasks presented. Table 9.2 illustrates such a typology of shows.

Quiz Show Audiences

Quiz show audiences are active, participatory viewers. Better-educated viewers use these shows to test their academic knowledge, whereas viewers with less formal education (no college) try to keep up with contestants as a measure of their abilities by engaging in self-rating or competing with others who have college degrees.[234] Game show fanatics, called *jipters,* love answers in the form of questions, sequential answers, multiple choice answers, and so on. Their enthusiasm includes trying to get around the network rules that limit individuals to just three game show appearances every 10 years. Winning money on game shows has become the avocation of hundreds of Jipters, whose lives are dominated by outfoxing the trivia-meisters. One such fact-head, Leszek Pawlowicz, never lost a match during his quest for the title of the 1992 *Jeopardy! Tournament of Champions.* And he won a cool million on GoldPocket.com, an Internet trivia game. So why should these folks be limited to three appearances in a decade?

According to producers, audiences don't want an intellectual hero like Pawlowicz; they'd rather see regular people answering questions about Madonna and Hillary in real time.[235] Viewers want to think that they might be able to grab the big prize themselves. Projection keeps audiences coming back. Have you tested your knowledge against that of a show's contestants recently? How well did you score? Did your score influence your decision to watch or not watch the show in the future? Why?

Talking and Telling

We see another form of reality by tuning in to television talk shows. A tradition advanced by Phil Donahue, talk shows are now open season for talk about everything and anything personal, disgusting, abnormal, and perverse. During the 1995 season, 24 daytime TV talk shows presented interpersonal conflicts, emotional crises, and disclosure of very private information.[236] Although their hosts became very brazen in their attempts to survive among the competition for viewers, only about half as many remained on the air seven years later.

An audience keeper, sexual themes are the second most common topic of discussion on television talk shows. Blunt discourse about sexual orientations and deviances cause critics to characterize talk shows as sordid, immoral, and sleazy.[237] Such shows rely on self-disclosure of personal information usually revealed only to one's close friends, family, clergy, or therapist. One third of disclosures are made by participants, one third are presented by the host or hostess, and the other third are revealed by audience members. Sleaze talk, a polite name for obscene discussions, gave us Jerry Springer, Ricki Lake, and Howard Stern. These hosts listen as guests present their grotesque character traits and absurd lifestyles to gasping, hooting audiences. These talking and question-asking events foster angry confrontation that passes for entertainment.

Springer has had to contend with violence among his contestants. One divorced woman who appeared on a "secret mistresses confronted" segment was misinformed about her role on the show. Thinking she was coming to reconcile with her husband, she arrived at the studio to find out that he had remarried and brought his new wife. The on-screen violence resulted in the divorced contestant's murder. Springer calls his show "chewing-gum TV,"[238] claiming that he's not responsible for any unforeseen consequences. He says it's a freak show, and no one who watches or appears as a guest should have any qualms about anything. This philosophy may be a little hard for some viewers to swallow. Romans used to pit gladiators against one another until death; today, we use talk show contestants to give us our violence fix.

Talk Show Audiences

We can approach talk show audiences in two ways: in a conventional/traditional style, where the viewer is an individual who witnesses a *debate* conducted by others, and in a more innovative style, where the viewer is regarded as a citizen who is encouraged to feel part of a *dialogue*. The debate style is competitive with a win-lose outcome, whereas dialogue shows focus on problem solving. Forming the basis of most talk shows, these styles reflect a classical dichotomy in journalistic values. We provide a closer look at these oppositional formats here.

Dialogue	Debate
Collaborative	Oppositional
Common ground focus	Objective is to win
Look for strengths	Identify weaknesses
Reveal and reevaluate assumptions	Defend assumptions as truth
Personal involvement	Alienation

SOURCE: Based on Study Circles Resource Center, Pomfret, CT. See Charity, A. (1995). *Doing public journalism.* New York: Guilford Press.

Talk shows that approach viewers as citizens produce a common experience, in contrast with shows that approach viewers as isolated individuals. Dialogue shows, such as *Charlie Rose* on public television, appeal more to women than to men; men prefer debate style, typical of *The Jerry Springer Show.* When the show's goal is to provide a unique experience for the viewer, traits like malicious delight, emotional outbursts, and freak-show performance often result. Common experience shows, however, are more concerned with consciousness raising than exposé. With audience-pleasing entertainment as the objective of most talk shows, we will continue to encounter debate-style performance that is effect driven, where hosts take no responsibility for the situation or spectacle.

In spite of the criticisms of debate-style talk shows and their supposed antisocial effects, studies of talk show audiences are minimal. Two studies shed some light on why viewers choose to watch talk shows. One study found that among the 27 gratification items used to score college students' motivations for watching talk shows, amusement and passing time were the two most prevalent reasons.[239] What is your reaction to talk show forums? Are you in favor of a "no limits" discussion format?

Researchers have also identified the following four effects of sexual discussions on talk shows:

☆   *Cultivation effects*—Viewers overestimate the prevalence of sexually related activities in society. In other words, we think that everyone is having extramarital affairs because they are discussed so regularly on television.

☆   *Disinhibition*—Viewers express more liberal attitudes toward sexual issues and diversity than they did in the past. For example, we don't get nervous during love scenes, as we used to.

☆   *Appreciation*—Is derived from viewer interest in programming with a sexual component. Viewers learn to pay more attention to broadcast intimacy than other forms of interaction.

☆   *Learning effects*—Images and language educate viewers about physical intimacy at an early age. For example, more children are likely to know what "oral sex" is than those of past decades.[240]

Audiences infatuated with reality TV in all its forms have turned hedonism into something fashionable; viewers' quest for undiluted pleasure is a top priority. We want what makes us happy. And we want it in all of our viewing encounters. Once again, in a true postmodern convergence of illusion and delusion, audiences may be predisposed to see everything on television as actuality.

News and Views

Americans are enthralled with live-action drama, especially in the form of news programming. Information has entered the entertainment arena head on in what we call *infotainment*. We have expanded our needs from local and national nightly news hours to news networks that broadcast around the clock. CNN personnel, long-standing experts of the continuing news format, brought us the Gulf War, O. J. Simpson's freeway chase and subsequent trial, and the hand-counting of ballots in Florida during the 2000 Presidential runoff. Like video junkies, we hang on every word as facts unfold, listening intently to opinions of the famous and infamous for hours and days.

News programming has three subgenres: investigation, dramatization and analysis. Investigative *news magazines* have become prime-time favorites. *Prime Time Live, 20/20, 60 Minutes,* and *48 Hours* are representative shows of this type. More sensational versions of the news exist in the form of *tabloid news,* which dramatizes events with actors and staged sets after the fact, often confusing audiences who are unaware of the show's fictitious nature. *News analysis* of politics, finances, current events, and celebrities crowd the airwaves in half-hour and hour segments. *The Capital Gang, Wall $treet Week, Meet the Press*, and *Entertainment Tonight* are among the most popular of this genre.

Enjoyed for its similarity to dramatic fiction, news programming is a popular choice among television viewers. But when drama *becomes* reality, the presentation changes. In fiction, drama is used to advance the plot. In news, drama unfolds and replays to update viewers. On September 11, 2001, for instance, television audiences accustomed to seeing fictionalized explosions and horror witnessed the shock of drama played out in real time as the World Trade Center was attacked by terrorists. Beginning shortly after 9:00 A.M. Eastern Standard Time, cameras from major networks focused on the events unfolding in the sky over Manhattan. Viewers found themselves witnesses to the unfathomable sight of passenger planes heading for and slamming into New York's tallest buildings. The scene was captured from multiple perspectives, and it was played repeatedly day after day. Every channel originated or carried footage of the attack. A rerun of a plane hitting a tower served as background for the lengthy commentary of news anchors and reporters in the field. And the attack was presented on split screens to accompany testimonies of heroic rescues and narrow escapes.

What differentiates news drama from fiction is the inescapable presence of news images. We can easily pop a video out of the VCR or change channels to remove scenes we don't want to watch. We cannot, however, erase the everpresent reality of disaster from consuming the airwaves. Events are replayed unrelentingly. Late-night hosts replace their comic formats with political discussions, network season premieres are postponed, and sensitive programming is removed from viewing schedules. Viewers are forced to rehash and review events over and over again. In times of catastrophic crisis, this uncanny blending of fiction and reality situates news programming as both compelling and troublesome.

Focus on Product News

According to a *New York Times* reporter, scandal products create the biggest buzz[241] among news viewers. Two recent scandals illustrate this point: the ballot-counting standoff in the 2000 presidential election and the impeachment trial.

Live news and entertainment sponsorship merged with nationally televised drama to deliver 462,000 ballots to the Florida State Capitol using a yellow Ryder truck on its 450-mile journey through Florida. Ryder appreciated its starring position in the presidential ballot-counting standoff videotaped from a news helicopter, especially because the brand's last big role was as the type of vehicle that carried explosives to the Oklahoma bombing. And the presidential impeachment trial was our first live Washington scandal featuring product placement, with brands like Zegna ties, DKNY, Black Dog, Gap, and Altoids.

What is the difference between news and the sensationalism of scandal? How have advertisers taken advantage of scandal in your city?

Many television viewers prefer to receive information in the form of lessons about food. Popular with wanna-be chefs and menu mavens alike, *cooking shows* have been around for a long time. Some recent additions have infused entertainment format variations into their recipes for success. *Two Fat Ladies* added a sprinkle of humor to the traditionally staid cooking-show genre in 1997. A few years later, cooking-as-competition was introduced by Japan's *Iron Chef*. Not to be outdone, Britain's *Naked Chef* features a 25 year-old host who plays drums in the rock band Scarlet Division. Shaggy-haired Jamie Oliver "strips down restaurant-quality food to the barest essentials of home cooking" by simplifying the process.[242] Featured on the Food Network, Oliver prepares meals with names such as "What to Serve Four Bandmates After a Gig," which appeal to younger viewers, who want food that's easy and simple, not fancy and complicated.

Nature-oriented programs (or "bug shows," as we call them) inform us about creatures and critters from around the globe. We have an animal channel (Animal Planet) as well as individual programs presented by public television (NOVA), the Discovery channel, and National Geographic. Viewers can also receive information on how to make home repairs, remodel an old house, fix a car, and plant a garden. The formula for the *how-to* genre's successful entertainment is clever hosts, humorous dialogue, and a bit of useful information. How have you used television to learn a new skill or improve a current one?

Infotainment Audiences

Who watches infotainment programs? Well-educated men and women who seek enrichment in an entertaining format. The plethora of information entertainment that is invading the airwaves may be indicative of viewers' willingness to enrich their lives with current events and supplement their knowledge by watching rather than reading about what's new or different. Information shows provide dialogue for social interaction, serving to ground viewers' personal identities and to establish them as informed citizens.

Another motivation for watching news as it unfolds was discovered during the terrorist attack on the World Trade Center and the Pentagon, when viewers huddled together before their televisions in mutual shock and horror. American viewers were connected to other viewers from around the world who shared their grief. A community of media viewers and empathizers was created around the globe. Crash coverage provided a common dialogue for millions of people worldwide and created a rhetoric of patriotism in America.

Prayer and Share

To reach mass audiences, religion took to the airwaves in 1960, when Pat Robertson started the Christian Broadcasting Network in Portsmouth, Virginia. *Religious programs,* such as Jerry Falwell's *Old Time Gospel Hour* and Robert Schuler's *Hour of Power* use entertainment tactics to attract audiences and solicit donations.

We can understand religious television by using the Source-Message-Channel-Receiver model of persuasion: who says what through what medium to whom. The message *source* is the clergy or show host who is a trustworthy representative of God. The *message* is an upbeat and inspiring sermon; its content emphasizes faith, hope, and charity. The *channel* is television, a popular and comfortable medium with production qualities for enhancement, including camera angles for intimacy, music for emotion, and living color for transformational images. The *receiver* is the viewer, who watches in the privacy of home surrounded by friends and family within his/her own time frame.

Although it's not a new phenomenon, televised religion reached its zenith with Trinity Broadcast Network's programming, which is carried by 1,000 stations worldwide. Since the network's beginnings in Tustin, California, in 1973, Paul and Jan Crouch have provided non-denominational Christian programming for what is currently the most all-inclusive, lifestyle-based religious network on the air. TBN offers shows on fitness, children's programs, Christian music videos, a marriage enrichment series, holiday specials, talk shows, and Christian dramas and movies. Show hosts and guests include pastors from America's largest churches, astronauts, champion athletes, movie stars, and country music entertainers.

Headquartered in a gigantic mosque-like structure adjacent to a major Orange County, California, freeway, Trinity Christian Center provides its studio visitors with Christian education, entertainment, and souvenirs. Visitors can shop to Christian music beneath dimmed lights, selecting from books, music, gifts, jewelry, accessories, health foods, medicine, and kid products. In addition, visitors can take a virtual time trip along the Via Dolorosa (old Jerusalem) to experience simulations of significant moments in the life of Jesus. And you can witness a virtual stoning, which is so real that it has been known to drive children to tears. Or you can visit TBN's Web site for directions to the corporate headquarters, programming schedules, virtual tours, and to make donations.

Religious TV Audiences

Viewers of religious programming tend to be middle-age women with low levels of education. A recent study of TBN viewers[243] reveals that watching religious television fills audiences' needs in five areas: spiritual, psychological, social, utilitarian, and media. The need most mentioned by viewers was media. Entertainment value was found to be TBN's strongest role for viewers, who sing along to music and delight to the strong visual images. Mentioned next in importance were social needs, which TBN meets in a variety of ways. Families watch programs together. Viewers see the Crouches as charismatic and inspirational leaders, and some audience members even form parasocial relationships with program personalities. By bonding with television actors, viewers feel that they have made new friends, and they feel socially fulfilled through the mediated interaction.

Although TBN specializes in spiritual enlightenment, this network functions best as a barometer for how viewers perceive their place in the vast concepts of God, religion, world, and self. As with other forms of mediated entertainment, the appearance, agenda, and content of televised religion offer few clues about why audience members watch. The fact is, they watch in large numbers, and they watch often. Religion has met the challenge of competing programming by providing entertainment that attracts and retains audiences.

Television Trends

Television is not the same today as it was in the '60s, and it will continue to evolve in the future. But how? We suggest three changes you might expect in the next several years: plot renewal, more music channels, and redefinition of the nuclear family. Dramatic events and advertising revenues also play a role in television's future, as you'll see in the next section.

A Search for Plots

Reality shows have flourished because they are cheap to produce, satisfy a voyeuristic urge, and have a frisson of authenticity. But those are not the only reasons networks jumped on the reality bandwagon. One major cause is that television is experiencing a deep crisis in narrative.[244] Most plot structures originated in folk tales and haven't changed much over time. Stories are structured like this: During some historical period, a protagonist takes action in a particular physical setting. One day, he confronts the antagonist, who is a source of conflict. In the end, the protagonist resolves the conflict and the story ends. All stories are a variation on that theme.

Over the past 25 years, plots have been depleted and worn out from overuse. With an increasing number of media outlets and demands for programming worldwide, story plots have not been able to keep pace with audience expectations. Because popular formulaic plots—love and adventure scenarios—elicit predictable responses from audiences, they are continually recycled. How many mad killers can we catch and arrest? How many romantic encounters can we endure?

Reality television, a temporary rescue for plot delivery, wore thin; eventually, *Survivor* and its counterparts became as formulaic as the plots they displaced. Next, networks tried to break the mold and lure young audiences with shows like *Popular,* which centers on high school cliques. But when the program's realism suddenly turned surreal (over the edge), viewers were convinced that the show didn't take narrative seriously. Wrestling was another plot alternative that became popular because such shows admitted their deliberate and shamelessly manipulated plots. Wrestling, aimed at adults, was successful because of its self-reflexive, post-modernist twist, where the manipulation itself became the plot.

In addition to plot variations, networks are looking to alternative storytelling formats. In NBC's comedy *Watching Ellie,* starring Julia Louis-Dreyfus, a single real-time scene was presented in 22 consecutive minutes for the spring 2002 season. Designed as a slice of life, the show presented a window into the life of a Los Angeles singer who performs in cabaret clubs and sings jingles for grocery stores. Another attempt at real-time format is presented in the popular Fox show *24.*

As it becomes a medium in search of a plot, television programs in the following genres are emerging: *humorous satire* (e.g., Comedy Central's *Bush*), *surrealism* (e.g., Fox's *Malcolm in the Middle*), *totally improvised dialogue* (e.g., HBO's *Curb Your Enthusiasm*) and *stories told in overlapping flashbacks* (e.g., Fox's *Grounded for Life*). Some programs also provide *hybrid formats*, allowing audiences to play along using the Web. In ABC's game/reality show, *Runner,* a person selected to be the object of a nationwide manhunt is armed with a car, a credit card, and a cell phone. If the runner escapes detection for 28 days, he or she wins $1 million. And the whole country can play along by visiting the Web site or watching the TV show, where clues are provided about the runner's location. Anyone who catches the runner wins up to $1 million. This single-plot show—despite its interactive potential—was a less than single season phenomenon.

A Competitor for MTV

MTV plays to a younger audience than most channels, and it is never at a loss for original programming. It is a brand name with global juice; MTV viewership has increased dramatically during the last 2 decades, with 16 stations reaching 342 million households in 140 countries. Since its inception in 1981, MTV has grown into a marketing titan and has set off a dramatic shift of power in the record industry. Because of MTV's grip on the coveted 12- to 24 year-old demographic, the cable outlet has clout among advertisers and record labels.

Based on the music channel's stellar performance, AOL Time Warner Inc. is discussing the possibility of launching a rival music channel. Owner of Warner Music Group, the media conglomerate has control of Linkin Park and Trick Daddy, as well as a vast cable network. Unfazed by the threat of a rival music channel, Def Jam Record founder Russ Simmons reminds us that "if it's hot today and on MTV, it'll be on fire tomorrow."[245] And any rival will have a tough time upstaging MTV, which has left its mark on politics with coverage of Bill Clinton, on culture with hip-hopera "Carmen," and on music videos with early trendsetters like Madonna.

Vanishing Nuclear Families

According to statistics from Children Now, the nuclear family is disappearing from network prime time even faster than in real life.[246] The national child advocacy organization that examines media messages to children says that only about 11% of recurring prime-time characters on networks are parents of any kind, and only 61% of them are still married. HBO, for instance, presents a family in *Six Feet Under* that includes a deceased dad, a whoring mom, a gay son and his psychotic brother, and a sister on crack. A quick look at the prime-time families suggests a similar trend: *Reba* (NBC), with a Texas soccer mom (singer Reba McEntire) whose dentist-husband leaves her for his hygienist; *Hack* (CBS), focusing on a divorced dad who makes a living driving a cab; and *Bram and Alice* (CBS), featuring a father and daughter who discover each other on the job. Capitalizing on the nostalgia craze, NBC offers a '60s family in *American Dreams,* and ABC's *Once and Again* presents a more traditional, family-oriented show. The WB (Warner Brothers) channel recast the '70s show *Family Affair,* with a new Uncle Bill and Mr. French supervising three orphaned children. In spite of all the family sitcom and drama alternatives, the hottest dad on the block is mobster Tony Soprano, and the most popular American family is a cartoon (*The Simpsons*).

Why has the family faded from the spotlight? Perhaps shows reflect demographic and cultural shifts. Or perhaps, because families rarely watch shows together, it's no longer necessary to satisfy everyone with the same show. And as the definition of family changes, advertisers have been forced to adjust as well. The Family Friendly Programming Forum, a group of ad executives, presented an improvement plan for improving television scripts for family shows; one of their suggestions was to replace divorced parents with widowed dads and moms. But for the foreseeable future, we'll continue to be entertained by our televised family counterparts, who often engage in gratuitous sex and use foul language, and who include a mix and match of combinations that are supposed to reflect real life.

Dramatic Events and TV Programming

After the terrorist attacks of September 11, 2001, network shows made an effort to rewrite their scripts to address public concerns and appear timely. NBC's *Third Watch* devoted several episodes to the World Trade Center disaster, and ABC's *NYPD Blue* also included pointed references to the attacks in the show's scripts as well as a dedication to New York City police and firefighters. *The West Wing,* also on NBC, offered an indirect, fictional response just 3 weeks after the attacks with an episode that was a thinly veiled history lesson about terrorism.[247]

Figure 9.1   The Nelson Family

Stars of *The Ozzie and Harriet Show,* where the dad worked, the mom stayed home, and the kids did what they were told; this show was the precursor of contemporary dramas and sitcoms, in which the family unit and its problems have changed.
© Bettman/Corbis.

Because the terrorist attacks were of such magnitude and the aftermath was so preoccupying, the war against terrorism and the fear of bioterrorism became part of the fabric of television. Watching a movie or live performance, audiences can escape current events. But on television, the topic intrudes everywhere. Show creators justify their programming by claiming responsibility to deal with the events, noting that shows involving police and firefighters would appear insensitive if they ignored the events. In today's post-modern world, here fiction and reality occupy the same television space, viewers are hard-pressed to differentiate between the two. How audiences receive and internalize this information/dramatic hybrid will be the subject of continuing research.

Focus on a Battle of the Networks: NBC's Strategy to Win

In response to audiences who have become distressingly fickle, NBC Entertainment hired Jeff Zucker to get them back. Formerly executive producer of the *Today* show in New York, Zucker, 36, knows how to create sensations. He has staged weddings in Rockefeller Plaza, and he dressed Matt Lauer in Jennifer Lopez's Versace dress to please viewers. As legions of viewers abandon network television, it has suddenly become an extremely complex game of chess. It's Zucker's job to determine which gambit will succeed.

In the absence of a clear solution, Zucker's philosophy is to use a few good gimmicks—such as adding 10 "Super-Size" minutes to some episodes of *Friends,* importing the British hit *The Weakest Link,* and scoring big with the sadistic *Spy TV.* Zucker is a believer in short-lived rating jolts and producing a creative mix of high and low, quality and cheap. Balancing novelty with tradition, Zucker offers as a counterpoint to *Will & Grace* the show *Fear Factor,* a cheaper, sillier, different breed of comedy that appeals to younger audiences. He also favored piloting *Scrubs,* a single-camera, no-laugh-track comedy that follows a medical resident and his fellow doctors, and *Emeril,* starring a famous chef. "I know everyone hates *Emeril,*" said Zucker. "He's not *Frasier* and never will be. But at least people know who he is, and that counts for something."[248]

His strategy also includes scheduling opportunities, such as starting *Third Watch* 2 minutes early on premiere night by rearranging the commercial structure to keep viewers from switching channels. In another masterful stroke, Zucker aired an episode of NBC's new reality show *Lost* alongside *Fear Factor* when CBS planned to air *The Amazing Race* 2 weeks early. Because the plots of *Lost* and *Amazing Race* are similar (people stuck in rugged terrain fighting it out for a cash prize) Zucker planned to snare *Fear Factor's* viewers for *Lost.*

Zucker wants young audiences, and he wants a promotable element. He loves catch phrases and running gags. And he wants to satisfy the bottom line. He develops his own set of rules, and *Fear Factor* lives up to all of them: Teens love it, it's cheap, and it's full of thrills that are easy to sell. Next, he revived *Battle of the Network Stars* after it had been off the air four years. One thing he promised not to do is a reality show in space—unless, of course, it will bring audiences to NBC.

What gimmick would you suggest to show creators to call attention to their reality shows? What other real situations might be used as backgrounds for a new season of programming?

Advertising Revenue and Network Stars

Cast members of *Friends* signed a contract to receive $1 million per episode for the 2002 season. As advertising revenues continue to diminish on network programs, this amount may be the pinnacle of star compensation. We believe that programming will reflect the loss of revenues by casting unknown starts in new shows to avoid the high cost of celebrity participation. Low-cost production and unknown cast members may be the wave of future seasons as the four networks face fierce competition from cable channels and pay TV. Innovations from HBO threaten the livelihood of traditional programming and give audiences more power in the choice of their viewing content.

WHILE WE WATCH: MEASURING EFFECTS OF TELEVISION VIEWING

In the early days of television, viewing was a communal experience where everyone enjoyed one of three available network programs. Today, television has become an isolated activity. Count the number of televisions in your home. You probably have a TV for every member of your household. Why? Because we all prefer different programming and, with hundreds of channels from which to choose, we demand constant viewing entertainment.

Television has become a window to the world for many of us. We begin our day with news and perhaps leave the TV on for background noise as we do household chores. During the day we discuss what we watched, and in the evening we tune in to our favorite sitcom and finish the day with David Letterman or Jay Leno. On weekends we watch movie channels and sports. Our lives often revolve around what's happening on TV. By bringing the world into our homes, television has changed the way the world uses media.

The impact of both real and fictional television on audiences is the subject of much ongoing academic and professional research. Six theoretical frameworks ground most studies on the effects of TV content on viewers:

1. *Schema theory*[249]—Assumes that information processing is constructive and that people modify mediated information in accordance with their beliefs in the context in which it is received. (We could investigate the role of televised political advertising on voting using this theory.)

2. *Cultivation theory*[250]—The repetitive pattern of mass messages and images forms a central core of common symbols, which in turn form the fabric of society. (This theory might be used to investigate how popular sitcoms affect everyday language.)

3. *Social learning theory*[251]—People imitate behavior they see on television. (MTV's impact on adolescent behavior could be investigated with this theory.)

4. *Agenda-setting theory*[252]—News shows set the focus of news thrust. (By comparing coverage of a single story around the globe, we could make some observations about how news anchors determine content, as this theory suggests.)

5. *Socialization theory*[253]—The social reality of TV is more real than reality itself. (By identifying parasocial relationships between women and soap opera stars, we might sustain this theory.)

6. *Uses and gratifications theory*[254]—Audiences make choices in media based on their expectations for satisfaction. This theory asks the question, "What do people do with the media?" (We can use this theory to determine what effect an unpopular episode of a particular sitcom has on the viewer's return to that show the following week.)

We offer these theories to illuminate how it's possible to arrive at common understandings of a topic. Theories help us to study how audiences make meaning and interact with television images.

A Word From Our Sponsor: Audience as Rating Point

Television audiences are most valued for their viewing presence. Nielsen rating systems measure who watches what shows. Programs with the largest audiences command the highest advertising revenues. Thus, successful networks and independent stations provide entertainment to please their audiences. Networks feed the masses with beverage spots and car commercials. Niche stations tempt smaller markets with medicines and exercise equipment. One thing viewers should never lose sight of is the reality of the bottom line. Programming has become a popularity contest, and the winning shows get the best commercials.

Advertising's function has shifted from selling a product to associating enjoyment with a brand. By providing enjoyable and technologically enthralling commercials, advertisers entertain rather than promote. The best spots revolve around a story or present a series of action vignettes that have little to do with the product and everything to do with how viewers feel about a brand. The Budweiser frogs croak to amuse us, and the Coke bears make us smile.

As we become resistant to blatant brand builders, advertisers make the transition to a softer, gentler form of branding: product placement. Brands now appear in almost every form of television programming. From *Seinfeld's* cereal boxes and J. Peterman (catalog retailer) character, to plots built around product characters, prime time has been loaded with logos. Here's one example. With a cast of Emmy award nominees, the NBC sitcom *Will & Grace* integrated a Mattel toy into the plot line of one episode. A Cher doll became the sidekick of the character named Jack, whose affection for the real Cher had been a running gag since the show debuted in 1998. This product's role in a TV series is emblematic of the rapidly blurring line between programming and peddling, and paid and unpaid content in media entertainment.[255] Although the marketing people claim this was not a product placement, viewers may see this type of product intrusion as content veering toward infomercial.

The grounding for product placement in sitcoms draws from three basic literary theories:[256]

☆ *Genre theory*, a type of classification method, enables sponsors to match plot and characters with products within a specific situation.
☆ *Feminist theory* looks at gender, specifically sex-based attitudes toward sponsors of particular products and placements in sitcoms.
☆ *Persona theory* looks at the personality of the speaking characters and focuses on the sponsor. Sponsors can be visible within the plot, meaning that characters interact with them, or invisible outside the plot as a commercial sponsor of the show.

By learning about audience attitudes toward the character and toward the product, placements can be accurately directed. Viewers of *Will & Grace* like Jack and are amused by his fascination with the actress-singer Cher. According to these theories, viewers should be receptive to the previously mentioned Mattel placement. Researchers found that attitudes toward characters who play permanent roles are much stronger than attitudes toward characters who play temporary parts in situation comedies, and attitude varies with gender. For instance, if a returning character is perceived to be overtly pushing a product, men often feel negatively toward that character. However, if characters who are perceived to be leaving the show or who are only appearing for one segment embrace a product, they are not subject to ill feelings from audiences of either sex. Because Jack is a regular character, the assumption is that his likability will not be tarnished from the endorsement of a Cher doll because of its natural fit into the story. Films also have their share of product placements, as you will read in the "A Closer Look" section later in this chapter.

Social Impact of Television

Television has provided Americans with role models and with heroes, with current events and with controversial points of view. Because we spend between 2 and 8 hours in front of the TV set each day, much of our conversation revolves around what we watch. Listen to the conversations of children, and you will hear them refer to cartoon characters by name. Teens cite brands worn by their favorite MTV artists. Adults discuss sitcom characters as if they were personal friends. Men refer to sports commentators' remarks about game action, and women discuss the dresses worn by the stars of *Sex and the City*. Television programming has become the vocabulary of modern society.

As American programming invades the global landscape, viewers question the values and ideas projected by its shows and stars. During the '80s, when *Dallas* was popular, global viewers thought all Americans had the cunning of J. R. and the fashion of Sue Ellen. *Baywatch* continues to be the most popular show worldwide, suggesting to foreigners that America is a land of beach beauties and monosyllabic dialogue.

And our views of the world are shaped by the images provided by Americans for Americans. We watch children starving in Africa and terrorists bombing civilians in

Palestine. We hear commentary from American news media broadcasting live from trouble spots, and we understand the world according to these perspectives. Think about the role television plays in your life and in your perceptions of the world. Can any other medium compare to the power of televised images for their influence on how we think about ourselves and our world? Although measuring it may be difficult, the social impact of television may best be reflected through the attitudes we hold toward ourselves, our culture, and our society.

Preview of Coming Attractions

Watch out for a new age of hybrid visual storytelling. Content of all forms is now delivered as made-for-TV movies by networks acting as producers, and as movies released directly to videotape and television networks. As technology improves, single-camera production will bring new reality to the cinema and our home viewing systems. Projected from flat screens and enhanced with surround sound, movies will carry messages from around the world into our living rooms.

In an effort to bring *new programming* to the screen, a company called LivePlanet is working to combine the up-to-the-second urgency of cyberspace, the drama of television, and the unpredictability of a live event while giving the audience a chance to feel like a part of the event.[257] By integrating film, TV, and the Web, LivePlanet is Hollywood's most ambitious attempt to integrate the Internet into mainstream programming. LivePlanet founders Ben Affleck, Matt Damon, and Chris Moore combine reality TV with online games (for example, *RealityRun,* which had 650,000 hits daily on its Web site when a contestant was let loose in Berlin in August 2001).

These visionaries want to succeed where Hollywood has failed. Producing traditional media based on live events that allow viewers to participate online sounds simple, but no other studio has tried anything quite like it. Two unsuccessful attempts were the *Zombie College* Web series, which flopped, and Pop.com, which never got off the ground. A hybrid of Internet start-up and traditional production company, LivePlanet looks to advertising and paid sponsorships to make money. Sam Adams beer, for instance, sponsored the Web phase of LivePlanet's *Project Greenlight* film and ran promotions when the movie was released and when HBO aired its documentary about making the movie. Of course, Affleck and Damon appeared as spokespersons in Sam Adams commercials.

A German company called GfK Group specializes in tracking and analyzing remote control clicking behavior on interactive TV to customize advertising. This new technology measures audience reactions to advertising, such as gender differences in computer use. By gathering such patterns, the company builds profiles called *silhouettes* of the computer users based on the ads they respond to. This new biometric monitoring is expected to penetrate 40% of American households by 2005, accompanied by $11 billion in advertising. Traditional demographic targeting used by advertisers will be rendered obsolete when this new technology enables cable advertisers to create specific targeting strategies based on actual consumer use.

FADE TO BLACK

Society has spoken. People want unscripted television and riveting story lines. As consumers of mediated images, we look to writers, directors, and producers to provide stimulating entertainment content. Entertainers are listening to society and developing new and innovative content for broadcast and film venues. Convergence is the watchword of 21st century content distribution. The bottom line is that viewing audiences will receive the visuals, narrative, and music provided in quality drama, comedy, and news in all forms of visual media. Audiences have spoken, and audiences have been heard. All we have to do now is position our remote, sit back, and enjoy.

 A Closer Look

TV as Radio[258]

Subscribers to cable and satellite TV may or may not be aware of the music channels available on their televisions. Time Warner Cable's digital service, for instance, has 40 music-only channels, each with 'round-the-clock commercial-free programming, allowing viewers to use their television sets as cutting-edge radios.

While you listen, the screen identifies the song that is playing, the name of the performer, and the title and label of the CD from which the track is drawn. And the sound is as good as the speakers through which you are hearing it. The programming is versatile and extensive. "Singers and Standards" plays Sinatra-esque tunes, "American Originals" offers bluegrass, show tunes and Dixieland, or you can listen to classical, jazz, and big band music channels.

One provider for this service is Music Choice, a small company based in Horsham, Pennsylvania, a tiny township north of Philadelphia. Their service may herald a significant change in the way Americans listen to music. Founded in 1990, Music Choice bills itself as "the world's first digital audio service offered via satellite to cable subscribers." The company serves 1,050 cable systems across the United States. Ten specialists maintain a group of playlists larger than those heard on ordinary radio stations. Their current-hit channels play between 500 to 800 songs each.

Soon, subscribers will also have access to album-cover artwork, artist biographies, and tour dates. And when you subscribe, you'll be able to buy whatever CD you're listening to just by using your remote control. Fans of this musical innovation claim that the wide-ranging genre and reliable quality make TV music a must-have for people who like to listen at home.

What kind of musical programming does your cable or satellite provider offer? What is the cost? What is the appeal of this form of music for you? For your parents?

DISCUSSION AND REVIEW

1. Do talk show hosts have a responsibility first to their audience or first to their guests? Why? What problems can arise from a misdirected priority?

2. What are the main distinctions between a news magazine and tabloid news on television? Are these distinctions easily recognizable to news audiences?

3. How does social learning theory explain the effects of violence on viewers? Is research conclusive about the nature of those effects?

EXERCISES

1. Watch a television talk show and discuss its content from the perspective of dialogue versus debate. How would you improve the content of the show?

2. Look at the product placements in a TV sitcom and analyze them using one of the three placement theories presented in the chapter. Which do you think is most effective?

3. Tune into a sports program and list the advertisers promoting products on the program. Then look at the commercials featured during a prime-time sitcom. How are the commercials different in content? What does the difference in brand types tell you about the viewing audience?

RECOMMENDED READINGS AND WEB SITES

Fiske, J. (1990). *Television culture.* London: Routledge.

Fowles, J. (1996). *Advertising and popular culture.* Thousand Oaks, CA: Sage.

Goldstein, J. H. (Ed.). (1998). *Why we watch: The attractions of violent entertainment.* New York: Oxford University Press.

http://timstvshowcase.com is a roster of every television series ever to air on network TV with cast lists, theme-song sound bites, and links for purchasing show memorabilia.

10

The Sound of One Hand Clapping

Performing Arts Live

Magic is the ability to take people out of their boring, problematic day and leave them in a moment of astonishment.

— David Blaine

Before media transmitted action electronically, all entertainment was performed live. Today, the performing arts must struggle to maintain a slice of the entertainment pie. Founded on ancient traditions that established the basis for dramatic theory, the performing arts are important because they directly reflect our Western heritage. Although many different arts are classified under the rubric of performance, in this chapter we will discuss those that are most important to 21st century leisure.

Live performances are different from other kinds of entertainment because they involve active audiences that become part of group and lived experiences (performances that occur live). As part of a group, individuals increase their power to achieve reinforcement and pleasure. Not only do audiences contribute to the shows' financial successes, they also make personal connections to them. Audiences have aesthetic experiences that involve attending to, perceiving, and appreciating performance for itself. The experience of being in the presence of performers is what drives audiences to attend live performances.

If you've ever been to a live performance, you understand the extent to which the show's success is dependent upon audience response. Laughter becomes infectious in a crowd although, if experienced alone, the same humor might leave you unmoved. Performance succeeds to the degree that the audience is excited. Viewers want to be thrilled, amused, or moved, and they want to know that other people are sharing their experience. When a performance succeeds, audience members subordinate their separate identities to the group. If the house is not full, the performance not only loses money, it loses force.

Live performance has demonstrated an unexpected tenacity in the face of competition from film, television, video, and other popular entertainment. During a live event, audience members are not simply media spectators—they become performers themselves. If the performance is to succeed, the audience must be active, must share with the performer, and must assist with the act of creation. Every audience member helps to make or break the performance. Because live performances can achieve a sense of occasion impossible for mediated events, they have retained their lure. Buying the tickets, planning the event, socializing with a group, and enjoying post-event activities produce a more enjoyable experience than is usually achieved by viewing a film or by watching a television show.

Audiences have levels of expectations for performance; they continue to attend depending upon how well the performers live up to expectations in the true sense of expectancy and uses and gratifications theories. Moreover, the socialization that takes place prior to and following performances lends itself to social theory. And, because each audience member takes away his or her own interpretation of the performance, the reception and reader response theories are also applicable here.

As the object of marketing and sales tactics, live audiences have been the subject of countless studies to determine how performing companies can best deliver exceptional entertainment to subscribers and supporters of the arts. Studies show that audiences want a spectacle in which they can participate. They want to share an experience as well as view a form of entertainment. Designing spectacles has become a paramount challenge for producers of live performance, who must continue to compete with mediated entertainment for their share of audiences.

First we look at experience of attending (or *consuming*) performing arts. Next, we divide the performing arts into two groups. One we call *classical performance* because of its popularity with traditional audiences, who often attend events for their social and lifestyle gratification. The other, *popular performance,* refers to events that are more accessible to mass audiences of varied socioeconomic levels and interests. Capitalizing on niche or narrow markets, popular arts performances draw audiences from geographic and demographic segments that are often more interested in the performance itself than in the spectacle surrounding it. As interactive performance increases in popularity, distinctions between the two sections become blurred. Live theater that incorporates video or animation into its performance is just one example of genre mixing that is gaining popularity among audiences of both classical and popular events.

CONSUMING PERFORMANCE: A MODEL OF LIFE EXPERIENCE

A unique combination of factors is involved in buying or consuming performance experiences. Each consumer responds to a particular aesthetic that lends to or prohibits enjoyment of a performance—for example, some like classical concerts, whereas others prefer raves. Experiences are a result of multiple motives, often unconscious (for example, attending an opera because doing so is seen as a high-status activity may be an unconscious motive). Some consumers enjoy the ritual behavior that accompanies performance (for example, formal attire and behavior are expected at opera performances). Attendance is often determined by situation-specific opportunities (for example, short-run performances limit our attendance options). Experiences are strongly influenced by social interaction, such as intermission criticism or post-performance conversation. Finally, recollections of events influence repeat consumption. In other words, if you enjoyed the event, you will probably attend another.

As yet, no theory exists to explain and predict the buying-consuming experiences associated with attending performing arts. A perspective called *general living systems theory*,[259] however, is appropriate for modeling consumer experiences. This theory suggests that all living systems are self-regulating, with a number of subsystems that are characterized by feedback loops. This means that information regarding behavioral outcomes can potentially form the basis for ongoing activities,[260] which is a suitable model for the interplay between consumers' experiences of the performing arts and the sociocultural environment of those consumers. Using this model, we can better understand the thoughts, feelings, and actions associated with attending performing arts.

The Consumption System

The system relevant for attending performing arts includes behavioral triggers, consumption motives, and consuming activities that are embedded in long-term memory and experiences of everyday lives. Behavioral triggers include such factors as the following:

☆ *Intro-personal factors* such as social class, occupation, ethnicity, gender identity, experience, involvement, and personality. For instance, a person's love of rock music with symphony is a taste typical of outgoing upper middle class baby boomers in affluent Western societies.[261]

☆ *Interpersonal factors* (which influence the social interaction that occurs while attending) include (a) the number of companions, (b) type of relationship between them, (c) content, frequency, and timing of interaction, and (d) knowledge of similarity in tastes and preferences.[262] A person may attend with another person to experience shared enjoyment of the performance form.

☆ *Product factors*, which include the attributes of performing arts.

☆ *Situational factors* that affect psychological and physical states, such as time, money, energy, health, mood, and so forth. An audience member may be relaxed because she has a reliable baby sitter during her theater date.

Consumption Motives

Research indicates that people have multiple motives for attending performances. Some of those motives and desired consequences include the following:[263]

☆ *Enrichment motives,* such as emotional stimulation, intellectual enhancement, and experiencing extraordinary states of being.

☆ *Reduction motives,* including a recovery of energy through relaxation and escapism from work and responsibilities.

☆ *Communion motives,* which give the participant a sense of attachment with others, friendship, and connecting with celebrities.

☆ *Distinction motives,* such as feeling unique, experiencing the power of choice, feeling superior to others, and comparing oneself to others through fashion or reaction to the performance.

Consuming Activities

One typology of consumption practices was made from an observation of baseball spectators; that observation viewed sport consumption as play.[264] The factors (or practices) from this typology are listed here because they are useful for explaining and predicting consuming experiences of performance audiences:

☆ *Acquiring practices*—Help audience members seek information, such as a critic's review prior to attending; planning for future events, such as buying a season subscription; making choices, such as deciding to have dinner after a show.

☆ *Experiencing practices*—Help audience members make sense of events, such as the translation crawler presented during an Italian opera; passing judgment through personal assessment of the performance quality; appreciating a performance though emotional responses to it.

☆ *Integrating practices*—Help consumers become informed, such as by attending preconcert talks; by contributing to the performance through laughter or applause; by personalizing the event for your own enjoyment.

☆ *Self-expression practices*—Help consumers express themselves, such as by bonding with fellow audience members; making oneself distinctive by sitting in a box seat; exhibiting status by wearing expensive jewelry.

☆ *Socializing practices*—Help consumers socialize, such as by sharing the experience with others during intermission; by dancing with others at a rock concert; or by telling jokes after the show.

Every consumer has different motives for attending a performance; these reasons may evolve and change as they become more avid audience members. Some consumers consume leisure conspicuously by using performance attendance to communicate status. Status of this type is associated with three types of effects, all of which result from bragging or flaunting the ability to pay, acquire tickets for, or attend an event to impress other people:[265]

1. *Veblen effects* occur when one pays an exorbitant amount for a ticket—for example, $400 to see Robin Williams perform live.

2. *Snob effects* occur when one acquires a scarce ticket—for example, to see Elton John perform in the Acropolis in Athens.

3. *Bandwagon effects* occur when someone attends an event—for example, a rave—because everyone else is attending.

A performing arts audience member stores information about the consumption before, during, and after the event that results in both implicit (unconscious) and explicit (conscious) memories. These memories influence their enjoyment of current and future performance experiences. By watching how people make sense of both their past and future experiences, we may better understand how consumers select and enjoy live performance.

FORMAL ATTIRE REQUESTED: CLASSICAL PERFORMANCE[266]

From the days of Greek theater, the performing arts have traditionally been categorized by events that appeal to either *elite* or *mass* audiences. Contemporary critics characterize elites (the upper class) as people who dress up in expensive clothing, pay high ticket prices, and attend only socially acceptable performances with their socially acceptable friends. For many elites, the spectacle is more important than the quality of the performance. Appearance at these events reinforces social status and proclaims identity as a member of the elite group. With the passing of the generation that embraced the elite tradition, however, this attitude is disappearing.

As attendance at expensive performance venues declines, arts marketers are devising creative ways to package the theater, ballet, and opera for younger audiences. The trend is away from stuffy, dark performance venues to open-air, well-lighted presentations. Preconcert discussions, out-of-venue performances, and star power are being used to reduce the audience intimidation factor and to compete with mediated and other forms of entertainment. Short performances are being presented in shopping malls, elementary and junior high schools, and in public parks free of charge. Opera arias are sung in urban parks, and the Santa Fe Chamber Orchestra even performs in a department store. Each of these events helps to bring performance to a wider audience and to build attendance at performance venues.

Sociologists study classical performance audiences and their lifestyles for attendance motivations. Based on the premise that identity is derived from association, audiences frequent events that fit their desired social status. Ticket prices and expected attire have promoted self-selection by audiences who are attracted to status-driven entertainment. With the encroachment of popular culture into even the highest-brow performances, however, audiences are becoming homogenized.

Important to the continuing health of all forms of classical performance is *corporate sponsorship*. Arts venue managers solicit corporate sponsors and individual donations to support these programs; only a few receive government assistance from the National Endowment for the Arts. Used as a public relations tool for troubled industries, arts philanthropy helps bolster the corporate image of companies suffering from poor associations. The benefits are not always mutual. As with their media counterparts, live concerts must incorporate brands into publicity and promotion for their financial survival. Corporations are attracted to performance sponsorships because of the image they reflect. By underwriting a ballet, for instance, an oil company may enhance its otherwise unfavorable image by associating with an upscale, classical event. Next time you attend a live performance, check the program to see who is sponsoring the event and what that sponsorship is intended to provide for the donor. One danger posed by sponsorship affiliation is the loss of creative freedom for arts organizations. There is a tendency among some corporations to "possess" their sponsorship partners; however, as long as audiences are not forced to suffer commercial breaks, no one seems to mind the marriage.

This section presents an overview of performances traditionally presented to audiences who appreciate classical arts: theater, musicals, opera, dance, ballet, and symphony. Each event has its own tradition and following, and all are important for the roles they play in shaping our social and cultural identity.

Curtain Rising:
Drama, Opera, Musicals, and Orchestral Concerts

Although we don't know exactly how the theater came into being, we do accept the traditions born in ancient Athens as dominant in Western theater. Basically, theater can be described at its most fundamental as the presence of an actor in front of an audience. The art of the theater is essentially one of make-believe, or *mimesis*.

Drama

We can trace the origins of *drama* to simple storytelling. The storyteller would disguise his or her voice or create characters through movement and costume. Modern dramatic theater is still concerned with live performances that use action to create a coherent and significant sense of drama. Aristotle suggested that drama (tragedy in particular) would affect everybody by eliciting the emotions of pity and fear, which would bring about a purging of these emotions. Such a notion, called *catharsis doctrine,* is the cornerstone of drama theory.[267]

For us to become involved in the plot, drama requires a degree of *plausibility.* The actors' ability to make the audience believe in their speech, movement, thoughts, and feelings determines believability. The connection established between the actors' impressions and the director's intentions contributes to this process. Make-believe is a factor of the distance that exists between actor and audience. To be successful, drama must contain realism, and the characters must seem plausible to reduce the distance and engage members of the audience in the action.

Opera

Opera is drama set to music. The story is presented in a series of vocal pieces with orchestral accompaniment, overtures, and interludes. With origins in drama of the Middle Ages, opera developed along national lines during the 19th century. Italy, Germany, Spain, and France were most active in producing operatic performances. Italian composer Giuseppe Verdi's famous *Rigoletto, Il Trovatore, La Traviata,* and *Aida* are perhaps the best-known operas presented to American audiences today. Originating in Germany, Richard Wagner's musical drama *Rings* revolutionized opera with the breadth and scope of its performance. French opera, noted for its beautiful melodies and incorporation of ballet, and Spanish operas, which combine the intoxicating rhythm of gypsy dancing with the passion of bull-fights, are presented less frequently in the United States. Beginning performances in 1878 in Central City, Colorado, American language opera has yet to be perceived as more than musical theater by opera aficionados.

Foreign-language operas once intimidated audiences but, with the advent of digitized text translations, Americans are becoming more willing to approach operatic performance. And the emergence of opera stars has popularized this genre's music. Public Broadcasting's televised presentation of the Three Tenors (Luciano Pavarotti, Placido Domingo, and José Carreras) attracted younger and more eclectic audiences to opera music. A performance by the Three Tenors brought 200,000 people to New York's Central Park in 1999, contributing to the integration of opera into our popular culture.

Originally intended as musical drama for the masses, opera was often performed outdoors for families, who sang along while they ate homemade bread and drank homemade wine. In Verona, Italy, you can still partake in such a spectacle during the summer season, when operas are performed in an ancient coliseum before thousands of enthusiasts. Operatic arias are often performed at no charge for the public in San Francisco's Golden Gate Park, continuing the Italian open-air tradition in an abbreviated format.

Musicals

Generally speaking, Americans prefer their opera "light." *Musical theater,* one of the most entertaining outgrowths of opera, receives the highest numbers of attendance, awards, and recognition of all operatic forms. The universal appeal of song and dance has rendered musical theater the most popular show type. America is credited with pioneering modern classic musicals such as *Oklahoma, West Side Story, My Fair Lady,* and *A Chorus Line.* The most recent musical versions to hit Broadway feature media stars and popular music, setting to music story lines from a variety of popular genres.

Operettas, vaudeville, and burlesque (also called *revues*) were forerunners of modern musicals; *operettas* alternate language and song, *vaudeville* is a series of variety acts, and *burlesque* satirizes other theatrical forms. Emerging strongly in the 1920s and 1930s, the musical comedies of Irving Berlin, Cole Porter, and Richard Rogers were very popular among theatergoers. Dance forms associated with the musical—such as tap, jazz, ballroom, and disco—were popularized by famous dancers and choreographers. Indeed, Fred Astaire and Gene Kelly took musical dance to the status of a genuine art form. In the past 2 decades, however, musical theater has become more fragmented and is slowly being replaced by conceptual musicals such as *Rent* and *Fosse*[268] or by musicals adapted from animated films, such as *The Lion King.*

Orchestral Concerts

Some audiences prefer listening to music for its own sake. A recent historical development, *orchestral concerts* were not a significant feature of musical life until the late 18th century. Moreover, the very concept of *listening* as a specific activity gained acceptance only after public concerts were popularized. For some people, listening to music is a means of self-fulfillment or self-actualization. To those who enjoy national anthems and military marches, it is an expression of choice and freedom. Although other motivations for attending symphonic concerts are still unclear, it is known that music has a profound effect on our emotions.

With the advent of DVD, cable radio, and surround-sound systems, electronic music is often preferred over live orchestral concerts. To revive the dwindling attendance at symphony halls, music directors are integrating popular vocalists and star performers into their concerts. And they are mixing media with live performance. A recent Los Angeles concert combined a symphonic orchestra with classic film cartoons projected on a large screen as a background for the accompanying music. Classical concert subscription sales are enhanced by preconcert lectures and events for single adults to create a social happening that competes with other forms of entertainment for audience attention.

On Your Toes: Ballet and Dance

Ballet developed out of the court spectacles of the Renaissance, in which social dances performed by royalty and aristocracy were presented in harmony with music, pageant, decor, and costume. In the century that followed, ballet became a vehicle of drama, and dancers became characters in a story. Dancers were trained in techniques of noble, comic, or grotesque according to their physique. Like opera, ballet was performed in opera houses for aristocratic audiences.

Figure 10.1 Dancers Perform Modern Interpretations of Ballet

© Corbis.

By the 19th century, Romantic ballet emerged, and the ballerina became an ideal stage figure. Scenarios for ballets were devised by professional writers, or *librettists*. Russian ballet came to the West in the early 1900s, bringing the Kirov and Bolshoi of Leningrad and Moscow on regular tours to the United States. After World War II, modern ballet incorporated diverse and complex dance styles of all kinds into performances. The effortless movement of ballet's Renaissance ancestor lives on in today's ballet, distinguishing it from other forms of dance.

Just in case you think ballet is still an activity for women wearing tutus, tune into one of the Public Broadcasting Service (PBS) broadcasts to preview the wonderful physical expression that has displaced typical toe dance routines. Modern dance brings new dimension to ballet dramas set to rock and big band music as well as classical pieces. Keeping to the tradition of dramatic performance, ballets tell a story where conflict is danced into resolution.

Traditional *theatrical dance* was developed in the United States and Europe late in the 19th century and received widespread success in the 20th. Today, dance is undergoing a tremendous metamorphosis, the result of a protest against both the balletic and the interpretive dance traditions. Based in ballet and yet related to the improvisatory forms of popular social dance, *modern dance* was defined by the choreography developed and performed by Twyla Tharp's company in New York.

As modern dance changes in the concepts and practices of new generations of choreographers, the meaning of the term *dance* grows more and more ambiguous. The separation of dancer and audience in theater dance has tremendous influence on the style of the dance itself and on its reception as an art form. The professionalism of dancer and choreographer, the presentation of movement, and the use of visual effects reach their most sophisticated levels in modern dance performances.

During the 1960s and 1970s, a new generation of American choreographers, generally referred to as *postmodernists,* replaced conventional dance steps with simple movements such as rolling, walking, skipping, and running. A primary influence on the development of *postmodern dance*, Merce Cunningham began performing in nontheater spaces. He incorporated repetition, improvisation, minimalism, speech or singing, and mixed-media effects into his company's dance routines. Unlike most modern dance performances, postmodern dance concerts are often performed in outside spaces rather than in theaters. In the spirit of Cunningham, postmodernists move in street clothes, use little or no set and lighting, and many performances take place outdoors or in lofts and galleries. Such avant-garde modern-dance companies are small and occupy a position on the fringe of the dance world, attracting only small and specialist audiences. Although mainstream modern dance now attracts large audiences in both Europe and North America, it too was for many decades a minority art form, often playing to only a handful of spectators.

Recently, new energy has invigorated theatrical dance. A look at any week's *New York Times* Sunday entertainment sections will evidence the innovations in modern dance performance. Here are two examples. Pilobolus, a company started by a Dartmouth College student in the early 1970s, combines acrobatics, athletics, and gymnastics with dance as a signature choreographic style. Characterized as *acrobatic mimes*,[269] Pilobolus performs worldwide to musical scores by Paul Sullivan, which bring a unique post-modern element to performance dance. Still appearing and renowned for their unique style, the Merce Cunningham Dance Company presented a run of six events in November 2000 consisting of one-time-only performances of 90 minutes without an intermission. With music and decor conceived and composed separately from the dance, each performance was different. Dancers didn't know for sure what they would be seeing and hearing until the curtain went up, resulting in a totally spontaneous program.[270]

COME AS YOU ARE: POPULAR PERFORMANCE[271]

Popular performance can be any dance, music, theater, or other art form intended to be received and appreciated by ordinary people in a literate, technologically advanced urban society. Popular art in general tends to reinforce mainstream beliefs and sentiments and to create identity in a social group. It is distinguished by rapid changes of style, by its revivals of earlier art periods, and by its constant borrowings from elite art, folk art, foreign cultures, and modern technology for its song tunes and lyrics, dances, trends, and fads.

The term *popular theater* denotes performances in the tradition of the music hall, vaudeville, burlesque, follies, revue, circus, and musical comedy, as distinguished from legitimate, high, or artistic theater. The singers, dancers, comedians, clowns, puppeteers, jugglers, acrobats, and ventriloquists of popular theater make up much of what is known as show business. Vaudeville, once known as "street voices,"[272] was marinated in American barrooms and British music halls. Music, humor, and movement are essential ingredients of what is commonly called popular theater. Music helps bring performer and viewer together in a shared event with no pretense of realism. Humor often distorts reality in the crudity of slapstick or in the mockery of a stand-up comic. Movement presents itself through eroticism, exaggeration, or acrobatics. Here, the distance between audience and actor is accentuated rather than diminished.

We present seven forms of recent trends in popular theater that both extend tradition and resist it: live art, rock concerts, comedy, magic, circus, rodeo, and dog shows. Although each genre has its own following and style, popular performances of all types have one thing in common: the support of passionate followers. As *fans* of popular culture, audiences integrate its fashion and idiosyncratic jargon into their lifestyles. Most fans actively support live performances and often participate in related activities such as Internet chat rooms, fan clubs, and reunions. The trends that continue to provide pop culture fans with innovative and unique forms of popular entertainment are presented in this section.

Unusual Stuff: Performance Art[273]

Performance art or *live art* comes in a variety of forms, including monologue, personal ritual, dance theater, and artists' cabaret. Performance art is differentiated from classical performance in that live art

- ☆ is relevant to current events,
- ☆ has a spontaneous level of creativity,
- ☆ involves small groups,
- ☆ costs little to produce, and
- ☆ has a brief duration.

The history of performance throughout the 20th century shows performance to be an experimental laboratory for some of the most original and radical art forms. Performance provides incomparable material for examining contemporary viewpoints on issues like the body, gender, or multiculturalism.

The term *performance art* implies a state of perpetual animation. We can see performance in works of artistic creation in Jackson Pollock's *action paintings,* which are developed to musical interludes during which he literally flings paint onto canvas. In the film *Pollock* (2000), Ed Harris in the title role depicts the artist's performance style, which is paramount for understanding and appreciating his art. "Earth artist" Christo, whose works are also considered performance art, wraps landscapes and buildings in various materials. Christo has wrapped forms such as 11 islands in Biscayne Bay near Miami, Florida, in 1983 (his Surrounded Islands project) and the Reichstag in Berlin, Germany, in 1995. His performances include planning, constructing, and dismantling the massive projects, which are photographed and preserved in books about each installation.

In recent decades, performance and live art have been very pervasive. In 1961, composer and fluxus (graffiti) artist Yoko Ono performed a work of text and sounds called "strawberries and violin" at Carnegie Hall. In 1972, Judy Chicago's performance art dealt with the trauma of rape using a soundtrack of women recalling their experiences. In the 1980s, actor Spalding Gray used the language of a monologue to describe a particular landscape, establishing his poetic journalistic form as a genre within performance art. Because of the continuing popularity of performance art, museums are now commissioning curators to mount major exhibits that include it.

Rock 'n' Rollin': Band Bashes

The audience for popular music (as distinct from the music of the concert hall) grew tremendously in the first half of the 20th century, partly because of technological developments. In 1954, electronic instruments accompanied Elvis Presley's nondenominational music, which incorporated everything from hillbilly rave-ups and blues wails to pop-crooner ballads. A term commonly used as a euphemism for sex, *rock and roll* became Presley's signature. His music oozed sexuality. The frenzied involvement of the adolescent girls in his concert audiences sometimes required ambulances to treat the fainting swooners. Teen audiences became the prime target for *concerts,* which people attended to hear most new forms of popular music.

An American rock band that played improvisational psychedelic music, the Grateful Dead was one of the most successful *touring bands* in rock history. The Grateful Dead combined jug bands with musicians in the San Francisco Bay area in the early 1960s. Remarkably eclectic, the Dead provided a key part of the free live music filling San Francisco during 1967's Summer of Love, when the city became a magnet for hippie baby boomers. The Dead created a new form of American performance follower: the groupie. Dead Heads, as their fans were known, epitomized the counterculture. Draped in flowing scarves and granny dresses, they danced for hours to the jamming band. The Dead pooled eclectic talents to pioneer an energizing blend of rock instrumentation and jazzy improvisation.

Meanwhile, other *psychedelic bands* were drawing their share of enthusiasts. The 13th Floor Elevators from Austin, Texas, reflected the darker, more psychotic frenzy of acid rock.

Acid was characterized by overdriven guitars, amplified feedback, and droning guitar motifs that were influenced by Eastern music. Pink Floyd was the leading group of the British scene, which revolved around venues such as London's UFO club and Middle Earth. Events like the 14-Hour Technicolor Dream drew counterculture celebrities such as John Lennon, Yoko Ono, and Andy Warhol. Although few psychedelic bands lasted, the impact of the genre was huge, revolutionizing fashion, poster art, and live performance.

Another aggressive form of music, *punk rock,* coalesced into an international movement between 1975 and 1980. Full of vital energy beneath a sarcastic and hostile facade, punk became an archetype of teen rebellion and alienation. If the names Slits, Raincoats, and 101ers are not familiar, brush up on your punk rock history at www.punkrock.org. You can check out bands and song titles on www.punkrockacademy.com or locate the latest performances on www.worldwidepunk.com. In the 1990s, Jimmy Buffet's audience flocked to his concerts in Hawaiian shirts to celebrate tropical fantasy in much the same manner as the Dead Heads had embraced their band decades before. The emergence of boy bands and rappers drew equally frenzied fans as the rock concert era continued to evolve into today's version of a high-energy musical event. Enhanced with giant video screens, light shows, and Dolby sound systems, musical concerts draw audiences by the thousands to large arenas and outdoor venues. Audience involvement in live band concerts makes them a popular form of live entertainment.

Yucks-R-Us: Comedy

Comedy has always been a form of popular expression performers used to deliver political and social messages to live audiences. Parodies, satires, off-color jokes, and slapstick have amused audiences for decades in nightclubs, county fairs, and amateur nights. Joke telling and comedy have grown to be acceptable performance formats for expressing opinions and critiquing society.

Comedy also can include humor used to ridicule people we dislike. According to Plato, the primary source of humor's amusement is its "display of vain conceit and self-aggrandizement where detested traits are humbled by a cutting punch line."[274] Why do we get pleasure from the misfortune of others? Because by making fun of other people's predicaments, we can forget our own. Mood management theory suggests that frustrated men and angry women tend to pick comedy more than people of other temperaments do. Through comedy, anger dissipates. For many of us, humor appears to hold promise as a mood repairer by offering up light-hearted solutions to adverse conditions. See Chapter 4 for other theories that explain our reactions to comedy and humor.

In times of stress, many people seek out laughter and relief. One place they can find a heavy concentration of humor in the form of jokes is a club specializing in comedy. *Comedy clubs* specifically dedicated to humor and improvisation have been around since 1960 and were very active until the 1980s when the proliferation of second-tier comedians who were neither funny nor affordable diminished audiences. The best-known venue for comedy was Chicago's Second City, where Bill Murray, John Belushi, and Chris Farley began their careers.

In a theater that seats 300, Second City performers still combine scripted sketches with bits improvised from audience ideas in shows performed every night of the week.

The Ice House, a San Gabriel Valley (California) folk music club, started featuring comedy in the 1970s when Lily Tomlin and the Smothers Brothers recorded albums there. The club recently added an annex to present weekend Comedy Clinics. San Francisco's Improv hosted comics like Robin Williams, who still appears there on occasion to try out new routines. Veterans of stand-up comedy, talk show hosts David Letterman and Jay Leno, use comedy to recast current events in nightly televised monologues to live audiences. *Saturday Night Live*, which began with an improvisational format, also features former club comics in its sketch-parodies.

Many "open mikes" are available in bars and malls, where aspiring comedians can perform before live audiences. Men and women aiming for television auditions often begin their careers with original material at open mikes, graduate to comedy clubs, and eventually get an agent to promote them. The newsgroup www.alt.comedy.standup, which is dedicated to communication among agents, writers, and comics, provides professionals with opportunities to interact and connect with one another—all in an attempt to amuse audiences with humor.

If it's funny, we laugh. But why? One researcher who recorded 1,200 laugh episodes concluded that most laughter is produced by speakers, not listeners.[275] In other words, we laugh more when our entertainer laughs. Also, a gender disparity in laugh rates was discovered, with women surpassing men. Ideally, then, performers should gravitate to female audiences for the most active laughter available.

For whatever reason, comedy has had an important place in entertaining live audiences since jesters and clowns became professionals. Requiring a quick wit, the ability to write, and nerve enough to perform before live audiences, today's stand-up comics are tomorrow's television and film stars. Their take on society, well crafted into funny anecdotes and characterizations, provides insight into ourselves and others that may be no laughing matter.

Now You See It, Now You Don't: Magic[276]

A magician is an actor who pretends to do something impossible. The fire-eater, for instance, uses a loosely woven rope specially treated with chemicals to catch fire when it's removed from his throat. Onlookers see the rope's glow as it is swallowed and believe in the illusion. Using the psychology of deception and timing, magicians have mystified audiences for centuries. Sorcerers were thought to use supernatural powers to gain control over natural forces. Closely akin to religion, magic as entertainment surpassed the appeal of magic in religious ritual as early as 2500 B.C. In the 4th century, Christian theology denounced magicians, and they were outlawed. By the Middle Ages, magicians were condemned as witches and devil worshipers, and they were tortured and killed.

Centuries passed before magic could again be performed in public. During the Renaissance, traveling entertainers began performing before royalty and, by the 16th century, there were professional magicians doing card tricks, reading minds, and making object disappear. Called *illusionists,* magicians passed the secrets of their trade from generation to generation by word of mouth. Not until 1612, when *Subtle and Pleasant Tricks* was published in English, were illusionary skills made available in print. When magic arrived in the British colonies of North America, Puritans condemned the idle amusement as the work of the devil. Only after the Revolution in 1776 was magic acceptable as a source of entertainment in America.

Called the father of *modern magic,* Robert Houdin introduced stage illusions using electricity, perfected the thought-transference trick, and used common objects to create illusions. A generation later, Harry Houdini took his name. A trapeze artist by trade, Houdini began performing amazing escapes in the 1890s. His routines began with getting out of straitjackets and handcuffs, and they progressed to an act in which he was shackled with irons and placed in a box that was locked, roped, weighted, and submerged underwater. Entertainers such as "the Coney Island Fakir" (a.k.a., the mind reader Joseph Dunninger) and hypnotic routines performed by "the Amazing Kreskin" dominated the 1940s.

After a wane in the popularity of magic, David Copperfield revived illusion by performing tricks at the age of 12 to enthralled television audiences. Best known for his ability for making large objects disappear (he made an airplane disappear from an airport runway), Copperfield staged an escape from Alcatraz prison in 1987. And taking up the trick planned but never completed by Houdini (who died first of a ruptured appendix), David Blaine is best known for his spectacle of entombment. He spent 72 hours inside a block of ice in front of the ABC building in New York, for instance. Most of his illusions are performed for individuals rather than before large audiences. To interest a kid on the street, Blaine will remove his baseball cap, reach inside, and pull out a large snake. And he doesn't charge admission. The antithesis of showman Copperfield, Blaine's style is low key—no stage, no lights, no smoke, no curtains. It's just himself and a random audience.[277]

One of the most famous venues for illusion is the Magic Castle, a 1908 Victorian mansion located in the hills above Hollywood. The Castle is a clubhouse for the Academy of Magical Arts, an organization established to encourage and promote public interest in the ancient art of magic. Although popular performances don't usually require a dress code, one is enforced at the Castle for audiences who come to watch performers create illusions that have the appearance of reality.[278]

Magic continues to captivate live audiences composed of people who have become numb to the visual deceptions of mass media. To keep magic alive, a computer consultant from New Jersey recently purchased the old Manhattan magic emporium once owned by Harry Houdini. The emporium began as a small toy shop in Germany run by the infamous Matrinka brothers that was known as the "Palace of Magic." A fellow named "Carter the Great" once kept a live lion in the palace's back room, scaring shoppers in front of the store with the beast's loud roars. Preferring a more commercial endeavor, the shop's new owner is reviving the emporium as an Internet magic retailer and online magic museum where neophyte magicians and collectors of Houdini memorabilia can buy products from the shop's archives.[279]

Figure 10.2 The Magic Castle in Los Angeles

The Greatest Show on Earth: The Circus

A descendant of Roman amphitheater performances, the modern *circus* was not organized into a distinct entertainment until the mid 18th century in England. Philip Astley, a trick rider, built a horse ring and engaged a clown, musicians, and other performers to stage dramatic attractions for commoners. Circuses were opened in Philadelphia and New York by 1793 and, within a few decades, circus families became prominent. Members of circus families were trained from childhood in the skills passed from one generation to another: riding, tumbling, ballet, and acrobatics. Aerial stunts, performed by the Walenda family on the flying trapeze, are examples of the traditions once popular in circus attractions.

Circus entertainment combines the suspense of acrobatics, the comedy of clowns, and curiosity about wild animals into a unique blend of enjoyment. Most Americans have heard about or have attended a Ringling Brothers and Barnum & Bailey Circus. These traveling shows were the highlight of pretelevision entertainment, causing young children to dream of joining the circus when they were old enough to leave home. The 130-year-old "greatest show on earth" still performs at Madison Square Garden and other venues around America. Although attendance at circuses remains steady, such large venues are hard to fill.[280]

Touring smaller towns in Northern New England, Circus Smirkus performs in recreation fields, town commons, and state parks rather than in large-capacity arenas. This circus, composed primarily of kids from 10 to 20 years old, begins practicing in June after school lets out. Smirkus begins with a spectacular opening act, a *charivori*, which brings out the full troupe in a rush of tumbling and acrobatics.[281] Smirkus provides a solid training ground of global coaching for circuses such as Big Apple, Ringling Brothers and Barnum & Bailey, and Cirque du Soleil.

Profile Peek: Circus OZ

As nostalgia of the circus fades, new forms of tent performances are emerging from around the globe. Australia has Circus OZ, a loopy, irreverent assortment of clowns, acrobats, and musicians who spritz water, walk upside down, ride flaming unicycles across a high wire, hang by their hair, and swing out over the audience in a trapeze act that brings a whole new dimension to the idea of catcher.[282] This show begins with its signature act, where members of the company, costumed like classical white marble statues, strike poses of balletic form while spraying themselves with mouthfuls of water. Accompanied by a funky onstage band, the troupe defies gravity by walking upside down high above the stage while drinking from a glass to Frank Sinatra's *My Way*.

As a descendant of slapstick, OZ brings elements of comedy and the unexpected to a traditional form of entertainment. In your opinion, does the inclusion of slapstick enhance or detract from a performance experience? Why? What kinds of audiences might enjoy a night out with OZ?

Devoted to performing for charity, Big Apple Circus is a nonprofit, one-ring show. The circus was created by the New York School for Circus Arts and has been supporting children's charity organizations since 1979. You can learn all about circus history, circus stars, and circus careers on Big Apple's Web site, www.bigapplecircus.org. Today, traditional circuses present only one performance a year in each city. In spite of the circus's new innovations, the children of technology are preoccupied with Game Boys and video arcades, rarely hearing about the big-top shows until they hit town. Still, for one of the most exciting and spontaneous live shows available today, the circus is your best bet.

Responding to a demand for technologically innovative entertainment, the circus's struggle to retain its popularity as a local attraction has yielded new hybrid forms of ringside entertainment. The most recent innovation, nouveau cirque, is circus without animals, clowns, or fire-eaters. Started in 1984 in France, the Cirque Plume pioneered the idea of blending theater, music, dance, magic, acrobatics, and comedy and calling it circus. The group's 2001 show, Melanges, casts 18 performers in a host of different roles—instrumentalists, comedians, magicians, and trapeze or tightrope artists—where inventiveness is favored over daring.[283]

Cirque du Soleil, a Canadian hybrid, was organized as a festival in 1984 by street performers in Quebec. The Boie St. Paul Fair brought performers together to exchange techniques, combining dance, music, and ballet. Now performing in 120 cities worldwide, Cirque employs 500 performers from four global headquarters. Recent shows include "Nauba" at Disney World in Florida, "O" and "Misterie" in Las Vegas, and "Dralion," which was performed around the world in 1999 and 2000. Best described as a kaleidoscope of adventure, Cirque du Soleil has performed in tents outside major cities to more than 23 million people. Although you can enjoy a portion of Cirque's attractions by visiting its Web site, www.cirquedusoleil.com, this theatrical hybrid can be fully enjoyed only by audiences who visit Cirque shows in person. Why do you think this circus shuns televising its performances? How would you judge Cirque's chances of continuing success without using mass media to reach audiences?

Buckin' Broncos: The Rodeo

By combining the thrill of circus acts with the primitive conflict of a sporting event, Westerners developed the *rodeo*. This series of contests and exhibitions in riding, roping, and other cowboy skills was developed between 1867 and 1887. Audiences cheered for bull riders, steer wrestlers, saddle and bareback bronco riders, and steer or calf ropers. Cheyenne, Wyoming, which claims to be the birthplace of the rodeo, has presented Frontier Days every year since 1897. For the past 25 years, the number of rodeos, attendance, and purse money has increased, and women now compete in their own rodeos, with barrel racing as the main event.

Horses and steers play key roles in rodeos as adversaries to chapped and hatted riders and wrestlers. After calves are released from chutes, calf ropers must rope them so that three hooves are tied together in under 15 seconds to be competitive. Champion wrestlers throw steers in record 10-second times. During riding events, contestants must stay on the horse for 8 seconds, holding on with one hand while being judged on a point system for their performance.

Rodeo audiences can relive the excitement of the Old West, watching as man is pitted against a beast in the ultimate competition to tame or be tamed. They cheer their favorite performers and partake in festivities that are reminiscent of frontier times. The lure of the authentic is a primary motivation for rodeo participants. A truly American form of entertainment, the rodeo has an established place in popular culture history and is still enjoyed by enthusiasts throughout the western United States.

Fido Follies: Dog Shows

Animal competitions have always been popular with American audiences, but the *dog show* craze has swept the nation. Parodied in the film *Best in Show* (2000), canine competitions pair dogs and owners or trainers against judges who rate the dogs for structure, coat, and movement. Dog shows—attended by prospective buyers as well as owners—feature barking noises, prancing movements, petting gestures, grooming rituals, and fancy trophies. Each breed is shown at a certain time in a special ring, and dogs are judged for their conformity to the breed standard. Dog fanciers attend shows every weekend, meeting friends and competing through their dogs. For participants, dog showing is much more than a hobby— it's a lifestyle. For audiences, dog watching is pure spectacle.

Breed rings present different levels of competition, and dogs that are not champions compete at the class level by sex. Each class—puppy, novice, American bred, bred by exhibitor, and open—has four placement awards. Winners of placement awards qualify for the next level of competition, which yields "Best" awards: Best of Breed, Best of Sex, and Winner. Best of Breed dogs are eligible to show in the *group*, the place where the real competition begins. Breeds are divided into seven groups: Sporting, Hound, Working, Terrier, Toy, Non-Sporting, and Herding. The winning dog in each group then competes for the grand prize, Best in Show. With the multiple judging stages that contestants need to progress through to win, competitors must devote significant time and energy to the showing process.

Dog ratings are compiled by dog publications or breed clubs and convey prestige to only the top dogs in the country. With 70% of Americans owning dogs these days, dog shows are popular events where people and pets meet and mingle amid the flurry of regimented fanfare. A walk through the grooming area provides a look at the best ambassadors of their respective breeds—perfect specimens. Everyone agrees: There is no substitute for the live action dog show extravaganza.

Identification theory provides one explanation for our K-9 fascination. Owners derive a sense of esteem through their pet's accomplishments. The pride of ownership that accompanies a blue ribbon has less to do with the animal's championship lines than it does with a human desire for recognition. A positive relationship is found to exist between the corresponding levels of recognition from winning and enjoyment of participation. In other words, winners have more fun. Spectators who compare owner to pet may notice an uncanny similarity between the two, which reinforces the notion of shared identity.

FADE TO BLACK

What you learned from this chapter is that when you turn off the television and log off the Internet to participate in live performances, you are in for a treat. The performance arts entertain us in ways that mediated forms cannot. As an audience member, you get to participate in what's happening, sing along, clap, stamp your feet, and cheer. And you get to do it with 10,000 of your closest friends. Performance has entertainment value, economic value, and social value. We can escape from routine for just a few dollars or even for free. We can laugh, cry, and lose ourselves in the experience of the moment. Most audiences agree that no other form of entertainment is as fulfilling as live performance.

We hope that live performance is not a dying art because it brings to us an element of the real that no other type of entertainment can. We get to feel, see, taste, touch, smell, and hear everything in person. As audiences, we can actively participate in performance success. Think about it: Real people performing real music, art, and theater in real time. What a concept! By supporting these events, we can maintain our connection with the aesthetic, with the beautiful, and with our cultural past. As the ancestors of mass media, the performing arts reflect centuries of talent and spirit. These arts are our heritage and our future; they also serve well as ambassadors to our global community.

 A Closer Look

Motivating Performing Arts Audiences[284]

How popular are the performing arts among people in their twenties and thirties? Accused of being media junkies, young adults are said to be uninterested in anything that isn't featured on the big screen. To test this criticism for accuracy, a class of college seniors attending a western state university asked potential audiences four questions about their entertainment preferences:

☆ Why do you think attendance is dropping at live performances?
☆ Who goes to these performances?
☆ Why do people go to live performances?
☆ How can the performing arts become more attractive to audiences?

Over a period of six weeks, students went to local entertainment venues, such as malls and cinema complexes, to identify people willing to talk to them for 30 minutes. Interviews were then set up, tape-recorded, transcribed, and analyzed for similarities and differences of responses. They interviewed 17 men and 42 women ages 24 to 37 with incomes averaging $45,000. Married persons accounted for 62% of the sample, and 43% of the participants had children.

This is a synopsis of responses to the four questions. For each answer, short quotes representative of typical answers are presented here.

People identified five reasons for not going to performing arts.

Reason	Statement
Money	"I'd rather go do something less expensive than pay $50 to see a play."
Planning	"Sometimes you have to get tickets 3 months in advance to attend a concert."
Exposure	"My parents never took me to a live show, so I really don't know what I'm missing. And kids don't get arts in school any more. How are we supposed to learn about it?"
Hi-Tech	"With 120 TV channels and 25 movie places around, you don't have to go out to a play or whatever to be entertained."
Lack of Promotion	"Movies have trailers, but shows just have small ads in the paper with a phone number to call for tickets. We really don't know what's out there by the ads."

The main reason people go to performing arts is previous exposure. Here are some sample responses that support this finding:

☆ "I had music and drama in boarding school, and we had to play in the orchestra. I think people who have had that training go to see live performances."
☆ "We saw plays in elementary school."
☆ "My parents took me every Christmas to see the Nutcracker ballet."

The main factor identified as motivation for attending performing arts is experience and appreciation. Here are some sample responses:

☆ "Someone who hasn't heard of Mendelssohn certainly won't sit through a violin concerto—they'd rather have sticks in their eyeballs."

☆ "When I heard Italian tenors in Italy, grown men were sobbing their eyes out. I didn't do that when the Rams moved out of LA."

☆ "Performance is a wonderful experience, a chance to see extraordinary talent."

☆ "Music is so emotional when it's live."

According to the survey, the two best ways to improve attendance are the following:

Expose kids early and often

☆ "With 2,400 kids at one high school, why not bring dance and music to the auditorium?"

☆ "If they won't go to *Swan Lake,* take *Swan Lake* to them."

☆ "Field trips to concerts should be mandatory for students in junior high."

Do better marketing

☆ "I think putting previews on TV would help people know what's out there."

☆ "Ticket giveaways on radio stations might help."

☆ "How about giving subscriptions as gifts at holidays by selling them to parents and grandparents?"

Student researchers reached the following conclusions about performance arts:

Exposure DRIVES experience.

Experience DRIVES appreciation.

Appreciation DRIVES attendance.

Only by conducting constant research can we understand what drives audiences toward or away from performing arts. Although it was not scientifically valid, this research exercise helped students to understand the complex issues involved in selecting entertainment choices.

How well does this research reflect your own views on attending live performance?

DISCUSSION AND REVIEW

1. Do highbrow and lowbrow distinctions exist today with regard to audiences? To entertainment types? How can you tell?

2. What role do humor and jokes play in sportscasting? In politics?

3. Discuss the marketing potential for televising and promoting dog shows to people who are not dog owners. What is the role for product endorsement and sponsorship opportunities?

EXERCISES

1. Using the calendar or entertainment section of your city's Sunday newspaper as a source, count the number of live performances offered this week. How does the number compare with the competing sports, film, and other entertainment offerings? Do your findings substantiate the chapter's notion of reduced offerings in the performing arts?

2. Visit a Web site dedicated to magic or comedy and consult the links as well as the content. If you were interested in attending a live performance, would the site help you locate a local venue? Does the site recommend places you can learn more about magic and comedy performances? Would you classify these events as suitable for elite or mass audiences? Why?

3. Recall a live performance that you have attended within the past few months, or attend one. Do you define it as classical or popular art? Was your attendance motivation social or are you interested in a particular performance genre? What role did the audience play in your enjoyment of the performance? Do you agree with the chapter's assertion that live performance depends upon audience reaction? Why?

RECOMMENDED READINGS AND WEB SITES

Anderson, J. (1999). *Art without boundaries: The world of modern dance.* Iowa City, IA: University of Iowa Press.
Christopher, M. (1973). *The illustrated history of magic.* New York: Crowell.
Cunningham, M. (1999). *Live and kicking: The rock concert industry in the nineties.* London: Sanctuary.
Kaye, E., & Barnes, C. (1991). *American Ballet Theater: 25-year retrospective.* Kansas City, MO: Andrews McMeel.
Wagner, R., & Ellis, W. A. (1995). *Actors and singers.* Lincoln, NE: University of Nebraska Press.
At http://cc.com, enter your zip code and find out about music, theater, and comedy shows, as well as other live entertainment performing nearby.
At http://memory.loc.gov/ammem/vshtml/vshome.html, find out how to access the American Variety Stage (1870-1920) multi-media anthology from the Library of Congress.
At www.geocities.com, find out what's happening in cities all over the United States.

11

Challenge or Chance?

Gaming and Gambling

For when the One Great Scorer comes To write against your name, He marks—not how you won or lost—But how you played the game.

—Grantland Rice

*G*aming is a term used to reference both games of competition and games of chance. From playing hide-and-seek as children to buying lottery tickets as adults, games continue to entertain us. Games of competition require skill; gambling activity, on the other hand, is based primarily on chance. Games of competition are classified as *agon*; racing, chess, and football are examples of agon games. Games of chance, such as flipping a coin, roulette, and lotteries, are classified as *alea*. Originating centuries ago, gaming today accounts for billions of dollars in business revenues. Studied as play, games are based on a mathematical theory that helps us understand rules and strategy. And technology provides us with the ability to accurately calculate probability and chance, and to play online.

This chapter concerns itself with a discussion of how gaming evolved, game theory, casinos, and the latest innovations in today's most popular pastimes: video games and Internet gambling. Lotteries, an ever-growing industry based on fantasy, are also included here.

HISTORICAL ROOTS

As explained in Chapter 1, play and games have been part of our global culture since ancient times. Several European countries developed the forerunner of what we play today. Gambling can be traced back to 2300 B.C., enriching history from the time of the ancient Greeks and Romans to the Elizabethan period. At the height of the Roman Empire, when gaming activity prevailed as the dominant leisure activity, all children were required by law to know how to gamble and throw dice. The French invented playing cards (individually handmade) in 1387, and a full deck of cards was printed by Johan Gutenberg in 1440 Germany.

The evolution of games into gambling occurred in the 16th century with the French working class, who adapted the Egyptian game of roulette. Blackjack caught the attention of Napoleon, and craps was developed by the English from an early form called Hazard. Poker was formed from and influenced by Persian, Italian, and English games of chance. The French refined betting techniques, but it was the British who developed the essential concept of bluffing. It's no wonder that Monaco, the oldest world capital of gambling, is located so close to France—its citizens had a leading role in the development and enjoyment of chance games.

THE PLAY'S THE THING

Every aspect of life has a pervasive sense of play attached to it. To argue that play is a part of the long journey of human civilization is not far from the universal truth, because evidence of play can be found directly in our daily lives. Studies in cultural sociology and anthropology show that play possesses cultural dimensions and exerts symbolic meaning in our society.

The cultural function of play revolves around a notion that the great archetypal activities in human society are all permeated with play.[285] Play has the following characteristics that separate it from other activities in human society:

1. Play is voluntary. Play is part of the natural process because it has a symbolic meaning of freedom. We cannot be forced or ordered to play.

2. Play is not ordinary or real. Rather, play is stepping out of real life into a temporary sphere of activity with a deposition all its own. Play is said to be "a paradox of everyday life in contemporary society."[286]

3. Play is distinct as to locality and duration, with limits in terms of time and place. It has a beginning and an end.

4. All forms of play are governed by rules.

5. Play has a persistent social community that remains even after the game is over. Play has a significant role in communication.

6. Play promotes the sense of secrecy and difference that distinguishes it from the common world. It has a sense of "insiders" and "outsiders" that deem play a distinct social behavior.

7. Play is a sacred and profound activity. It involves rituals, ceremony, and a venue for symbolic representation. (For example, football rituals include cheerleaders, ceremony features audience waves and flagpole climbing, and the gridiron represents gains and losses for opponents.)

As we learned in Chapter 1, games have been classified according to their degree of structure into four types of play. Games of competition, chance, simulation, and vertigo are placed along the dimensions of freedom from paideia (very free) to ludus (very structured). Because games are rule-based, researchers have studied them to develop strategies for winning in other aspects of our lives. Much of play research focuses on game theory.

GAME THEORY

Defined as a branch of applied mathematics, game theory serves as a guide for players and as a tool for predicting the outcome of a game.[287] Originally designed by John von Neumann and Oskar Morgenstern to solve problems in economics, game theory relates economics to a game in which the players anticipate one another's moves. This theory goes beyond the classical theory of probability because it stresses the strategic aspects of game.

Games are grouped into several categories, the simplest of which designates games as being one-person, two-person, or n-person (where n is larger than two). We play video games alone (one-person), play chess with another person (two-person), and play cards with a group (n-person). We also classify games according to the level of information available to players. In games of *perfect information*, such as chess, each player knows everything about the game at all times. Poker, on the other hand, is an example of a game of *imperfect information* because players do not know the cards the other players are dealt.

Games can also be classified as *zero-sum* and *nonzero-sum* by the extent to which the goals of the players are opposed or coincide. Poker is a zero-sum game because the combined wealth of the players remains constant. If one player wins, another must lose, because money is neither created nor destroyed. Nonzero-sum games, which involve barter or trading (such as with baseball cards), do not apply to our discussion of competitive games and gambling.

Finally, games are classified according to the number of decisions players must make. Games with a specific number of decisions to make are *finite*. Specific decisions are characteristic of most parlor games, such as poker, chess, and checkers. *Infinite* games such as lotteries, where there are either an infinite number of alternatives or decisions, are much more complicated than finite games. Our discussion of games and gambling is based upon one, two-person, or n-person, perfect and imperfect, zero-sum, finite games and games of chance, which may involve infinite alternatives.

Focus on the Prisoners' Dilemma

Game theory is often applied to real-life games, where cooperating rather than not cooperating results in winning. To illustrate the kind of problems that arise in games where the players are uncooperative, we offer the celebrated example of the *Prisoners' Dilemma*.[288] Two prisoners, A and B, suspected of committing a robbery together, are isolated and urged to confess. Each is concerned only with getting the shortest possible prison sentence for himself, and each must decide whether to confess to carrying a concealed weapon or remain silent without knowing his partner's decision. Both know the consequences of their decisions: if both confess, both go to jail for five years; if neither confesses, both go to jail for one year. And if one confesses while the other does not, the confessor goes free and the silent one goes to jail for 20 years.

To analyze the Prisoners' Dilemma, we apply the "sure thing" principle. Although A can't be sure what B will do, he knows that he does best to confess when B confesses (he gets five years rather than 20) and also when B remains silent (he serves no time longer than a year); B will reach the same conclusion. So the solution would seem to be that each prisoner does best to confess and go to jail for five years. Paradoxically, the two robbers would do better if they both adopted an "irrational" strategy of remaining silent, where each would serve only one year.

The irony of the Prisoners' Dilemma is that when each of two parties acts selfishly and does not cooperate (that is, when they confess), they do worse than when they act unselfishly and do cooperate (that is, when they remain silent). This principle applies to shopkeepers engaged in a price war or nations competing in an arms race. For shopkeepers, each knows that if he has lower prices than his competitor he will attract the other's customers, and both will earn smaller profits because they now make less on each sale. Similarly, if two nations keep buying more weapons in an attempt to achieve military superiority, neither gains the advantage, and both are poorer than when they started. It is only when the game is played repeatedly and neither player knows when the sequence will end that the cooperative strategy succeeds.

How can we apply the Prisoners' Dilemma to games of chance and gambling?

VIDEO GAMES[289]

Revenue from video games is now larger than profits generated by the film industry. Video game industry energy is expressed by its name, the Prometheus Engine, a unique piece of software used to automate characters, which was inspired by a god in Greek mythology who is believed to have given humans power.[290] Similar to other forms of entertainment, video game players are influenced by the dramatic worldview (see Chapter 1) because they identify with the dramatic structure of plots, conflict building, and resolutions that lead to particular

Figure 11.1   Video games are simulated or virtual reality.

© Corbis.

outcomes. And video games supply players with an array of dramatic consumption that serves their schematic reality.

In video games, digital computers are combined with primitive games for a new breed of finite play. The last three decades witnessed the fast-growing development in Silicon Valley that fosters the changing nature of video game playing.[291] Video games allow high degrees of computerized control, isolate players from other people, and move closer to a hyper-realistic territory. Because video games are simulated or virtual reality, we call them *hyper-real*. Games we played 100 years ago are still being played today, but in an electronic format—sport, board games, and fighting are all part of video game play.

Considered a form of interactive media, video games allow players to engage in a reciprocating exchange of three-dimensional visual communication messages. As modes of popular culture, video games are novelties mass-produced by entrepreneurs for the gratification of a paying audience. Games are created for public consumption, exerting strong emotional impacts on players through various psychological mechanisms. We define *video games* as interactive communication that players engage in while controlling a mediated video content, and games played on a dedicated console or computer screen. Video game types include (a) arcade games (e.g., *Pac-Man*), (b) home-console games (e.g., PlayStation 2, Xbox, and GameCube), (c) handheld games (e.g., Game Boy Advance), and (d) PC games (e.g., *Star Wars Jedi Knight II: Jedi Outcast*).

Video games conform to one of a hybrid of the following genres:[292]

☆ Role-playing games with a plot, based on history or literature stories (e.g., the *Final Fantasy* series)
☆ Real-time strategies involving two groups that fight with each other (e.g., *Starcraft* and *Missile Command*)
☆ First-person shooters who fight with an enemy (e.g., *Doom, Time Crisis,* and *Alien vs. Predators*)
☆ Shoot-'em-up/shooting games (e.g., *Space Invaders, Defenders, Robotron, Galaxian,* and *Battlezone*)
☆ Beat-'em-up/fighting games (e.g., the *Street Fighter* series, *Mortal Kombat, Ready 2 Rumble Boxing,* and *Pro Wrestling*)
☆ Racing games (e.g., the *Grand Turismo* series and *Project Gotham*)
☆ Sport games (e.g., *ISS Pro Evolution, Tony Hawk's Pro Skater,* and *Madden NFL 2001*)
☆ Platform games/exploration games with a series of levels (e.g., *Donkey Kong, Sonic the Hedgehog, Super Mario Brothers,* the *Castlevania* series, the *Tomb Raider* series, the *Mega Man* series, *Myst,* and *Raven*)
☆ Puzzle games (e.g., *Tetris*)
☆ God games (e.g., *Sim City, Sim Theme Parks, Populous, Civilization,* and *Flight Simulator*)

The interactivity of video games engenders a new type of learning experience by allowing players to control subjectively the input in relation to the output. The video game experience is complicated and skill-driven, containing these ingredients:[293]

☆ Players need to use attention to control perception.
☆ Players need to make mental maps of the game-space to notice landmarks and causal relations.
☆ Players need to coordinate visual attention and motor actions (mouse, joystick, or keyboard).
☆ Event-induced arousal is linked to the player's own ability to cope with a given problem.
☆ Players will get a continuous satisfaction from performance.
☆ The game processes are driven by the player's motivation for performing—success and failure are attributed to the player, not to the game-world.

All types of games have multiple levels of difficulty that represent the criteria for judging the player's own performance. Learning also involves self-esteem because a sense of worth evolves as a player judges his or her own competencies. Three characteristics—challenge, curiosity, and fantasy—are important ingredients for enhancing the player's intrinsic motivation in learning to play. Finally, sophisticated technology provides the player with interactive devices that foster learning through a ladder of challenge that shapes self-esteem.

Table 11.1 Narratives of Video Games

Print Narratives (Books)	Interactive Electronic Narratives (Video Games)
Author tells, reader listens	Player is part of story
Author is creative for reader	Designer is creative for player
Cold medium (low participation)	Hot medium (high participation)
Words based	Visual images and sound based
Imagination	Immersion
Strong characterization	Weak characterization
Endings strong	Endings weak or problematic
Reader external to events	Player internal to events
Participation by identification	Actual participation
Characters have freedom	Characters select from available choices
Illustrations simple	Graphics, music, and sound powerful
Story construction hidden	Story construction discovered
Many kinds of structure	Mazes and tangled rhizomes

SOURCE: Adapted from Berger, A. A. (2000). *Video games: A popular culture phenomenon.* London: Transaction Publishers.

Like other media, video games have specific narratives or story lines. In all games, the player must be able to manipulate something; otherwise, it's not a game, it's a movie. The use of interactive elements changes how story narratives are communicated. Table 11.1 provides the differences between print and interactive electronic narratives.

The gaming media have invoked graphic enhancements and microprocessors for a life-like gaming experience. One company that revolutionized gaming graphics is 3DFX, which introduced a graphics card for PCs that is able to generate extreme display pixel enhancements. The Voodoo product line relies on an FX engine chip and a Texture engine that provide an infrastructure for expansion. The latest card in the Verto series currently sets the standard in generating lifelike pixel depth. Not to be outdone, Intel's Pentium 4 processor has a chip structure that delivers the highest performance in video graphics and multimedia that is changing the way we view 3D graphics.

High-Tech Highway

Video game development and impact are a direct result of four factors of technology: advanced computer information processing, machine interactivity, player isolation, and reality simulation. Each is discussed here for its effect on contemporary society.

Advanced Computer Information Processing

Technological advancement in computer information processing is a main contributing factor to the enhancement of video game playfulness. The higher the processing capacity of microcomputer chips that video games contain, the wider the range of spectacular form, content, and interaction the games provide players. The Atari system, released in 1977, dominated the market when computer technology was still in its embryonic period. A milestone in video games history was the release of Nintendo's 8-bit processor entertainment systems in 1985. That same year, Sega began using a Dynamic RAM that allowed more memory access than conventional RAM in its new portable game, Nintendo Game Boy. In 1989, Sega introduced the Genesis system, featuring a 16-bit processor that provided higher graphic resolutions and faster processing ability than ever before. Super Nintendo, which came out in 1991, stayed in the lead until 1995, when Sega introduced a 32-bit processor. Not to be outdone, Nintendo responded with a 64-bit processor in 1999, followed by Sony's PlayStation 2 in 2000, and Microsoft's Xbox in 2001. Although the 64-bit generation still drives the market, future generations will feature chips with up to 132 bits.

Machine Interactivity

Three conceptual components dominate today's games: *sound and fury* (vivid information that attracts and holds our attention), *death and destruction* (war games), and *computer control*[294] (*Pong* was the first game where computer control was entirely electronic). Control is facilitated by machine interactivity, a component that makes video game experiences playful and enjoyable. Joysticks, which players control as input devices, are one way for players to interact with video games. In the analog mode, different pressures yield different responses—pushing a button hard results in a character jumping higher than pushing it softly. The dual-shock mode allows players to feel the vibrations in joystick controllers when interacting with some intense and suspenseful situations, such as those found in horror or adventure games. These are just a few of the technological advancements in design that have diversified and dramatized video game consumption in terms of human-machine interaction.

Player Isolation

One aspect of technology that affects video game consumption is the isolation of players from socialization. A study on playing effects found that players rated video games playing higher than contact with human companions. Technology has come to substitute for people by providing gadgets or equipment for playing solitary games such as cards, crossword puzzles, and video games, where competition is with oneself or against a machine. Creating the illusion of intimacy with on-screen characters, technology often keeps players from being with other people. Because video games require that we interact with machines, players become an active audience of game consumption.

Reality Simulation

A high quality of graphic and sound presentations now exists in video games. Technology brings players closer to a realistic gaming world. Abstract characters in classic games such as *Space Invaders* and *Donkey Kong* have been replaced by 3D characters that look like humans, such as Lara Croft, the heroic icon of *Tomb Raider.* Also, game background environments imitate real-world landscapes, such as the Las Vegas Strip, streets in Rome, and the Grand Canyon. *Driver2* takes players through cities like Chicago, Havana, and Rio de Janeiro. Such simulation of the real world, called *hyper-reality,* allows players to realize, construct, and live in synthetic or virtual reality. Games such as *Myst, Raven, Fight Simulator,* and *Sim Theme Park* are examples of the hyper-realistic conditions present in video game play. And recently, artificial intelligence methods have started being incorporated into gaming to create virtual characters. What do you think future games have in store for their players? Addiction? Isolation? Cultural enhancement?

Cultural Playground

Video games serve the same cultural function as other kinds of play in human society, and they contain the same theoretical characteristics described previously in this chapter. Assuming that all forms of leisure activities are voluntary and have a symbolic message that conveys the meaning of freedom, players are not forced to play video games—they play because they want to play. Playing video games is experiential consumption of entertainment. Video game consumption is not real; video games are played for amusement. Once the box is activated, video games take players to another world for a fixed period of time and, when the experience ends, players are transported back to their ordinary world.

Video games have common rules to which players must adhere. Adventure games such as *Mega Man 5* or *Castlevania: Symphony of the Night* end when the life bar of a heroic character is empty, or if a player defeats a big boss at the end of each stage. In sports games such as *Tony Hawk's Pro Skater* or *Madden NFL 2001,* the rules are as similar to the rules of the real sports as possible to make the playing experience realistic. In fact, different genres of video games have different sets of specific rules that players have to learn to take advantage of the complete playing experience.

Video game consumption creates a sense of persistent social community, meaning that players use video games as a method for interacting with other people. Fan clubs and game communities—such as the Videotopia Society, Street Fighter Fans, arcade games in multiplexes, and various online gaming communities—are popular. Despite the isolation video games foster, they also produce a social mechanism for players to converse and share experiences. The language of gaming is a source of communion for players worldwide.

Video games are a type of play that expresses a significant cultural function, as do other forms of play. Video game consumption is a form of modern hedonism because it relates to the multisensory, fantasy, and emotional aspects of our experience with products.[295] As our society becomes more *hedonistic* (focusing on immediate gratification) we exchange our nationality for an identity of consumption for pleasure. As a contemporary phenomenon, consumption is an important cultural movement, and entertainment is a vital part of its foundation. Entertainment and arts media are well suited to the context of *hedonic consumption,* which relies on the investigation of mental events dealing purely with subjective aspects of consciousness. *Hedonism,* then, is the fun that a consumer derives from a product—the pleasure that the product evokes—and an appreciation of the product for its own sake.[296]

What role does gender play in gaming? Men and women have very different innate survival mechanisms and survival behaviors, the most prominent of which, for men, is the hunting instinct. An entire range of hand-eye coordination characteristics and skills is needed to hunt. When men use these skills, they are rewarded with the sensation of pleasure. Women, however, do not experience the same chemical sensations.[297] The chemical release experienced from action and sports games has become a common way for men to exercise their instinct for hunting. Designed by and intended for men, aggression-based computer games provide stimulation that is easily adaptable to a peaceful society.

Whether they act as fantasy, thrill, intellectual and emotional challenges, psychological control, creative art, or enjoyment, video games are a perfect venue for providing a dramatic construction through catharsis and tension release. Game players subconsciously identify with the dramatic structure of plots (good vs. evil, heroes vs. villains, gods vs. monsters, and so on) and conflict building and resolutions (*agon*) that lead to particular outcomes in video games. Games also provide an array of dramatic consumption that serves players' schematic reality.

Video games, like other forms of play, fulfill a person's need to interact and are substitutes for what is missing from a person's self-definition and self-identity that cannot be found in a bureaucratic workplace. At work, we encounter stress and tension; at home, video game playing in the virtual world gives players emotional arousal, sense of power, and release from the stress of real-world problems. Players call video gaming one of the purest forms of pleasure.

Game Trends

This year, for the first time, video games will outperform the domestic box office of movies. Some selected titles, with estimated production costs and gross, are presented in Table 11.2.

Video game popularity begins with the very young. What is the major theme of the games children play? A 1992 study of the 47 top-rated Nintendo games found that only seven did not have violence as their major theme. And what about gender? The covers of these games portray a total of 115 male and 9 female characters, and 13 of the 47 games contain scenarios with women being kidnapped or having to be rescued. Once you know that the majority of game designers are male, you understand the motivation behind the violent themes and gender roles—guys design games for guys. Mainstream artists have warmed up to the video game platform, especially the free game-building tools that are shipped with bloody action games like *Quake* and *Unreal*. Just like the '90s female artists who designed *Quake* "skins" that changed the game's main character into a woman, artists have found that they can bring their own agendas to games to subvert traditional game rules. Artists say they like the sense of space conveyed by video games and the way the games draw the participant into the field of action. Now that the video game business and its icons have become part of the American cultural landscape, artists can use imagery to critique elements of contemporary society, such

Table 11.2   Movies vs. Games

Costs and Gross Revenue

	Movie	*Video Game*
	GoldenEye	GoldenEye (Nintendo)
Development cost	$60 million	$4 million
Domestic gross	$106 million	$230 million
	Austin Powers: The Spy Who Shagged Me	Legend of Zelda (Nintendo)
Development cost	$33 million	$6 million
Domestic gross	$201 million	$205 million
	Wild Wild West	Tomb Raider 1, 2, and 3 (Eidos)
Development cost	$160 million	$6 million
Domestic gross	$111 million	$192 million

SOURCE: From I prefer my stars to be interactive. (1999, August 30). *Newsweek,* p. 10.

as violence or consumerism. Other artists have gone further, creating game modifications that turn the original games on their heads. Even museums see video games as a medium that encourages visitors to interact with art at a fundamental level. According to one artist, "What really matters are pieces of hardware and digital personae because nobody has made any art with such stuff before."[298]

Mining a largely PG audience, gaming giant Electronic Arts (EA) is the biggest player, with more than double the share (20.8% of all games sold)[299] of either of its closest competitors, Activision and Nintendo. EA makes games for every platform but has built its dominance by emphasizing titles for Sony's PlayStation 2 console and the PC—a smart move, because PlayStation 2 titles make up 66% of console games sold and 38% of all games. The PC is the next-largest platform, with a 26% share, and it has the added benefit of stability, unlike console systems that rely on hardware upgrades.[300] EA has a massive internal studio system of 2,500 game developers in five countries. See Table 11.3 for a list of top-selling games by platform.

Sci-fi conspiracy title *Majestic,* an online game hub supported by advertising and subscriptions to deliver experiences that blend story telling, game playing, and communication, received lukewarm reception from players and cost EA.com $368 million. That loss could be turned around if *The Sims Online* (which debuted December 3, 2002) proves to be as big a hit as industry observers predict.[301] Role-playing games (RPGs) now put gamers at the helm in historical settings such as ancient Rome, ancient Egypt, and the Battle of Gettysburg. Players

Table 11.3 Top-Selling Games in 2002 by Platform

PlayStation 2	PC
1. Grand Theft Auto 3	1. WarCraft III: Reign of Chaos
2. Madden NFL 2002	2. The Sims
3. Medal of Honor Frontline	3. Medal of Honor Allied Assault
4. Spider-Man: The Movie	4. The Sims: Vacation Expansion
5. Final Fantasy X	5. Neverwinter Nights

GameCube	XBox
1. Super Mario Sunshine	1. Halo
2. Super Smash Bros. Melee	2. Spider-Man: The Movie
3. Sonic Adventure 2: Battle	3. Max Payne
4. Resident Evil	4. James Bond 007: Agent Under Fire
5. Spider-Man: The Movie	5. Elder Scrolls III: Morrowind

SOURCE: From Keighley, G. (2002, December). The Next Disney? *Business 2.0,* p. 112.

act as Julius Caesar, who builds an empire over centuries. Strategy games based on history transform a historical period into the stuff of interactive experiences. Players are immersed in building pyramids or fighting the Civil War. Accused of departing from accurate historical accounts, game makers argue that the purpose of such games is to entertain and perhaps tempt players to find out more about the actual event. Sometimes referred to as god games, games such as *Civilization* (ancient Rome) and *Age of Empires* (ancient Egypt) provide a springboard for player fantasy with an injection of historical reality. According to the game designer, the staying power of these games relies on foregoing the restraints of accuracy for the sake of entertainment.[302]

Growing in popularity every year, *online games* invite Internet users to play against themselves or thousands of potential opponents from around the world. In addition to providing players with amusement, Internet games may also serve as advertisements. Ads disguised as games are the rage among online marketers desperate to grab the attention of surfers who have grown numb to banner ads. Pepsi-Cola, LEGO, Levi Strauss, Ford, and DaimlerChrysler are seeding the Web with simple but addictive games to boost their brands and collect consumer data. Toyota, for instance, has three racing games hosted on Zone.com, a site run by Microsoft; more than 400,000 people downloaded one game called *Tacoma Adrenaline* from the site. Because games are attractive to children, companies must take care not to run afoul of the Children's Online Privacy Protection Act of 1998, which requires Web sites to obtain parental consent to collect information about children under the age of 13.

Games are obtained in one of three ways: purchased outright for less than $50,000, licensed by companies that pay a monthly fee to sponsor the game, or built from scratch for as much as $400,000. Pepsi's site, Pepsiworld (www.pepsiworld.com), is loaded with games ranging from simple races to complex baseball games. Even at their most expensive, advergames are cheaper than other forms of advertising. For instance, a 30-second spot aired on the *X-Files* costs a minimum of $250,000 to produce and $265,000 to place on the show. Full-page ads in magazines cost about $200,000 to produce and cost between $100,000 and $200,000 to run in magazines such as *Rolling Stone* and *Sports Illustrated*. An online advergame, on the other hand, can be obtained for under $50,000 and costs only $5,000 to place. The only drawback to switching ad dollars to games is that their effectiveness has not been thoroughly tested. No one knows whether or not advergames increase brand recall or sales. However, in today's fragmented media environment, all options must be tested. In the meantime, advertisers have generated something fun and creative.[303]

Here is a sample of gaming that was available online at the time of this writing:

— http://beallcenter.uci.edu/shift/textonly/main.html
    Shift-Ctrl was an exhibition presented in fall 2001 at the University of California, Irvine, that focused on game modifications and original game artworks.

— http://Thesims.ea.com
    At Sims Online, players pay $10 a month to create a virtual home in Simsville and fill it with characters whose daily lives they control. The game allows players to become the dolls and play house with other gamers anywhere in the world.

— www.arcademachine.com
    You can find more than 500 games to play at this fun Web site.

— www.gamespy.com
    With more than 200 games, GameSpy entertains visitors with the hottest multiplayer retail games, such as *Quake* or *Half-Life,* or adaptations of the timeless board games, including Monopoly, and backgammon.

— www.lostchange.com
    Levi's game site created to promote its Silver Tab denim line.

— www.shockwave.com/games
    Relive the glory days of the video arcade at Shockwave Games, which features classic 1980s video games, including *Centipede, Defender,* and *Satan's Hollow*. You can also try your luck at casino play and board games featured here.

Like television, electronic games have enabled players to withdraw from society and live in their own worlds. Although board games and games of sport can be played with a partner or a team, video games are solitary pastimes. One form of gaming is usually enjoyed with other people and often relies upon social interaction for its entertainment—we call it gambling.

GAMBLING

The whore and gambler, by the state Licensed, build the nation's fate.

—William Blake

Gambling occurs when players bet something of value on the outcome of a game or uncertain event whose result may be determined by chance. They risk money in the hopes of winning the game or contest. Gambling activities range in complexity from a coin toss to betting on cards in poker. Outcomes may be determined solely by chance (craps and roulette) or by a combination of strategy and chance (poker). Gamblers may participate while betting on the outcome in card games and craps, or they may be restricted from participation in the cases of lotteries and sports.

Concerned with the analysis of random phenomena, *probability theory* states that the outcome of a random event cannot be determined before it occurs; it may be any one of several possible outcomes. The actual outcome is considered to be determined by chance. Outcomes of games of pure chance are all equally probable—as in the lottery, where every player has the same chance of winning as any other player. In such games, each instance is a completely independent one, meaning that each player has the same probability as each of the others of producing a given outcome. The distinctive feature of games of chance is that the outcome of a given trial cannot be predicted with certainty, although the collective results of a large number of trials display some regularity. Probability found in games of chance can be expressed as a formula: probability (p) equals the total number of favorable outcomes (f) divided by the total number of possibilities (t), or $p = f/t$.[304]

In gambling games, probability is expressed as "odds against winning," or the ratio of unfavorable possibilities to favorable ones. Players get into trouble when they falsely assume that each play is NOT independent of the other, and that outcomes of one sort should be balanced in the short run by the other possibilities. The lure of a *winning streak* is an example of why some gamblers keep throwing the dice rather than settling for a single win. Gamblers invent "systems" based on this *Monte Carlo fallacy*; in reality, most game advantages go to the dealer or some other participant.

Short Stack: A Mini History of Gambling

Often perceived as a recent phenomenon, gambling actually dates back to antiquity. Dice have been recovered from Egyptian tombs, and the Chinese, Japanese, Greeks, and Romans were known to play games of chance for amusement as early as 2300 B.C.[305]

Used as instruments of divination, dice were thrown by Egyptian priests to see if the gods were on their side in decisions regarding topics from war to family planning. Perhaps the first cheaters emerged as priests loaded dice to outsmart their gods. Another cheater, Palamedes, used dice games to relieve the boredom of his fellow soldiers during the siege of Troy. Using what is known today as *riding the dice* (being caught up in winning and totally distracted), this Greek mythical hero was said to have been stoned to death for losing the battle.[306] The notion that a person who is winning a game of chance has the gods on his or her side originated from these myths.

Centuries later, both Native Americans and European colonists integrated gambling into entertainment rather than into religion, which shaped American views and practices regarding gaming. Native Americans developed games and language describing gambling, believing that their gods determined fate and chance. Following the 1980s, when gambling experienced a period of unprecedented growth, Richard Canfield, called the Prince of Gamblers, developed the technique of putting police and politicians on the payroll to protect his gambling venues. He is credited with making gambling into a respectable form of entertainment for the wealthy and for royalty, and his early casinos were prototypes for future Las Vegas houses of gambling.

Casinos were originally public halls for music and dancing but, by the 19th century, they became known as a collection of gaming and gambling rooms.[307] One of the first casinos was opened in 1861 in Monte Carlo to provide a major source of income for Monaco. Las Vegas, Nevada, has been operating casinos since the late 1940s, and gambling was introduced in Atlantic City, New Jersey, in 1978. By the 1980s, casinos began appearing on riverboats and Indian reservations. In 1999, $58.2 billion in profit was generated from the total gaming industry of wagering, lotteries, bookmaking, and gaming.

Increased public acceptance of gambling is reflected both in opinion polls and in the willingness of Americans to allocate considerable time and money to gambling pursuits. Five key factors explain gambling's increased presence and commercial success:

1. Voters are for the *voluntary tax* (pledged contributions based on revenues) collected from gaming locations.

2. An increasing number of people choose gaming as their leisure activity of choice.

3. Retirees are the single largest segment of the casino market.

4. Casino marketers are now attracting a "low roller" segment not previously targeted.

5. Gambling can be done in a diversity of locations using a variety of technologies. You can gamble in casinos, riverboats, and Indian reservations. Product innovations include video lottery terminals, slot machines, racetrack-based gaming devices, and video poker machines, as well as online gambling.

Four broad gaming segments are emerging, each with a somewhat different profile:

☆ *High rollers,* composed of sophisticated gamblers who tend to be wealthy, older, and male. They tend to play games of skill rather than chance.

☆ *Day trippers,* dominated by retirees who make several short trips to venues within easy driving distance; they mostly play the slots.

☆ *Low-stakes/new adopters,* who have recently discovered gaming as leisure diversion. Most are aging boomers and their parents with time and money to spend for enjoyment, and young women seeking a new diversion.

☆ *Family vacationers,* who gamble as an offshoot of a family vacation to a theme park or other attraction.

An important sector of America's economy, gambling employs about 380,000 people nationwide. And $3 billion in gaming tax revenue was paid in 2000 to states and communities where casinos operated, providing funding for programs benefiting schools and seniors. Noted for their philanthropy, casino companies give more than $10 million annually to United Way campaigns and donate more than $58 million to charities each year.[308] For every $1 million in revenues generated by the casino industry, 13 jobs are created.[309] No wonder Las Vegas is the fastest-growing city in America.

Neon Castles: Casino Gambling[310]

Casinos are legalized establishments where commercial gambling operators make their profits by regularly occupying advantage positions against players. Concentrated in pockets around the world, casinos are built in areas with relaxed legal restrictions supposedly enacted to combat cheating. Actually, more laws have been passed to derive tax revenues from gambling than to control cheating.

Casinos typically offer card games such as poker, baccarat, and blackjack. Many also have slot machines and roulette, as well as wagering on sports events. Although casino operators maintain Web sites as marketing devices and reservation systems, they are not in the business of providing online gambling. The biggest news in gambling is *merger*. MGM Grand bought Mirage Resorts to create a virtual triumvirate of mega-casino companies. Casino operators are rushing to consolidate because voters haven't been legalizing new gambling jurisdictions, leaving publicly traded companies few avenues for growth other than buying up their rivals.

Casinos, riverboats, and Indian reservations are meccas for American gambling. In the race to develop entertaining themes, Las Vegas casinos invested in expensive properties that have driven investments and stocks down in value. Its many billion-dollar properties load on huge shopping malls, theaters, spas, restaurants, and thousands of hotel rooms to lure guests. Atlantic City, still unable to overcome its seedy image, is not a popular destination resort for tourists. Instead, casinos bus in middle- and low-income gamblers from nearby cities and states to gamble. Still, MGM Grand and Mirage are planning to build casinos to compete with Trump's Taj Mahal, Plaza, and Marina, which dominate the New Jersey shoreline.

A popular Southeast casino location that provides legalized gambling is Tunica, Mississippi, which is now the country's third largest gambling destination. Other American locations are racing to catch up. Detroit and, across the river, Windsor, Ontario, are expected to become a significant gambling market as part of a group of several mega-casinos being built along the Detroit River. Casino operator Park Place Entertainment is buying up locals-oriented riverboat and land-based casinos in the Southeast and Midwest.

Connecticut is currently the nation's top *tribal gambling* market, with the most profitable casino in the United States. Foxwood Resort Casino, operated by the Mashantucket Pequot Tribal Nation, averages more than 55,000 patrons each day and more than 20 million visitors each year. The nation's largest casino, Foxwood employs more than 10,000 people. In the West, Harrah's Entertainment and Trump Hotels have each cut deals to develop and operate tribal casinos in California. Elsewhere, tribes in New York, Florida, and Minnesota reap hundreds of millions each year from gaming operations.

Locations worldwide are fast incorporating gambling into their national economies. In developing countries such as Slovenia, casinos are positioned adjacent to Italian border towns and cater to Italian gamblers by accepting lire and using Italian-language dealers. International destinations such as Macao, Isla de Margarita off the Venezuelan coast, and Bermuda tempt tourists from around the world to gaming tables. Casinos have the potential to lure travelers and bring tourism to areas devoid of natural wonders, historical monuments, or recreational resorts.

In spite of their active role in the global economy, casinos are also a source of personal tragedy. Contemporary society faces pervasive *gambling addiction*. Like alcoholics, gambling addicts are powerless against their compulsive behavior. Twelve-step programs and free clinics established to help addicted players are constant reminders of gambling's powerful lure.

A Virtual Roll of the Dice: E-Gambling

Owned by American individuals and partnership companies, most online gambling Web sites run their businesses offshore for legal purposes.[311] Sites offer casino-style games such as blackjack, craps, roulette, and poker. However, when e-gambling began, the question of how games are conducted over the computer screen invited game fixing in the interest of the casino Web site. Today, poker is the game of choice because the online casino does not have an interest in who wins money; players are playing each other, not the house. Online casinos take their profits by *raking the pot* (taking a percentage or fixed amount of the pot that everybody plays for), or through a fixed amount a player gives to the casino for a given number of hands played.

ParadisePoker.com is at the forefront of making gambling available to players worldwide. By downloading casino software, players compete against poker players all over the globe. Players buy chips with their credit cards. Based in Spain, Paradise Poker provides poker games that can be played for different amounts of money, and players do not have to play on the Web site. Both real and fake money are betting options, and Internet users can watch any other game that is being played concurrently. Using four Webmasters to oversee its server, Paradise uses a computer synchronization that makes the play the same speed for all of the users, no matter what speed their Internet connection may be, to eliminate modem speed advantages. Recent competitor Ultimatebet.com enlisted professional gamblers to promote their site, which offers real-money games.

The success of Internet gambling is attributed to combining two popular activities— betting and computer access—and giving a world of players access. Although Internet gambling has a minimal effect on Las Vegas and traditional casinos everywhere, it can only profit from the new generation of sites and relaxed governmental regulations. Taking advantage of this trend, Harrah's paired with iwin.com to form iwinHarrahs, and MGM linked with machine maker Silicon Gaming to create WagerWorks. In Nevada, it's now legal to gamble on sports on the Internet, and San Diego–based Vertgame.com offers wagering on horse racing and football. Because of opportunities available for global gambling operators to expand into online markets, Australia is now positioned as the world leader in its aggressive approval of Web gambling. Britain's Hilton Group, which owns Ladbroke Racing, is fast expanding into Internet betting as well.

Dreams for Sale: Lotteries

Lotteries, a more subtle form of gambling than casino betting, have a long history in the United States. As early as the 17th century, British colonization of America was partly financed through lottery proceedings. Because lotteries were viewed as a popular form of voluntary taxation in England during the Georgian era, they became popular in America as European settlers arrived. A half dozen lotteries sponsored by prominent individuals such as Ben Franklin, John Hancock, and George Washington operated in each of the 13 colonies to raise funds for building projects. Between 1765 and 1806, Massachusetts authorized lotteries to help build dormitories and supply equipment for Harvard College; many other institutions of higher learning, including Dartmouth, Yale, and Columbia, were also financed through lotteries. A lottery was even approved to finance the American Revolution. Today 38 states have lottery gambling systems.

Regular players spend an average of $830 a year, or $16 a week, on lottery tickets. Heavy players buy more than 20 tickets in a contest's first 45 days.[312] Those who buy tickets are usually poor people, minorities, or less-educated persons; they spend a greater portion of their income on tickets than higher-income, better-educated people do. For them, it's a chance at realizing their fantasies—buying a home, taking a vacation, taking care of elderly parents. In 2001, the lottery accounted for the largest percentage of the $600 billion Americans spend on gambling each year—more than on movies, theme parks, and sporting events combined.[313]

So why do we play? Playing the lottery is about dreaming, it's about equal opportunity, and it's about wanting it all—right now. A Gallup survey found that 61% of us believe daydreams help us to cope with emotional stress.[314] When we're not stressing, we're looking for an easy way to make money. Short-term gratification predominates.

To convince people to play lottery games, 38 states now spend nearly half a billion dollars each year on advertising.[315] Ads promise to give everyone a decent life—the rich and easy life. Ads feature ordinary people and their dreams, which of course are fulfilled by winning the lottery. Some ad campaign scenarios feature people who have achieved their wildest fantasies— like telling your boss you've just bought the company, and he's fired. Or driving a taxi to amuse yourself in between trips to your private island and your Italian villa. If you spend a dollar, one state's advertising claims, you may earn a 2,600% return on your money. What these ads don't tell you is that the odds are greater that you'll be struck by lightning than that you'll win the lottery. If you bought 100 one-dollar tickets a week your entire adult life (18 through 75 years of age), you'd spend $296,400 and still have only a 1% chance of winning the lottery.[316]

As long as people have dreams and a dollar to bet, lotteries will profit. And as jackpots soar toward the hundred-million-dollar mark, people will continue to line up for a chance at fame and fortune. Who cares about odds and reality when dreams cost as little as a dollar?

THE EFFECTS OF GAMING

We all enjoy games that are played in a variety of forms, venues, and technologies. We play for enjoyment, we play to compete, and we play to realize our dreams. Play has fascinated us for centuries and, in all likelihood, it will continue doing so well into the future. When considering the impact of game playing on our lives, it is important to focus on the *outcome of play*. Are we happier? Are we more astute? Are we winners or losers? What gratifications are derived from playing games? Outcomes are often studied as effects, and gaming outcomes are no exception. To illustrate the role of effects of gaming, we expose negative effects and contrast similarities and differences in emotional, self-esteem, and pleasure outcomes of playing video games with those of gambling.

Studies of video games focus on possible *negative effects*, arguing that interactivity makes players personally responsible for atrocious acts and implicates players in morally dubious actions. Games of action (which elicit strong arousal through violent images), aggressive player reactions, and point-of-view editing (using the camera to present a particular perspective) are critics' most popular targets. Likewise, gaming also can lead to negative outcomes, such as gambling addiction. To all pathological gamblers, the game takes hold of their lives and refuses to let go. Players who succumb to the idea of winning may become addicted to betting. The result is excessive gambling debt that often leads players into depression, withdrawal, and even theft to cope with the results of their addictive play. Society's focus on consumption and spectacle are identified by sociologists as prime motivators for the growing number of gambling addicts.

Interactivity in video games and participation in gambling are often preconditions for eliciting strong emotions in players. Competition in both activities can provide stimulation that causes physical arousal, a general physiological process that creates emotions.[317] Playing video games stimulates emotions that are close to real-life experiences. Gambling stimulates emotions of anticipation that transcend reality and become fantasy.

Interactivity and participation are directly related to levels of self-esteem. In games of skill, players are responsible for their wins and losses. Losing may cause loss of self-esteem because losing is linked to the player's assessment of his or her own performance. Because of the element of chance, gamblers may not feel personally responsible for winning or losing. Therefore, higher levels of self-esteem may be maintained by gamblers than by video game players, even as they face devastating financial loss.

Finally, the pleasures derived from immersion in virtual reality and gambling are passive pleasures. Interactive-game players, however, may switch to an active control of their emotional states, whereas gamblers have little opportunity for control over a game's outcome.

FADE TO BLACK

Taking chances may be inherent in human nature, and games of all sorts give us an opportunity to challenge fate and enjoy the glory of winning. Formed to create a better understanding of gaming, the American Gaming Association (AGA) provides information to the public, elected officials, and the media through education and advocacy. Part of the association's mission is to address the problems of underage gambling. With more Americans going to casinos than visiting major league baseball parks or attending movies, Broadway shows, and concerts, the AGA has a growing role in publicizing the downside of gambling. And their evidence suggests that gambling revenues will continue to increase dramatically in the future.

 A Closer Look

Using Psychographics to Promote the Lottery[318]

Using a system developed and revised by the Stanford Research Institute (SRI), advertisers are zeroing in on the values and lifestyles of potential lottery ticket purchasers; they aren't just relying on flair and humor. Research is key to targeting the right market segments. What follows is a sampling of how three state lotteries used research to drive successful advertising campaigns that peddled tickets:

☆ Virginia lottery research indicates that scratch ticket customers tend to play the lottery on impulse, are guided by what others will think, and watch TV in late morning and late evening. Marketers classify game prospects as *belongers, emulators,* or *achievers* according to Values And Life Styles (VALS) II typology. To attract high rollers, who prefer dice and card games, a *Star Trek* theme was designed to appeal to upscale enthusiasts. In the state's most popular campaign, Lady Luck engages in all sorts of clever promotional tricks. One ad featured the lady coming down the chimney to stuff Christmas stockings with instant scratch tickets. Another version showed a man and woman rejoicing at her knock on the door in anticipation of becoming winners, only to have their hopes dashed when they realize no one purchased the ticket that week. Lady Luck reminds the losers that they missed out on $50,000 a year for every million dollars in the jackpot by not buying a ticket. Lady Luck was responsible for selling millions of tickets for Virginia.

☆ Maryland has segmented keno players into three subclusters: *fragile egos, entertainment seekers,* and *solitary gamblers.* Researchers learned that Pick 3 Numbers players are superstitious; they dream a number or get a hunch. With this information, advertisers crafted a campaign to exploit superstitions, including taking advantage of the fear of failing to play a lucky number every day. A spot called "Linguine" featured a diner customer who sees a number 6 in the waitress's hairdo, a 2 in his pasta bowl, and a 0 in the water ring under his glass. When he fails to play the 6-2-0 combination that night, that sequence turns out to be the Pick 3 winner. "Your numbers," a voiceover says, "are out there." Another state study concluded that Maryland players care far more about total winnings than the likelihood of winning—a prescription for bigger jackpots and longer odds. When they learned from focus group participants that players preferred using lottery winnings to "do with my time anything I like" rather than buying luxury items, the state's ad agency created a TV commercial for the million-dollar Big Game. It showed a winner lounging happily in his lawn chair while his neighbors trudged to work in lockstep to the tune of *Sixteen Tons*.

☆ Washington, D.C., used a commercial for Powerball to suggest that a winner's lifestyle could be magically transformed by winning a life-altering multimillion dollar jackpot, omitting the fact that players' odds of winning are 1 in 55 million. Whereas marketers identified the big-jackpot Powerball as better suited for reception by middle-income folks, they identified the target for small-stakes Lucky Numbers as blue-collar workers. Then, the ad agency asked players to submit strategies that would motivate people to play Lucky Numbers who might not ordinarily play the game. They created a new campaign that featured animated reenactments of players' stories and suggestions.

What are the lottery advertising themes in your state? What research might have been conducted to create these themes? At which psychographic segment are the commercials aimed?

DISCUSSION AND REVIEW

1. What role do zero-sum games play in casinos? In video games? Do most gamblers know the difference? Is this a problem?

2. How does e-gambling fit into the scheme of gambling addiction? How can this addiction be curtailed?

3. What arguments would you use to convince an advertiser to switch his or her product placements from film to video games?

EXERCISES

1. Visit the sites listed in this chapter to play an online game of skill and a game of chance. What role do technology and new media play in gaming? How do you think technology will structure gaming of the future?

2. Invoke the uses and gratifications theory to explain player fascination with action games. Use expectancy theory to explain human fascination with gambling. Are the two theories interchangeable? Why? Are games and gambling interchangeable? Why?

3. Buy a dollar lottery ticket at a convenience store during a time when the jackpot is high. Describe the other ticket buyers at this location in psychographic terms using the VALS II system (as described in most advertising principles textbooks) or create your own subcategories. What kind of advertising campaign would you use to persuade these players to play more often?

RECOMMENDED READINGS AND WEB SITES

Liebert, R. M., & Spiegler, M. D. (1994). *Personality: Strategies and issues.* Pacific Grove, CA: Brooks/Cole.

Reeves, B., & Nass, C. (1996). *The media equation: How people treat computers, television, and new media like real people and places.* Cambridge U.K.: Cambridge University Press.

Stevenson, L., & Haberman, D. L. (1998). *The theories of human nature* (3rd ed.). New York: Oxford University Press.

Zillmann, D., & Bryant, J. (1994). Entertainment as media effect. In J. Bryant & D. Zillmann (Eds.), *Media effects: Advances in theory and research* (pp. 437-461). Hillsdale, NJ: Lawrence Erlbaum.

www.gambling.com has 16,500 links to relevant sites.

12

Sports Mania

One of the reasons for professional sports' popularity is that it produces winners and losers, heroes and villains. Even when viewed as an individual exercise such as running or biking, sports produce emotions and performances that are frequently hard to generate in most other pursuits.

—Sports marketers Rick Burton and Dennis Howard[319]

SPORTS AS ENTERTAINMENT

Sports have become a part of everyday life in most Western cultures. Even people who do not watch or play sports are subjected to sports in the news, in movies, and on billboards, T-shirts, and bumper stickers. For some individuals—such as coaches, professional athletes, commentators, and officials—sports are work. For most enthusiasts, however, sports serve as entertainment. *Entertainment* is commonly defined as something diverting or engaging. Similarly, Merriam-Webster's dictionary defines *sport* as "a source of diversion . . . or physical activity engaged in for pleasure."[320] Whether we are watching a movie, listening to a CD, or attending a basketball game, we are being entertained.

Today's sports organizations embrace their role as entertainment providers wholeheartedly. Reporter Keith Epstein of the *Washington Post* explains that professional sports events have become blowout entertainment extravaganzas. "Chants will blare from loudspeakers: 'Who let the dogs out? Woof-woof-woof-woof.' Crowd-rousers will lead dances and cheers. And before kickoff, fireworks will explode from the two end zones. . . . It's pageant. It's spectacle. It's theater. It's ear-pounding."[321]

A BRIEF HISTORY OF SPORT

It is difficult to determine what the first sport or sports were. It is a fairly reasonable assumption, however, that sports began the first time a person used physical activity for recreational purposes. Historians speculate that such sport could have been hunting or fishing for pleasure. What little is known of sports in Western cultures prior to the high civilizations of Greece and Rome comes from drawings of sports-like activities in Egyptians tombs, Cretian frescoes, Etrurian graves, and painted pottery from Sumeria and Assyria. The activities portrayed in these drawings often appeared to be combative or martial, like boxing, wrestling, fencing, and archery. They also included demonstrations of agility and courage, like bull leaping and bull-fighting practiced by the Minoan culture of Crete. A Minoan fresco also shows what appears to be a spectator's box in which well-dressed, presumably aristocratic women watch events. It is unclear where such events were held or how the spectators behaved, but researchers speculate that the events functioned to bolster community pride and identity and to consolidate political, religious, and military power.[322]

First recorded in 776 B.C., the ancient Olympic Games are often considered the birth of organized sports. These games included 5 days of sporting events that were primarily religious ceremonies. The games were expanded to include additional contests, reaching their height in 5th century B.C. Men competed in the nude in running, wrestling, the pentathlon, horse riding, and chariot racing. Women were barred from watching or competing; they were even put to death if they were caught doing so. Athletes who were victorious were crowned with olive wreaths, immortalized in statues, and treated like heroes for the rest of their lives. Theodosius the Great decreed an end to these games in 394 A.D. Sports, however, remained resilient. By 1200 A.D., sports for amusement and diversion re-emerged in some countries, although the authorities restricted many of the rougher games.

When the Olympic Games were revived in 1896, sports had reached a new level of sophistication. By the 19th century sporting activities had become very organized. Sports were formalized in leagues and clubs with rigorous training and competition schedules, and governing bodies were built for activities ranging from local softball and bowling leagues to the international Olympic Games. The first modern track-and-field meet happened in England in 1825. The first intercollegiate competition was held in 1829, when Oxford and Cambridge universities competed in a rowing match. Expanded coverage by newspapers, radio, and eventually television firmly entrenched sports as a mainstay of popular culture.

SPORTS AS DRAMA

Spectator sports follow the same basic theories of drama that characterize other forms of entertainment, as discussed in Chapter 4. Audiences may develop positive and negative dispositions toward a player, a team, or even toward a specific sport more generally. Consistent with disposition theory, audiences enjoy the victories of favored players or teams, and the defeat of despised opponents. Sports marketers Rick Burton and Dennis Howard appear to embrace this philosophy, as seen in this chapter's opening quote. This sentiment—that sports produce emotions and create heroes and villains—captures the essence of the notion of sports as drama.

Although sports have much in common with other forms of entertainment, they also have some unique characteristics. One important way in which sports differ from other entertainment forms is their immediacy:

> There's good reason why sports is a TV staple: It's human drama at a base level, it's cheap to produce and it's live. One can't minimize the power of immediacy in this time-shifting era when sports are the last remaining live coast-to-coast events—The Oscars, the Emmys, even *Saturday Night Live* are delayed to the West Coast. Only sports has the nation, and sometimes the world, watching the same thing at the same time, and if you have a message that's a potent messenger.[323]

Sports are spontaneous. Most dramas have scripts and most music has a score, but the action in sports is spontaneous and uncontrolled by its participants. Although other forms of entertainment include elements of surprise, they usually follow general expectations. We expect to be scared by a horror film, to laugh at a comedy club, and to cry along with a sentimental country music song. With sports, our emotions are much more difficult to anticipate; however, our reactions are often equally—if not more—intense. At the beginning, we feel eager anticipation, uncertain as to whether the game or contest we are about to watch will be a fast-paced thriller, a drawn-out tragedy, or perhaps even an unexpected comedy. As the game unfolds, if it is a close match, we might ride a roller coaster of emotion—from elation to anxiety to despair and back again. In a more one-sided contest in which one team or player completely dominates over the other, we might experience one long, rolling wave of triumph or disappointment, depending on which side we are rooting for. Although reality programming has introduced many new forms of live, unpredictable entertainment, these programs have rarely succeeded in evoking the intense, spontaneous audience reactions that sports generate with ease.

Because of its spontaneity, however, sports producers face challenges that are different from those of most entertainment providers. No one goes to a game hoping that their team will lose, yet it is the threat of losing that fosters the suspense audiences crave. In traditional drama, producers controls the content, setting the tempo and sequence of events to create suspense and outcomes that will satisfy their audiences. In sports, however, those that are selling the entertainment, including sports franchises and sports media, have little control over these factors. Nonetheless, sports producers are always looking for ways to maximize the drama and entertainment value of a sporting event. In some cases these efforts are obvious, such as in professional wrestling, which some might argue has become as much a soap opera as it is a sport. Rather than protest such comparisons, professional wrestling has seemingly embraced them, as reflected in the sport's new corporate title (as of May 2002): World Wrestling Entertainment. One way this shift has been accomplished is by focusing as much if not more attention on what the wrestlers do outside the ring as what they do in it. This focus allows for more character development and greater control to maximize dramatic appeal (see box "Wrestling Mania").

Focus on Wrestling Mania

Nowhere is the concept of sports as drama more evident than in professional wrestling. Wrestling as entertainment has survived in some form for more than 100 years, first as a carnival spectacle and later as a television spectacular.[324] Many of the characteristics of theater can be found in professional wrestling. The ring is like a stage, and the ropes, turnbuckles, and chains that form the ring are stage props. The theme of the drama—the vengeance of justice—is expressed in a plot of confrontation between good and evil. The wrestlers are portrayed as heroes or villains. These characters are developed through a combination of the wrestler's name, costume, and behavior. In soap-opera fashion, however, these roles are subject to change at any time. Good characters go bad, and bad characters reform. Romances, alliances, and conspiracies frequently realign. Interestingly, the amount of time spent on the actual wrestling during these matches has decreased in recent years, with more and more time spent on the posturing, taunting, and drama that take place between the wrestlers and other characters. Consider this report of one World Wrestling Federation live broadcast:

Baseball legend Wade Boggs was in the house; the nation's No. 1 author, a man in a leather mask

Figure 12.1 Shamelessly drawing on classic dramatic devices like stage names, stock characters, fancy costumes, grudge matches, and choreographed moves, professional wrestling *is* world wrestling *entertainment.*

© Duomo/Corbis.

named Mankind, was scheduled to wrestle; the women's chocolate-pudding match was good to go. Yet all was not right: not for the WWF and not for Vince McMahon, its chairman and mastermind. On the previous week's broadcast, his real-life daughter, Stephanie, had been "tricked" into marrying his arch nemesis, the wrestler Triple H. Now McMahon was running into the ring with a sledgehammer, out for blood. Stephanie had a surprise for him. She was in love with Triple H, she told him. And further, they were taking control of the company. She said, "Triple H outsmarted you by making business personal. That's something you know all about."[325]

And, like more traditional drama, most of the action is at least loosely, if not entirely, scripted. Most wrestling fans accept that the wrestling matches are faked, but this does not prevent fans from enjoying them. In fact, the number of wrestling fans has been growing. According to one report, in 1999, two Monday night wrestling programs each lasting two hours attracted 35 million viewers. Although males aged 12 to 34 make up the vast majority of viewers, the number of female viewers has been increasing.[326] Besides watching wrestling on TV, fans attend live events, subscribe to wrestling magazines, visit wrestling Web sites, and buy T-shirts, theme music, and autobiographies of wrestling superstars. Audiences, however, are forever fickle and, by the end of 2002, program ratings and event attendance suggested World Wrestling Entertainment might be losing some of its audience. As with all forms of entertainment, the popularity of professional wrestling may fluctuate over the years, and the sport will continue to change and evolve as it attempts to attract and retain audiences.

What do you think? Is professional wrestling more sport or drama? Watch a wrestling match and see what comparisons and contrasts you can draw between wrestling and other sports, and wrestling and other forms of drama, such as an action film or a soap opera. Why do you think professional wrestling became so popular at the beginning of the 21st century?

In other sports such efforts may be more subtle, but they reflect similar dramatic techniques. To promote sports as drama, "character development" is enhanced by profiles on the athletes provided in game programs, sports articles, and game commentaries. Fans are given not only the athletes' sports performance statistics, but also personal information about their lives and families. Over the years, the sports themselves have changed and evolved to promote spectatorship. Rules for football, baseball, and basketball were modified in the 1970s to favor dramatic offensive action, thus enhancing spectator appeal and fitting more efficiently into the requirements of television programming.

Rules and schedules are continuing to change. To better fit within fans' typical leisure-time schedules, baseball includes more night games, and the World Series begins on a week-end. The pitcher's mound was lowered to make the curve and slider pitches more effective and more exciting to watch. In basketball, rule changes were designed to facilitate scoring because fans tend to find high-scoring games more exciting. Similarly, in the National Football League, to emphasize higher scoring and forward drive, the goal posts were moved back to the endline, kickoffs now begin at the 35 yard line rather than the 40, and the penalty for offensive holding was reduced from 15 to 10 yards. In addition, sudden death overtimes were instituted to intensify the pace and maximize the excitement of tiebreakers. And schedules were changed to increase the number of games played by better teams in bigger television markets.

Sports franchises must work to keep audiences entertained even when the action is slow or the home team is suffering a long losing streak. Most of the techniques used today to enhance the dramatic value of sports are not new, just improved. Cheerleaders, mascots, and music help sustain momentum during game lulls, as they always have, but with twists that add pizzazz. Players are no longer simply announced over the public address system as they take the field or court—they are introduced with theme songs and elaborate video presentations. Teams have flashier team colors, logos, and uniforms, and new stadiums are designed to maximize entertainment with luxury boxes, jumbo video screens, VIP clubs, novelty stores, a vast array of dining options, and better camera angles for the television viewing audience.

Current Trends

A Word from Our Sponsor

Sports is big business these days—a business of endorsements, sponsorships, broadcast rights, and licensing agreements. Professional athletes like Michael Jordan, Shaquille O'Neal, and Tiger Woods endorse products ranging from burgers to briefs. The International Events Group (IEG) reported that corporate sports sponsorship grew 12% in 1999, compared with a 6.8% increase in advertising and a 7.4% growth in sales promotion. IEG estimated that as much as $22 billion would be spent for sports sponsorships worldwide in 2000 including $8 billion spent in North America, with approximately 68% of the money going to sports figures and events. Corporations are putting their names on stadiums and convention centers, from Philadelphia's First Union Center (home of the NHL Flyers and the NBA 76ers) to Landover, Maryland's FedEx Field (home of the NFL Redskins) to the Staples Center in Los Angeles (home of the NBA Lakers and Clippers and NHL Kings).

Although FedEx and Staples enjoy high name recognition, purchasing stadium rights can give even lesser-known entities much-desired advertising. Donna Ramer, managing director at the public-relations firm Makovsky & Co., cites 3Com Corp., the computer company that purchased the naming rights to then-Candlestick Park, host of the NFL's San Francisco 49ers. "Nobody really knew who 3Com was when they bought the rights. But it enabled them to get vital name placement and awareness. Companies want consumers to associate their product with a city," Ramer said.[327] In just the first six months, that $500,000 investment netted 3Com an estimated $48 million in national publicity at a time when 3Com's networking company was trying to establish itself as a nationwide leader in its field.[328]

The economic downturn that began with the new millennium forced some companies to consider making cutbacks in their sponsorship deals. In 1999, PSINet Inc. signed a deal to pay $105 million to put its corporate logo on the Baltimore Ravens' new football stadium. Less than 3 years into its 20-year contract, the Ashburn, Virginia–based company admitted that it soon might run out of cash and be forced into a bankruptcy filing, and they ended their original sponsorship deal. Meanwhile, Miami's Pro Player Stadium began looking for a new sponsor in the spring of 2000 when Pro Player's parent company, Fruit of the Loom, filed for bankruptcy.[329] And, 3Com opted not to renew its contract with Candlestick Park.

When these deals fall through, the negative publicity sports franchises suffer for being associated with this failure can be as painful as the financial losses. It seems likely that sports sponsorships will remain a critical component of professional and amateur sports alike; however, both sponsors and sports programs are also likely to become more sophisticated and cautious in their dealings.

Growth in Media Coverage

Billions of fans attend sporting events each year, but even more fans watch sports on network and cable television or listen to sports on the radio. Television networks are trying to keep pace with the demand for sports programming. Networks paid close to $18 billion for NFL broadcasting rights in 1999, and NBC spent a record $2.3 billion in total for the broadcast and cable rights for the Olympic Games in 2004, 2006, and 2008.[330]

Nielsen ratings for 2000 Super Bowl XXXIV estimated that 43.5 million homes in the country's 47 largest TV markets watched the Rams seal a 23-16 win on the final play. Roughly 62% of U.S. homes with their TVs on at that time were tuned to the game.[331] According to Nielsen, 21.5 million viewers watched NBC's prime-time coverage of the summer Olympic Games in Sydney, Australia.[332] Interestingly, although these numbers are impressive, ratings for both the Super Bowl and the Olympics were significantly lower than previous years, with viewership for the Olympics down as much as 35% from 1996. Although many explanations have been offered for this decline, most analysts would agree that increased competition resulting from the proliferation of televised sporting events and other media offerings has taken its toll. Even the most avid sports fan cannot and probably would not want to watch all televised sports offerings.

The introduction of sport-specific stations adds a new element to the mix. Networks must now compete not only with a growing number of ESPN channels, but also with niche networks such as the Golf Channel and SpeedVision. In addition to traditional sports media, now other outlets such as the Internet, pay-per-view cable television, and satellite stations such as Primestar and DirectTV allow viewers to play a more active role in customizing the sports programming they wish to see. This practice of *narrowcasting* (reaching smaller, more specific audiences) appears to be the future of sports media.[333]

Going to X-tremes

Extreme (or X-treme) sports represent another recent trend. If something is dangerous, it is interesting. Many extreme sports originate as new, daring twists on more traditional pastimes such as the downhill, off-road spin-off on traditional skateboarding pictured in Figure 12.2. The extreme sports movement, however, has changed a lot since it began more than a decade ago with isolated collections of athletes using bikes, boards, and blades in unique ways. Consider the steadily increasing popularity of snowboarding, one of the original extreme sports. Snowboarders earned a reputation as rebellious troublemakers and were initially despised by traditional skiers because of their grungy attire and unorthodox maneuvers. Today, ski resorts welcome snowboarders as young and old alike convert from skis to boards.

The trend is toward riskier and more dangerous endeavors. Take epic accomplishments like the climbing of Mount Everest; climbers George Mallory froze to death and Edmund Hillary and Tenzing Norgay nearly died. Now every corporate executive from around the world seems to be planning to attack Everest. But that's not enough. To up the ante, getting to the top of the highest peak in the world now means doing it without oxygen or racing up in record time or staying at the top longer than anyone else.

Figure 12.2 Athletes and spectators alike thrive on the adrenaline rush of pushing the limits with innovative and obscure extreme sports like the downhill, off-road spin-off on traditional skateboarding, pictured here.

© Jaime Budge/Corbis.

Extreme athletes are getting braver, bolder, and crazier. Those who want to push the limits are now pursuing activities such as *free flying* (a speedier, less disciplined form of sky-diving) or *free soloing* (scaling mountains and icy ledges with no harnesses or ropes). Today, *extreme* is what was once considered *insane*. And the athletes themselves will tell you why they enjoy extreme sports. "I'm totally addicted to adrenaline," explains Travis Tripp, who competes professionally, hurtling downhill at 72 miles per hour on an 8-foot-long board called a street luge.[334] Although extreme sports are largely youth dominated, one line of thought suggests that these sports simply reflect a larger, recent societal obsession with risk and excess that has also characterized the business world, with its big dot.com ventures and stock market gambles.[335]

Some people believe that extreme athletes just like the attention, but psychologist Jennifer Taylor disagrees. "They're not doing it for popularity or publicity," said Taylor, an Arlington sports psychologist. "They do it to challenge themselves physically and mentally to see if they can withstand the pressure and . . . get in touch with who they are." She adds that athletes who risk their lives are masters of their craft, with exceptional mental and physical brawn. They push the limits to test their skill. According to Taylor, these sports even provide some with a spiritual sensation or an inner peace: "They're doing something larger than themselves by meeting a challenge that other people aren't up to." But Taylor does find it difficult to justify the gamble these athletes take with their lives. "Part of me says that these people are crazy."[336]

The athletes themselves are not the only ones crazy about these sports. The number of extreme sports fans is growing rapidly. Many of these fans have never tried these sports, although often only because their parents or other loved ones will not let them. Extreme sporting events such as the X Games draw sellout crowds. Following the new sportainment trend, these events are often large-scale celebrations with headlining bands, celebrity appearances, and rows of vendor booths. Extreme athletes are signing lucrative sponsorship and endorsement deals, and extreme sports films and bootleg videos also do well. Although many diehard extreme sports fans resent this commercialization, the appeal of extreme sports is not surprising. The more danger there is, the more suspense and excitement there is, the more entertaining it is. Sports writer James Sullivan sums it up: "The X Games, now in their sixth year, have spoken for the entire culture of the West: From loud, fast music to guerrilla film-making and outrageous ad campaigns, pushing the envelope is the mark of the era."[337]

WELCOME, ATHLETES AND SPORTS FANS

Think about the sports and recreational activities in which you have participated recently. Maybe you have gone skating, skiing, or biking, lifted weights, or played golf or tennis. As discussed earlier in this chapter, participating in sports and games has been one of the most long-standing traditions of civilization.

Playing Sports

Today, millions of people participate in a variety of physical activities every year. Research suggests the following three basic reasons why individuals participate in sports:

☆ *Personal improvement.* Release of tension/relaxation, sense of accomplishment, skill mastery, improved health and fitness, other people's respect for one's athletic skill, release of aggression, enjoyment of risk taking, personal growth, development of positive values, sense of personal pride.

☆ *Sports appreciation.* Enjoyment of the game, sport competition, thrill of victory.

☆ *Social facilitation.* Time spent with close friends or family, sense of being part of a group.

Although this list suggests that many individuals participate in sports for reasons other than entertainment, most people who play sports do so because they enjoy it. Certainly sports-related games such as miniature golf or even sports video games are designed for little more than entertainment value. (For more on video games, refer to Chapter 11.)

Spectator Sports

Fandom

Sports as entertainment is usually more closely tied to watching rather than playing. Not surprisingly, research suggests that people watch sports for many of the same reasons they enjoy other forms of entertainment. Wann has identified eight basic motives fans have for watching sports; see Table 12.1. Although "entertainment value" is isolated as a single factor on this list, virtually all the motivation factors that are identified reflect general leisure or entertainment functions.

According to Webster's dictionary, a *fan* is "an enthusiastic devotee (as of a sport or a performing art) usually as a spectator."[338] Although some individuals consider themselves general sports fans, most fans are more strongly devoted to certain sports than others. Why do some people prefer football or hockey, whereas others prefer golf or auto racing? Research suggests that differences in one's motivations for watching sports may explain differences in sports preferences. Some evidence suggests that individuals who are motivated by *aesthetics* express preferences for individual and nonaggressive sports, whereas those motivated by *eustress* and *self-esteem* prefer team sports, and those motivated by *economics* prefer aggressive sports. Research also shows that men generally prefer more aggressive sports than women do.

Although sports preferences may be influenced by internal personality factors and other characteristics, they are also affected by external sociological influences. Individuals tend to reflect sports preferences that are consistent with the preferences of their family, friends, and local and national culture. Preferences are also shaped by situational factors, such as one's geographical location. For example, individuals who live near the water are more likely to show a preference for water sports. As with all industries, sports producers and marketers conduct extensive research on these factors so that they can better target and tailor their sporting events and products to appropriate audiences.

Fanaticism

Sports lovers follow their teams with something akin to religious zeal, as evidenced not only by the amount of money they are willing to spend on game tickets and sports

Table 12.1	Fan Motivation Factors
Self-esteem enhancement	Fans are rewarded with feelings of accomplishment when their favorite players or teams are winning.
Diversion from everyday life	Watching sports is seen as a means of getting away from it all.
Entertainment value	Fans enjoy the drama and the uncertainty of sports.
Eustress	Sports provide fans with positive levels of arousal. It is exciting to the senses. It gets your adrenaline going.
Economic value	Some fans are motivated by the potential economic gains associated with gambling on sporting events.
Aesthetic value	Sports are seen by many as a pure art form—people appreciate the beauty and "ballet" of athletic performances.
Need for affiliation	The need for belonging is satisfied by aligning with a sports team, particularly if important reference groups, such as friends and family, are also fans.
Family ties	Some fans feel sporting events can promote family togetherness by providing opportunities for families to spend time together.

SOURCE: Adapted from Shank, M. D. (2002). *Sports marketing: A strategic perspective* (2nd ed., pp. 188-193). Upper Saddle River, NJ: Prentice Hall.

merchandise, but also by the quirky traditions and ritualistic behavior they exhibit at all levels of sports, from little leagues to the pros. Like followers of different religious denominations, fans for different teams worship according to their own unique traditions. They chant war cries and wear "lucky" caps. In Wisconsin, fans pledge team allegiance by adorning their heads with cheese slices. Fans around the world don war paint from head to toe in team colors. Dennis Perrin, author of *The American Fan,* equates this fanaticism with primal behavior:

> In Indiana basketball tribalism is particularly extreme. So manic are the fans that one might view them as insects at a feast. . . . To sit in a crowded small-town gym as the boys run the floor is to experience the insect collective at fever pitch . . . and should the game go to overtime, the conscious mind fades and it is hours before one's mammal senses return.[339]

Athletes themselves have their own traditions. Consider some of the pregame rituals of key NBA players. For Larry Bird such rituals meant locking his eyes on the retired number 4 jersey of Boston Bruins hero Bobby Orr hanging from the Boston Garden rafters while the national anthem played. For Bailey Howell it meant brewing a cup of tea and then sipping—pinkie extended—until the cup was empty. For Kareem Abdul-Jabbar it meant sitting by his locker and reading a book, often in the buff. At Florida State, football tradition includes

> **Figure 12.3** Like ancient warriors, sports fans engage in their own unique rituals of costume and war paint, chants and charms, BIRGing in reaction to their teams' victories, and CORFing in reaction to their defeats.

© Corbis.

taking a piece of sod from the opponent's football field following key victories and burying it in a cemetery next to the practice field.

Through their dedication and rituals, fans in a sense move beyond serving as mere spectators to become active participants. This participation makes them feel as though they are part of the team, and this sense of belonging enhances their enjoyment. Psychology offers several explanations for this phenomenon. According to social identity theory, people are motivated to behave in ways that will boost their self-esteem. It is reasoned that sports fans feel that they can get this boost by identifying with a sports team. Fans identify with their team by *Basking in Reflective Glory (BIRGing)* and *Cutting Off Reflective Failures (CORFing)*. When our team wins, we like to bask or BIRG by proudly wearing team sweatshirts and displaying team posters. By identifying with winners, we feel that we are winners. When our team wins, "we win." In contrast, when our team loses, we CORF. Our rhetoric changes; "we" don't lose, "they" do. We disassociate ourselves from our team. When our team is struggling, we may also CORF by *blasting,* or criticizing and downgrading other teams. Sports fans tend to reflect *in-group, out-group biases,* where characteristics of the in-group (the fan's team) are automatically seen as good, and characteristics of the out-group (the competition) are automatically bad.

Fans also demonstrate a process called *deindividuation*, where people lose their self-awareness and have decreased concern for how those around them evaluate their actions. People seem to lose or change part of their identity, taking on the team identity when engrossed in sports. They are swept up in the moment and act as a group rather than as individuals. Among athletes, this loss of individualism can be advantageous because team members are willing to sacrifice their bodies for the good of the team. It is also in this state that mob violence or rioting may occur among both athletes and fans.

SPORTS AND SOCIETY

Sports entertainment does not occur in a vacuum. Like all entertainment, it both shapes and reflects other aspects of society. Similar to other forms of entertainment, including the arts—such as theater, dance, literature, and music—sports has shared a delicate relationship with religious and government practices. Research has examined these relationships as well as other societal implications associated with watching and playing sports.

Sports as Religion: Play and Pray

Many comparisons have been drawn between sports and religion. This is perhaps an obvious connection, considering that the original Olympic Games served as religious rituals in which the athletes were also representations of the gods. Although modern sports spectators live in a relatively secular age, today's fans are said to be as passionate about their sports and as devoted to their teams as religious followers are regarding their spiritual leaders and beliefs. In fact, it is suggested that contemporary sports fill the vacuum left by the decline of religion.

In the United States, football is often isolated for these comparisons. Media analysis scholar Arthur Asa Berger notes that "the passionate feelings people have about football (and their teams) and the intensity of our collective interest in the games leads me to think that football has a dimension far beyond that of simply being a sport."[340] He argues that in today's secular societies, many religions have become increasingly more rational and continue to demythologize themselves, becoming more scientific and less ritualistic, while football has become superstitious with folklore and complex rituals that are compared to traditional religious theology. According to Berger, "people seem to have a need for myth, ritual, mystery and heroism, and football perhaps more than religion in contemporary societies, is helping people satisfy these needs."[341] Thus, it is suggested that sports functions for many people as an alternative to religion. Table 12.2 points out some interesting parallels between football and religion.

Sports and Politics: And the Winner Is . . .

Considering the parallels between sports and religion, it is perhaps not surprising that religious and political leaders have exhibited somewhat fickle attitudes toward sports,

Table 12.2 Football as Religion

Professional Football	Religion
Superstars	Saints
Sunday game	Sunday services
Ticket	Offering
Great merger (into a single league in 1920)	Ecumenical movement
Complex plays	Theology
Players on the way to the Super Bowl	Knights in search of the Holy Grail
Coaches	Clergy
Stadium	Church
Fans	Congregation

SOURCE: Adapted from Berger, A. (1982). *Media analysis techniques*, p. 129. Beverly Hills, CA: Sage.

alternately embracing and opposing sporting activities. This flip-flopping has largely centered on the question of whether sports support or threaten morality and good citizenship. Historically, sports organizers "often incurred the wrath or moral concern of dominant political and religious forces who abhorred the wasteful and dissolute behavior—drunkenness, wagering, violence and sexual promiscuity—that often accompanied [sporting events]."[342]

In 394 A.D., the Christians forced the Roman emperor to end all pagan rituals, including the Olympic Games.[343] In 1365 King Edward III issued an order that "able bodied men" who were at "leisure" on feast days should engage only in militarily useful "sport" using bows, arrows, and other approved weapons. Those who engaged in "vain games of no value like stone throwing, handball and football did so under 'pain of imprisonment.'"[344] Commitments to work and restrained leisure similarly led to the banning of the ancient football game in Ashbourne, Derbyshire, in 1860.[345]

Many authorities, however, worked to promote sports and physical activity as a way to "discharge unhealthy urges among the citizenry."[346] This view held that keeping the working class occupied with sports was preferable to allowing them to remain idle, free to engage in other vices or to become too weak to work or defend the country. Sports were seen as a means of promoting discipline, cooperation, leadership, and purity. It was this line of thought that led to the re-emergence of the Olympic Games in the late 1800s.

Today, sports and politics remain difficult to separate. National, state, and local governments allocate funds for school sports programs and other sports organizations. Local governments fund recreation facilities for public and professional sports use. Governments also pass legislation banning discriminatory practices in sports and restricting sports-related advertising and sponsorship of alcohol and tobacco products. Scholar David Rowe suggests an interesting role for the relationship between sports and government:

National governments . . . have invested heavily in sports and sports television (through national, public broadcasters) because of the highly effective way in which sports contribute to nation building. In countries divided by class, gender, ethnic, regional and other means of identification, there are few opportunities for the citizens of a nation to develop a strong sense of "collective consciousness," of being "one people."[347]

It is argued that events such as the Olympics are used to build patriotism and loyalty. Ironically, although there is some thought that countries that excel at sports appear more powerful and more capable of waging war effectively, it is also thought that international sporting competitions enhance international understanding and make actual military combat less likely. Similarly, sports is a popular diversion used to try to "straighten out" wayward youths. Again, it is reasoned that, in addition to keeping kids occupied and away from crime and violence, sports teach discipline, responsibility, and teamwork.

Not everyone, however, shares this optimistic view of modern-day sports. Marxist and Neo-Marxist critiques of sports include accusations of racism, commercialism, militarism, nationalism, and imperialism. This disdain is usually limited to sports as practiced in capitalistic societies; in contrast, they embrace sports in socialized societies (such as the former Soviet Union) as benevolent, community-building activities. Many Neo-Marxists are even more skeptical than Marxists; they disapprove of all sports, reasoning that governments use sports to divert potentially revolutionary energies away from political action. The argument, in essence, is that sports distract audiences from political problems and keep them occupied so they have no energy or interest to rise up against their government. Or, as one author puts it, "the protest against political and economic injustice is drowned out by the spectators' mindless screams of ecstasy and rage as they identify with the gridiron gladiators and the stock-car drivers."[348]

Sports and Violence:
Hit Me With Your Best Shot

To many fans and critics, modern-day sports seem more violent than ever. Anecdotal evidence of violence, where athletes attack not only each other but also referees and fans, abounds even in noncontact sports such as baseball and basketball. Of even greater concern to many is the fact that athlete violence doesn't always end when the games end. The media delight in reporting the skirmishes athletes get into off the court or field. In fact, ESPN began including a daily crime report in its broadcasts. Nonetheless, others contend that today's sports and their athletes are relatively tame compared to the life-and-death gladiator matches of yesteryear.

It has always been difficult to separate sports from violence. Indeed, research suggests that many audiences, particularly male audiences, enjoy sports more if they contain high levels of violence and roughness. The logic is that aggression heightens the drama and suspense of sports and acts as a cue to observers that athletes are so highly motivated to win

Figure 12.4 Critics point to skirmishes like this riot at a soccer match as evidence of sports-induced violence, yet the question remains whether the cause for such violence rests more on the sporting events themselves or the societies that breed them.

© Reuters, Inc./Corbis.

that they are willing to take life-threatening risks. Some argue, however, that it is not the actual degree of violence in a game but the viewers' perceptions of violence that influence their enjoyment of sports. Interestingly, research suggests that sports commentary is capable of altering viewers' perception of violence such that when commentators stress the roughness of the play, it appears even rougher.

Even more disputed than the perceived amount of violence in modern sports is the question of how this violence affects those who view it. The relationship between sports and societal violence has received significant attention in both popular and academic literature. As is true for other depictions of violence, however, theorists are split in their views.[349] According to one view, aggressive sports can have a cathartic effect on audiences, reducing their own aggressive urges and thus minimizing actual violence. Evidence for this effect, however, is rather weak. A more popular view maintains that viewing sports may promote spectator violence. Theories supporting this view are reviewed in Chapter 5.

The Evidence

Incidents ranging from parent brawls at youth league games to full-scale riots at professional sporting events are pointed to as examples of sports-induced violence.[350] In Sarasota,

Florida, a man was arrested and charged with battery after storming the field to punch the referee in his 7-year-old son's flag football game. In Salt Lake City, two women were charged with assault after allegedly attacking a mother, leaving her unconscious, following a youth baseball championship game. At a National Football League game in Cleveland, the referees literally had to run for their lives as angry fans hurled beer bottles and other debris at them for making a delayed call that dashed the Browns' playoff hopes. And in New Orleans, the mother of a Duke University basketball player suffered a concussion after fans at the University of Maryland hurled water bottles and other debris because the Terps had lost the game. Perhaps most alarming is the case of a 44-year-old American man who killed a fellow parent while they were watching their sons take part in an ice hockey practice match in Cambridge, Massachusetts.

Backing up these examples of fan violence, empirical research suggests that sports violence can make spectators more aggressive. This research suggests, however, that audiences may react differently to televised sports than they do to live events. Sports commentary and other features of mass media may influence audiences more than the violence itself. If sportscasters speak favorably of the violence, as they often do, then observers may be more apt to learn and perhaps perform violent behaviors than if the sportscasters condemn the violence or if there is no commentary at all. So the aggressive effects of watching televised sports may be greater than the effects of watching live sports. Yet because television viewers are often more isolated from others, they do not face the same crowd situations that tend to provoke aggression at live events.[351] Nonetheless, the evidence found in these studies poses a significant dilemma for sportscasters. If they want to enhance the entertainment value of a sporting event, research suggests that they should emphasize violence and roughness. However, if they do so, they risk encouraging violent behavior in their audiences, an impact that many would argue runs counter to the journalistic creed to promote the public good.

Sports Heroes:
Where Have You Gone, Joe DiMaggio?

Criticisms of the violent behavior of modern-day athletes go hand and hand with criticisms of the athletes themselves. These critics argue that today's sports do not produce heroes like Joe DiMaggio, whose achievements include a 56-game hitting streak in 1941 that may never be surpassed. "It is hard to think of anyone today, in sports or out, who comes near [DiMaggio's] sustained dignity (hoopster Michael Jordan seems to have qualities of that gold, but this will take some years to validate). In the arena of public affairs, there's hardly a name that does not come with an asterisk."[352] Psychologist Frank Farley identified six character traits he believes define the essence of heroism (see Table 12.3). Not every hero may have them all but, according to Farley the more, the better. It is not the athletic prowess of today's athletes that most critics question, for clearly we have many remarkable sports stars— impressive risk takers who possess courage and strength, skill and expertise. It is their moral fiber—their honesty, kindness, and generosity—that is considered questionable. According to one critic, contemporary athletes "merely reflect the heroic attributes of physical vitality

Table 12.3 What Does It Take to Be a Hero?

Six Important Character Traits

Courage and strength.	Whatever a hero is, he or she isn't a coward or a quitter. Heroes maintain their composure—and even thrive—under adversity, whether it be the life threatening sort that war heroes face or the psychological and emotional strains that politicians and business leaders must endure.
Honesty.	It's no coincidence that "Honest Abe" Lincoln and George "I cannot tell a lie" Washington are among our nation's most cherished figures. Deceit and deception violate our culture's conception of heroism.
Kind, loving, generous.	Great people may fight fiercely for what they believe, but they are compassionate after the battle is over—toward friend and foe alike.
Skill, expertise, intelligence.	A hero's success should stem from his or her talents and smarts, rather than from mere chance—although, for the sake of modesty, a hero might well attribute his or her hard earned achievements to luck.
Risk taking.	No matter what their calling, heroes are willing to place themselves in some sort of peril.
Objects of Affection.	We might be impressed on an intellectual level by somebody's deeds. But admiration is not enough—heroes must win our hearts as well as our minds.

Consider how today's top sports figures compare against this list.

SOURCE: Adapted from How to be great! What does it take to be a hero? Start with six basic character traits. (1995). *Psychology Today*, 28(6), p. 46.

and unconquerable spirit on the surface. Yet beneath these superficial characteristics, modern athletes lack the ethical uprightness necessary to qualify them as real heroes."[353]

Consider the focus on morals. Some might be surprised to learn that politicians rate first as the most commonly mentioned heroes. Neck and neck for second place are entertainers (Barbra Streisand is big among women, Clint Eastwood among men) and family members. Religious figures rank fourth, whereas most of the rest come from the military, science, sports, and the arts.[354]

There are several possible reasons sports figures rank so low. One factor may be the sheer number of them. It was much easier for Joe DiMaggio to become a hero when baseball and football were the only sports of any popularity. Another consideration is that sports have become big business, with athletes seemingly motivated as much by financial gains as by athletic ones; for example, they often charge fans for autographs. Others argue that sportswriters and tabloid journalists are to blame. This line of reasoning suggests that today's sports figures, as well as others in the public eye, are no more or less noble than they have been in the past. It is simply that today's journalists spend more time focusing on human failings and frailties than on nobility and heroics.

Heroes are thought to have depth. "Depth," it is argued, "is that timeless, mythical, almost otherworldly quality that marks a hero. It's hard to articulate exactly what this is . . . but we all know it when we see it—it's what makes even physically diminutive heroes seem larger than life."[355] Thus some might argue that an overemphasis on athletic prowess at the expense of education and other pursuits has created a generation of one-dimensional sports stars. Psychologist Frank Farley wonders if public disillusionment with pro athletes means that most of tomorrow's sport heroes will be fictional characters like Rocky.

Who Needs Heroes?

Heroes are said to be the window into the soul of a culture. If you look at a nation's top heroes, you'll get a pretty good idea of its citizens' values and the ideals they cherish. American heroes tend to be individualists and risk takers. But in China, heroes might be more likely to uphold tradition. These distinctions have important implications for everything from international business dealings to political and military negotiations.

In this context, a recent survey reporting that nearly half of American children have no heroes at all has ominous implications.[356] There is concern about how these kids will learn to transcend adversity—such as poverty or racism—without the example of the great men and women who came before them. "The great American story is the person starting from nothing and becoming something," Farley says. "We need more depictions of that."

According to Farley, "Being inspired by people who do great things is one of the oldest, most reliable forms of motivation."[357] In reviewing Farley's work, one author notes that "we sorely need heroes—to teach us, to captivate us through their words and deeds, to inspire us to greatness. . . . Above all, they spur us to raise our sights beyond the horizon of the mundane, to attempt the improbable or impossible."[358]

Contemporary Sports Icons

Although some may bemoan a lack of modern-day sports heroes, others suggest that today's heroes are bigger and better than ever. Clearly, one of the most notable current sport icons is Michael Jordan. If heroics were to be measured in dollar figures, his value would be unquestionable. It was estimated that Michael Jordan had a $10 billion effect on the United States' economy while he was playing in the National Basketball Association (NBA) from 1984 through 1998. The success of Gatorade's "Be Like Mike" campaign certainly supports Jordan's heroic status.

Figure 12.5 Some people argue that today's pool of potential sports heroes has never been greater, particularly with the rise of female sports stars like soccer player Tiffeny Milbrett, whose play for the United States has served as inspiration for young women across the country.

SOURCE: Photo courtesy of Linda Milbrett.

And even if late 20th-century America was in short supply of heroes, some would argue that today's pool of potential heroes has never been greater. Following on Jordan's heels was the neck-and-neck home run record race between baseball's Sammy Sosa and Mark McGwire, and Tiger Woods's domination on the golf course. Women's sports have also produced inspiring athletes, such as soccer players Mia Hamm and Tiffeny Milbrett, and basketball's Sheryl Swoops. In addition to athletic prowess, in true heroic fashion, these athletes have been noted for their poise and sportsmanship. Nonetheless, many critics and fans remain cynical about whether or not today's athletes are suitable heroes or role models.

FADE TO BLACK

Archaeological records suggest that sports may be some of our earliest forms of entertainment. Although sports are more spontaneous than many other forms of entertainment, they follow the same dramatic principles as most other forms of entertainment. In fact, their capacity for generating suspense and captivating audiences has made them big business. People may be motivated to play and watch sports for many reasons. Fans and athletes alike may pursue their sports with almost religious fervor. Sports can also be very political. Governments have differently condemned and promoted sports over the years. Indeed, sports can have powerful cultural and societal impacts. And, as with many other forms of entertainment, a significant body of research has studied both the potentially positive and negative effects of sports.

A Closer Look

Show Us the Monkey

Football, basketball, hockey, and wrestling fans have all appeared to wholeheartedly embrace the new sportainment approach. In baseball, however, the response has been less enthusiastic. Although many diehard fans seem to prefer a more traditional game atmosphere, some critics argue that baseball is too outdated for contemporary audiences, who seek fast-paced action. Although baseball still maintains a reasonably strong fan base, professional teams continue to search for ways to increase support.

Disney applied some of its magic to the Anaheim Angels baseball team, with mixed results. Disney signed a deal to buy the Angels in 1996 for $140 million and then spent $90 million to renovate Anaheim Stadium. Edison signed on as a corporate sponsor with an agreement rumored to call for the company to pay Disney about $1.4 million for 20 years in exchange for its name on the stadium. Disney initiated its takeover with the slogan "Kiss your big 'A' goodbye," referring to the landmark big "A" marquee at the stadium.

Not surprisingly, the ballpark now has a family entertainment theme similar to Disneyland, which is located just a few minutes up the road. Gigantic bats and batting helmets frame the main entrance to Edison International Field, serving as an imposing backdrop for the games. The outfield is garnished with "Home Run Extravaganza," a landscaped fountain area resembling Disney's old West "Thunder Mountain" ride. Angels home runs are celebrated with fireworks, music, and 80-foot geysers. And when the kids grow fidgety in their seats, they can drag their parents out to "The Perfect Game Pavilion" beyond center field, where they can match their base-running speed to that of Angel Darin Erstad, try to hit a home run like Tim Salmon in a homer contest, or order up a peanut butter and jelly sandwich at the "Rookie Table Restaurant."

And, at first, these changes seemed to work. Headlines read "Disney's Magic Works on Angels"[359] and "Disney's Wonderful World: First-Place Angels Aren't the Only Attraction at the Ballpark."[360] "It's awesome," 9-year-old Jason Anderson said between bites of a ketchup-dripping corn dog.[361] Of course, the Angels were winning then. And even so, not everyone was charmed by the Disney transformation. Disney's approach provides a stark contrast to the nearby Los Angeles Dodgers, who continue to host traditional ball games, playing organ music and selling Dodger dogs in their 1950s stadium. Many longtime Angels fans criticized the cheerleaders and rock music Disney offered as an alternative.

Then came the rally monkey. According to sportswriter Bill Shaikin, "The irony is delicious. Disney, the team owner that put cheerleaders and bands on the dugout roof and fake rocks in the outfield, finally found something to stir the interest of Angel fans, purely by accident. It is, well, a picture of a monkey jumping up and down."[362]

During an Angels game, all of the announcements, video clips, and between-inning entertainment are overseen by Rod Murray, Angels director of entertainment, and his staff. They prepare for each game as one would for a play. Everything is run according to a script, complete with dialogue for announcers and cues for music and video. The Angels are known for producing top-quality video clips, which are shown during the game, and each player has a theme song that is played as he comes up to bat. Baseball games, however, are unpredictable, so the crew must be flexible and creative.

The legend of the rally monkey began in June 2000 as the Angels were losing to the San Francisco Giants. Video crew members Dean Faulino and Jason Humes were working hard to whip up some crowd support. They found a video clip from the 1994 hit movie *Ace Ventura, Pet Detective*, starring Jim Carrey, that showed a monkey jumping up and down. They fixed the clip so it would run in a loop, superimposed the words "Rally Monkey" over it, and flashed it on the JumboTron. The Angels rallied, scoring two runs in the last inning to win, and the crowd went wild.

Fans began to demand the monkey, and the "Show me the monkey!" battle cry was born. The monkey became an Angels game regular, rallying the team to come-from-behind victories in 18 of their next 31 wins. To avoid copyright infringement, the Angels hired Katie, the capuchin monkey featured on "Friends," to film a series of Rally Monkey promos. A master of mass merchandising, Disney did not anticipate fan demand for the monkey. Angels staff scrambled to find souvenir monkeys to sell at games. The first shipment of 96 stuffed monkeys sold out within hours. "We've been going crazy just trying to keep up with the demand," said Timothy Fisk, who was charged with the duty of locating wholesalers. "Our biggest problem is finding the exact one shown on the scoreboard."[363] Less than one month after the craze began 3,500, toy monkeys had been sold at Edison Field.

The Angels Rally Monkey shows that entertainment, particularly spontaneous entertainment like sports, can often be more of an art than a science. Even entertainment veterans like Disney may find it difficult to anticipate what audiences will enjoy.

DISCUSSION AND REVIEW

1. How do sports compare to other forms of entertainment? Review the comparisons made in the text and add some of your own. Look to both historical and current sports trends for comparisons.

2. Ask different people you know who play and watch sports why they enjoy doing so and see how their answers match up with the lists in this chapter. If you enjoy playing and/or watching sports, consider which of the reasons and motives apply to you.

3. This chapter discusses many implications of the relationship between sports and other aspects of society. Review and react to this discussion. Discuss any other ways that you feel that sports shape and reflect the rest of society.

4. Some people say that sports decrease violence, whereas others say that sports foster violence. List as many arguments as you can for each side. What is your opinion?

5. Do you think sports figures are good heroes or role models? Should they be? Why or why not? Review the six character traits of heroes discussed in this chapter. Think of any well-known sports figures and evaluate how they measure up to this list. Do you think this list accurately reflects heroic characteristics? Are there some characteristics that you would add or delete?

EXERCISES

1. Do some research and trace the evolution of one sport. Where did it start, and how has it changed over the years? Reflect on why these changes occurred. Look for societal

influences such as religion, politics, or legislation, as well as efforts to increase the sport's entertainment value. Can you make any predictions for the future of this sport?

2. Watch a sporting event on television and pay attention to the commentary. Pick a contact sport (such as hockey or football). Can you identify strategies sportscasters use to increase the entertainment value and drama of the event? Pay attention to their reactions to any aggressive acts. Do they react positively or negatively to these actions? Consider the implications for societal violence.

3. Attend a live sporting event. Can you identify any fan or "fanatic" behavior? What rituals do you see? How does the event compare to religious practices?

RECOMMENDED READINGS

Crabb, P. B., & Goldstein, J. H. (1996). The social psychology of watching sports: From ilium to living room. In J. Bryant & D. Zillmann (Eds.), *Responding to the screen: Reception and reaction processes.* Hillsdale, NJ: Lawrence Erlbaum.

Guttmann, A. (1986). *Sports spectators.* New York: Columbia University Press.

Perrin, D. (2000). *American fan: Sports mania and the culture that feeds it.* New York: Avon.

Rowe, D. (1999). *Sport culture and the media.* Philadelphia: Open University Press.

Shank, M. D. (1999) *Sports marketing: A strategic perspective.* Upper Saddle River, NJ: Prentice-Hall.

13

Seeing the World

Tourism and Travel

The tourist is the other fellow.

—Evelyn Waugh

Tourism is the largest employer in the world. The industry provides services such as lodging, food, souvenirs, entertainment, and transportation to people who travel. Travel includes a journey to some destination and the services that facilitate that journey. Tourism is an industry that interacts with every aspect of the travel process—that is, people leave home, travel to a destination, act as guests to hosts who serve them, collect souvenirs, and return home. The important elements of the tourism process are presented in Figure 13.1.

In this chapter, we approach tourism historically and structurally, and then we discuss the guest, the host, and the destination. After identifying some problematic issues related to tourism, we look at the role of travel for the entertainment industry, the theories that drive the industry, and tourism's impact on global culture.

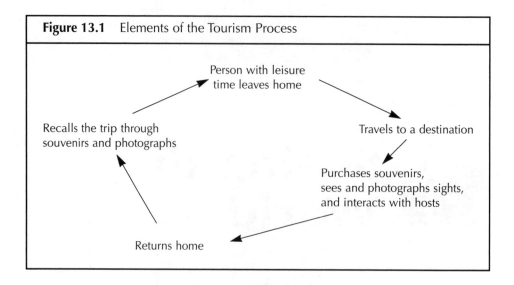

Figure 13.1   Elements of the Tourism Process

AROUND THE WORLD
IN 80 DAYS: EARLY TOURISM

We credit the Romans with creating the first resorts built for the purpose of tourism. These resorts, which were on the coast of Italy, combined leisure activities with health in thermal spas, places where citizens could escape from the moral codes that constrained their everyday lives.[364] The loud parties, excessive drinking, and nude bathing found at these resorts were the precursors of today's activities at spring break destinations. By the Middle Ages, people were traveling to see art and architecture, and to learn the languages and cultures of European countries. Italy was the favored destination for these trips, which were the origin of the *Grand Tour* (global trips supported by the wealthy that began in the 17th century and continued for three centuries). By the 18th century, members of the middle class were sightseeing in short journeys and visiting commercialized spas for fashion, social activities, and gambling. Tourism in the Middle East began in the 18th century and continues today, mainly in the form of religious pilgrimages to important sacred sites such as Mecca, where the Muslim tourist flow is the largest single annual movement of tourists in the world, and Jerusalem, which is a holy city for both Jews and Christians.

Modern-day travel originated in such pilgrimages as well as trade routes over which spices and silk were brought from Asia into Europe. Travel by animal-driven carts was slow and dangerous, and few citizens were willing to venture into unknown territory. The purpose of travel was business, not pleasure. Eventually, adventurers voyaged by boat in search of new lands. Shipping became the transportation of choice for traders and explorers alike.

The introduction of railroads in the 19th century and transatlantic cruises in the 20th century laid the foundation for modern tourism to, from, and within Europe. Today, Europe is the most popular continent as a destination for international tourists, although it is losing ground in the world market to other regions, such as the Pacific Rim, where Australia and New Zealand have a long tradition of *outbound tourism* (tourists leaving the country for destinations outside the country itself).

AROUND THE WORLD IN 8 DAYS: MODERN TOURISM

We attribute the founding of modern tourism to British entrepreneur Thomas Cook, who began packaging tours in the mid 19th century. Cook created new markets for tourism, changing the nature of the relationship between travelers and their hosts forever. Travel agencies were developed to mediate tourism and to create demand where it had not previously existed. In Europe and the United States, railroads and steamship lines provided access to places previously inaccessible to the average traveler. Early hotels and resorts that catered to tourists were managed by railroad companies, and the American West became a favorite destination for city dwellers. Steamship companies replaced their cargo with passengers and were transformed into the first cruise lines dedicated to ocean experiences. European and American resorts, which were founded as retreats for church groups, provided transformative experiences at beach and mountain resorts, where visitors learned how to "worship" the sun.

Contemporary tourism has social and economic implications, spreading modernity to rural parts of the world. By organizing mass travel and providing new rationalizations for traveling, founders of the modern tourist industry used nationalism and cultural pride to transport citizens around the countryside. During the 1950s, people were urged to discover America and to "see the USA in our Chevrolet." The imagery used for recreational tourism focused on spiritual and physical well-being and glossed over the risks and discomforts long associated with travel.

The 1990s travel explosion, which reported expenditures of more than $5 trillion on tourism worldwide, can be attributed to several factors, including the following:

☆ Economic prosperity and increases in disposable income
☆ Advances in travel technology
☆ Increase in leisure time
☆ Access to credit and charge cards
☆ Professional packaging of tours, cruises, and vacations
☆ Awareness of distant lands provided by travel channels and nature-oriented programming

The trip has become a commodity, the tourist a consumer, the world a supermarket of travel opportunities. Whether vacationing for an inversion of everyday life, consuming travel as imaginative pleasure seeking, or delighting in the inauthenticity of the normal tourist experience, 21st century travelers are embracing tourism. The motives of tourists are deeply rooted in their pattern of expectations, goals, and values. The promised experience must materialize if tourists are to successfully escape from their routines and problems. Existing marketplace goals and values serve to motivate and gratify tourists, suggesting that compliance with the theory of uses and gratifications is alive and well in the tourism industry.

Tourism Types

Tourism is an activity serviced by a variety of industries. Although we focus our discussion on only a few types in this chapter, we can identify the following as capturing a viable segment of the tourist industry:

1. *Business tourism*. Travel conducted in work time rather than leisure time, business travel includes travel to meetings, training, conferences, fairs, exhibitions, and incentive travel (reward for performance).[365] Often a business traveler will extend a business trip for pleasure or share a trip with an accompanying family member.

2. *Cause tourism*. Here, tourists work for no compensation on projects such as conservation, building, or teaching local populations.

3. *Day trips*. People travel short distances to theme parks, zoos, museums, outlet malls, beaches, and so forth. Day trips may involve an overnight stay.

4. *Educational tourism*. This category includes travelling to learn a new language, study history, art, or drama on location, or take a class. School and university trips and specialty camps are also classified as educational travel.

5. *Hedonic tourism*. Experience is based on pleasurable activities, including shopping and social interaction.

6. *Health tourism*. Travelers visit spas and therapeutic resorts that provide programs to improve one's health or appearance.

7. *Pilgrimage tourism*. Groups of worshipers or spectators travel to religious sites or to sporting events. Trips to visit relatives or to attend class reunions are included here.

8. *Virtual tourism*. People travel via the Internet without leaving home.

9. *Wilderness tourism*. Travelers journey to ecologically sensitive locations, go backpacking or camping, participate in cycling or sailing, and travel where outdoor activities prevail.

For all but three (business, hedonic, and virtual) of the above tourism types, packages are available to travelers. *Packaged holidays* are remedies for stress. Many travelers never question why they leave a comfortable home to visit some unknown place in potential discomfort. They just know they can get a deal on an exotic location, a place to spend time and money away from home. Some vacationers never even leave the confines of their hotels. Instead, they search the new space for familiarities.

Tourists sign up in record numbers for tours and packaged trips. Three recent innovations that facilitate the packaged travel market are the following.

☆ *Inclusive holidays,* which allow distant destinations to become accessible to a mass market. Professionals plan sightseeing, accommodations, and transportation so that all travelers need to do is pack.

☆ *The Internet and electronic devices* enable more independent travelers to personalize packaging without assistance—that is, to obtain their own tickets, hotels, and rental cars.

☆ *Consortia* organize smaller hotels so they are competitive with large chains. Marketing consortia provide access to regional groupings or specific market segments with bulk purchasing. Airlines, hotels, and credit cards package trips to take advantage of consortia relationships.

Regardless of what kind of traveler you are or what kind of package you choose, the process of becoming a tourist can be understood in terms of flow and regions.

Flow and Go

The flow of tourism has three route options. Access to the destination is most often a direct route by plane or other means of rapid transportation. The route home may be more circuitous, involving side trips or stops along the way. Another option is to view travel to or from the destination as a recreational and integral part of the trip itself.[366]

The flow to and from destinations has three regions. The *generating region* is where our trip begins. Marketing activities, booking transportation, and making hotel reservations are essential for planning the trip. Upon leaving our point of origin, we enter the *transit region.* The time between departure and arrival is spent checking into and traveling on a particular mode of transportation. Tourist attractions are located at our *destination region,* where tourists arrive to be entertained. We conceptualize tourist flows and regions in Figure 13.2.

After a person leaves home to travel on a mode of transit to a tourist attraction, he or she becomes a tourist in search of locals, souvenirs, and memories. This person who goes off to experience a new place and who returns home enriched from the experience is essential to all types of tourism. The next section will help you understand basic tourist needs and motivations in the context of our entertainment culture.

HAVE CAMERA, WILL TOUR

The Barbarian of yesterday is the Tourist of today.

—Neal Mitford, 1959

Today, anyone traveling for pleasure or leisure can be called a tourist or a guest in places other people call home. Although the term *traveler* is often used to refer to a tourist, we

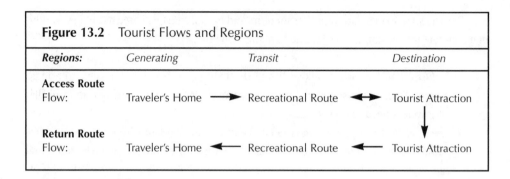

Figure 13.2   Tourist Flows and Regions

Regions:	Generating	Transit	Destination
Access Route Flow:	Traveler's Home ⟶	Recreational Route ⟷	Tourist Attraction
Return Route Flow:	Traveler's Home ⟵	Recreational Route ⟵	Tourist Attraction

differentiate between the two terms from an activity perspective: A traveler actively engages in a purposeful journey, whereas a tourist takes a more passive and consumptive approach to travel. For our purposes, tourists use travel and leisure for entertainment, and our interest is in what entertains tourists and why. By understanding tourist motivations, the entertainment industry can maximize the travel experience.

The Tourist Gaze

Tourists develop a particular *gaze* directed to features of landscape and townscape which separate them from their everyday lives.[367] While gazing, tourists capture these views through photographs, postcards, camcorders, and so forth. Tourists set out in search of something new and different, whether authentic or simulated, to amuse themselves. Tourists gaze upon the objects of their travel in various ways. They may gaze romantically at one another, they may act as spectators or sightseers of street activity, or they may act socially as a collective. Gazes can also be directed at nature or at cultural antiquities.

Tourists are named according to their particular gazing characteristics. We call tourists on packaged tours who gaze as a collective *groupies*; people who travel for adventure on their own gaze as *explorers*; those with no planned activities, called *wanderers,* gaze randomly.[368] Whereas explorers and wanderers prefer more casual and spontaneous accommodations, groupies usually stay in predetermined locations. They sometimes act as children, following tour guides, going where they are told to go, and doing what they are told to do. In such cases, tourists seemed to be playing childlike games that involve breaking traditional adult rules. Excess, for example, is one taboo tourists break—they eat too much, spend too much, stay up too late, and wear outrageous clothes.

Some tourists seem to enjoy "playing tourist" by preferring simulation to experiential reality. Such tourists prefer fakery and contrived experiences (Las Vegas, film locations, theme parks, and so on) over more genuine travel experiences.[369] If modern tourism is shaped by McDisneyization, is it any wonder that tourists seek travel experiences that reflect superficiality?[370] On the other hand, tourists may seek to escape the mediated or themed associations that occur in their daily routines.[371] The quality of this escape experience depends in part on how entertaining it becomes for the tourist.

Regardless of what we call them or what they seek, tourists are people at leisure, and tourism encompasses the activities they engage in while at play.[372] A *touristic process* begins with the desire to leave home, travel to other places, and encounter people from different cultures. During this process, tourists engage in a series of transactions with people who serve them, such as travel agents, hotel managers, shopkeepers, and others who work in the tourist industry. To facilitate the touristic process, tourist travel is generated through the marketing efforts of this industry. At the other end of the tourism process is the host society, which depends on tourist-generating areas to send them visitors. Understanding the social relations between guests and their hosts is essential to marketing and delivering a successful tourist experience.

Hosts and Hosting

People who live in tourist areas and districts are called *hosts*. The relationship that develops between hosts and guests depends on several conditions, including the following:[373]

☆   The number of tourists visiting a place in relationship to the size of the host population. Small towns with large numbers of tourists are more encumbered than large cities.

☆   The type of tourist gazing that takes place. Tourists are welcome to observe objects, but hosts are uncomfortable with observations of people.

☆   The organization of the industry that develops to service tourists (commercial, ecological, local crafts, and so on).

☆   Economic and social differences between hosts and guests. Wealthy tourists invading developing countries have a profound impact on inhabitants.

☆   Effects of tourism on host economy and lifestyle. Tourism often changes the nature and quality of life for residents of tourist destinations.

☆   The extent to which tourists can be identified and blamed for undesirable economic and social developments. Overcrowding and negative outcomes are easily attributed to visiting guests.

Examples of these conditions are presented later in this chapter in "A Closer Look," which features an actual case study of tourism and its effects on a small seaside community.

Local residents become a tourist resource, providing entertainment and curious pleasure for outsiders. A tension develops between locals and guests, who are at odds in their preferences for the context of leisure time. In other words, guests seek beauty and exoticism, whereas locals may long for escape, progress, or economic growth. Locals sometimes feel that their space has been invaded by the tourists who come to gaze on them. They accuse visitors of depleting the town's natural and commercial resources.

Residents living in tourist destinations usually approach tourism in one of two ways: active encouragement of it or passive acceptance. Acceptance or resignation separates locals from guests both spatially and socially. These locals patronize places tourists do not frequent, or they leave town to avoid them. Such an attitude may deter tourism but rarely ends it. A more desirable approach is active encouragement, which fosters local enterprise, arts, and entertainment through marketing and promotion. When tourism becomes a location's primary source of revenue, services appear and grow to meet demand, which increases tourism, which increases demand. As the cycle expands, the destination has no longer any choice but to grow with it.

IF IT'S TUESDAY, IT MUST BE TURKEY: PROGRAMMED TRAVEL

One leisure hypothesis says that people seek kinds of stimulation in their leisure environment opposite to those they have at work. Another hypothesis suggests that tourists seek the same kind of stimulation and enjoyment their work provides for them.[374] Whichever is the case, the main element of tourist space is that of *perceived space,* which is the place in their minds— their expectations. Travel fulfills those expectations.

The Going or the Getting There

We usually travel to specific destinations. Three types of journeys provide clues for understanding travel and its relationship to the destination region:[375]

1. *Departure is the destination. Flight* is the key here. Travelers simply want to get away from home. In this case the trip rarely yields deep or lasting effects for the traveler.

2. *Arrival is the destination.* This is travel as *amusement and acquisition,* where travelers prefer going somewhere without having to change locations after they reach the destination. These travelers prefer the replacement of firsthand experience with simulation. Often photographs used to document the destination are the sole purpose of the trip. Las Vegas, theme parks, and packaged experiences prevail.

3. *The destination is undetermined.* These travelers prefer *exploratory or experiential* trips that are spontaneous or impulsive rather than planned or packaged. Even getting lost can be fun for these folks.

For our purposes, arrival destinations are most important for their role as entertainment. People arrive to sightsee; sightseeing has become a regular tourist ritual.

Destinations serve as temporary residences or overnight stays as well as places to go on day trips. Identified as sun, sand, and sea locations, beach destinations are often capital-intensive tourist attractions.[376] Destination attractions include specific geographic districts, retail or commercial establishments, and ethnic or cultural groups.

Tourist attractions allow tourists to form a relationship with a sight and a marker or piece of information about the sight.[377] One distinguishing characteristic of an attraction is the presence of markers or souvenirs. Urban areas of tourism have specific *tourist districts*. New York's Soho, Paris's Latin Quarter, and San Francisco's Haight Ashbury are examples of such districts. After a district has gained tourist status, it tends to replicate what tourists expect in terms of new architecture and commerce, calling into question what is real and what is authentic. For example, Sante Fe, New Mexico, is a city that tore down its original adobe structures and replaced them with new adobe structures that currently serve as shopping plazas. In spite of physical alterations, the town still serves its residents in much the same fashion as it did before it became a mecca for tourism.

Ethnic districts of cities also draw tourists. Tom Robbins describes just such a district—Chinatown in any American city—in his book *Half Asleep in Frog Pajamas*:

> In Chinatown, neon is not just so much electrified signage, it is theme music, a visual soundtrack to the neighborhood. Tourists are yanked into Chinatown by shivering tentacles of unnatural color, to be swallowed up by a radiant carp maw infected with exotica . . . Neon gas courses through images of dragons and pagodas, hues of hibiscus and ginseng, silkworm and firecracker. Neon pushes its embroidery needle in and out of the sky above Chinatown, decorating the canopy that will both protect and advertise it, setting it apart from other parts of town" (p. 358).[378]

Functioning *establishments* also act as tourist attractions. Fisherman's Wharf in San Francisco began as a working pier and has gradually changed to accommodate tourists at the expense of the fishing industry. An example of a complete transformation is the train terminal in Paris, which was recently converted into Musee D'Orse, a modern museum housed within the arched transportation center. Unlike districts that retain their original purpose, establishments are most often transformed from what they were into a tourist attraction. One exception is the Empire State Building, where offices and tourist tower function in harmony.

And then there's Hollywood, which has recently undergone a substantial renovation to keep tourists coming. Betting on Hollywood Boulevard, Disney renovated the El Capitan Theater and purchased a next-door address for its live-action spectacles. Nine million dollars was spent renovating the Pantages Theater for the extended run of the blockbuster musical *The Lion King*. A consortium of studio power brokers raised $14 million to restore the Egyptian Theater, transforming the waterlogged venue into a majestic showcase for film preservation. And a real estate developer is spending $567 million on a facility that includes a luxury hotel, restaurants and shops, a broadcast studio, and a deluxe theater to serve as the permanent home of the Academy Awards. Attempting to return Hollywood to its former glory, Mann's Chinese Theater attracts visitors who can't resist comparing handprints and footprints with 150 screen legends.

Even *groups of people* can become tourist attractions; a Hari Krishna community is one example where group members are objects of sightseeing. Occupants of Chinatown lure tourists, as do Native American pueblo dwellers. People become attractions because of the cultural or ethnic differences from those who visit them. Perceived as oddities, groups of human beings have lured tourists since the days when so-called circus freaks were promoted to attract audiences.

Roadside Attractions

Some attractions are found or occur during a journey to or from a destination. Hip, post-modern tourists look for virtual reality through the roadside popular culture. Called *roadside attractions,* small theme parks like Flintstones Village (Foothills Highway, South Dakota) and curiosities such as the Snake Pit (Ansted, West Virginia) and the Showman's Rest Circus Cemetery (Hugo, Oklahoma) pepper our highways. Antique shops and swap meets also serve as popular stops for travelers. A sort of museum for the eccentric, the Museum of Jurassic Technology in Los Angeles parodies real museums with its pseudo-scientific exhibits, which feature information about people and phenomena no one ever knew they wanted to know. By making use of information that lies on the edges of our cultural literacy—things we've heard of but don't know much about—the museum seduces us with exhibits on bat radar, ultraviolet rays, and aspects of kitsch culture. A few other museums that are worth stopping for include: the Cockroach Hall of Fame in Plano, Texas; the Museum of Bathroom Tissue in Madison, Wisconsin; and the UFO Museum in Roswell, New Mexico. These and other populist museums deserve attention for their homemade artifacts, not usually perceived as important tourist attractions.

Road Kitsch

A road trip highlight is the random sighting of vernacular works of art—stuff ordinary people create for their yards, or outlandish communal decorations. For instance, Alabama travelers on their way to Birmingham can stop at the Ave Maria Grotto to see and buy models of global religious architecture on Brother Joseph Zoettle's property. Other attractions, visible for miles, are commercial landmarks, such as cone-shaped ice-cream stands, hamburger-shaped diners, or life-sized animals.[379]

Travelers also like to visit places that were made famous by the media. Four such places are the Washington town that was home to the TV sitcom *Northern Exposure,* the ranch featured in the TV show *Dallas,* the bar from the TV series *Cheers,* and the frat house at Dartmouth captured in the film *Animal House. The Sopranos,* a popular HBO TV series, created quite a cash cow for commercial providers in Kearny, New Jersey. Tour high spots include an auto body shop, a pork store, and a sleazy dance joint that serve as locations for, respectively, Soprano hangouts Big Pussy's, Satriales, and the Bada Bing! nightclub (where one can buy T-shirts and Sopranos trivia). Tourists happily pay $30 to see some of the least attractive sites in New Jersey just because they are places where the fictitious Tony and his gang conduct their business.[380]

Scenes of infamous crimes also lure tourists; among them are the condominium of murdered celebrity wife Nicole Simpson in Los Angeles; the Lorraine Motel in Memphis, where Martin Luther King was assassinated; and the clinic in Florida where a Pensacola abortion doctor was murdered. These and other places that house roadside popular culture attractions provide amusement for people traveling between here and there.

Kodachrome and Candy

As amusing for tourists as travel itself are the finding and purchasing of *souvenirs* or *markers*. Collecting artifacts, an essential part of the tourist ritual, provides travelers with tangible symbols of their experience. The symbolic significance of artifacts is important for understanding the total tourist experience. Souvenir artifacts can be classified as follows:[381]

- ☆ *Pictorial images* (e.g., postcards, snapshots, books, etc.)
- ☆ *Pieces of the rock* (i.e., things saved from the natural, gathered, hunted, or taken from a built environment)
- ☆ *Symbolic shorthand* (e.g., manufactured miniatures or oversized objects)
- ☆ *Markers* (i.e., souvenirs that in themselves have no reference to a particular place or event but are inscribed with words that locate them in place and time)
- ☆ *Local products* (e.g., indigenous food, food paraphernalia, liquor, local clothing, and local crafts)

A relationship exists between the degree of travel experience and the type of authenticity people need from souvenirs. Souvenirs with obvious or public meanings have *conspicuous authenticity,* whereas *idiosyncratic authenticity* comes from private meanings that tend to focus on the symbolic, intangible elements of souvenirs.[382] Global revenues from conspicuous souvenir sales topped $100 billion in 2000 and are expected to continue rising as tourism expands. Sales of Hard Rock Cafe T-shirts, for instance, surpass food revenues in all its international locations; here visitors willingly pay for a marker that advertises their patronage. Wisconsin cheese, California wine, and Minnesota wild rice are a few American products packaged for tourists to commemorate their visits to a destination. Miniature Eiffel Towers, stuffed Florida alligators, polished and painted seashells, and visually stimulating postcards are examples of conspicuous souvenirs less experienced tourists purchase to commemorate place.

More seasoned travelers prefer locally produced or naturally gathered artifacts that signify the experience rather than the place. The production of arts and crafts for tourist consumption is often associated with a destination's rural population. Craft industries may grow and prosper with tourism because they retain what is perceived to be an authentic rather than a mass-produced quality. Local artists may also benefit by associating their art with a regional ecology, such as California's Wyland, who is known for his "whaling wall" murals and porpoise statues. This artist's sea creatures are widely collected by international tourists, who display Wyland marine art to symbolize both their excursions and their ecological philosophical

Figure 13.3 A Wyland "Whaling Wall" depicts ocean creatures that act as tourist souvenirs.

© Wyland Galleries, Laguna Beach, CA.

allegiance. In Wyland's case, native art has grown into an international, multimillion-dollar industry, bringing about the true form of what is best described as *tourist art*.[383]

Tourist attractions must be complemented by a variety of tourist services if revenue from tourism is to flourish. Services established for tourists often benefit locals, who are able to enjoy retailing and restaurants that cater to visitors. During the off season, tourist services often depend upon residents to sustain them through the lean months until tourists return.

THE TOURISM INDUSTRY

When destinations foster tourism, services become part of the landscape. Service can be thought of as *mediation* because of its role in facilitating tourism. The mediation of tourism by individuals and institutions stands apart from the host/guest relationship. Service providers may not even live in or near the places where tourism occurs. Mediators are people who service tourists, including but not limited to planners, promoters, agents, artists, guides, investors, hotel managers, pilots, lifeguards, taxi drivers, clerks, restaurants, and on and on. Everyone who travels or encounters travelers can be considered contributors to the travel industry.

The business of tourism as developed by pioneers such as restaurateur Fred Harvey (who placed his Harvey Houses along the Sante Fe Railroad line west of the Missouri River in 1860) is twofold. One task is telling potential tourists what they want and how to get it (for example, "you want food and we have a restaurant"). The other is to produce places that conform to the expectations and desires the industry has helped create (for example, providing good cooking at reasonable prices).[384] Both components turn to elements of entertainment for their success.

Chambers of commerce, convention and visitors bureaus, and travel consortia employ marketers to produce brochures, films and videos, and promotions to encourage people to travel. AmEx Corporation integrates elements of transportation and lodging to entice travelers who are on a budget. Advertising agencies create amusing commercials to inform potential travelers about destinations and transportation options. Vacation time-shares are created to facilitate distance travel, and pageants are performed to lure visitors. Travel writers, public relations agents, and video producers entice citizens to leave home for adventure and excitement.

After people are persuaded to travel, they must be satisfied with their choices of transportation and destination. Industries that provide methods of travel as well as accommodations and experience are competitive and prosperous. Airlines promise on-time arrivals, trains extoll the virtues of scenic transport, and ships lure us with gourmet dining. Hotels provide free movies and workout facilities, parks present 12 different types of water activities, and cities offer gambling, games, and gifts.

Leisure, a crucial component of entertainment, is itself an industry. Cartoon characters attract and amuse visitors, surreal jungles make dining more fun, and giant roller coasters thrill us. To make travel from home to our destinations palatable, airlines entertain us with in-flight films, and ships have live performances. Our hotel offers us games, and places we visit provide venue-specific gifts. Without entertainment, travelers may become bored and seek other methods of amusement. To prevent boredom, the industry embraces entertainment to ensure pleasant and lucrative travel experiences.

TOURIST SPACE

Tourist spaces are specific locations where people congregate to experience the unfamiliar. Entertainment providers must consider the issue of authenticity and how it determines the nature and quality of tourist space.

Is It Real or Is It Memorex?

Tourists' curiosity for what is perceived to be real causes them to purposefully seek out behind-the-scenes places in tourist locations. Wandering into residential neighborhoods, peeking into private spaces, or probing hosts for answers to intimate questions are some examples of this phenomenon. Visitors are often heard asking directions to "places where the locals go." Tourists sometimes hide their cameras and try to look like they belong by shedding stereotypical identities. Tourism capitalizes on the quest for what is real by establishing the perception of authenticity.

The tremendous expansion of tourism has diminished much of what we consider to be authentic. To compensate, the tourism industry manufactures what is called *staged authenticity*

Table 13.1 Types of Tourist Space

	Tourist Impression of Scene	
	Real	Staged
Nature of Scene		
Real	**A.** Authentic and recognized as such	**C.** Suspicion of staging, authentically questioned
Staged	**B.** Failure to recognize contrived tourist space	**D.** Recognized as contrived tourist space

SOURCE: From Cohen, E. (1979). Rethinking the sociology of tourism. *Annals of Tourism Research, 6*, 18-35.

and *pseudo events.*[385] The success of Las Vegas's replicated cityscapes (New York, Venice, Paris) attest to tourists' preference for visiting the fake place because it exists without the hassles and discomforts—traffic, poverty, dirt—they are certain to encounter in the real place.

Mediated experiences also facilitate reality through replication. Visitors to the Grand Canyon may visit the IMAX version of a helicopter tour located on the south rim and return home feeling just as gratified as if they had actually hiked its Bright Angel trail. If tourists prefer well-produced visual exploits over authentic adventures, imagine the possibilities open to mass media for providing virtual tourism.

Four types of tourist spaces have been identified, as shown in Table 13.1. Experienced tourists seem to know they are playing the tourist game in the obvious absence of what is truly authentic (type D in Table 13.1). And they don't care. Visitors to Gettysburg understand that they are not time travelers, nor are they savages on Hawaii's tropical beaches, nor can they be invisible observers in foreign lands. They know that colorful brochures don't portray long lines of people waiting to enter amusement parks, nor do they discuss the confusion of exchanging local currency. Today's tourists may even revel in the confusion and disorientation that typify prefabricated destinations. The more elaborately staged the experience, the happier the tourist. At least that's what packagers of leisure travel depend upon to lure and retain vacation consumers.

NEW AND EMERGING TOURISM MARKETS

Tourism worldwide is undergoing great change in terms of the demand for new product, popularity of older established forms of tourism, changes in the way product is purchased, and growth of outbound tourism countries not previously generating travel. Twelve trends and new markets are highlighted here.[386]

The All-Inclusive Vacation Concept

In the early days of 20th century tourism, packaged tours were the norm. The "if it's Saturday, it must be Belgium" approach to travel provided tourists with security, no-hassle accommodations, and a pleasant introduction to a foreign country. Since 1960 we have seen a resurgence of all-inclusive tourism, ranging from travelers with specific expenditure or duration requirements to the luxury end of the market. Club Med is an example of a high-end vacation package geared around a single destination. Another form of this concept, cruises, often provides guests with theme-oriented activities while on board. Both educational cruises, which include computer and language instruction, and dance cruises, which feature "brain food" (intellectually stimulating activity) as well as sightseeing, provide a broadly appealing experience. In addition, the incentive travel business is instrumental in packaging and promoting destinations as rewards for company executives and high achievers.

Children's Holidays

The summer camp and school or group trip movement designates children as tourism consumers in their own right. Some interesting camps featured by the *Wall Street Journal* for summer 2002 were the following:[387]

- ☆ *Secret Agent Camp*—In Lake Arrowhead, California; teaches the art of espionage in 3-week sessions that cost $3,220.
- ☆ *Camp Lindenmere*—In Pennsylvania's Pocono Mountains; offers weekly programs in music, theater, circus, and magic for $800.
- ☆ *Blue Dorado Adventures*—Offers 3 weeks aboard a 45-foot yacht in the Caribbean for $3,980.
- ☆ *Camp Namanu*—In the foothills of Mt. Hood, Oregon; offers fishing and rafting activities, where campers learn how to choose the right lure and casting technique, at $325 per week.
- ☆ *Belvoir Terrace*—In Lenox, Massachusetts; an arts camp for girls who learn acting techniques, directing, and production skills for 2 months for a cost of $7,400.
- ☆ *Summer Law Institute*—At UCLA in Los Angeles; prepares tomorrow's attorneys by having students attend trials and learn techniques of persuasion, debate, and discussion for $1,100 per week, including room and board.

As influencers, children will continue to play a large role in determining which camps they will attend and which vacations their parents should schedule.

The International Wedding Market

Honeymoon travel, big business in the United States, is also flourishing in Japan and the United Kingdom, where Las Vegas, New England, the Caribbean Islands, and Cyprus are popular destinations. A honeymoon package includes ceremony, video, flowers, music, food, and drink at a destination. Exotic wedding companies promote underwater, parachute, bungee jump, and ice cave ceremonies. The popularity of distance honeymoons and the low air fares have this business jumping.

Pop Culture Travel

An outgrowth of location filming, visiting places where TV dramas or films were shot is popular with tourists. The film *Sleepless in Seattle*, the book *A Year in Provence* (France), and both media versions of *Angela's Ashes* (Limerick, Ireland) are examples of media that popularize certain locations.

No-Frills Travel

Mediterranean and Gulf of Mexico cruises are available for travelers on a budget. Airline tickets and cruises are priced competitively and are often offered online for the traveler's asking price.

Couples-Only Market

High disposable incomes and childless couples have launched romantic tours and bed-and-breakfast destinations to attract travelers to adult-only venues for weekend to week-long getaways. Sandals, which caters to couples, Club Med, dedicating specific locations or time periods to adults, and Golden Door Spa, priced to restrict attendance to adults, are examples of such offerings. Most cruise lines also offer senior vacations worldwide.

Travel for Health

One of the oldest trip motivators, health travel includes a variety of products such as holistic 'health farms,' resort-based fitness vacations, natural mud and mineral water treatments, and weight-loss spas.

Eco-Tourism

Some people are motivated to travel to see wildlife and experience natural wonders. Eco-tourism feeds on the growing concern for rainforests and endangered species. Wildlife and travelogue programs have increased awareness of habitat adventure. Belize in Central America is noted as a major site of eco-tourism development for its forest reserves, Mayan archeological sites, and the second-largest barrier reef in the world. Sustainable development is achieved in part through attention to preserving wildlife habitats.

Religious Retreats

Worshipers and travelers searching for spiritual experiences are traveling to retreats such as Mount Athos in Greece, and to cults and sects in Asia. Meditation and harmony are the products of these destinations. Religious retreats continue to grow in popularity.

National Parks

Travel to natural wonders lures ground-transported visitors and campers to areas policed and controlled by rangers and park officials. The U.S. National Park System employs more than 36,000 people to serve more than 270 million visitors each year. Parks receive their revenues from appropriations from entrance fees, camp site fees, and concessionaires. Popular with families and so-called armchair travelers, parks provide brief exposures to wilderness and offer a break from commercialism for those on a budget. International visitors are housed in park lodging and guided by bus into Yellowstone or by mule into the Grand Canyon. Overcrowding has caused parks to limit their visitors in peak seasons.

Adventure Travel

A plethora of new adventures is available to those with time on their hands and challenge in their hearts. Wilderness Travel, a 22 year old company out of Berkeley, California, is just one of many companies providing travel to remote destinations with comfortable lodging or camping and good food "without sacrificing the spirit of adventure." For those with the resources and a sense of adventure, hundreds of new companies have sprung up to meet those needs. Space Adventures is taking deposits toward sub-orbital rides into space for about $100,000. Or one can take a two-week dog sled trip with Northwest Passage for $25,000, or climb Mt Everest for $65,000 with Alpine Ascents. Other adventure options include skiing cross country at the South Pole ($45,000 for two months), taking a 25 day trek into Bhutan for $6,000, helicopter skiing in Canada in the Cariboo range for $105,000, or riding the rapids of the Zimbabwe River for $3,000 excluding airfare.

Business Travel

Municipal tourism is fostered by convention operations that actively promote their cities as destinations for trade shows, meetings, and conventions. Effective marketing strategies in cities such as Boston, San Antonio, and San Francisco have created a lucrative business by involving private-sector businesses in promoting the city with cooperative advertising and a dynamic convention and visitors' bureau.

THEORETICAL APPROACHES TO TOURISM

The "build it and they will come" theory of travel no longer ensures financial success in the tourism industry. Careful planning and execution have replaced the haphazard approach.

Proven theories, marketing principles, and aesthetics are invoked to successfully persuade people to travel, to tell them what they want while they're away, and to convince them to return. Highlights of these theories and principles are provided here.

The *4Ps principle* is invoked to market all components of tourism. The *product* (venue or transport) must be well conceived and tested for its desirability; the *price* must be competitively determined for mass or niche appeal; the *place* (location of the venue or transport) must be easily accessible; and *promotion* (PR, advertising, direct sales, sales promotion) must be executed with skill. Because most tourists are experienced consumers, they have high expectations for each aspect of this marketing mix.

Branding is also an essential component of tourism. All modes of travel, places of accommodation, and tourist locations are brands. Disney has created and maintained one of the most successful examples of international brand identity ever developed. After all, doesn't everyone recognize and embrace Mickey? Recognition is only one aspect of brand success. Effective brand management is necessary to build lasting relationships between travelers and tourist industry brands.

To make us to feel good about their brands, marketers use aesthetics. The term *marketing aesthetics* refers to the marketing of sensory experiences in corporate or brand output that contributes to the brand's identity.[388] Attractiveness of the venue is one aspect of aesthetics. Another more important aspect of that concept is the aesthetic that tourism provides by functioning as a symbol for pleasure and gratification. Gratification can be provided by the inherent qualities and structural features of a brand or by the meanings communicated through the brand. If we feel good about the Marriott—by being satisfied with the visual appearance of the hotel and the memories we attach to staying there—we are gratified by the Marriott brand.

A *theory of uses and gratifications*[389] elaborates upon this concept. It suggests that, as consumers, we expect certain levels of gratification and, if we are not satisfied, we discontinue our use of a particular product. Because tourists are said to be "fantasists or escapists"[390] in their flight from routine and problems, marketers promise a relief from that routine through tourism. To be successful, each component of the tourism industry must meet the tourists' expectations of that fantasy or escape.

Marketing aesthetics, like uses and gratifications theory, draw from communications research by attending to *peripheral messages* (giving us information through entertainment). They also draw from *product design* (form and function) and *spatial design* (structure and symbolism). Arguing for aesthetics as a provider of tangible value for a brand, marketers suggest that attention to message and design creates loyalty, allows for premium pricing, cuts through information clutter, and protects against competitive attacks. The *Design Management Journal* is dedicated to providing information on how to use marketing aesthetics that have specific applications for the tourism industry.

Tourist-specific methods of *target segmentation* have been developed for promoting travel and tourism.[391] They are the following:

☆ Purpose of travel. (Why are they taking the trip?)
☆ Traveler needs. (What basic requirement do they have for the trip?)

☆ Motivations and benefits sought. (What do they expect to receive during the trip?)

☆ Traveler characteristics. (What are their economic, geographic, psychographic, and demographic traits?)

☆ Price. (What do they plan to spend on the trip?)

Many tourism businesses have to deal with multiple travel segments. By directing their messages toward one or several segments, marketers are able to address the specific desires of tourism consumers and entertain them appropriately.

TOURISM'S EFFECTS AND POLICY DEVELOPMENT

Tourism does not operate in a vacuum. Immigration and migration patterns and numbers affect destinations at all levels—socially, economically, environmentally, and politically. An overview of these effects may help you understand the complicated process of making policies that ensure a sustainable global environment.

Social Effects of Tourism

Visitors to a region or country create social relationships that typically differ from those within the indigenous population. Tourist-host relationships affect individuals, families, and societies involved in the tourism process. Individuals may experience different degrees of rewarding and educational cultural contact. Travel experiences have profound effects on travelers because their experiences often are among the most outstanding memories of their lives. Families experience memorable adventures when they travel together.

But tourists can also become victims of crimes perpetrated by locals. In Italy, boys on motor scooters grab purses from unsuspecting women while they shop on city streets. In Spain, tourists in cars are stopped along the road and robbed of their possessions. Such incidents create bad feelings about the host country and the people who live there.

Tourism's effects on societies may be equally disconcerting. The presence of tourists changes the living patterns of locals in both positive and negative ways. It may enhance their economic status yet deprive them of the privacy they desire. In developing countries, tourists may influence locals' ways of dressing, consumption patterns, desire for products, sexual freedoms, and world outlook. Tourism development may even affect the natives' entire way of life, fostering prostitution, gambling, drunkenness, and other excesses.

Negatives acknowledged, travel and tourism are primary ways in which members of different cultures may get to know one another. Interactions with local people can dispel the stereotypes formed by media portrayals or historical profiling. And immersion in a foreign nation can provide a new perspective of your homeland. Students who take a year to travel after finishing college return with a different perception of democracy and America than they had before they left home. Tourism is our best hope for fostering peaceful coexistence.

Economic Effects of Tourism

Occasionally, events occur that affect the travel and tourism industry on a global basis. Gas shortages curtail travel by car, economic recessions cause vacancies at hotels, and natural disasters lay waste to destination attractions. But the greatest setback to the tourism economy to date occurred as a result of the terrorist attacks on the World Trade Center and the Pentagon in 2001. After September 11, air travel declined to the point that many airlines were forced to merge with other companies or go bankrupt. Hotels with hundreds of empty rooms laid off servers and staff members. Restaurants, small businesses serving travel-related enterprises, and transportation companies suffered severe cutbacks.

The threat of international terrorist attacks kept people from leaving home for months following the event. In spite of increased security by airlines, discounted hotel rates, and inexpensive packaged tours, the industry suffered tremendous losses in revenue. But as time passes and consumer confidence is rebuilt, tourism is expected to rebound. The quest for adventure, the lure of the unknown, and the need for relaxation can stimulate travel, even following a disaster. The size and extent of the travel and tourism industry renders it one of the most important economic generators of our time. The fact that even after a terrorist attack tourism can recover relatively quickly is evidence of the magnitude and power contained in this global service industry giant.

Environmental Effects of Tourism

The most devastating impact of tourism from the perspective of host countries is its effect on the physical and natural environment of a tourist location. *Carrying capacity* is a key concept in analysis of the potential environmental impacts of tourism. The concept has three elements:[392]

☆ *Physical capacity* is the limit in terms of the actual number of tourists that can be accommodated in a region. Yosemite National Park is frequently jammed with bumper-to-bumper traffic during peak tourist seasons, despite seasonal caps on the number of people admitted.

☆ *Environmental capacity* is the limit in terms of the number of users that an area can endure before visitors notice a decline in the area's desirability. The beaches of Miami, Florida have become over crowded and littered during winter months, reducing their attractiveness to sun worshipers.

☆ *Ecological capacity* is the maximum number of users that an area can accommodate before ecological damage is incurred. Hikers in the tens of thousands that swarm to the Waterton-Glacier Peace Park on the Canadian-U.S. border have all but destroyed the alpine plant life of that location.

Carrying capacities are determined by (a) the number of visitors, (b) the amount of use by the average visitor (day visit versus extended stay RV camping), (c) the quality of resource management and facility design, and (d) the number of area residents and their quality-of-life needs. With careful planning and management, governments can control and monitor carrying capacities for the mutual benefit of both hosts and guests. Controlling environmental damage begins with policy development.

Tourism Policy Development

Governments working together to preserve natural terrain and resources at a global level is called *sustainable tourism*. Sustainability pertains to the ability of a destination to maintain the quality of its physical, social, cultural, and environmental resources. Immigration policies, policies on wages and welfare, foreign investment regulations, zoning laws, currency exchange rates, legal system policies, and policies that limit growth and access to sensitive areas affect the appeal, attractiveness, competitiveness, and sustainability of a tourism destination. To help with this effort, destination management organizations work at the national level as the National Tourism Organization (NTO), at the state level as a State Tourism Office, and at the municipal level as a Convention and Visitors Bureau.

Tourism policy consists of a philosophy and a long-term vision for the destination. The vision guides the development of objectives, which in turn provide a basis for formulating long-term development strategies for the region. There are four major components of the policy formation process:[393]

☆ During the *definition phase*, policymakers develop explicit statements that define the tourism system. Planners determine tourism development policies and objectives; then they survey and inventory the existing situation.

☆ The *analytical phase* is composed of internal reviews as well as audits and analysis of survey information. An external, macro-level review of current and future demand and promotion policies is evaluated.

☆ Identification of strategies, implications, and policy recommendations is accomplished during the *operational phase*. Here, policymakers determine the scope of tourism development needed to achieve objectives, and they make recommendations for specific projects in specific locations.

☆ Finally, these recommendations and programs are executed during the *implementation phase*, where responsibilities are allocated, funding support is identified, and a time line is put into place. Plans are monitored to determine if objectives are being achieved, and modifications of the plan are made as objectives change. Research methods are used to examine, plan, and evaluate policies during all four stages of development and implementation.

When regulation and management of resources fall short, the ecology of the physical landscape will suffer. Residents of desert communities complain as all-terrain vehicles (ATVs) destroy natural habitat, and forest rangers worry about fire danger from careless campers. In developing countries, tourist litter can also be a problem. Prior to 1990, Budapest, Hungary, had no trash receptacles because citizens carried their own grocery sacks and containers for prepared food. After McDonald's opened, the city was inundated with Styrofoam containers and food wrappers flung in the street. The presence of fast-food retailers poses problems for countries that opened their cities to free enterprise after communist control ended.

The U.S. policies involved in dealing with certain countries, or the politics in the countries themselves, can cause difficulties for travelers. The U.S. policy on not offering direct flights to Cuba forces visitors to fly through Mexico or Canada to reach the island. Welcoming the revenue from tourism, Cuba does not police American citizens who visit. However, the United States levies fines on travelers if and when they are caught coming back into the country. Another example is Egypt, a heavily traveled country, where extremists have attacked women tourists who do not wear traditional dress. In an effort to preserve tourism, the Egyptian government has dedicated police to protect women as they tour Cairo and attractions along the Nile.

FADE TO BLACK

This chapter presented distinct methods and models for conceptualizing tourism and its main components: tourists, hosts, and destinations. The tourist industry is integrally related to leisure and entertainment activities. Studies on the sociology and psychology of tourism provide useful insights for understanding tourist motivations. Market segments and the marketing mix can be used to approach tourism from a consumption perspective. By conceptualizing a tourist destination as a brand, we can understand the role of promotion and consumer satisfaction for successful tourism experiences.

Industries related to tourism exist to stimulate desire for travel, to take travelers safely to their destinations, and to accommodate guests at the destination site. Packagers and promoters are hired to reflect consumer fantasies in their advertising and incentive promotions designed to generate travel. Air, rail, bus, and rental car businesses incorporate entertainment into the transit experience. Hotels, sport venues, theme parks, malls, zoos, museums, and so forth require operations personnel and hire workers for every kind of occupation conceivable to function as an integral part of the destination experience.

By entertaining travelers through enticing advertising, enjoyable travel, and amusing destinations, the tourism industry will continue to expand and thrive. Creative application of tested theories can provide industry managers with successful and profitable returns on efforts expended in all regions of tourism.

🔍 A Closer Look

Laguna Beach Tourism

If we look closely at a resort town and its problems, we see how theories and models are used to analyze the situation and make recommendations to solve those problems. After reaching maximum saturation from tourist traffic during the summer of 1999, Laguna Beach, California, asked for solutions to issues concerning access to its attractions and residents' attitude toward this destination.

Figure 13.4 Laguna's Main Beach Recreation Area

© Corbis.

Location

Tourism is the primary industry of Laguna Beach, a Pacific Coast town of 45,000 people, where beach, sun, and sand and a Pageant of the Masters performance attract inlanders who come from a 50-mile radius to visit the city on day trips, and tourists who come for stays of between 4 and 10 days. Each year, more than 200,000 people attend the pageant, which is a re-creation of famous artworks depicted on stage by volunteer actors. Held in conjunction with a Festival of the Arts since 1942, the pageant is a world-renowned event staged to attract visitors and tourists to the city.

More than 500 registered artists live in Laguna Beach, exhibiting arts and crafts at three separate venues from Memorial Day to Labor Day. In addition, incredible vistas, quaint shops and galleries, and world-class hotels attract millions of tourists annually. The city can be easily accessed from north and south or from inland. Traffic congestion and parking problems plague the city during summer months, when tourists arrive by bus and coach to take advantage of the arts offerings and natural environment.

According to a survey conducted by the visitors' bureau, who polled guests at 13 local hotels, the average stay in Laguna Beach is 4 nights, and the primary reason for visiting the city is to attend the pageant (46%). The top four activities in the city are using the beach (77%), attending art venues (59%), shopping (39%), and visiting art galleries (36%). Eighty-four percent of survey respondents plan to return. Those who do not anticipate returning cite parking and crowds as primary reasons for their dissatisfaction with the overall experience.

Hosts and Guests

By applying the host/guest relationship criteria presented in this chapter, we can make some observations and identify several of Laguna's destination problems:

1. *Criterion:* The number of tourists visiting a place in relationship to the size of the host population

Problem: During summer months and weekends all year, tourists outnumber residents two to one.

2. *Criterion:* The type of tourist gazing that takes place

Problem: Tourists park on residential streets for beach visits, preventing hosts from accessing their homes and invading their privacy.

3. *Criterion:* The organization of the industry that develops to service tourists

Problem: The city tourist bureau and chamber of commerce don't currently work together to develop tourist-related facilities. Instead, pageant and festival activities are determined by a board of directors.

4. *Criterion:* Economic and social differences between hosts and guests

Problem: Hosts locate in this community for its upscale lifestyle. Most tourists are of lesser socioeconomic status and come to Laguna to experience "the good life."

5. *Criterion:* Effects of tourism on host economy and lifestyle

Problem: Residents may resent visitors because of parking issues, traffic gridlock, and because tourists can fill beaches with litter and destroy tide pools.

6. *Criterion:* The extent to which tourists can be identified and blamed for undesirable social developments

Problem: Congestion and crowding are visible results of visits by day trippers, weekend visitors, and seasonal travelers, preventing residents from maintaining their lifestyles.

Tourist Regions and Segments

Laguna's destination region is severely affected by the transit region that services it. If transportation (cars and buses) cannot reach the city, destination activity declines with revenues. Laguna caters to two tourist segments—day trippers and hedonic tourists—who come to attend the festival, to shop for art, and to enjoy the beach.

Besides being a sun, sand, and sea destination for amusement, Laguna is a location of acquisition, providing tourists with a plethora of souvenirs of all types. Pictorial festival posters cost $10; seashells are so-called pieces of the rock and can be collected for free; symbolic shorthand is available as a miniature Hotel Laguna; Laguna Beach T-shirts are visitation markers; and local crafts provide some authentic artifacts for tourists seeking more meaningful souvenirs.

Marketing

Laguna Beach's brand is synonymous with the Festival of the Arts. A review of the *marketing mix* identifies some problems with Laguna's brand image today. Although the festival is popular and well produced, the city as a *product* has some weaknesses in terms of the deteriorating image of its user-friendliness. Ingress and egress (*place*) issues as well as local discontent with outsider invasions are having a negative effect on the visitors' perception of gratification. Costs to dine, park, and attend art venues (*price*) are high and discouraging to travelers on a budget. Because of a limited advertising budget, *promotion* efforts are limited to a Web site, gallery location brochures, visitors' bureau collateral materials, and listings in local newspapers' event calendars. Given the competition from adjacent beach locations and the threat of the pageant moving to another city, Laguna Beach would be well advised to rethink its transit and destination spaces.

Recommendations

Planning and policy making must occur to set objectives for all three tourist regions, to set objectives and strategies for reaching those objectives, and to monitor their implementation. Specific objectives, strategies, and tactics of the planning process are stated next.

Generating Region

☆ *Objective*: To stimulate tourism from regions outside of Orange County.
☆ *Strategy*: Promote price discounts and benefits of group travel.
☆ *Tactics:* Tourist center brochures. Internet site information.

Co-op promotions between retailers and tourist venues. Hotel discounts to encourage seasonal patronage from visitors outside the 50-mile radius of the city. Hotel shuttles to provide ease of access from airports and bus depots to final accommodation destinations.

Transit Region

☆ *Objective:* Restrict automobile traffic into the city to provide stress-free beach and event access to sustain current visitations from day trippers.
☆ *Strategy:* Improve visitor transportation facilities.
☆ *Tactics:* More shuttles running between existing parking lots and town. Five-minute lapses between trips to improve the service.

Destination Region

☆ *Objectives*: Control parking and traffic flow in commercial and residential areas.
☆ *Strategies:* Offer controlled parking options for both hosts and guests. Restrict out-of-towners from attending city-sponsored activities (such as Sunday free concerts at Bluebird Park) to simultaneously retain attendance numbers and sustain local support.
☆ *Tactics:* Additional parking structures to accommodate day trippers. Stickers for parking in residential areas. Short-term access to local shopping for residents. Proof of residence to gain access into city-sponsored events intended for hosts.

To evaluate the success of these programs, city officials should conduct surveys to determine levels of satisfaction with the tactics by tourists and residents alike. These results will enable plans to be modified to best accommodate the needs of both hosts and guests.

DISCUSSION AND REVIEW

1. How do the three types of destination regions contribute to understanding the impact of tourism on a local or national economy?

2. What threats exist for development in national parks and game reserves, and how can they be managed?

3. What role does sustainable tourism play in developing tour packages that are marketed as eco-tours?

EXERCISES

1. Visit a local travel agency and collect brochures for three locations or cruise lines. Compare these materials for similarities in visuals and rhetoric. Are differences significant enough to help you make a selection? What factors would affect your selection decision?

2. Log on to the Web sites of Lonely Planet (www.lonelyplanet.com) and Rough Guides (http://travel.roughguides.com) to research what tourists might find when they visit Paris. Compare each site's approach to recommending accommodations and places to visit in the city. What did you learn about Paris from these sites?

3. Rent a travel video of a place you have visited. After viewing, mentally compare what you saw during your visit and what is presented on the tape. What aspects of the place are omitted in the videotape? What does this comparison tell you about place marketing?

RECOMMENDED READINGS AND WEB SITES

Chambers, E. (2000). *Native tours: The anthropology of travel and tourism.* Prospect Heights, IL: Waveland.

Cooper, C., Fletcher, J., Gilbert, D., Wanhill, S., & Harlon, R. (1998). *Tourism: Principles and practices.* New York: Longman.

Lippard, L. (1999). *On the beaten track: Tourism, art and place.* New York: The New Press.

MacCannell, D. (1999). *The tourist: A new theory of the leisure class.* Berkeley: University of California Press.

www.highwayproject.com is a collection of photographs that documents the disappearing culture of the American roadside.

www.planetware.com provides travel photographs for planning personal journeys.

www.recreation.gov is an integrated site able to search any recreational opportunities on federal public lands. A one-stop shopping informational service.

14

Themed Environments as Fabulous Fakes

Disneyland, Mall of America and Las Vegas foster surrogate experience and surrogate environments that have become the American way of life. Distinctions are no longer made, or deemed necessary, between the real and the false.

— Ada Louise Huxtable

Since the end of World War II, theming has altered our everyday environment. As cities became less desirable places to raise families, the trend toward suburbanization broke down the urban/rural dichotomy. Tracts of homes encroached upon farmland until the transition between them was almost indistinguishable. *Suburbia,* a concept that erupted in the mid 20th century, created *edge cities,*[394] where residents could display signs of their wealth and status by planting green lawns and building multiple-car garages. People became comfortable with representing themselves through these and other environmental symbols taken from television and film. Urban places contained offices and commerce, and residential spaces housed families who took public transportation to their places of work or play.

Today, both metropolitan and suburban spaces feature themed environments that merge contemporary, commercialized popular culture with the entertainment media.[395] To embrace the spirit of merging, we define *themed environments* as spaces that serve as containers for human interaction where the public can mingle, and where themed material forms are used as symbols to convey meaning to those who use them. Staging themed environments to convey meaning has become big business. By staging experiences within themes, companies are able to *engage* consumers, not simply attract them.

This chapter takes a closer look at the places we shop and visit through the perspective of themed experience. After we explore themed environments in general, we take you to the staged indoor worlds of malls and restaurants, and we visit outdoor amusement parks and entire cities. All these are places where theming has become a way of life for Americans. As you read about themed environments in this chapter, try to identify one or more of the symbols that contribute to the success of each staged reality.

CREATING SYMBOLIC REALITY

Prior to the 1900s, thematic content was limited to symbols of ethnic enclaves, religious institutions, and business-oriented buildings. At the turn of the century, designating class status became a major social marker of a population. Since the 1960s, symbolic differentiation has been accomplished with material objects, façades, and motifs. Symbols moved way beyond ethnic, religious, and class distinctions to an expanding repertoire of meanings. Derived from our popular culture, today's themes come to us directly from novels, television, films, and music. By fusing commercialized popular culture with entertainment, we get themed environments.

Today, nothing escapes theming. Sports stars and logos pepper our competition venues; national parks are converted into idealized versions of Mother Nature; music characterizes a city (Nashville), immortalizes rock and roll as a restaurant (Hard Rock Cafe) and promotes singers as theme parks (Dolly Parton). And to indulge our fantasies, the entire city of Las Vegas provides miniature cities and ancient motifs to amuse us. As cultures, cuisine, and countries become familiar to us through theming, we feel connected to what otherwise would be an alien experience.

Realms of Experience

Theming encourages different realms of experience and both active and passive levels of participation.[396] As audiences and consumers become bored with passive types of entertainment experiences, they actively seek the unusual and unique. Staging experiences within the context of specific themes enhances consumption activity and promotes commerce. Themed environments can be educational, escapist, or aesthetic in purpose. An *educational experience* requires absorption and active participation. Exploratoriums (science museums) are edutainment[397] venues where visitors learn while they play. An *escapist experience* involves supreme immersion for the actively involved participant. Consumers escape into theme parks, casinos, and virtual environments for an ultimate experience. In an *aesthetic experience*, consumers are passive about their immersion in a staged environment. Visitors to the Rainforest Cafe, although immersed in a jungle scene, are more interested in eating than in exploring the staged reality.

All three realms of staged, themed experiences characterize our lives whether we live in the central city or the suburbs. We eat lunch in the nostalgia of Hard Rock Cafe, buy sneakers at Nike World, and vacation in Las Vegas. Forms of symbol-ridden environments occupy all aspects of our daily lives. Themed spaces, defined by media culture motifs, characterize our cities, suburbs, shopping places, airports, and recreation spaces (such as sports stadiums, museums, restaurants, and amusement parks). Each environment is designed to entertain us within a commercial enterprise so we are amused while we spend our money.

Staging Reality

Themed environments strive to look *authentic*, which is often taken to mean untouched by the marketplace. Here, we define the term as something that is accurate and representative, but not necessarily real—hyper-real retail, perhaps—and some attempts at realism are better than others. As technology improves an architect's ability to reproduce and imitate, the copy is often a more enjoyable experience than the real. Visitors to New York, New York in Las Vegas claim to prefer the clean, safe, and abbreviated experience of the replica to visiting the actual city. An artificial place like this one can yield a very authentic experience for willing participants.

Five principles for developing a themed environment are:[398]

1.   An established sense of place that visitors recognize as different.

2.   An altered sense of reality in space, time, and matter where size, past/future, and sensation are manipulated.

3.   A cohesive, realistic whole where a completely new reality is created.

4.   Multiple places within a single space that put the visitor in motion in the experience.

5.   A theme that reflects the character of the enterprise and gives visitors what they expect from the venue.

Semiotics, the science of signs and symbols, helps researchers to study and understand how theming affects our perceptions of reality. Many people understand popular culture through themed experiences. By incorporating recognizable symbols into everyday environments, theming provides a way for us to experience at will a historical era, faraway place, or exotic culture. According to researchers, the presence of symbols enhances our enjoyment of almost every activity in which we engage. We can understand the entertainment value of theming by comparing attendance at themed versus nonthemed environments—the former far surpasses the latter because people enjoy the familiar and respond positively to symbols of their own reality as provided by all forms of mass media.

RETAIL SPACES

Capitalizing on a combination of fantasy and the familiar, themed environments lure us to shopping malls, airports, restaurants, and branded venues. Marketers, understanding our need for socialized consumption, provide us with a plethora of opportunities to experience themes that can be educational, entertaining, escapist, aesthetic, and—most of all—profitable. Some of these opportunities are discussed next.

Themed Buying: Shoppertainment

A highly regulated, private, commercial space designed to make money, the mall is a stark contrast to public, city shopping. Some malls, called *gallerias,* are replicas of the Palazzo Vecchio in Florence, Italy, a shopping area with two levels and no roof that was constructed in the Middle Ages. Galleria malls in America (e.g., Houston, New York, San Francisco) are enclosed spaces and may have more than two stories. Accounting for more than half of all retail sales in America, modern gallerias and malls in general use thematic appeals in their design and advertising to attract business in a very competitive marketplace.

Malls are not only centers for shopping—they are highly organized social spaces for entertainment, interaction, and other types of consumer excitement.[399] Disenchantment with traditional shopping centers caused designers to create retail entertainment complexes that integrate entertainment and aesthetic experiences with the shopping experience.[400] Most theorists view malls as the embodiment of the postmodern condition, stressing their theatrical and hyper-real character.[401]

The first mall that was conceived as a shopping destination is the Mall of America in Bloomington, Minnesota, which opened in 1992. The largest in the United States, this 76 acre mega-mall has more than 400 specialty shops, a 14-screen movie theater, nightclubs, bars, 9 family entertainment areas (e.g., Camp Snoopy, Golf Mountain), 22 restaurants, and 23 fast-food outlets. You'll also find a theme park with 23 amusement rides, a roller coaster, high–tech, virtual-reality simulations (e.g., interactive virtual-reality laser game Star-Base Omega) and Underwater World Aquarium. To encourage tourism, Northwest Airlines allows cross-country passengers to enjoy a one-day stopover at the mall for an additional $50.

A more manageable themed mall is located in Ontario, California. Ontario Mills Mall (OMM) publicity claims that it offers "the art of shopping in an entertaining environment and shopping that is diverting, engaging, pulsating, dynamic and vibrant."[402] Patrons of the 38-football-field-sized mall may drive on a virtual car track or tee off on a virtual golf range at Dave & Buster's game place. The mall employs a director of tourism to maintain high levels of motor coach business. Tour buses bring shoppers of many nationalities to the 10 color-coordinated "neighborhoods" (retail zones), which cater to tastes from upscale adult to grungy adolescent. Overhead, 65 giant screens run an endless series of commercials produced by the mall's studio, Mills TV. OMM's destination shopping provides everything to lure and entertain shoppers within one cutting-edge architectural space.

Figure 14.1 A Shopping Mall

© Owen Franken/Corbis.

Department stores, although not overtly themed, often characterize themselves for specific audiences. Paris's two largest department stores, Le Bon Marche and Les Galeries Lafayette, use three domains of cultural manipulation to differentiate themselves: public space (the surrounding area), social space (store windows), and personal space (store itself).[403] Located in the Left Bank neighborhood within a modern building, Le Bon Marche fashions itself as an upscale shop for local and Parisian shoppers; the theme is local status. Les Galeries Lafayette, on the other hand, caters to tourists and mass shoppers by providing a historical setting that is by itself an attraction in the fashionable area adjacent to L'Arc d'Triumph; it uses the historic tradition theme to attract consumers.

Malls were instrumental in developing social shopping, which allows a break from routine peppered with sensory stimulation, exercise, amusement, and fantasy. Formed on the uses and gratifications theory, shopping has become recreational and hedonic; simple barter has become browsing satisfaction and consumption pleasure. The act of buying—an appropriation of signs—becomes a means of self-realization; a shopper is both the audience and the performer of the show.

Shopping areas—*marketscapes*[404]—have become the dominant socializing space in our postmodern society. The primary dimension of sociality practiced in malls is observing and being observed. Participants become actively immersed in social communication, enjoying an escapist experience. Teenagers (also called *mall rats*), use the mall as a stage, whereas seniors see it as an exercise center. These social arenas possess characteristics of both leisure sites and public spaces, and are enjoyed by shoppers and browsers worldwide.

Focus on Airports: Straighten Up and Fly Right!

Large metropolitan airports build themed interior spaces to amuse their annual 3.2 billion passengers[405] between flights and to persuade travelers to select them for trip departures. No longer amused by the experience of air travel, passengers look to airports to define their journey's pleasure. Emulating the massive expanse and retailing atmosphere of malls, airports cater to passengers with time on their hands. The McCarran Airfield in Las Vegas has slot machines in every available place throughout the concourse area. There's a winery and tasting room at Dallas-Forth Worth International. Art exhibits and concourse exhibitions, such as the type presented in the O'Hare and San Francisco airports' United terminal, are an attempt at nonpaid entertainment. These spaces lure travelers to the places where they can buy replicas of what is currently being exhibited.

Innovations such as "guaranteed street pricing," duty-free shops, banking services, health club facilities, fine dining restaurants, food courts, and family fun centers make sanitized airport environments excellent retailing opportunities. Chicago, Dallas, Denver, Pittsburgh, and Los Angeles are examples of airports that embrace the mall concept. Outdoing its American counterparts, Frankfurt, Germany's airport is the ultimate stopover, with an underground mall of its own. If you're traveling with children, a layover at Amsterdam's Schiphol Airport offers a low-light nursery with cribs to keep baby safe while parents visit the nearby casino and art exhibitions.

How do themes enhance the travel experience for tourists? For seasoned travelers? What other amenities might airports include to enhance air travel?

Themed Restaurants: Eatertainment

The way people eat has significantly changed in the last twenty years. No longer reserved for special occasions, eating out is a leisure activity enjoyed by millions of people on a regular basis. Faced with endless competition, restaurant owners choose the most popular strategy for differentiating themselves from the competition: theming. Their goal is to have diners absorbed by the restaurant's aesthetic experience.

We can identify three common traits among themed restaurants:[406]

☆ Themes are drawn from popular culture genres such as film, sport, popular music, and ethnic cultures.
☆ Theme narrative is communicated through the use of props, artifacts, sound, menu, and merchandise.
☆ Eating is not the central focus of a visit.

An offshoot of the roadside diner or decorated shed, themed restaurants began as hamburger stands or freeway stops like Stuckeys. Specialty restaurants—such as the Cannery in Newport Beach, California—have converted factories into eateries, with artifacts as décor. Using photographs of the historic site, artifacts from the original building, and navigational equipment typical of the times, such cannery restaurants are crafted in the theme of a fish-processing factory.

Restaurants have used themes of nature, adventure, and celebrity to differentiate them-selves. The Rainforest Cafe seats diners in safari animal-skin chairs under a faux sky that promises occasional storms, complete with lightning and rain. Dive restaurants feature going underwater in a submarine, allowing diners to avoid getting seasick and claustrophobic. Now-defunct Planet Hollywood overwhelmed patrons with media memorabilia, perhaps to camouflage the mediocre food they served.

Launched in England, the Hard Rock Cafe is the best-known fully themed restaurant. The rock music industry motif includes nostalgic elements from the '50s when rock began. The restaurant's exterior is framed by large neon guitars, and the front end of a 1950s Cadillac convertible is embedded in one interior or exterior wall. Copies and original memorabilia of the rock industry—gold records, concert posters—serve as wall decor. The rock music theme has proved very successful; today, more than 30 years after the first Hard Rock Cafe opened in London in 1971, it still attracts both diners and lookers. Marketing's role is evident by the fact that profits from merchandise bearing the Hard Rock Cafe logo often surpass food revenues.

Restaurants with ethnic themes are common: Italian (e.g., Olive Garden), Mexican (e.g., El Torito), and Japanese (e.g., BeniHana) are among the most popular. And nostalgic diners have become themed: Ruby's Diner (soda shop theme) and Mel's Diner (deli theme), franchised throughout California, offer burgers, fries, and sandwich fare. *Reflexive theming*,[407] when the theme is a brand and the brand is the theme, is commonly found in franchises. Here, the brand becomes a symbol of the dining experience. McDonald's, Burger King, and KFC are themes that are also brands.

Diners experiencing the aesthetic of themed eateries acknowledge the venues as fakes but are amused by the staged reality. How many restaurants have you visited lately that do not have a theme? The low number should tell you something about the aesthetic experiences expected by those who eat out.

Branded Theming: Logotainment

Like reflectively themed restaurants, branded venues rely on the brand to produce the theme (Nike = sports, Sony = electronic games) and the theme to reinforce the brand. Introduced in 1991, Nike Town (Chicago) is a menagerie of themes, styles, and images revolv-ing around sports. It is a retailing experience that enhances those who visit this sport theme park. Shoppers become immersed in this atmosphere's aesthetic. Built around the "Just do it" slogan, every design element of the Nike servicescape[408] encourages impulsive behavior and invites instant gratification. Resembling a "spiritual gymnasium"[409] or a cathedral of con-sumption,[410] Nike Town is a combination of an amusement-centered themed environment and a mega-boutique.

What happens in this place is more subliminal than active commercialism. Parents show their kids around in the same way they might point out exhibits in a museum. The sales staff

Figure 14.2 The Hard Rock Cafe features a theme of rock and roll set in the nostalgic '50s.

© Robert Holmes/Corbis.

doesn't apply pressure; in fact, they are more informative than persuasive. The educational and aesthetic experiences enjoyed in this logo monument will, in theory, be transferred to the Nike brand. Visitors are encouraged to increase their *brandscape* through their engagement with this environment. Brandscapes are "material and symbolic environments that consumers build with marketplace products, images and messages."[411]

Sony's Metreon, a 350,000-square-foot center in San Francisco, is billed as four floors of "ultimate entertainment experience." Derived from the roots of two Greek words, *Metreon* means a nurturing urban environment and an important place of public assembly. Its attractions are based on the works of three award-winning artists and authors: Jean "Moebius" Giraud (*Airtight Garage*), David Macaulay (*The Way Things Work*), and Maurice Sendak (*Where the Wild Things Are* and *In The Night Kitchen*).

Located in the city's South of Market district, Metreon's fourth floor is dedicated to the magical world of Sendak's children's books. *Where the Wild Things Are* features a mysterious forest where visitors meet goblins, a bubbling cauldron, a crazy hall of mirrors, strange sounds, flying birds, and a giant, interactive 17-foot-tall Wild Thing. *In The Night Kitchen* is a diner set in the dreamy world of moonlight and stars that forms the backdrop for his book of the same name. These storybook re-creations allow children to become escapists as they become immersed in the environment of make-believe.

Airtight Garage is an interactive adventure zone with three electronic games created especially for Sony: *Quaternia* (team capture-the-flag game), *Badlands* (demolition derby), and

HyperBowl (combines miniature golf, bowling, and a TV sports event) provide escapist experiences for all active participants. In *The Way Things Work*, visitors use both sides of their brains to explore new ways of looking at everyday technology with a three-screen, 3-D investigation of mechanics and machinery, featuring the illustrator's famous woolly mammoth. Combining education with aesthetics, visitors experience the ultimate in entertainment.

Each floor provides shopping for Sony music, Sony electronics, and brand extensions of products from the three branded artist attractions. Products from sponsors Citibank, Pepsi, Levi's, Intel, Mercury, and others are sprinkled among the shop offerings. Five themed restaurants feed visitors to the Metreon and its theaters. As Nike is the main brand for Nike Town, the Sony brand is the hero of the Metreon venue. Rather than thinking about Sony as a product, we are expected to experience Sony as a pleasant diversion—as a brand that belongs in our lives.

Other brandscapes include Coke and M&M stores, retail venues that present brand histories and brand memorabilia for nostalgic viewing and purchasing. The primary purpose of themed venues is to provide entertainment for potential consumers within the context of a brand that becomes synonymous with enjoyment, fun, and wonder. The innovative brand stores and retail entertainment complex link names and logos of major companies to exhibits and attractions to develop cross-marketing opportunities in which retailers and sponsors promote each other inside and outside the mall.[412]

URBAN PLACES

By taking themes into larger spaces, marketers lure consumers with entertaining, experiential places to conduct everyday business as well as to spend leisure time. From our suburban neighborhoods to the urban metropolises and the parks situated between them, themed environments clamor for our attention and our cash. Although you have probably experienced one or more of these places, this section offers an opportunity for you to view them as marketplaces that provide educational, entertaining, escapist, and aesthetic experiences.

Themed Neighborhoods: Archetainment

Regions where activities are conducted in centers that are functionally specialized and separated by travel time of 15 to 30 minutes are labeled as *postsuburban* areas.[413] Residents travel by car across city boundaries for work, socializing, and shopping. Postsuburbia consists of separate spaces for living (neighborhoods), shopping (malls), and working (industrial parks).

One such postsuburban space is Orange County, California, home of Disneyland, several major universities, large destination shopping malls, the Crystal Cathedral, and the Mighty Ducks hockey team. Orange County is dotted with neighborhood shopping centers, upscale malls, swap meets, and consumer warehouses (Costco), each of which plays a different role in the postsuburban marketplace. Theming prevails in offices, health spas, universities, and religious buildings. In fact, some call Orange County a 786-square-mile theme park, where the theme is "you can have anything you want."[414]

The town of Mission Viejo, known as a super-dormitory and home of the perfect high dive (home of nine gold, two silver, and one bronze Olympic swimming and diving medalists), is billed by its developer as "the California promise." Recognizable residential themes such as Greek Island, Capri Villa, and Uniquely American punctuate the "promise." Viejo clones have sprung up throughout the county, with names like Aliso Viejo (locals characterize the town as straining over the hills for an ocean view), Rancho Santa Margarita (their motto: "Where the West begins again"), Coto de Caza (an outgrowth of a tennis and riding resort), and Monarch Beach (which revolves around a golf course billed as world class). And for 21,000 retired elderly people, Leisure World, the largest retirement community in America, has sprouted businesses such as brokerage houses, banks, and money handlers in a supermarket of financial services.

Orange County's Knott's Berry Farm in Buena Park is designed as a city that imitates a city. Even as a toy city, it has a studied illusion of reality that takes over as you walk down the streets. It pretends to be real, like wax museums that pretend to feature real people—real fakes. (Acknowledged copies are *real fakes,* and creations not based on reality are *fake fakes*.) The oldest themed amusement park in the world, Knott's celebrates the "wholesome aspects of an idealized and simpler America." The farm is a stark contrast to the hyper-modern county that surrounds it. Knott's neighbor, Disneyland, makes it clear that within its magic enclosure visitors are in a *fantasy,* not a mere reproduction.

Emerging as an important economic region, Orange County has become an information-oriented, postsuburban society, with shopping environments that serve as a metaphor for life in general. Thanks to the advanced credit system, which supports and drives consumption activities, Orange County—like its many counterparts across the country—will continue to support themed spaces for their social, commercial, and psychological needs.

Themed Cities: Faketainment

Hershey, Pennsylvania. is an eastern city all dressed up for visitors to the chocolate capital of America. Complete with its own chocolate river, Hershey is adorned with street lamps in the shape of kisses and retailers that expand the brand motif with brown decor and chocolate souvenirs. Such a brandscape relies on tourists with a sweet tooth who come to eat. According to a *New York Times* writer,[415] surrogate experience and synthetic settings have become the preferred American way of life.

Environment has become entertainment. A replica of New York City, built in Las Vegas as a skyscraper casino with Coney Island rides, is a "crowd-pleaser without the risk of a trip to the Big Apple."[416] If we were to rank fakes on a scale of 1 to 10 (10 being the best), Las Vegas would get an 11. Here, imitation has become an art form. Vegas's outrageously real fake (that is, intentional copies, as opposed to fake fake creations not based on reality) has developed its own style from the ground up to become an urban design frontier.

The famous Vegas Strip is itself a linear theater, evolving over the past 90 years in a uniquely American way. The opposite of a modern city with an identifiable center, Vegas is constructed around the Strip, on which theme hotels become way stations to energize the consumer in motion. Now thought of as a family destination, Las Vegas offers casino hotels, amusement parks, and shopping malls, all themed, prefabricated, and available as a packaged vacation. Plus, you get Wayne Newton and animatronic dinosaurs as well. Such extravaganzas—Caesar's Palace with its heroic Styrofoam statuary, Luxor's sphinx and mirror-glass pyramid, Bellagio's art masterpieces, Venecia's canals, Paris's Eiffel Tower—are but a few of the city's monuments to simulation. Ironically, the faux New York, a colorful Gotham hodgepodge of a casino hotel, was built in 1997 without the twin towers of the World Trade Center. After the terrorist attacks of September 2001, the Vegas replica suddenly became more accurate for its omission.

Viva Las Vegas

Since *gambling* was renamed *gaming* in the 1970s, it has become one of America's favorite pastimes. Casino billboards advertise entertainment shows as "the world's most daring," "most sensual," or "most exciting." Neon superlatives like "best," "largest," and "biggest" dominate the landscape and dwarf people and cars, evoking the materialization and megalomania of the town.[417] The place radiates hope, humor, and extravagance, endlessly repeating the myth of instant wealth available to anyone who'll play. Neon dollar signs are interrupted by exploding marquees that preach the mantras of the Strip: SHOP SHOP SHOP, WIN WIN WIN. A true postmodern space (see Chapter 15), the Strip is composed of vastly incongruous architectural styles that are forced into senseless proximity. Medieval Excalibur is a few blocks from Caesar's Palace of ancient Rome, which isn't far from modern New York. Centuries and continents are mixed together in the ultimate faux-travel experience. None of it makes any sense, which is okay because it's not supposed to.

A farcical theater-of-the absurd character of contemporary life, Las Vegas is neither intended to be nor taken seriously by tourist consumers. Visitors receive an escapist experience, becoming immersed in fantasy. Banking on our desire to return to our childhood, Las Vegas lets us play the game of dress-up, pig out, and stay out all night. Our quarters feed the slots, and our fantasies of winning the ultimate jackpot give us the freedom to keep on pretending that we don't have to grow up. Vegas is a playpen for the middle class and middle aged; what makes it unique is simply the scale of the carnival.[418]

Themed Amusement Parks: Mousetainment

Born as Coney Island (New York) at the turn of the 19th century, the first theme park had a recipe for entertaining large crowds: play, escape, release, fantasy, thrills, and family outings. This forerunner of Disney made important contributions to outdoor amusement in each of its three Coney Island parks:

☆ The idea of structuring amusements around sea animals, water rides, and aquatic exhibitions began with Sea Lion Park, created in 1895 by Paul Boynton. Today, every major amusement park contains some kind of water slide, like Shoot the Rapids (Cedar Point, Ohio), Mill Chutes (Venice Beach, California) or Log Flume (Six Flags nationwide).

☆ Steeplechase, a technology-driven fun center featuring Human Roulette Wheel, Earthquake Floor, Blow Hole, and Electric Seat, was developed in 1897. This pattern of mechanical rides, sideshows, midway, fun houses, audience participation, and voyeurism were to become the industry standard.

☆ In 1903, Luna Park was created with a concern for physical appearance, illusion, crowd control, live spectacular shows, and ambiance. This amusement park blended foreign cultures, pleasant atmosphere, staged events, and illusion rides into a new, more successful version of commodified leisure. Dreamland, the final construction of the Coney Island amusement parks on 15 acres of oceanfront property across from Luna Park, survived after Luna burned down in 1944 and was considered its replacement in a sense.

Coney Island Parks made three great contributions to formulating amusement centers: structuring amusements around water rides and aquatic exhibitions; linking technology to amusement with mechanical rides, sideshows, fun houses, and a midway; and emphasizing physical appearance, crowd control, and ambiance. During the next half century, no other amusement park in America resembling Luna/Dreamland was ever built.

A decade after Luna's destruction by fire in 1944, Disneyland appeared looking like a new park, although Disney's formula represents an extension of that of the Coney Island parks of the early 20th century. Disney was a master of displaying popular images, such as Medieval Castle and World of Tomorrow, which were inspired by the 1930 World's Fair. Disney's practice of parading employees in mouse or duck costumes was patterned after Luna Park's storybook characters Alice in Wonderland and the Mad Hatter, who mingled with park visitors. Disneyland was designed to deviate from the vulgarity, clowning, and exuberance Coney Island was famous for. Ironically, former Disney employees are building a new park at Coney Island that conforms to its historic past.[419] Today, the Disney theme park form is the most popular attraction on earth.

Unlike Las Vegas, which is fake, Disneyland is a *fabricated* entity of its own. It is not a copy; it is an original concept duplicated in several geographic locations around the globe. Disneyland hides all things fake. In Disney terms, *imagineering* designates the creative process of "making the magic real"—that is, translating fictions and fantasies to concrete themed architecture and attractions.[420] Disneyland is a master of planning, crowd control, and crowd movement. After standing in line and performing obediently to the prescribed traffic control, one critic warned: "What you and your 10 to 20 thousand cohorts are performing is a huge, choreographed, aesthetically quite arresting species of close-order drill."[421]

By blending common mass culture symbols and an appealing physical design, Disneyland has had a profound impact on the construction of themed environments across America. Visitors leave their usual modes of transportation and enter the park as pedestrian travelers. The main attraction of theme parks is their stark contrast to the everyday lives of the people who visit them. Traits of the park, such as the following, act as liberators from daily constraints:

☆ Theme parks are *crime free,* unlike many cities and urban areas.

☆ Parks offer a *contrast to routine, at-home dining* with a festival of food varieties.

☆ The experience *encourages family interaction* in a child-centered environment.

☆ Entertainment is a *festival,* not a spectacle provided by encounters with mass media.

☆ Leisure and play clothing allows people to *cast aside fashion rules* they adhere to in the workplace.

☆ Parks provide an *illusion of escaping* from the demands of personal economy. Once the admission price is paid, all rides are perceived as free.

☆ Visitors encounter *fantastic architectural structures* that provide themed entertainment in themselves.

Combining retail and park theming, Disney Village at EuroDisney presents authentic representations of four American nostalgia themes so that Europeans may experience in a single location the Old West, rock and roll, '50s sports, and famous American places of the past. Displaying bows and arrows, guns, and Indian artifacts, Disney Village captures visitors' hearts with an accurate depiction of Buffalo Bill's Wild West show, which was performed in England and France between 1883 and 1913. A red-and-blue motif is the backdrop for vintage cars and Hollywood memorabilia reproduced to entertain park and Village visitors.

With parks in America, France, Japan, and soon Hong Kong, Disney has captured the minds and hearts of consumers with an age-old formula to provide carefully fabricated fantasy and social interaction for families across cultural and geographical boundaries. Visitors become immersed in an escapist experience that allows them to visit any place on earth—and they can even take a virtual voyage to space.

So where do we go from here? Disney-jaded tourists who balk at the $58 a day entry fee to interact with a mouse may want to make a pilgrimage to ancient Jerusalem in Orlando's new Holy Land Experience for only $17 a ticket.[422] Fulfilling the need for synthetic history that is tidier and sweeter-smelling than the real kind (e.g., camel hoof prints but no camel dung), this theme park's virtual history has engendered controversy. Christian leaders criticize the park for trivializing religion, and a Baptist minister was accused of intending to use the park to convert Jews to Christianity. When the park opened amid heavy security and a barrage of TV news crews, the fake seemed not very different from its Israel prototype.

▨ FADE TO BLACK

Disney and other extensions of theme environments sell experiences to people who draw on the cultural codes they know for entertainment that is both enjoyable and meaningful. Toy stores, bridal salons, hair salons, grocery stores, and even wilderness attractions also rely on themes and staged aesthetics to attract and retain consumers.

The success of themed environments is based on their instructive sign and symbol systems, which minimize the work visitors must do for successful interaction. We are not strangers in a strange land inside a themed mall or park because we understand how to navigate and negotiate the space. We find comfort in the familiar and enjoyment in our skills at achieving consumption success.

We must not underestimate the importance of motifs for marketing and entertainment. They provide an experience that comes from our highly developed, image-driven, and commodity-driven popular culture, which is fostered by the merging of commercial retailing, advertising, and mass media. Themed environments work because they offer consumers a spatial and visual experience that is both entertaining and fantasy driven. Because they work, and because they are profitable, themes will dictate the nature of the vast majority of our interactions from now forward.

 A Closer Look

Theming Australian Cuisine

The Outback Steakhouse, with 535 outlets in 46 states,[423] uses cultural symbols to fashion what might be called *reality engineering*.[424] For some diners, these simulations may be their only contact with a foreign culture; restaurants' stylized culture becomes a surrogate for authentic culture. A group of researchers[425] wanted to know how these symbols are interpreted across cultures and how we use them to learn about the foreign culture. They wondered: Are these environments authentic?

Using stereotypical prototypes of Australian artifacts, Outback uses symbols as a kind of cultural shorthand that is easily interpreted by visitors. Some standardized "authentic" atmosphere symbols include

☆ Koala bears and kangaroos

☆ Foster's Lager beer signs

☆ Snakes and boomerangs

☆ The Great Barrier Reef

☆ The Sydney Olympics

☆ "Down under" music

The menu includes

☆ Walkabout Soup

☆ Jackeroo Chops

☆ Crocodile Dundee Steaks

☆ Shrimp on the Barbie

☆ Kookaburra Wings

☆ Wallaby Darned Drinks

Research was conducted to answer these questions:

1. If Outback Steakhouse were to open in Australia, how would Australian consumers respond?
2. What types of food and decor would Australians include in an Australian-themed restaurant?
3. What do American diners think of the "authentic" Outback Steakhouse?
4. How much do Americans learn about Australia from the symbols?

Step 1: Australians' Responses to Artifacts

To answer these questions, researchers showed the symbols used in Outback's decor, uniforms, and menu to Australians for comments on cultural authenticity. Here are some of their comments about those artifacts:

☆ "I would choose a decor that represents the way we live, not something stuffed with kangaroos and koalas and that sort of tacky stuff. We're multicultural now. We're more adventurous. We expect variety."
☆ "The old *Crocodile Dundee* image has been done to death. Australians live at the beach, not in the bush. The Sydney Opera House is far more appropriate than the desert."
☆ "It is a bit corny. It conjures up an image that's from the past. I think Australians are a bit more sophisticated these days."

Step 2: Australian Representations

The Australian students produced collages depicting their interpretation of a traditional Australian theme restaurant, including uniforms and a menu. Australian alternative collages contained these images:

1. The koalas, kangaroos, and Aboriginal artifacts were replaced with ochre-colored desert scenes, beaches, and cityscapes.

2. The uniforms were "outback" casual.

3. An emphasis upon fresh food was common.

These collages were then shown to 80 male and female Australians ranging from teenagers to retirees.

Those who agreed with the images in the collages said things like the following:

☆ "I would feel right at home here. It's real Aussie, mate. Looks true blue with dinkum bush tucker."

Those who did not agree expressed feelings such as the following:

☆ "I don't think Australia needs an Australian theme restaurant because our food includes so many traditional foods from around the world. What is traditional Australian these days anyway?"

Those surveyed had the following opinions of their countrymen's menus:

☆ "I like the idea of seafood. The menu should reflect the Australian diet, and we don't eat T-bone and burgers only."

☆ "The idea of unique local foods was great. I liked pavlova and damper on the menus."

Step 3: American Interpretations

The Australian collages were digitized, placed on the Web, and reviewed by American students. The Americans almost all commented on the lack of the "typical" Australian icons in the collages. In many instances they did not understand the meanings represented or did not feel that they matched their perceptions of "traditional Australian." Here are some views the Americans offered on various topics.

On Authenticity

☆ "The first collage is very authentic because of the pictures of the deserts, safari hats, emus, kangaroos, and snakes. On the other collage, I think the fish needs to be replaced with a kangaroo or a koala bear. They would better represent the Australian image."

☆ "This is very Australian. It has included many Australian things that people who do not live in Australia have come to expect from seeing movies like *Indiana Jones*. It has the typical hat and whip, Australian animals, and pictures of the desert. To me, someone who has never experienced the culture of Australia, this looks very Australian."

☆ "I think the restaurant should have things like stuffed kangaroos and koala bears and road signs, like kangaroo crossings. I would also include pictures of the Great Barrier Reef. I would focus on the sports of Australia, like boomerang throwing."

☆ "For uniforms, I think of all the typical Australian clothing. I think of the khaki shirts and shorts that the host of the *Crocodile Hunter* [TV series] wears. They could also improve their uniforms by having a necklace or some kind of jewelry made of crocodile teeth that is truly Australian."

Perceptions of Food

☆ "I would have a hard time finding something to eat. There were things on the menu that I have never heard of. But they also had things that were truly Australian, like kangaroo chops. Americans would compare this to the Outback Steakhouse and expect the same kinds of food."

☆ "The snail snacks, reptile toasters, and oxtail soup are not exactly what I would have selected. I would think of having shrimp, cheese fries, and definitely a bloomin' onion. I would also have some type of brownie and ice cream on the dessert menu."

☆ "For beers I would add Heineken, Sam Adams, Bud Light, Budweiser, and Coors Light. I would keep the wines listed but add White Zinfandels and Merlots to the list. I would exclude the Bush Grub because it does not fit the outback menu, and I would add sweetened and unsweetened tea."

Step 4: American Alternative Collages

Twelve American students created collages depicting their interpretation of an authentic Australian restaurant. According to the photos chosen for those collages, the American students preferred the idealized version of Australia. To a large extent the Americans "played back" the Outback images.

So What?

From this study, we learn three specifics about what Australian and American diners at the Outback expect from the restaurant:

Australian consumers would not welcome the Outback to Australia.

1. The Australians disliked the clichéd cultural icons that were used to represent their culture, whereas Americans indicated a preference for these.

2. Australians felt that the Outback restaurant failed to capture the real Australia, ignoring the modern multicultural aspects of the country in favor of historical representations and those depicted by the media.

3. In some cases, Australians felt that the Outback Steakhouse was more American than Australian.

4. They concluded that the success of this restaurant in Australia would be limited to tourist locations frequented by international tourists, such as the Gold Coast of Queensland.

American diners thought the Outback Steakhouse was authentic.

1. Outback Steakhouse icons were accepted by Americans as proto-types of the real thing.

2. In most cases they expressed a preference for an environment that incorporated elements of their own culture, rather than one that was truly Australian.

Americans learn about Australia from the symbols they get from the media.

1. Americans' interpretation of Australia has been heavily influenced by media-depicted images of idealized and fantasized Australians, such as Crocodile Dundee and the Crocodile Hunter.

We might conclude from all this that Americans have become conditioned to expect staged environments, such as themed restaurants. What was once presented as hype is now accepted as real. Given this assumption, we have several questions left unanswered. Should restaurant designers include "real real" or focus on the "fake real"? And what effect will this simulated hyper-real have on our authentic environment?

DISCUSSION AND REVIEW

1. Why are so-called fake amusements so attractive to many tourists?

2. What themes are most popular for dining? For adventure? Which themes depend upon violence for their success?

3. Discuss the role of themed brand retail outlets for promoting products and for generating image. Which factor is more important, sales or brand equity? Why?

EXERCISES

1. Visit an ethnic themed restaurant and make a list of all the icons, artifacts, and symbols of the theme. Then ask 10 friends what icons, artifacts, and symbols they would choose for that theme. Compare the two. What conclusions can you draw from this comparison?

2. Visit a themed mall and list all the experiential realms available there. Which experiences are tied to brands? Which are linked to age demographics, such as children? What role do the mall restaurants play in supporting the theme? What evidence can you see of reality engineering?

3. Develop a new theme for a mall, park, or Las Vegas hotel. Describe the space, retail venues, and artifacts you would incorporate into this destination. What audience would you target for your venue? List factors from the chapter that helped you make your selection.

RECOMMENDED READINGS

Gottdiener, M. (1997). *The theming of America: Dreams, visions and commercial spaces.* Boulder, CO: Westview.

Halter, M. (2000). *Shopping for identity: The marketing of ethnicity.* New York: Schocken.

Pine, B. J., & Gilmore, J. H. (1999). *The experience economy.* Boston: Harvard Business School Press.

Ritzer, G. (1998). *The McDonaldization thesis: Explorations and extensions.* London: Sage.

Schmidt, B., & Simonson, A. (1997). *Marketing aesthetics: The strategic management of brands, identity and image.* New York: Free Press.

Sherry, J. F. Jr. (Ed.). (1998). *ServiceScapes: The concept of place in contemporary markets.* Chicago: NTC Business Books.

15

 # The Ecstasy of Communication

Postmodern Entertainment

Today we live in the imaginary world of the screen and networks. All our machines are screens. We too have become screens. We live everywhere in an "aesthetic" hallucination of reality.

—Jean Baudrillard

Many people talk about postmodernism, but few people agree on just what it means. For that reason, we present our own notion of the term. The use of the prefix *post* implies that what this word is describing follows modernity, the epoch of late 19th and early 20th centuries that came into being as the capitalist-industrialist state. Property, labor, manufacturing, and services grounded modernism. Central to the shift from modernity to postmodernity is a type of social order brought about by new forms of technology and information, where simulation takes priority over reality.[426] In other words, postmodernists duplicate rather than create. They dwell upon the future rather than the past, and they replace a desire for truth with a quest for meaning.

In a contemporary society of 7-second sound bites, we prioritize access to entertainment and experiences over the ownership of things. We organize our 21st-century lives according to commodified experiences rather than product commodities. This chapter begins by rejecting the notion of reality and concludes with specific examples of postmodern architecture and experience. We suggest that our worlds are constructed with options and scenarios, simulations and experiences, that fall within the rubric of entertainment.

Because we can apply postmodern criticism to every genre of entertainment, it is appropriate to study postmodernism in its own right. After we define the postmodern condition, we present specific postmodern examples in the cultural spaces and places of marketing, media, architecture, and museum exhibitions. The impact of postmodernism on entertainment and society often alters our perceptions and our reality. By understanding the nature of this phenomenon, we become better consumers of entertainment and of our mediated society.

OUR POSTMODERN SOCIETY

Postmodernism is a way to describe our society. Theming, as discussed in Chapter 14, is a prime example of postmodern expression. Here, the disorientation of time and space are combined with representations of what's real as well as with symbolic or virtual reality to produce a postmodern condition. Many forms of mass media are considered to be postmodern, especially the contemporary cinema of David Lynch, Steven Soderberg, and Oliver Stone.

Definitions

Postmodernism has been defined in a variety of ways, including the following:[427]

1.   A nostalgic, conservative longing for the past, coupled with an erasure of the boundaries between the past and the present (e.g., Hard Rock Cafe)

2.   An intense preoccupation with the real and its representations (e.g., Las Vegas)

3.   A pornography of the visible (e.g., violent cinema, such as *Blue Velvet*)

4.   The commodification of sexuality and desire (e.g., Calvin Klein advertising)

5.   A consumer culture that objectifies a set of masculine cultural ideals (e.g., purchasing the biggest televisions, the fastest cars, and guns that are designed to kill people rather than shoot game)

6.   Intense emotional experiences shaped by anxiety, alienation, resentment, and a detachment from others (e.g., video games and Internet or computer entertainment)

Central Features of Postmodernism

Evidence of postmodernization is everywhere—you just have to know how to recognize it. To that end, we highlight five central features of postmodernism in the entertainment arts you can identify during your journey through the 21st century.[428]

Disappearance of the Boundary
Between Art/Entertainment and Everyday Life

What this means is that amusement is an integral part of our lives and that we cannot really separate what is performance from what is reality. Our cities are centers of consumption, play, and entertainment, saturated with signs and images to the extent that anything can be represented. Leisure activities (such as visiting theme parks, shopping centers, malls, museums, and galleries) converge to fill our spare time.

Collapse of Distinction Between
High Culture and Popular (Mass) Culture

People of all classes attend similar performances, watch similar television shows, play similar sports, and take similar vacations. Few true so-called highbrow activities are practiced today. Mass culture dominates the attention of audiences from all lifestyles in what can be called a "hypermarket of culture."[429]

Playfulness and the Celebration of "Surface" Culture

We enjoy what is often called *kitsch* (the mundane or mementos of bad taste) such as hanging dice, *Reader's Digest,* airport paperbacks, soap operas, and tabloids. Barbie collectors and fan clubs meet and tell stories about their dolls; Beanie Babies are hoarded the moment they are discontinued, then traded as icons. Science fiction movies (such as *Revenge of the Killer Tomatoes*) are featured at film retrospectives. We embrace and love the mundane.

Decline of Originality

Ideas, rather than being new, are most often a reshuffling of what already exists. We draw from all eras of the past and combine materials to come up with different forms, such as Disneyland and Club Med. We succumb to fads—take a look, for example, at the explosion of sport utility vehicles (SUVs) on the roads of America—and jump on bandwagons. We flock to the same tourist places everyone else is frequenting and attend the same movies—all of which are created in the image of some other popular or successful place or film.

Assumption That Art/Entertainment Can Only Be Repetition

Cities like Las Vegas are reproductions of other places that are created so we can experience them without actually visiting the true location. We duplicate and fabricate exactly; most aspects of our existence are McDonaldized (franchised). Inner cities are becoming gentrified by members of the dot.com generation, who develop them as sites of tourism and consumption. This happens in most major metropolitan areas; San Francisco's South of Market area is an example of this phenomenon. If you woke up not knowing where you were, then ventured out into any global metropolis, you would have trouble identifying the location because the franchises, sports, and musical messages you encounter are like those of all other cities. You'd probably wonder, "Where am I?"

HYPER-REALITY

Assuming responsibility for the postmodern condition, the media take control of and permeate our lives, bombarding us with instructions, solicitations, education, politics, and news. The intensification of media messages creates a state of being fast-forwarded, of confronting a very hyper reality every day of our lives. Time is fragmented into a series of perpetual presence, with no sense of time, and reality is a series of visual images.

Media are our new technology. Interaction with all forms of mediated communications is our reality, according to postmodernists. Taking Shakespeare literally, postmodernists claim that commerce has made the whole world a stage and all experience a simulation. And in fact, for many children spending between 5 and 6 hours each day watching television, using the Internet, and playing games causes media to become more real than any of their other activities. To some people, an event is not even real until it has appeared on television, been featured in the news, or hit the Internet. Indications of hyper-reality can be found in most realms of our lives. Here we present a few examples—promotion, lifestyle, architecture, and museums—that demonstrate the pervasiveness of the postmodern condition in entertainment and life.

Marketing, Advertising, and Sponsorship

The *commodification* of everything (i.e., everything is for sale) has empowered marketing and advertising to levels never before experienced. To get audiences to frequent entertainment venues, tourists to travel, spectators to watch sports, and so forth, promotion is necessary. As consumers of signs, we need to be shown what to do by who is endorsing, providing, or underwriting the activity so we can make sense of it. *Marketing* is the means by which the whole culture is searched for potential meanings that can be changed by entertainment into paid-for experiences. Spending more than $1.5 trillion a year on marketing (advertising is $15 billion and promotions more than $450 billion of the total), U.S. businesses pay to solicit our patronage by transferring cultural values onto experiences that we will buy. The money that used to be spent marketing products is now spent marketing entertainment in all of its forms. Selling products is secondary to selling the experience of those products by weaving bits and pieces of culture into products and selling them as lived experiences. We buy a Jeep branded by Eddie Bauer so we can fantasize about rugged overland adventures (even if we never leave the freeway).

Rather than sell us products, *advertising* endeavors to entertain us. How many times have you paused before changing channels because an interesting visual or musical piece stopped you before you discovered it was an ad? Ads no longer try to sell us anything; they try to make us feel good about a brand by entertaining us. Here is a historical example of how advertising and entertainment are fused. In 1990 in Budapest, Hungary, just after the communists left, commercials were first shown in 10-minute segments between programs. Disenchanted with the dull shows provided by the state, viewers gathered around their sets especially for the commercials, which were much more entertaining than what came between. Today, advertisers know that viewers are in control, so they engage film directors like Woody Allen and George Lucas to produce 30-second movies with a particular brand in the starring role.

Because they know that we consume symbols, not products, companies now spend more than $19 billion a year on *sponsorship* of community and cultural events around the world. No amusement, activity, or sport is immune to the corporate stamp. Product brands cover NASCAR vehicles and fly on the sails of America's Cup boats. Brands name events—such as the Nokia Sugar Bowl, Carlsberg Soccer Cup, and John Hancock Boston Marathon. Companies tie themselves to local educational institutions and cultural events because such activities are close to the lives of their potential customers. In an effort to create a lifelong relationship with niche communities and interest groups, companies position themselves as active cultural partners.

Postmodern Lifestyle

We understand *culture* to represent the shared meanings and practices of a group of people. In addition to being a shared way of life, culture is also the shared arts and experiences of a group. Groups are often defined by their lifestyles. Turning away from a focus on lifestyle as class-based, we view *lifestyle* as the active stylization of life, the playful exploration of experiences and surface aesthetics.[430] In the class-based view of culture, ticket prices restricted entry and fostered stratified lifestyles; stratification fostered highbrow and lowbrow types of entertainment, which divided rich audiences from poor ones.

With postmodernism, traditional distinctions and hierarchies are collapsed, multiculturalism is acknowledged, and globalism is embraced. We celebrate difference rather than sameness. What this means is that all stories, religions, histories, news interpretations, and so forth can coexist because they all have relevance, and no single perspective dominates. Here's an example: While you watch a football game, you see an ad for beer, get a weather report, learn that a bomb has exploded (killing hundreds), get a preview of the newest movie release, and experience replays of fumbles and touchdowns. How can viewers attribute importance when each mediated experience receives equal weight and significance?

To understand the essence of postmodernism, you must grasp its key notions of identity and possessions. French philosopher Jean Paul Sartre identified three aspects of personal identity: "being, doing and having."[431] During most of the 20th century, *having* possessions preoccupied us. We used cars and clothing and logos to help us define ourselves. The transition to an entertainment economy will see a shift from having to *doing* as the most important marker of our personal identity. Where we travel, what events we attend, what clubs we enjoy, and in what sports we participate will become significant parts of self-concept (our *being*) for citizens of postmodern, post-capitalist countries.

Indications of the trend away from *having* and toward *doing* can be found in personal behavior. For instance, a Boston geologist decided to purchase a used car rather than a new one so he'd have enough money to travel to Bali. For her son's sixth birthday, a mother in San Diego purchased passes to Legoland and the zoo instead of toys. A Chicago e-commerce executive selected a less expensive house so he could join a golf course. These actions are testimony to a new reality—we are no longer identified by what we have but by what we do for recreation, entertainment, and play.

Play, according to Sartre, releases subjectivity. As soon as a person is free and wishes to use freedom, then the activity becomes play. When people want to discover themselves as free, they are not concerned with possessing an object. Rather, through sports or games, we can attain wholeness. In other words, by wanting to play, we are exercising our desire to exist in the world. By using our resources to purchase play instead of objects, we capture the essence of freedom and fantasy.

Here is where the distinction between reality and play becomes fuzzy. Sartre assumes that play and reality are separate. Yet in our entertainment society, our reality is often defined through our play activities, so they become overlapped and indistinguishable from one another. Fashion as play is one example. Today, there is no single fashion standard. Fashions exist without rules and with multiple choices.[432] You can wear hiking boots with a full-length period skirt and a see-through branded T-shirt, and wrap yourself with a mink pelt from the '40s. We combine eras and fabrics without regard to rules of ensemble.

Fashion has always played a role in personal identity. We embrace logos for what they say about us. Yet in New York or Istanbul, you can get exact copies of brands and logos for a fraction of the cost. At a shop in Greenwich Village that sells faux designer purses, you can buy a slick shoulder bag for $18, and the clerk will affix any logo you want to it. A watch shop near the world's largest covered bazaar in Istanbul boasts a sign saying: "Authentic Fake Watches." Rolex, Tag Heuer, Cartier—you name the brand—are available for $25 (less if you bargain) and can pass for the real thing on your wrist.

Because they are ceasing to be significant for personal identity purposes, logos are being replaced by fashions of outrageous designs, mismatched fabrics, and copies of designer outfits, making dress an affordable and entertaining activity. Style enables us to create, maintain, or change our identities at will; we may step in and out of reality by simply changing our clothes.

Postmodern Places

Our built environment is an essential element in any discussion of postmodernism. Given the emphasis on our visual consumption of the urban environment, here we consider the changing patterns and forms of architecture and building and their roles in entertainment. All sorts of places have come to construct themselves as the objects of tourists gaze, as sites of pleasure; one of those places is the museum, which has recast history through the variety and nature of exhibition content.

Figure 15.1 Guggenheim Museum in Bilbao, Spain designed by Frank Gehry

© Yann Arthos-Bertrand/Corbis.

Architectural Forms

Architectural space in postmodernism is localized, specific, context-dependent, and particularistic. Postmodernity can be visualized best by looking at buildings designed by Frank O. Gehry. Architect of the famous Guggenheim Museum in Bilbao (Spain), which is a showcase of contemporary art, Gehry explains his creations as "wrappings." Critics have not been good to Gehry, describing Bilbao as "a luxury liner from an art deco tourist poster, docked beside an oil refinery that's died and gone to heaven"[433] and his Seattle Experience Music Project as "open-heart surgery gone awry."[434]

The first major project of Gehry's career was remodeling a Santa Monica tract house in 1979, where the old house was the core and the new house was the wrapper. He used a number of inexpensive materials—metal, plywood, glass, and chain-link fencing. Composed of three types of space, the house begins with a group of small rooms with stairs, bedrooms, bathrooms, and closets. Next, the major spaces of the old house have become the living room on the ground floor and master bedroom on the first floor. Finally, the spatial wrapper has entry, kitchen, and dining areas that are five steps below the living room. His "hyperspace"[435] features numerous contradictory perspective lines going to numerous vanishing points above and below a wide variety of horizons . . .[436] nothing is at right angles, nothing seems to vanish to the same point. Gehry's world vanishes to a multitude of points, and he does not think that any are related to a standing human being. His sense of center no longer has its traditional value.

The features that render Gehry's house as postmodern are its strange feeling of the absence of inside and outside, the bewilderment and loss of spatial orientation, the messiness of an environment in which things and people no longer find their place.[437]

Gehry is just one of many architects combining past and present to provide the inter-action of design and art that house activity spaces and workplaces. In particular, the campuses of the University of California at Irvine and Santa Cruz integrate architectural styles and creations by a variety of designers to provide interest and diversity in educational environ-ments. Today, form does not necessarily follow function; rather, it manifests hyper-reality by entertaining audiences.

Breaking the rules of hotel design, postmodern architect Philippe Starck says he wants to "bring some originality, creativity and a sense of humor back to the hotel landscape."[438] To do so, he gave San Francisco's Clift Hotel a facelift that is "a strange cocktail of classicism, surre-alism and modernity."[439] For instance, he integrated a 1937 Man Ray inspired wheelbarrow chair with a faux fireplace and orange plexiglass coffee table cubes in the hotel's Penthouse Suite. In the bar, Starck installed five redwood-framed, wall-mounted plasma TV screens that project digital images of famous works and original video art. Visitors to the lobby notice a stool fashioned after a black bowler hat and a green apple, an 18-foot-high bronze fireplace, and a stylized version of a Louis XVI chair—three times its actual size. According to Starck, "the perfect lobby is not about how it looks, but how it makes you feel. I want people to feel glamorous. I want to blow people away and try to lift their spirits. Hotel are not places to just come and sleep, but to have unique experiences."[440]

Retailers have also embraced architecture as a means of getting customers into their stores and entertaining them while they buy. Two New York stores, Prada and Toys "R" Us, are good examples of how architecture is being used to re-infuse brands with a sense of excite-ment. Prada architect Rem Koolhaas believes that shopping is the last remaining form of public activity. He favors the idea of retail design *epicenters*, which become devices to renew the brand by counteracting and destabilizing any received notion of what the brand is, does, or will become.[441] The store he designed in Soho cost $40 million and features hard-edged late modernism, with technology such as glass-enclosed dressing rooms that turn translucent at the touch of a button. The elevator, a cylinder of glass perched on a hydraulic piston, was fabricated in Italy for a cool $11 million. Merchandise is displayed in metal cages hung from the ceiling that move around so the store is constantly redesigned—another expensive solution to a fairly simple problem.

Much less pretentious, the Toys R Us Times Square store features a 60-foot-high ferris wheel that blends entertainment and the hard sell. It has 14 passenger cars, each with an indi-vidually themed cab—one car is based on Mr. and Mrs. Potato Head, and another on a Tonka truck. Mr. Monopoly has a car, as does Barbie. Much of the store is divided into environments with special themes. The store's glass façade, which is sometimes transparent and sometimes covered with a series of images on automated panels that roll down like shades, is a continu-ously changing billboard. Because both of these stores can be more fully appreciated when they are empty, retail architecture seems to have become more of a private indulgence than a public space.

A Medley of Museums

Venues of performance and exhibition, museums provide us with transformations of historical time to the space in which we live. Nearly 15,000 museums entertain millions of Americans each year, and one in every 28 Americans is a member of at least one museum. Museums in the United States, as a group, average 865 million visitors each year, or 2.3 million visits a day. The largest museum in existence is Washington, D.C.'s Smithsonian Institution, with more than 140 million items.[442] Although museums have never been more important as entertainment alternatives, they are also suffering from an identity crisis. They encompass a universe of places so different in size, budget, and orientation that it's hard to say what links them together beyond the need for visitors. That common need, however, is the prime motivator to offer more than just "dead stuff" for public consumption. To meet the need, museums are modifying their traditional role of education to one of entertainment.

The final evolution of the modern museum into a postmodern museum has only occurred in the last 5 or so years with the rapid expansion of the Guggenheim Museum franchises in Berlin and Bilbao and coming soon to Paris (France), Salzburg (Germany), and Geelong (Australia). An alliance between the Hermitage Museum (St. Petersburg, Russia) and MoMA (the Museum of Modern Art, New York) was recently established to create an independent for-profit e-business to curate international exhibitions drawn from both collections. The postmodernization of these museums reflects two specific aspects of postmodern culture—the postmodern corporatization of the museum and the notion of museum as ritual entertainment.

The postmodern *corporatization* of the museum combines modern corporate ideals of efficiency and rationalization with postmodern audience (target markets) marketing drives in relation to exhibitions, merchandise sales, food and beverage outlets, and commercial advertising. The postmodern museum also actively pursues other forms of income, including consulting, creative fundraising, and joint ventures with businesses that are not art related. For example, for a 10-year period starting in 2000, MoMA is consultant to the design and management of a new 65,000-square-foot museum in Japan, the Mori Art Centre. The key element of postmodern museum corporatization is that it aims for a wider audience base through specific audience targeting. This is reflected through aggressive advertising and marketing campaigns, which in turn reflect the nature of the postmodern museum as entertainment provider. In a curious postmodern twist, the audience-targeting strategies of the museum cause it to be an audience-driven entity, entrenched in commercialization and fulfillment of the postmodern audience's demand for an essential postmodern museum experience—that is, ritual entertainment.

Postmodern audience-driven *ritual entertainment* is an evolution of the modern museum ideal of aesthetic contemplation, which is an evolution of the early museum ideal of art as ritual. Ritual entertainment embodies both the early museum ideal of art as ritual and the postmodern audience-driven ideal of museum as comprehensive entertainment center. Consequently, we find the interesting situation of an audience expecting both value for its entertainment dollar and some form of sedated pleasure and spiritual nourishment. The postmodern museum as audience-driven entity is left with little choice but to accede to these demands by providing the complete museum entertainment experience—symptomatic of a certain Disneyfication of the postmodern museum. For example, although a modern museum may have introduced bookshops and cafes to increase its bottom line, the postmodern museum regards parties, hired-out functions, and the promotion of other forms of the arts as part of its responsibility as a comprehensive entertainment center. The audience-driven necessity for the postmodern museum to provide an all-encompassing experience reflects the blurring of boundaries between postmodern art spaces.

Often called secular cathedrals, museums have become storehouses of collective values and diverse histories—places where we seem to want to spend our free time. They are our new theaters of conscience, memorials to suffering, choreographed places of ritual genuflection—and they offer packaged units of morality that are guiltlessly entertaining. Vacillating between being a university and a Disneyland, museums are places to show things to people that they didn't know they wanted to see. And, as such, they are entertaining places.[443] As postmodern museums integrate art, artifact, and replica, they are often indistinguishable. Michelangelo's *David*, the statue housed in Florence, Italy, is often mistaken for a copy, and the replica located in a public space is perceived to be the authentic statue. Does it matter to visitors whether they see the original or a copy? Should it matter?

Museums have to do with curiosity that serves the pleasure of the spirit. One of the few places one is supposed to be able to experience something authentic is in a museum. Museums display objects that exemplify originality, authenticity, and truth, providing an experience that a reproduction cannot. Museums use two approaches regarding the display of objects: object as culture and object as art. Objects important as part of a larger whole, or as representative of a culture, are often displayed in ethnographic museums, where the object is assimilated into its total environment. Reconstructed villages and mannequins provide realistic displays that serve primarily as backdrops for the objects themselves. They assist viewers in understanding the objects' social role. A Brussels museum dedicated to artifacts of the former Belgian Congo integrates drums and masks into realistic settings that feature native dwellings and animals typical of the region.

Culture-based museums contain objects that are widely separated in time and space. Time, however, is manipulated, whereby the past is made to converge with the present, often obliterating the distinction. Mannequins constructed to "breathe life" into surrounding objects may remind us of zombies rather than actual beings. Synthetic bodies in frozen behavior with items that are supposed to represent things belonging to actual people end up being constructions of the unreal, regardless of the authenticity of the objects on display in those scenes. Museums invent a version of reality by suggesting that authenticity is based on the details they have created to display objects. This mixture of modernity and antiquity, art and reproduction, space and display has contributed to a postmodern rendering of history and its implications for the present.

Art objects, after they are recognized by specialists or the marketplace, tend to be exhibited alone, displayed as an aesthetic form rather than a source of cultural information. The world's largest cut emerald is featured in Turkey's Topkapi museum inside black glass and illuminated indirectly to emphasize its beauty. Regardless of the fact that the emerald has great historical significance, its aesthetics and monetary value have cast it as a work of art.

Museum shops, located in shopping malls, sell reproductions of art antiquities that serve owners as *objets d'art*. You can buy a plaster cast of the nose of the *David* statue for $30 from the British Museum, or an Incan bathrobe from the Smithsonian Institution for $150. People buy these things to commemorate their visit, to show they have "done" the museum. Things and lifestyles, the past and present, are collapsed together into an appealing package that can be purchased by the consumer who wants to be considered as worldly by others. We are all able to become time travelers, experiencing the past without ever leaving the comfort of the present—a truly postmodern activity.

Eclectic, Eccentric, and Erotic: Museum Variety

Museums that reflect the obsession with fantasy are the essence of Las Vegas, where visitors can find a gambling museum, a neon museum, and two museums devoted to performers who have come to personify the city: Liberace and Elvis. Inside the Tropicana Hotel's towering neon sign is a panel that invites revelers to visit "the world's largest gambling museum," a venue that contains more information about Las Vegas than about gambling. The only other cultural icon of this city is neon, so it is fitting that a dedicated museum presents examples of neon, which has been called the only indigenous visual culture on the North American continent.[444] The neon museum is really just eight pieces of neon signage on display along a pedestrian mall—outdoors and on view 24 hours a day. It serves as a graveyard of signs that have been discarded and rescued for posterity. The Liberace museum, like its namesake, focuses on lavish excess and becomes a parody of itself. Visitors can see the musician's pearl-and-rhinestone cloaks, mirror-paneled cars, and jewelry dripping with diamonds. Somewhat more professional in presentation, the Elvis-a-Rama museum is devoted to artifacts belonging to the city's secular saint. Not to be outdone, casinos such as the Bellagio are incorporating exhibition halls for the display of art masterpieces. The Venetian now presents works from Guggenheim and Hermitage collections; the first exhibit was "The Art of the Motorcycle."

Museums are also venues for charity events and fashion shows. Clothing as art recently appeared in installations by Issey Miyake at the Ace Gallery in New York, Versace at the Metropolitan, and Armani designs at the Guggenheim. The 2000 Giorgio Armani fashion retrospective polished up a familiar facet of urban life: the grand promenade through flattering reflections of ourselves (superimposed on fantasies of how much better we would look if we could afford nice clothes) that we take on the great shopping streets of Paris, Milan, and New York.[445] Star worship feeds the frenzy of museums' clothing auctions, where a dress worn by Diana, Princess of Wales, when she danced with John Travolta at the Reagan White House sold for $222,500. Both the Metropolitan and the Los Angeles County Museums of Art hold fund-raisers for fashion luminaries, who donate their attire.[446]

Some critics are fearful that art museums are being reduced to the level of social historians and commodity showrooms. They worry that curators put sponsors, attendance figures, and historical narratives ahead of art.[447] One art critic believes that museums displaying artifacts such as guitars (Boston), motorcycles (New York), and *Star Wars* memorabilia (Houston) are "swindling the public" by using the prestige of art to collect money for exhibits that have only superficial appeal.[448] Opposing that view, the head of the American Association of Museums claims that "museums today are taking the tact that they need to broaden the perspective of what is valued in culture, instead of saying only certain kinds of art should be shown."[449]

Three recent museum exhibits reflect critics' concerns. First, the Los Angeles County Museum of Art's millennial celebration, "Made in California: Art, Image and Identity, 1900-2000," presented a historical retrospective that mixed painting, sculpture, photographs, film, video, clothing, and furniture with rock concert posters and travel brochures. Second, "Face to Face" was an exhibition as department-store make-up counter sponsored by Shiseido, the Japanese cosmetics giant, in New York University's Grey Art Gallery. Finally, Brooklyn Museum of Art's "Hip-Hop Nation: Roots, Rhymes and Rage" featured an exhibition that was part product showroom, part history lesson. Accused of betraying art and artists, museums that succumb to material culture or inferior artwork are said to become rental exhibition halls rather than to be custodians of aesthetic masterworks. Should museums commemorate the past? Should they glamorize the present? What is a museum's responsibility to its public sponsors?

Some museums feature *historical journeys* through a profession or trade, or *parody* scientific achievement; they make no claims that they are art custodians. Entertainment venues such as Madame Tussaud's Wax Museum in Times Square provide replicas and memorabilia of famous people. Here you can see Larry King gossiping with a colleague, Woody Allen alone in a corner, and Barbra Streisand sitting on a fountain. Certainly reality here is in the eye of the beholder.[450] Museums that cater to the unusual include the American Sanitary Plumbing Museum in Worcester, Massachusetts; the National Museum of Dentistry in Baltimore; the Museum of Jurassic Technology in Los Angeles; and the Hays Antique Truck Museum in Woodland, California.

Focus on Museums as Movie Stars

Museums are often pieces of art in their own right, such as New York's Guggenheim, a spiral gallery designed by Frank Lloyd Wright. This and other museums have provided the backdrops for movie scenes. A few examples are the following:

☆ *The Mummy* (1932), with Boris Karloff, who visits the Cairo Museum to see a mummy

☆ *Bringing Up Baby* (1938), with Cary Grant and Katharine Hepburn, who are reconstructing a brontosaurus skeleton at the Stuyvesant Museum of Natural History in New York

> ☆ *Topkapi* (1964), Melina Mercouri's classic heist of a dagger from the museum in Istanbul
>
> ☆ *Rocky* (1976), with Sylvester Stallone running up the stairs of the Philadelphia Museum of Art
>
> ☆ *Batman* (1989), in which Jack Nicholson's Joker runs wild in Gotham's art museum, the Metropolitan Museum of Art
>
> ☆ *A League of Their Own* (1992), in which Tom Hanks's team visits the Baseball Hall of Fame in Cooperstown, New York
>
> ☆ *The Thomas Crown Affair* (1999), in which Pierce Brosnan breaks into the Metropolitan (1999)
>
> What films have you seen that feature or use museums as props? What does the presence of a museum in advertising do for product image?

An exhibit that was particularly indicative of postmodern tradition took place in the Laguna Beach Museum (California) in 2001. Called "In Smog and Thunder: Historical Works from the Great War of the Californias," this exhibit featured a one-man show by Sandow Birk, who presented a faux history museum dedicated to a fictional historic event. An intersection of fantasy and power, this epic exhibition of paintings, drawings, political propaganda posters, models, maps, and other artifacts was called "an alienated spectacle of thematized entertainment par excellence" by a reviewer.[451] Using labels, legends, wall texts, an audio tour, and the works themselves, Birk documented an apocalyptic civil war between Northern and Southern California.

The battle between Fog Town (San Francisco) and Smog Town (Los Angeles) depicts both cities as total war zones, with recognizable cultural landmarks such as Taco Bell, the Getty Center, San Francisco MoMA, and Pizza Hut. His parody of the styles of historical painting and posters depict surfing, punk rock, and street life in Latino neighborhoods. The wild juxtapositions of Mickey Mouse waving a "Free ATM" banner beside a farmer with a rifle, rake, and laptop computer are fantastic. Birk's work has been called a "comedic examination of the illusion industry, its institutions and icons of propaganda, whether disguised as high art, mass media entertainment, religious symbolism, political persuasion or corporate advertising."[452]

In the recent past, museums were nationally recognized for the quality of their collections; today, the evaluation criteria are different. The top 25 American museums were recently ranked according to "the goods, display, building, shopping, food, and fun factor."[453] Because shopping and fun qualify as entertainment, we provide a list of the top five museums in each category in Table 15.1.

Table 15.1   Most Entertaining Museums

Best Shopping	Most Fun
1. Museum of Modern Art, New York City	1. Menil Collection, Houston
2. Nelson-Atkins Museum, Kansas City	2. American Visionary Art Museum, Baltimore
3. Dallas Museum of Art	3. Denver Art Museum
4. Detroit Institute of Art	4. Museum of Fine Art, Boston
5. Los Angeles Museum of Modern Art	5. San Francisco Museum of Modern Art

SOURCE: Delp, L.; Ryan, C., & Sanders, L. (2000, November). Museum smackdown, *Travel Holiday*; excerpted from a list on p. 107.

Noteworthy for their entertainment value, some museums offer special environments to visitors. The Frick (New York) is housed in one of 5th Avenue's only remaining mansions. The architecture of San Francisco's Museum of Modern Art takes visitors through a catwalk that simulates being in a giant eye, and their cafes feature trendy fare. Renovated in 1997, the Denver Art Museum is a model of comfortable, user-friendly venues with its discovery libraries, a great collection of American Indian art, and interesting shopping. The Menil, often referred to as the country's most sophisticated museum, combines modern art with ancient and tribal art in an urban neighborhood of art sites. In spite of its rating as 7th best overall, the authors are partial to the Metropolitan Museum of Art in New York City; they are always entertained when wandering through its vast collections, tomb rooms, or the shop's fascinating array of gifts. The Met introduces visitors to the art world in such a way that we become swallowed up in a marvelous menagerie of immortalized art and sculpture, indulging our fantasies and outdoing our expectations of what it means to visit a museum.

As old-guard curators and directors retire, we can expect exhibitions that illuminate something about objects on view, regardless of whether they are paintings by Monet or a Nike swoosh. As audience-driven and ritual entertainment, museums are responding to their publics with sophisticated marketing programs that rival those of their entertainment competitors. The controversial role of museums as keepers of art will continue, we suspect, for at least a few more decades. Until then, we shall see the lines between high art and popular culture continue to blur in a true postmodern fashion.

LYNCH AS POSTMODERN CINEMA AND VIDEO

> *The postmodern would be that which searches for new presentations in order to impart a stronger sense of the unpresentable.*

—Jean-Francoise Lyotard

Our mediated culture also reflects the postmodern condition. Movies and television shows include representations of sexuality, violence, and nostalgia for a past where melodrama defines the relation between the sexes. We focus on David Lynch's *Blue Velvet* (a 1986 film) and gothic soap opera *Twin Peaks* (a 1990-1991 TV show on ABC), which are examples of mediated postmodern philosophy.

Located in small-town America, both of these works contain all the terrors and simulated realities characteristic of the postmodern definition. Both texts display an absence of boundaries between past and present, as well as a treatment of time that locates viewers in a perpetual present. Lynch, called the quintessential postmodern director, puts the unpresentable (brutality, insanity, homosexuality, sadomasochism, drug and alcohol abuse) before viewers in ways that challenge the boundaries that ordinarily separate private and public life.[454]

In *Blue Velvet*, nostalgia for the past is presented as '50s and '60s rock 'n' roll, suggesting that the music of our comfortable youth may lead to destruction and violence. Here, the past as sacred and profane is moved to the present and future, where the hyper-real is always real. The film exists both as a parable of sin[455] and redemption and as pornographic cult.[456] Lynch locates the meaning of his film in the viewer's experience with the context. Viewers see his work as either cinematic art or as trash—reviewers are equally split in their opinions. One reviewer even equated the film to religious, symbolic art.

Each postmodern trait is identifiable in Lynch's text. Beginning with Bobby Vinton singing *Blue Velvet*, the film parodies the past and present. It mocks the icons of the past by placing them in the present. As the film opens, Jeffrey discovers a rotting ear in a vacant lot while Dorothy and Frank engage in sadomasochistic rituals—the *unpresentable*. Women appear simultaneously as playmate and wholesome types. They are sexual objects and slaves as well as mothers and honored wives, exhibiting the dichotomy of female portrayals characteristic of postmodern commentary. The film ends by focusing, as in its beginning, on an ear—symbolic of Lynch's path into the unconscious, perhaps?

Twin Peaks, a television soap opera, had all the ingredients of traditional soft-core fare: sex, violence, murder, and adultery. In just a short time, the program became a cult phenomenon, watched faithfully by people who did not normally watch prime-time television. Lynch's version of violence and sexual expression hit the airwaves with a vengeance, prompting viewers to keep wondering, "Who killed Laura Palmer?"

Lynch's voyeuristic visions look into the future and see technology and violence, so he takes refuge in the fantasies and nostalgia of the past. His dreams are postmodern solutions to life in the present. He implies that small towns are no longer safe from urban evils. The nice thing about his postmodern drama is that things usually turn out all right in the end. Villains die and fallen heroes repent and go home. His characters confront reality through the lens of conservative ideology, and viewers can enjoy the characters' myths, sex, and violence as entertainment. His latest film, *Mulholland Drive* (2001), is 2 hours and 25 minutes of macabre thrill, highly charged erotica, and indelible images focused on Hollywood and the film industry. What films have you seen that might be considered postmodern?

The problem with postmodern cinema is that audiences may view such works not as postmodernity but as mirrored reality, where the stars' identity becomes our own. As we continually seek entertainment that presents unique visions of reality, we may be held hostage to the creations of directors like David Lynch without proper defense mechanisms. An understanding of postmodernism as a societal critique helps to defray the confusion and promotes informed viewing. This chapter was designed to arm readers with enough knowledge to embrace postmodernity in all its forms with an objective and critical eye.

FADE TO BLACK

As computer hypertext causes the "death of the author,"[457] computer communication turns the private solitude of reading and writing into a public network.[458] As Internet technology proliferates, we may not know who is writing what we read or who is reading what we write. Using online personas in cyberspace through virtual communities helps undermine the notion of real self, perpetuating postmodernism. Men and women casting about for new life experiences open their minds to being everywhere at once and play into the aspect of life as a paid-for performance. The change in our roles as productive workers into creative performers represents a change in our social relationships.

People like Ralph Lauren and Martha Stewart prepare costumes and sets that we use as backdrops for our life performances. We can outfit ourselves in Quicksilver and become surfers, or wear Armani and become professionals. Our image managers allow us to act out whatever fantasies we like and amuse ourselves by theatricizing our lives. Lauren and Stewart can do this because the theater is typical of what goes on in society all of the time. As actors on our own stage, we are all entertainers, and we are all audiences.

If this sounds a bit hard to swallow, check out the magazine racks, TV guides, and fashion outlets for evidence of the presence of those who help us create a reality designed as fantasy or vice versa. Welcome to hyper-everything.

 A Closer Look

Frank Gehry's Postmodernity

In June 2000, the Experience Music Project (EMP) opened in Seattle. The 140,000-square-foot museum by Frank Gehry includes 80,000 artifacts, from rock memorabilia to a 30-foot sculpture made of more than 500 guitars. It also contains interpretive and interactive exhibits that trace the history of rock and allow visitors to play instruments and mix their own music. EMP, which is located on the 74-acre site of the 1962 World's Fair, includes a monorail running right through it that is a handy way to avoid traffic during sporting events.

The "swoopy" exterior forms—red, blue, purple, silver, and gold, indicative of guitar finishes—were designed by a 3-D computer modeling program originally designed to develop Mirage fighter jets. Intended as a memorial for Seattle-born rock star Jimi Hendrix, who died in 1970, the museum features a Hendrix gallery that consists of his original written lyrics for the album *Electric Ladyland* and an interactive multimedia kiosk devoted to his songwriting. You can even buy a copy of his Stratocaster guitar in Olympic White for $1,650 with case from www.fender.com.

Financed by former Microsoft mogul Paul Allen, EMP is the first major structure ever designed almost from its conception to final parts fabrication entirely with a computer. Its forms—five billowing multicolored techno-morphs—are clustered around a bulging asymmetrical breadbox core. Curved aluminum, copper, and steel fish scales reflect Seattle's filtered oyster light. Allen calls the museum "rock 'n roll architecture that, even if you don't like the design, you have to appreciate for the exuberance and the audacity of the structure."

Gehry's design reflects a post-modern approach to entertainment for the following reasons:

☆ Gehry blurs the boundary between entertainment and life in his presentation of a musical icon within the context of an interactive museum housed in a building that is itself a work of art.

☆ Highbrow patrons of architecture and popular culture music fans can both enjoy the experience of this museum.

☆ The museum celebrates our mundane preoccupation with stardom and celebrity.

☆ Gehry has taken shapes from reality and fantasy to create an amalgamation of the past and future.

☆ Gehry's forms are repeated and fabricated from materials that have been used many times before for similar and dissimilar purposes. EMP memorializes rock music and repeats the musical theme in every element of the building and its contents.

You can experience the EMP yourself by logging on to www.emplive.com.

DISCUSSION AND REVIEW

1. In what ways is your life postmodern? What elements of the past, present, and future occupy the same time and space in your daily entertainment activities?

2. Compare kitsch (or surface culture) with popular (or mass) culture. How are they alike and different? What role do they play in entertaining us?

3. What sponsorships or brand associations can you identify that link a product with an activity? How does the product or brand become part of the entertainment experience?

EXERCISES

1. Log on to the Museum of Jurassic Technology Web site, www.mjt.org, and describe the museum in terms of the postmodern condition as presented in this chapter. What is the museum's purpose? Would you visit its location on Venice Boulevard during a visit to Los Angeles? Why or why not?

2. View Oliver Stone's movie *Wall Street* and analyze it using the postmodern terms from this chapter. Is the film a work of art or trash? Why?

3. Locate and read Jean Baudrillard's *The Ecstasy of Communication*. Summarize the subject of his essay. Do you agree with his postmodern perspective? Why or why not?

4. Visit a local museum and characterize the nature of the exhibit as historically significant or a slice of popular culture. How do the exhibits inform visitors? How are visitors entertained? What is the primary responsibility of the museum to its visitors?

RECOMMENDED READINGS

Baudrillard, J. (1987). *The ecstasy of communication.* New York: Semiotext(e).

Cross, G. (2000*). An all-consuming century: Why commercialism won in modern America.* New York: Columbia University Press.

Featherstone, M. (1991). *Consumer culture and postmodernism.* London: Sage.

Jameson, F. (1991). *Postmodernism.* Durham, NC: Duke University Press.

Root, D. (1996). *Cannibal culture: Art, appropriation and the commodification of difference.* Boulder, CO: Westview.

16

 # Futuretainment

I don't know what entertainment will be like in 100 years' time. But it would be nice to have a piece of hardware that you could scrunch up like a cloth, chuck in your bag, then unscrunch so that it would deliver entertainment to you any time and anywhere.

—British celebrity Carol Vorderman[459]

What does the future hold for entertainment? Will "going to the movies" or "programming the VCR" seem as old fashioned to tomorrow's children as the notion of "sounding like a broken record"[460] and taking "an E-ticket ride"[461] might seem to children today? Many of the chapters in this text have discussed trends in different forms of entertainment and speculated about what the future may hold for them. Often, these speculations have involved evolving new media technologies. This chapter reviews and continues this discussion, with a primary focus on new media and their implications for more general entertainment trends, to see if we can catch a preview of coming attractions.

NEW MEDIA

Beginning with print and continuing with radio, film, and television, advances in mediated communication have opened new avenues for entertainment. Virtually all communication media have the potential for use as entertainment. It is perhaps not surprising, therefore, that today the term *futuretainment* is often used in reference to predictions involving the use of the Internet and other new media as vehicles for entertainment.

Figure 16.1 Disney's Classic E-Ticket

The term "E-Ticket Ride" is still used to describe new, exciting forms of entertainment—even though Disney did away with their ride tickets long before many of today's entertainment-hungry audiences were born.
© Disney Entertainment, Inc. Reproduced with permission.

What Are New Media?

The term *new media* is difficult to define. Listed here are several definitions that have been offered by various researchers and organizations:

☆ A range of interactive digital products and services that offer new ways to trade, market, educate, and entertain, delivered through the Internet, CD-ROM, DVD, interactive TV, and intranets.[462]

☆ The convergence of traditional media, such as films, music multimedia, games, and entertainment.[463]

☆ Interactive applications that combine moving pictures or sound (or both) with graphics or text.[464]

☆ Information and communication technologies relative to the convergence of computer technology and telecommunications, such as e-mail, the World Wide Web, electronic publishing, video conferencing, computer-supported communications services, and personal communication services. In relation to the Internet, new media include hypertext literature, Web pages, and all virtual reality systems used for work and leisure.[465]

Many people equate new media with advances in media technology. Indeed, many of the definitions just mentioned allude to technological advances such as the Internet, CD-ROM, and the like. According to these definitions, however, the most central feature of new media is not the technology itself but the convergence or combination of media technologies. Thus, in simple terms, *new media* (sometimes called *multimedia*) refers to products or services that incorporate a variety of media. More often than not, these technologies are combined in a way that permits interactive use.

Types of New Media

A new media product or service combines elements of computing technology, telecommunications, and content. Web sites on the Internet are good examples of new media because they are accessed through telecommunications technology and they invariably incorporate a variety of media, including text, audio, and animation. Virtual reality devices, handheld computers, mobile phones, and electronic book readers like eRocket, Glassbook, and Microsoft Reader similarly fall within the new media category in that they are combinations of several forms of media. Virtual reality devices often combine visual, audio, and other technology. Handheld computers and mobile phones can be used for multiple media purposes—sending and receiving information, recording information, game playing, and so on, and electronic book readers combine traditional print with electronic technology.

Consistent with the new media concept of convergence, emerging forms of new media are rapidly becoming interdependent, and many of them connect back to the Internet. Handheld computers and mobile phones can be networked with traditional computers, and many have wireless Internet access. E-books can be downloaded from the Internet. And, of course, all of these types of new media can be, and often are, used for entertainment. Today, traditional forms of entertainment—such as books, films, music, sports, and games—can all be accessed in some manner through new media and the Internet. Thus, the evolution of the Internet and other new media technology is influencing almost all forms of entertainment.

As with so many other advances in communications technology (such as in print and radio), the Internet was not originally designed as a vehicle for entertainment or for commerce of any sort. The Internet is really nothing more than a network of computers developed by the Department of Defense to be used in case of a nuclear attack. Government officials wanted to be sure they would have access to their information if one computer or network was down. Universities and professors then began using the Internet to spread and gather information.

In 1989, software engineer Tim Berners-Lee created a system of codes and protocols he called the *World Wide Web* to serve as a system to allow physicists from around the world to be able to access each other's computer networks, data, and documents. The Web served as the basic platform that opened up the Internet for a larger number of users. A product called *Internet in a Box,* introduced in the United States in 1994, further opened up the Internet for general use by enabling people to connect with the Web from their home computers. Although the Internet was initially designed for government intelligence and research, after general Web access was established, entertainment and other commercial uses soon emerged. In fact, entertainment appears to be rapidly becoming the most popular use of the Internet (see the "Focus on Internet-tainment" box).

Focus on Internet-tainment: The Net's Not Just for Information Anymore[466]

According to a poll conducted by Greenfield Online, more people log onto the Internet to play and be entertained than to gather information. In the company's biannual Netstyles survey, it was reported that more than 80% of the approximately 3,000 people surveyed viewed the Internet as a source of entertainment rather than as a source for news and information.

The study revealed several popular entertainment uses. Of those surveyed, 80% played games on their computers, both online and offline, and 66% of the respondents with multimedia capabilities used the Internet to download music. More respondents subscribed to sites that provided joke or game updates (52%) than to sites that provided daily news updates (43%), e-mail newsgroups (31%), business updates (30%), or stock market updates (22%).

Interestingly, the report also indicated that almost half of those interviewed claimed to be watching less television since the time when they established Internet access at home. Nearly 75% of those polled log on to the Internet after work, displaying similar habits to those who "crash" in front of the television after work.

The Internet provides access to entertainment in two primary ways: through *Web site portals*, which provide access to entertainment products or services that can be purchased for delivery or downloaded, or through *Web site services*, which provide direct entertainment experiences. Portals include sites such as Amazon.com, Sony.com, and Ticketmaster.com where individuals can buy books, videos, video games, music, or tickets. In this case, the Internet is used more as a directory or gateway for entertainment than for entertainment itself, although many people may enjoy simply browsing a Web site's offerings as a form of entertainment. Other Web sites, however, provide direct entertainment experiences. Yahoo.com, Games.com, and numerous other sites allow users to play a range of video games, and sites such as Sony's EverQuest.com and Ultima Online (uo.com), which host complex, interactive, multiplayer role-playing games, are becoming increasingly popular. In addition to playing games on the Internet, you can listen to music, create music, watch videos, dress up Barbie, build cities, meet people in chat rooms—the range of Internet entertainment experiences is almost limitless. Many sites, such as Sony.com and Disney.com, function both as portals and direct services, where individuals can purchase or download entertainment or enjoy entertainment offerings directly on the sites.

Driving Forces

It is probably safe to say that new trends and advances in Internet entertainment, indeed all futuretainment, will continue to push the limits of what technology and the law will allow. Innovators looking for ways to create, reproduce, and blend different forms of entertainment will experiment with every new gadget or software application. Some ideas will succeed; others will fail. Some projects will flop due to lack of interest, others because the developers cannot find a way to legally make money from them. If you want to try to predict the next entertainment hit, you need to identify who the successful innovators are and pay attention to what they are doing.

The Power of Porn

Interestingly, some of the most profitable and innovative Web sites are adult entertainment sites. In fact, many experts argue that adult entertainment—what some might call pornography—is one of the most powerful technological forces driving new media. Technology is driven by demand. Cutting-edge firms develop products they think will sell fast. According to the experts, some of the strongest demand comes from porn "manufacturers" because they are looking for technological advances that will help them get over the one big problem their industry faces—the shame factor.[467]

Malcolm Hutty, general director of the Campaign Against Censorship of the Internet in Britain, explains that although demand for porn is high,

> [porn] doesn't travel well. People want porn, but they want it in the comfort of their own home, not seedy backstreet cinemas or sex shops, and they don't want anyone else to know about it. Technology helps bring it straight to you. Each advance seems, at least, to bring you closer to the fantasy, and guarantee more privacy. The more private it becomes, the more comfortable consumers feel, particularly women. They enjoy it more, so they buy it more.[468]

Adult entertainment is credited with driving many advances in new media, including better privacy and security guarantees for financial transactions online as well as better video streaming technology. Adult entertainment Web sites were the first to introduce start/stop video streaming, thereby allowing customers 24- to 48-hour windows to view purchased online videos, and adult sites also pioneered technology for downloading still and moving images on handheld computers and mobile phones. Adult entertainment providers have become so good at developing technology and making money online that mainstream e-businesses—including not only entertainment, but also commerce from banks to supermarkets—are now asking its leading practitioners for advice.[469] Thus, emerging trends in adult entertainment may serve as a useful gauge for all forms of entertainment.

Shall We Play a Game?

Another innovator to watch is the gaming industry. Video games are growing increasingly popular. In 1997, video game sales began outperforming domestic box office movie sales.[470] As discussed in Chapter 11, not only do video games generate more gross revenue than motion pictures, they cost significantly less to produce, creating the potential for a significantly more favorable profit margin.

One of the more impressive aspects of the gaming industry is the multitude of platforms that exist for game play. There are handheld devices, television, computer, and Internet platforms as well as large–scale, self-contained game units. Large-scale game units include those featured in arcade venues, which range from the small portable video game machines found in pizza parlors and gambling machines in casinos to the large-scale gaming theaters found in multiplex gaming centers like Dave and Buster's and GameWorks. Although video games have traditionally been considered children's entertainment, multiplex gaming centers cater to all ages.

As discussed in previous chapters, gamers are a fickle lot. They thrive on novelty. Thus, the gaming industry also has extra incentive not to become stagnant, but to remain innovative. The gaming industry has led the way, with many advances in areas such as animation technology and software programming that, in turn, are often adopted by other entertainment industries. Ironically, then, it would seem that futuretainment is being guided by two of the most unlikely partners—adult entertainment on one end of the spectrum and on the other end, gaming, which (apart from gambling) has functioned predominantly as a youth-oriented form of entertainment.

Uses and Effects

New Media Users

Researchers find that new media users in the United States tend to be younger, more affluent, and better educated than the U.S. population as a whole. An early study of Internet use in 1996 found that more than 65% of Internet users had household incomes of $50,000 or more, compared with 35% of the U.S. population as a whole, and more than 75% of Internet users had attended college, as opposed to 46% of the total U.S. population.[471]

More recent studies continue to reflect these trends.[472] Internet use appears to be lowest among the elderly, the poor, and those with the lowest level of educational achievement. A study conducted in 2000 found that 68% of residents in American households with incomes under $25,000 did not use the Internet, and 67% of Americans who have not completed high school did not have Internet users in their households. Of those aged 65 and higher, 70% lived in households that did not use the Internet. This study also found that young people not only use the Internet more, they are also more likely to use it as one of their primary sources of information, with 67% of Americans aged 18 to 24 using the Internet to gather key information, compared to an overall nationwide average of just 46% who use the Internet for that purpose.

None of these trends should be particularly surprising. Younger individuals, as well as those who are affluent and well educated, are likely to have more exposure and better access to the Internet than others might typically have. Research does, however, indicate little racial disparity for new media use. Internet usage by white, black, and Hispanic households is approximately equal, with only 43% of white households, 43% of black households and 38% of Hispanic households lacking Internet access.

Effects and Impacts

Because new media are just that—new—relatively little research has specifically examined impacts that it might have on audiences. Nonetheless, many researchers speculate about such impacts. Considering that young people make up a significant portion of new media users, it is not surprising that many of these speculations have centered on how new media may affect children. New media have no doubt resulted in many positive impacts, including increasing access to limitless information and entertainment as well as facilitating the production of new information and entertainment. While surfing the Internet or satellite television channels, children and adults alike may be exposed to new ideas and information that may increase their knowledge and perhaps spark their own creativity and innovation. By playing on the Internet or with entertainment software, children can also improve their general technology and computer literacy. New media technologies have also been enlisted as helpful learning aids in most disciplines—math, language, sciences, arts—for almost any age based on the belief that the interactive nature of new media can help make learning more engaging and fun.

In addition to these potentially positive impacts of new media, there are also some concerns. Many concerns echo traditional worries about the impact of television, films, music, and the like—that is, that new media entertainment may have negative impacts on children's psychological and physical health. The fear is that children will spend all of their time surfing the Internet or playing games online instead of getting exercise playing outside or learning how to socialize with other playmates. There have also been reports of children developing repetitive strain injuries from using computer keyboards and video game controls that affect muscles, nerves, tendons, joints, ligaments, cartilage, or spinal discs (such as tendonitis and carpal tunnel syndrome).[473]

Another concern is the difficulty in blocking children from access to pornography, violence, and other materials found on the Internet, in satellite programming, and in other new media. Although new software and devices like the V-chip for television are providing parents with more mechanisms to help them patrol and restrict their children's access to such material, none of these remedies is foolproof, and parents may have little or no control over their children's access to these materials outside their own homes.

One of the biggest concerns, however, is Internet crime, including (a) the trafficking of child pornography and (b) adult sexual predators who target children surfing the Web. The FBI, along with several state as well as international agencies, maintains special units devoted to preventing, investigating, and prosecuting Internet crimes. For example, in September of 2000, Italian police confiscated approximately 3,000 tapes, CDs, and DVDs of child pornography, including some involving children only several months old (see Figure 16.4). Police said they had arrested eight Italians who were thought to be members of a child pornography ring that traded videos over the Internet, including films of Russian children who were abused to death. Police specializing in Internet crime told reporters that their 19-month investigation had given them enough information to begin investigations into 1,700 people suspected of buying the material over the Web. Similarly, in March 2002, the FBI's "Operation Candyman" broke up a pornography ring and brought charges against more than 89 people for trading and propagating child pornography.

The development of new media has also opened the door for other forms of criminal activity. Primary concerns include credit-card fraud and stolen identities. By making online purchases or even by simply clicking on a Web site, individuals are providing valuable

Figure 16.2 In 1975, young and old alike were wowed by technology that turned their televisions into video games.

© Huiton-Deutsch Collection/Corbis.

information that could possibly be intercepted and used fraudulently. Many recent technological advances do appear to provide better information security. Nonetheless, Internet crime will likely continue to be an important concern, but perhaps no more or less so than similar crimes not related to new media.

New media are at the heart of the heated battle over intellectual property rights. Some of the primary advantages of many forms of new media entertainment are that they allow for

Figure 16.3 Today, the gaming industry continues to lead the way for many other entertainment industries, with advances in areas such as animation technology, software programming, portable computing, and internet applications.

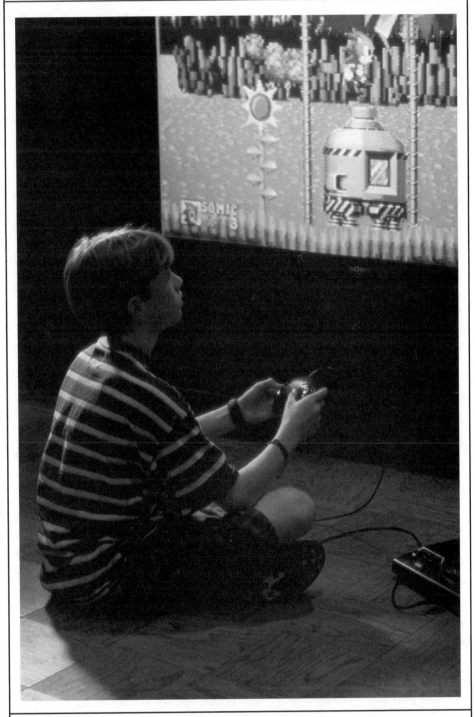

Figure 16.4 Italian police confiscated approximately 3,000 tapes, CDs, and DVDs of child pornography suspected of belonging to a child pornography ring that traded videos over the Internet.

© AFP/Corbis.

easy, quality duplication, manipulation, and circulation. Unfortunately, this advantage is what concerns many intellectual property owners. Most forms of entertainment consist of intellectual property. The content of books, movies, video games, and music can all be considered intellectual property. As discussed in Chapter 7 (on music and radio), many authors, artists, and others who own this property argue that new media make it too easy for others to copy their work without properly compensating them.

Meanwhile, other would-be authors and artists argue that, as the result of these concerns, rules governing intellectual property rights are becoming too strict, limiting artistic and creative freedom. As we have seen, many new forms of entertainment incorporate elements from entertainment that has come before them. Old stories are made new with updated characters and new twists. A new song might include melodies or lyrical references to older songs. The question becomes: When are such adaptations close enough to the original that individuals must get permission from and provide compensation for the owner of the original work? The fear is that if permission and compensation requirements are set too rigidly, it may stifle innovation and creativity, particularly among newcomers who lack the financial backing that large, established entertainment producers have for compensation and legal fees. This debate will likely continue to be an important concern for years to come.

A Focus on Futuretainment Post 9/11: Our Wounded Culture[474]

On the first anniversary of September 11, 2001, the *New York Times* published some reflections about the impact of the terrorist act upon American culture in general and upon entertainment in particular. Contrary to predictions that our culture would be indelibly altered by terrorist events, ironically, very little had changed in the year post September 11. Instead of moderation, film and television violence still thrived. Playboy bunnies were doing *Fear Factor* stunts, and media stars were beating each other's brains out on *Celebrity Boxing*. Big-screen blow-em-up extravaganzas flourished, including films like *The Sum of All Fears*, which showed us the nuclear destruction of Baltimore. Instead of family bonding being shown on TV, we got the sitcoms *The Bachelor* and *Meet My Folks*, which turned sexual discourse into prime-time entertainment. Shark attacks made a comeback on TV news. And our magazines still deconstructed Jennifer Lopez's wardrobe and Tom Cruise's love life.

Films released in the summer of 2002 percolated with subtexts of terror. *Signs* played to anxiety about the unknown, and *The Panic Room* suggested there is no place safe to hide. Even the title and topic of the second installment of the Tolkien trilogy, *The Two Towers*, resonated with new associations (the World Trade Center towers).

Produced in response to September 11, pieces of musical and fine art either produced raw eloquence or reeked of exploitation and bad taste. Bruce Springsteen's songs memorialized the victims. Country music produced titles like *Courtesy of the Red, White and Blue*. And hip hop songs that question the war in Afghanistan (like *Home of the Brave*) showed a marked departure from rap's recent focus on sex and money. An outpouring of photographs, drawings, and collages of the event were exhibited around New York City. In a piece performed at the Museum of New Art in Detroit, an artist poured flour over herself (symbolic of ashes), then wrapped herself in an American flag and donned a gas mask. The question that comes to mind is: Should art trivialize or demean history, or bear witness to it with dignity?

Given a shrinking economy, fall 2002 television programming reflected a tendency to stick with traditional genres like franchise sequels, star vehicles, and remakes of old hits like *The Beverly Hillbillies*, or to choose low-cost programming like reality TV. And in response to the success of the movie *Spider-man*, film makers have more than a dozen superhero movies in development or production. Films intended to generate good, clean escapist fun include *Incredible Hulk*, *Fantastic Four*, *Daredevil*, *Iron Man*, *Catwoman*, and *Ghost Rider*. (The plots of these movies echo the good-guys-versus-bad-guys language that recurs in the rhetoric of President George W. Bush, in which Americans are portrayed as heroes and the enemies of America are depicted as villains.)

Also enjoying a renaissance are spy movies with government employees as heroes. Ben Affleck (*The Sum of All Fears*), Matt Damon (*The Bourne Identity*), Chris Rock (*Bad Company*), and Al Pacino (*The Recruit*) star as CIA operatives while Tommy Lee Jones (*The Hunted*), Tom Hanks (*Catch Me If You Can*), Ed Norton (*Red Dragon*) and Antonio Banderas (*Ecks vs. Sever*) have been cast as G-men.

In spite of what's playing at this writing, Hollywood and Broadway producers have decided that what Americans want is "comfort entertainment" in the form of nostalgia that reminds viewers of simpler, happier times. ABC and WB scheduled shows in which grown-ups travel back to their high-school days in the 1980s. NBC (*American Dreams*) and Fox (*That '70s Show*) have family-based shows set in the '60s and '70s, an era that had similar traumas to our own, such as the Kennedy assassination and the Vietnam War. And CBS was making its own television movies about such '50s and '60s icons as Lucille Ball, Jackie Gleason, Dean Martin, and Jerry Lewis. On Broadway, a candy-colored hit musical, *Hair Spray*, draws on fond remembrances of the *American Bandstand* era. New Broadway revivals include *Man of La Mancha, Gypsy, Flower Drum Song, Little Shop of Horrors, Dinner at Eight,* and *Our Town.*

Picking up on the nostalgia theme, Roger Ebert, film critic for the *Chicago Sun-Times,* is focusing on the past for current entertainment. In his "Great Movies" series, Ebert reviews old pictures because, he said, "So much of the new stuff is just not very challenging for an intelligent viewer." And he's not the only one who thinks so. NPR veteran Susan Stamberg, who thinks there is a dearth of anything fresh and original in contemporary pop culture, has broadcast extended essays on cultural touchstones like the Mamas and Papas' hit *California Dreamin'* as part of her "Present at the Creation" series. On TV, VH1 is broadcasting *Ultimate Albums* in a series about genre-defining CDs because they claim audiences are hungering for cultural comfort food in a post September 11 world.

A century ago, being culturally educated meant being familiar with a few widely accepted works. Today, roughly 30,000 new CDs are released each year to compete with films, television, video games, and the Internet for teenagers' attention. With such an entertainment smorgasbord, media audiences who can hardly keep up with the present take comfort in the past. Stamberg notes,

It's been such a chaotic time in this past year that there's something very reassuring in these revisits to the past. It's so much harder to create these days, harder for artists to really pull themselves together and find new things to say because they are still recovering." If this is true, perhaps the revivals of the old will ultimately yield to more creativity in all entertainment genres.

What is your prediction for the next 5 years?

CHARACTERISTICS OF FUTURETAINMENT

Although it is difficult to predict exactly what the future will hold for entertainment, a review of emerging trends may provide some ideas of where we might be headed. Many of these trends are tied closely to new media, but they have implications for all forms of futuretainment.

Multipurpose

Perhaps the most obvious trend is the multipurpose nature of new media themselves. Emerging new media entertainment products seemingly do it all—you can send e-mail, surf the Internet, call a friend, play a video, and listen to the stereo all with one handheld device. Some gadgets even allow you to record audio and video in addition to playing it. Devices that can deliver multiple forms of entertainment better, faster, and cheaper will likely be favorites with consumers.

Products and services that infuse entertainment into other tasks will also likely fare well. One of the most recent trends is advertisement gaming, where simple Internet advertising banners are being replaced by online games designed to keep audiences entertained while other products and services are being marketed to them. Even providers of traditional leisure activities are looking for ways to maximize their entertainment value. An article published as part of a series on new entertainment trends discussed what museums are doing to try to attract and retain audiences. The article began by stating that "the museum of the future could be a cross between a theme park and a piazza, crammed with gizmos, fantasy, exclusive restaurants and a dizzying array of merchandise."[475]

Along these lines, teachers and educational programs are increasingly looking for ways to combine entertainment with instruction. Researchers and educators began holding Entertainment Education (EE) conferences as far back as 1989 to allow participants "to share their own professional experiences and challenges and to exchange the 'do's and don'ts' of EE practice, science, and policy."[476] The Netherlands boasts an Entertainment-Education Foundation dedicated to studying ways to infuse education with entertainment (and vice versa), such as the radio soap operas produced to promote safer sex in Africa and other countries, as discussed in Chapter 5. Not surprisingly, many of the ideas discussed involved traditional and new media entertainment.

Even religious groups are infusing their worship with entertainment. Author and motivational speaker Ken Davis blended entertainment with religious inspiration in his recent video *Is It Just Me?* advertised as "guaranteed to have you laughing as well as leave you encouraged with a simple message of God's love."[477] Many new services offer resources and advice for ways to incorporate entertainment into religious teachings and gatherings. For example, boasting "comedy so clean you can eat off it," the Christian Comedian Index began "providing a resource for Christian event planners" in 1999.[478]

Figure 16.5 Researchers test a video helmet and virtual reality gloves that engage multiple senses; experts claim that complete virtual world experiences of the sort featured on *Star Trek*'s holodeck are not far off.

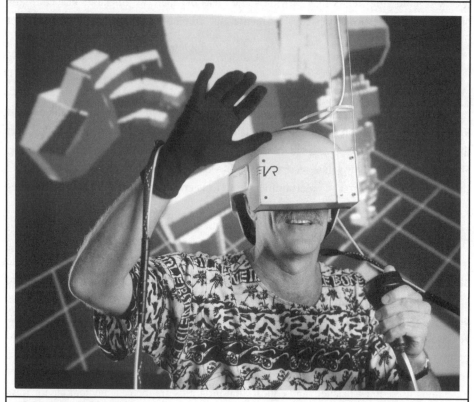

© Roger Reesmeyer/Corbis.

Multisensory

For many years now, mediated entertainment such as television and film has been able to stimulate our optical and auditory senses with sights and sounds. Some forms of new media, however, even engage our senses of touch and smell. In Figure 16.5, researchers test a video helmet and virtual-reality gloves. The view the wearer sees is projected on the screen behind him. Wearers become immersed in the computerized scene and use the gloves to pick up and move simulated objects. Many virtual reality games and rides now allow audiences and players to feel motion and tactile sensations—the rumble of an engine, the sinking feeling of a fall, or the slam of an impact. New media may also include aromas, such as Disney's "Soaring Over California" attraction, where audiences smell orange groves and pine forests while enjoying a simulated hang-gliding experience across the countryside. Makers of emerging forms of entertainment will likely continue to experiment with ways they can simulate and manipulate reality by stimulating our senses. Experts claim that complete virtual world experiences of the sort featured on *Star Trek*'s holodeck are not far off.

Audience Autonomy

The very term *mass media* reflects the nature of traditional mediated entertainment. Once upon a time audiences were at the mercy of many entertainment providers. Television and radio audiences could choose from only a limited selection of programs offered at specific times. If you wanted to watch or listen to a specific program, you had to be sure to watch or listen at a specific time. If you wanted to watch or listen at 2 p.m., you had to make do with what was on at that time. Live entertainment was similarly limited by time and place. Thus, we all experienced the same entertainment, at the same time, en masse. Entertainment producers and programmers dictated the entertainment we could have and when we could have it. Recently, however, control has shifted from entertainment producer to entertainment consumer. Audiences are no longer held hostage by the dictates of entertainment programmers.

Demassification

New forms of entertainment are increasingly individualized. For many years now, entertainment has been tailored to niche audiences. Music, movies, television programs, magazines, video games, and nightclubs are all designed for specific groups of people. Simply by virtue of the increased number of entertainment options available at any given time or place, individuals have more control over their entertainment experiences, and these trends are likely to continue.

Entertainment on Demand

Inventions such as the VCR and TiVo gave audiences even more control so that today people can have almost any entertainment they desire when they desire it. They can program television systems to find, record, and play programs they want to watch. Entertainment offerings on the Internet are typically available 24 hours a day, and new search engine technology allows users to build tailored, individualized profiles that can be used to alert them to new content, such as Web site postings or new music related to their own interests. Individuals are also not restricted by where they can enjoy entertainment. They can enjoy movies, games, music, and the Internet not only in theaters, arcades, automobiles, offices, and living rooms but also on the bus or a park bench, thanks to high quality portable devices.

Interactivity

The interactivity of many emerging forms of entertainment gives audiences additional control over their entertainment experiences. In role-playing video games, individuals may have control over everything from the planet they play on to their character's favorite flavor of ice cream. Individuals can participate in chat rooms with people halfway around the globe. Providing ultimate control, new media also allow individuals to create their own entertainment software and hardware, slide shows with sound tracks, digital videos, cartoons, music, even their own video games and virtual cities.

Audiences also have the choice NOT to interact but, instead, effortlessly sit back and let others entertain them. Audiences enjoy all these forms of control, and they are often willing to pay premium prices for them. Thus, products and services that increase audience autonomy will likely continue to figure prominently in futuretainment.

Signs of the Times

New entertainment trends will also continue to shape and reflect the economic, political, and social environments from which they are born. Just as today's stories, songs, games, and pastimes reflect today's people and issues, tomorrow's entertainment will similarly reflect the people and issues of the day. Chapter 15 explored how today's entertainment reflects the post-modern era we live in. Postmodernism suggests a breakdown and recombination of tradi-tional structures, and our entertainment reflects this with genre and era mixing in drama, music, art, and even in dining, where restaurants feature *food fusion* (combinations of differ-ent flavors and ethnic dishes). New media, with their endless possibilities for breaking down, converging, and re-creating entertainment, are almost postmodern by definition.

Nonetheless, invariably, the pendulum will swing. Today's "anything goes" philosophy may eventually be replaced by new lines of thinking. Thus, the final, perhaps bold, prediction we will make for futuretainment is a *return to basics*. Following an era of funny horror films and dark comedies, popular alternative music and Peking duck pizza, some individuals may begin to yearn for firmer boundaries, where horror movies are truly scary and comedies are truly funny, alternative music is truly alternative and pizza comes with pepperoni.

Some people will welcome these boundaries, while others will continue to shun them. As long as emerging multipurpose, multisense entertainment continues to promote audience autonomy, however, both camps should have plenty of entertainment options to suit their respective tastes.

FADE TO BLACK—CUT AND WRAP

This brief chapter has focused predominantly on how new media are shaping the future of entertainment. New media entertainment is defined as entertainment that incorporates a variety of media, and it is suggested that new trends in entertainment might be identified by paying attention to innovators in new media technology. Predictions for futuretainment include continued focus on multipurpose and multisense products and services that maxi-mize audience control over the entertainment experience as well as a possible return to more traditional entertainment offerings.

New media, of course, are not the only significant force shaping the future of entertainment. Throughout this book, we have traced numerous ways that developments in entertainment have been shaped not only by technological advances but by the political, cultural, economic, and legal realities that existed at the time. And, in turn, we have also explored how entertainment can exert a significant influence on the creation and perception of those realities. Future entertain-ment will likely be no different in this regard. The evolution of entertainment is forever intertwined with the evolution of the societies in which it resides.

A Closer Look

PricewaterhouseCoopers' Predictions for Futuretainment[479]

The Entertainment & Media (E&M) Practice of PricewaterhouseCoopers, one of the world's leading professional services organizations, issued a report at the dawn of the new millennium titled "The Future of the Entertainment & Media Industries."

According to Kevin Carton, Global Leader of PricewaterhouseCoopers' Entertainment & Media Practice,

> In the next five years, the entertainment and media industries will encounter unprecedented change due to the advance of digital technologies. The report's findings and predictions can help industry decision makers take steps now to be better positioned in the digital future.

The report offers the following eight recommended "survival steps" for those who want to be successful in the entertainment and media industries in the 21st century:

1. *Pursue new revenue streams as content control ebbs.*

Companies must replace the idea of *re-purposing content* with the concept of *strategic authoring*. All new content should be designed from the outset for multiple purposes rather than just one. The traditional concept of product-release windows will be dropped in favor of staging multiple, closely timed releases for fast introduction and exploitation of new products.

2. *Organize to reflect connections, not traditions.*

As product connection opportunities replace release-window thinking, organizations will need to adapt structures to support these new models. Organization design needs to maintain flexibility to chase new connections.

3. *Balance production demands between art and technology.*

The act of creating is far more valuable than the technology for recording, and flexibility in use of media will remain important in attracting creative talent. E&M companies should separate truly creative endeavors from processes that can be systematized.

4. *Look for competition from unlikely foes.*

The era of content oligopolies as mediators of what reaches the public is over. As traditional industry boundaries continue to blur, some of the companies now experimenting with content-as-entertainment may become the next generation of entertainment-as-content companies.

5. *Merge for stronger experience offerings, not just savings.*

History hints that synergy has eluded large media mergers, partly because creativity does not seem to understand the benefits of scale. In the future, intra-company cooperation and collaboration are essential, but the fundamental reason for mergers should be better product and service offerings.

6. *Approach ancillary markets as primary markets.*

In the fully connected world there are no ancillary markets. Markets will still be distinguished by means of distribution, but not by time. Exploitation approaches need to account for this new simultaneity.

7. *Let advertisers know: What have you sold for them today?*

Advertising spending is not likely to decline, but instead of targeting audiences by gender and age bracket, advertisers will aim to target audiences by consumption patterns and buying proclivity. This will lead to new trends, such as results-based pricing and better personal interest/affinity group targeting.

8. *View retailers and customers as "virtually" inseparable.*

Brick-and-mortar will remain the dominant distribution model because retailers will stay as close to their customers as is necessary to survive. Content providers need to recognize that this linkage will continue to exist and that they must facilitate it.

The PricewaterhouseCoopers report makes another major prediction: *the death of e-business.* Within the next 10 years, according to the report, commerce will have merged predigital and digital business models in a seamless way of doing business. Electronic business will no longer be "E"— it will just be.

What do you think? How does the report compare to the discussion throughout this text? How does it compare to what you see happening in the world right now?

DISCUSSION AND REVIEW

1. Review how the text describes new media. Based on this description, come up with your own definition. Compare similarities and differences between qualities of the Internet and other forms of new media entertainment and traditional media. Give examples to illustrate your points.

2. What industries are leading the way for futuretainment and why? Can you think of other industries—both entertainment and nonentertainment—that may play a large role in shaping futuretainment? Explain.

3. Discuss the characteristics of futuretainment reviewed in the chapter. Do you agree with each of these? Use examples to make your case. Try to come up with other characteristics or trends that you think are emerging or will emerge for futuretainment.

EXERCISES

1. Look up terms like "futuretainment," "the future of entertainment" or "new technology and entertainment" on an Internet search engine and in a news database like ProQuest or Lexis Nexis. Report what you find. Select one or two articles that you find particularly interesting and discuss them.

2. Have a friend write down at least 20 things people do for entertainment. Review the list and see how many currently involve new media. For every item on the list, speculate ways that new media might be used to enhance, imitate, or modify these forms of entertainment.

3. Try several forms of new media entertainment. Prepare a written critique of each the way a critic might review a film, toy, or restaurant. Describe your experience. Did it meet your expectations? Review pluses and minuses and make suggestions for improvement.

RECOMMENDED READINGS

Darly, A. (2002). *Visual digital culture: Surface play and spectacle in new media genres* (part of the Sussex Studies in Culture and Communication series). New York: Routledge.

Manovich, L. (2001). *The language of new media*, Cambridge, MA: MIT Press.

Pavlik, J. V. (1997). *New media technology: Cultural and commercial perspectives* [part of the Allyn & Bacon Series in Mass Communication]. Boston, MA: Allyn & Bacon.

Weibel, P., & Druckrey, T. (2001). *Net condition: Art and global media* (Electronic Culture: History, Theory, and Practice). Cambridge, MA: MIT Press.

Notes

1. Rifkin, J. (2000). *The age of access.* New York: Penguin Putnam.
2. Ibrahim, H. (1979). Leisure in the ancient world. In H. Ibrahim & J. S. Shivers (Eds.), *Leisure: Emergence and expansion* (pp. 45-77). Los Alamitos, CA: Hwong Publishing.
3. Huizinga, J. (1950). *Homo ludens.* Boston: Beacon Press.
4. Stephenson, W. (1988). *The play theory of mass communication.* New Brunswick NJ: Transaction Books.
5. CircusWeb: Circuses Present and Past. (1996). History of the Circus. Retrieved from http://circusweb.com/cwhistory.html. November 8, 2002.
6. McLellan, D. (2000, August 13). Circus atmosphere: First woman big-top publicist tells tales of three rings. *Los Angeles Times,* p. B8.
7. Arancibia, M. (1995, July 3). Jesters: Laughter in the court. *Cambio,* p. 16.
8. Retrieved from www.britannica.com August 13, 2000.
9. From A brief history of puppetry, www.sunnieunniezz.com/puppetry/puphisto.htm, Oct. 13, 2000.
10. Mergen, B. (1984). *Cultural dimensions of play, games and sport.* Champaign, IL: Human Kinetics Publishers Inc.
11. Wolf, M. J. (1999). *The entertainment economy.* New York: Times Books.
12. Ibid., p. 4.
13. A concept introduced by Erving Goffman in 1974 in *Frame Analysis: An essay on the Organization of Experience.* New York: Harper Colophon.
14. A concept originated by George Herbert Mead in 1934 and expanded by Herbert Blumer and the concepts of Darwinism and Behaviorism.
15. A perspective first provided by Alfred Schultz in 1967; it is discussed in M. Natanson (Ed.). (1967). *The Collected Papers of Alfred Schultz.* The Hague: Martinus Nijhoff.
16. Wolf, M. J. (1999). *The Entertainment Economy: How Mega-Media Forces are Transforming Our Lives.* New York: Random House, Times Books, p. 4.
17. Wolf, M. J. (1999). *The Entertainment Economy: How Mega-Media Forces are Transforming Our Lives.* New York: Random House, Times Books.
18. Noam, E. (1995). Visions of the media age: Taming the information monster. Paper presented to the Third Annual Colloquium, Alfred Herrhausen Society of International Dialogue, Frankfurt, Germany.
19. Goldhaber, M. H. (1997, April 7). The attention economy and the net. *First Monday, 2*(4). Online journal accessed December 9, 2002, at www.firstmonday.dk/issues/issue2_4/goldhaber/index.html
20. McChesney, R. W. (1999, Nov. 29). The new global media: It's a small world of big conglomerates. *The Nation.* Retrieved March 24, 2002, from www.thenation.com/doc.mhtml?i=19991129&s=mcchesney
21. Wolf, M. (1999). *The entertainment economy: How mega-media forces are transforming our lives.* New York: Random House, Times Books.

22. Ahrens, Frank (2002, October 24). These Giants hope to dump Angels and more; Media conglomerates say non-core assets must go. *Washington Post,* p. E01.

23. Ibid.

24. Mulkern, A. C. (2002, November 24). Feds may propel media mergers: Views differ on impact of relaxing rules. *Denver Post,* p. K01.

25. Wolf, M. (1999). *The entertainment economy: How mega-media forces are transforming our lives.* New York: Random House, Times Books.

26. Ibid.

27. Ibid.

28. Berry, M. (2000, November). Keynote address. Proceedings from Entertainment Day, event hosted by the California State University, Fullerton.

29. *Nintendo GAMECUBE and Game Boy advance to reinvent video gameplay for 21st century.* (2001, May 16). Canada Newswire, Ottawa.

30. Strategy Analytics: Games console sales to hit 41.9m units in 2002; PlayStation 2 dominates global market with 63 percent share. (2002, October 17). *M2 Presswire;* Coventry, p1.

31. Snow, S. (1993, August 7) Pop/Rock: The morning report. *Los Angeles Times,* p. 2.

32. Quoted in Barron, K. (March, 2 1999). Theme players. *Forbes,* v.163(6), p. 53.

33. Cited in Brownfield, P. (1999, May 16). It's not easy leaving "Home": series swan song saddens Tim Allen. *Special from the Los Angeles Times Record,* Bergen County, NJ., p. y03.

34. Goldhaber, M. H. (1997, April 7). The attention economy and the net. *First Monday, 2*(4). Online journal accessed December 9, 2002, at www.firstmonday.dk/issues/issue2_4/goldhaber/index.

35. Johnson, Roy. S. (1998, June 22). The Jordan effect. *Fortune,* 124-132.

36. Ibid.

37. Ibid.

38. Adler, R. P. (1997) *The Future of Advertising: New Approaches to the Attention Economy.* Washington, D.C.: The Aspen Institute.

39. Statistics obtained from the Travel Industry November 11, 2002, from www.tia.org/

40. Wolf, M. J. (1999). *The entertainment economy: How mega-media forces are transforming our lives.* New York: Random House, Times Books.

41. Ednalino, P. (2001, September 19). Public finds an escape in books, film; Denverites flock to venues in days after terrorist attacks. *Denver Post, Rockies Edition,* p. F.09.

42. Entertainment (Company Town; IN BRIEF): Video rentals soar for second week (2001, September 28). *The Los Angeles Times,* p. C5.

43. Adapted from Wolf, M. J. (1999). *The entertainment economy: How mega-media forces are transforming our lives.* New York: Random House, Times Books.

44. Based on a typology by Abercrombie, N., & Longhurst, B. (1998). *Audiences: A sociological theory of performance and imagination.* London: Sage, which uses the terms 'simple, mass and diffused' audiences.

45. McQuail, D. (1997). *Audience analysis.* Thousand Oaks, CA: Sage, p. 7.

46. From Elliott, P. (1974). Uses and gratifications research: A critique and a sociological alternative. In J. G. Blumler & E. Katz (Eds.), *The uses of mass communications: Current perspectives on gratifications research* (pp. 249-268). Beverly Hills, CA: Sage.

47. McQuail, D. Blumler, D. J., & Brown, J. W. (1972) studied different radio and TVD programs in Britain. See their study, Explaining audience behavior, in D. McQuail (Ed.), *Sociology of mass communications* (pp. 135-164), Harmondworth, UK: Penguin.

48. From Katz, E., Blumler, J., & Gurevitch, M. (1974). Utilisation of mass communication by the individual. In J. Blumler & E. Katz (Eds.), *The uses of mass communications: Current perspectives on gratifications research* (pp. 19-32). Beverly Hills, CA: Sage.

49. From Herzog, H. (1944). Motivations and gratifications of daily serial listeners. In W. Schramm (Ed.), *The process and effects of mass communication* (pp. 50-55). Urbana: University of Illinois.

50. See Weiss, W. (1971). Mass communication. *Annual Review of Psychology,* 22, pp. 309-336.

51. See McQuail, D. (1985). With the benefit of hindsight: Reflections on uses and gratifications research. In M. Gurevitch and M. R. Levy (Eds.), *Mass Communication Review Yearbook,* 5, 125-141.

52. From Lindlof, T. (1988). Media audiences as interpretive communities. In J. Anderson (Ed.), *Communication Yearbook II,* (pp. 81-107). Newbury Park, CA: Sage.

53. McQuail, D. (1997). *Audience analysis.* Thousand Oaks, CA: Sage, Chapter 3.

54. Kershaw, B. (1996). The politics of postmodern performance. In P. Campell (Ed.), *Analysing performance: A critical reader.* Manchester, UK: Manchester University Press, p. 166.

55. Gurvitch, G. (1955). The sociology of the theater. In E. Burns & T. Burns (Eds.), *Sociology of literature and drama.* Harmondsworth, UK: Penguin, 1973.

56. McQuail, D. (1994). *Mass communication theory: An introduction.* London: Sage.

57. Carey, J. (1975). A cultural approach to communication. *Communication,* 2, pp. 1-22.

58. A notion of Debord, G. (1994). *The society of the spectacle.* New York: Zone Books, p. 9.

59. From the ideas presented in Lasch, C. (1980). *The culture of narcissism.* London: Sphere.

60. See Sennett, R. (1997). *The fall of public man.* New York: Knopf.

61. From Narcissus and necessity: Why are we creating virtual realities? Retrieved November 9, 2002, from www.transparencynow.com/virtual.htm

62. A phrase coined by Umberto Eco.

63. See Rubin, A. M., Perse, E. M., & Powell, E. (1989). Loneliness, parasocial interaction and local TV news viewing. *Communication Research,* 14, pp. 246-268.

64. Abercrombie & Longhurst, op. cit., p. 131.

65. For a close look at research techniques appropriate for entertainment, see Sayre, S. (2001). *Using Qualitative Methods for Marketplace Research.* Thousand Oaks: Sage.

66. For more information on the ethnography of media consumption, see Moores, S. (1993*). Interpreting audiences.* London: Sage.

67. See Lull, J. (1990*). Inside family viewing: Ethnographic research on television's audiences.* London: Routledge.

68. See works by David Morley (e.g., *Television audiences and cultural studies.* (1992). London: Routledge).

69. See works by John Fiske (*Television culture.* (1987). London: Methuen) and Ien Ang (*Remote control: Television audiences and cultural power.* (1989). London: Routledge).

70. From Stevenson, N. (1995). *Understanding media cultures.* London: Sage, p. 183.

71. McQuail, D. (1997). *Audience analysis.* Thousand Oaks, CA: Sage, p. 41.

72. From Blumler, J. G. (1985). The social character of media gratifications. In K. E. Rosengren, P. Palmgreen, & L. Wenner (Eds.), *Media gratifications research: Current perspectives,* (pp. 41-59). Beverly Hills, CA: Sage.

73. McQuail, D. (1997). *Audience analysis.* Thousand Oaks, CA: Sage, p. 131.

74. Based on a process described in Schultz, D. E., & Barners, B. E. (1999). *Strategic brand communications campaigns.* Lincolnwood, IL: NTC Business Books, p. 99.

75. Chaney, D. (1995). *Fictions of collective life.* London: Routledge.

76. Abercrombie & Longhurst, op. cit. (1998), Chapter 6.

77. Neuman, W. R. (1991). *The future of the mass audience.* Cambridge, UK: Cambridge University Press, p. 104.

78. McQuail, D. (1997). *Audience analysis.* Thousand Oaks, CA: Sage, p. 150. Edited from a list presented in Table 9.1.

79. From McKinley, J. C. Jr. (2000, August 11). It isn't just a game: Clues to avid rooting. *New York Times Sports,* p. C1.

80. Cited in Simpson, J. B., comp. (1988). *Simpson's Contemporary Quotations*. Boston: Houghton Mifflin. Accessed January 22, 2002 at www.bartleby.com/63/

81. Freud, S. (1925). Formulations regarding the two principles in Mental Functioning. In Collected Papers, Vol. IV, Ch. 1. London: Hogarth Press. As cited in Stephenson, W. (1998). The play theory of mass communication. New Brunswick, NJ: Transaction, Inc., p. 52.

82. *Merriam-Webster's Collegiate Dictionary (10th ed.).* (2001). Springfield, MA: Merriam-Webster, Incorporated. Accessed January 22, 2002, at www.m-w.com/cgi-bin/netdict?drama

83. Zillmann, D. (1996). The psychology of suspense in dramatic exposition. In P. Vorderer, H. J. Wulff, & M. Friedrichsen (Eds.), *Suspense: Conceptualizations, theoretical analyses, and empirical explorations* (pp. 199-241). Mahwah, NJ: Lawrence Erlbaum Associates.

84. Carroll, N. (1996). The paradox of suspense. In P. Vorderer, H. J. Wulff, & M. Friedrichsen (Eds.), *Suspense: Conceptualizations, theoretical analyses, and empirical explorations* (pp. 71-91). Mahwah, NJ: Lawrence Erlbaum Associates.

85. Zillmann, D. (1996). The psychology of suspense in dramatic exposition. In P. Vorderer, H. J. Wulff, & M. Friedrichsen (Eds.), *Suspense: Conceptualizations, theoretical analyses, and empirical explorations* (pp. 199-241). Mahwah, NJ: Lawrence Erlbaum Associates.

86. See for review Zillmann, D. (1980). *The entertainment functions of television*. Hillsdale, NJ: Lawrence Erlbaum.

87. Vorderer, P., & Knobloch, S. (2000). Conflict and suspense in drama. In D. Zillmann & P. Vorderer (Eds.), *Media entertainment: The psychology of its appeal* (pp. 59-72). Mahwah, NJ: Lawrence Erlbaum Associates.

88. Zillmann, D. (1991). Suspense and mystery. In J. Bryant and D. Zillmann (Eds.), *Responding to the screen: Reception and reaction processes* (pp. 281-304). Mahwah, NJ: Lawrence Erlbaum Associates.

89. Freud, S. (1958). *Der Witz und seine Beziehung zum Unbewussten* [Jokes and their relation to the unconscious]. Frankfort: Fischer Bücherei. (Original work published 1905).

90. Zillmann, D., & Bryant, J. (1980). Misattribution theory of tendentious humor. *Journal of Experimental Social Psychology, 16*, 146-160.

91. See for review, King, Cynthia (in press). Humor and mirth. In J. Bryant, J. Cantor, & D. Roskos-Ewoldsen (Eds.), *Communication and emotion: Essays in honor of Dolf Zillmann*. Hillsdale, NJ: Lawrence Erlbaum Associates.

92. Deans, J. (2000, May 22). New Media: Gagging to get on the net: TV comedy producers are investing in new entertainment ideas designed to make the City take them seriously. *The Guardian*.

93. Ibid.

94. Ibid., paragraph 9.

95. McArthur, T. (1992). *Oxford's companion to the English language*. Oxford: UK: Oxford University Press.

96. Lucas, F. L. (1958). *Tragedy: Serious drama in relation to Aristotle's poetics*. NY: Macmillan, p. 175.

97. Ibid.

98. Goldsmith, W. (1975). Beloved monsters: A psychodynamic appraisal of horror. *Journal of Contemporary Psychotherapy*, 7:17-22.

99. Zillmann, D., Weaver, J., Mundorf, N., & Aust, C. (1986). Effects of an opposite-gender companion's affect to horror on distress, delight, and attraction. *Journal of Personality and Social Psychology, 51*, 586-594.

100. See, for review, Tamborini, R. (1991). Responding to horror: Determinants of exposure and appeal. In J. Bryant & D. Zillmann (Eds.), *Responding to the screen: Reception and reaction processes* (pp. 305-327). Hillsdale, NJ: Erlbaum.

101. Johnston, D. (1995). Adolescents' motivations for viewing graphic horror. *Human Communication Research, 21:4*, 522-552.

102. Rosenbaum, R. (1979). Gooseflesh. *Harper's Magazine,* 86-92.

103. Stephenson, W. (1988). *The play theory of mass communication.* New Brunswick, NJ: Transaction Books, p. 45.

104. Ibid., p. 46.

105. Carter, B. (2001, July 22). TV this fall means taste has changed, analysts say. *The Sunday Patriot,* Harrisburg, PA, p. E01.

106. Lowry, B. (2001, May 2). Smile, you're in "assisted reality." *The Los Angeles Times,* p. F1.

107. Cited in Carter, B. (2001, July 22). "TV this fall means taste has changed, analysts say." *The Sunday Patriot,* Harrisburg, PA, p. E01.

108. Cited in ibid.

109. Cited in ibid.

110. Quote found on p. 74 of Steuer, J. (1992). Defining virtual reality: Dimensions determining telepresence. *Journal of Communication, 42* (4), 73-93.

111. Haley, K. (July 23, 2001). More. Better, Different. [Showtime management strategy to include interactivity and expanding digital multiplex]. *Multichannel News, 22* (30), 12A.

112. Cited in ibid.

113. Cited in ibid.

114. Vorderer, P. (2000). Interactive entertainment and beyond. In Zillmann, D., & Vorderer, P. (Eds.), *Media entertainment: The psychology of its appeal.* Mahwah, NJ: Lawrence Erlbaum Associates.

115. Adapted with permission from Terrapin Children's University Web site on Roman drama at www.wam.umd.edu/~mdwebb/terps/clas2.htm

116. Winn, M. (1985). *The Plug-in Drug.* New York: Penguin Books, p. 4.

117. Kuhn, T. (1970). *The Structure of Scientific Revolutions* (2nd ed.). Chicago: University of Chicago Press.

118. Lippmann, Walter. (1922/1934). *Public Opinion.* New York: Macmillan.

119. Lowery, S. A., & DeFleur, M. L. (1995). *Milestones in mass communication research.* White Plains, NY: Longman.

120. Lazarsfeld, P. F. (1941). Remarks on administrative and critical communications research. *Studies in Philosophy and Social Science, 9,* 2-16.

121. Katz, E., & Lazarsfeld, P. F. (1955). *Personal influence: The part played by people in the flow of communications.* New York: Free Press.

122. The Bobo doll studies are detailed in Bandura, A. (1977). *Social learning theory.* Englewood Cliffs, NJ: Prentice-Hall.

123. Hovland, C. I., Lumsdaine, A. A., & Scheffield, F. D. (1949). *Experiments on mass communication.* Princeton, NJ: Princeton University Press.

124. Klapper, J. T. (1960). *The effects of mass communication.* New York: Free Press.

125. Iyengar, S., & Kinder, D. R. (1987). News that matters: *Television and American opinion.* Chicago: University of Chicago Press. Also, McCombs, M. E., & Shaw, D. L. (1972). The agenda-setting function of the mass media. *Public Opinion Quarterly, 36,* 176-187.

126. Cohen, B. (1963). *The press and foreign policy.* Princeton, NJ: Princeton University Press.

127. Bandura, A. (2002). Social cognitive theory of mass communication. In J. Bryant & D. Zillmann (Eds.), *Media effects: Advances in theory and research* (2nd ed.) (pp. 121-154). Hillsdale, NJ: Lawrence Erlbaum Associates.

128. See Roskos-Ewoldsen, D. R., Roskos-Ewoldsen, B., & Carpentier, F. R. (2002). Media priming: A synthesis. In J. Bryant & D. Zillmann (Eds.), *Media effects: Advances in theory and research* (2nd ed., pp. 97-120). Hillsdale, NJ: Lawrence Erlbaum Associates, p. 97-120. Also, Jo, E., & Berkowitz, L. (1994). A priming effect analysis of media influences: An update. In J. Bryant & D. Zillmann (Eds.), *Media effects: Advances in theory and research* (pp. 43-60). Hillsdale, NJ: Lawrence Erlbaum Associates.

129. See for review, King, C. (in press). Humor and mirth. In J. Bryant, J. Cantor, & D. Roskos-Ewoldsen (Eds.), *Communication and emotion: Essays in honor of Dolf Zillmann.* Hillsdale, New Jersey: Lawrence Erlbaum Associates. Also, Zillmann, D. (2000). Humor and comedy. In D. Zillmann & P. Vorderer (Eds.), *Media entertainment: The psychology of its appeal* (pp. 59-72). Mahwah, NJ: Lawrence Erlbaum Associates.

130. Rogers, Everett M., & Shoemaker, F. Floyd (1971). *Communication of Innovations: A Cross-Cultural Approach* (2nd ed.). New York: The Free Press.

131. Faules, D. F., & Alexander, D. C. (1978). *Communication and social behavior: A symbolic interaction perspective.* Reading, MA: Addison-Wesley, p 23.

132. Berger, P. L., & Luckmann, T. (1966). *The social construction of reality: A treatise in the sociology of knowledge.* Garden City, NY: Doubleday.

133. Adapted from Baran, S. (2001). *Introduction to mass communication: Media literacy and culture.* Mountain View, CA: Mayfield Publishing Company, pp. 334-335.

134. Calvo, D., & Abramowitz, R. (2001, November 19). Uncle Sam wants Hollywood, but Hollywood has qualms. *Los Angeles Times.* Available at http://pqasb.pqarchiver.com/latimes/

135. See Singer, D. G., & Singer, J. L. (Eds.). (2001). *Handbook of children and the media.* Thousand Oaks, CA: Sage.

136. Adapted from Baran, S. (2001). *Introduction to mass communication: Media literacy and culture.* Mountain View, CA: Mayfield Publishing Company. Also, Singhal A., & Rogers, E. M. (1999). *Entertainment-education: A communication strategy for social change.* Hillsdale, NJ: Lawrence Erlbaum Associates.

137. From an item by Daniel Sanger in the *New York Times Sunday Magazine*, December 9, 2001, p. 67.

138. Maryles, D., & Riippa, L. (2001). How they landed on top, *Publishers Weekly, 248*(12), p. 31.

139. Spano, S. (2000, December 10). Whodunits by women make great travel books, and it's no mystery why. *Los Angeles Times,* p. L7.

140. Ha, J. (2000, May 9). The wow factor. *Los Angeles Times*, p. B2.

141. Carvajal, D. (2000, November 27). Boing! Pop-up books are growing up. *New York Times,* p. B1.

142. Wild about Harry. (1999, September 20). *Time Magazine.*

143. The opinion of Roberts, G. G. (1990). Contemporary book limited editions: Popular culture turned elite. *Journal of Popular Culture, 24*(3), 167-176.

144. The opinion of Schickel, R. (2000, December 10). The frenzy of renown. *Los Angeles Times Book Review,* pp. 1-2.

145. Dame Rebecca West said this as quoted in www.britannica.com.

146. As quoted in www.britannica.com.

147. Statistics from Picard, R., & Brody, J. (2000). The structure of the newspaper industry. In A. Greco (Ed.), *The media and entertainment industries.* Boston: Allyn & Bacon, p. 46.

148. Quoted in an article by Kuczynski, A. (2001, September 10.) The new feminist mystique. *New York Times,* p. C1.

149. Encyclopedia Britannica entry for "comic strip." Retrieved December 8, 2000, from www.britannica.com/bcom/eb/article/

150. Jules Feiffer as quoted in Mitchell, E. (2000, July 25). They oughta be in pictures. *New York Times,* p. B1.

151. Lang, J. S., & Trimble, P. (1988). Whatever happened to the man of tomorrow? *Journal of Popular Culture, 22*(3), 157-173.

152. Lee was quoted in Raphael, J. (2000, July 16). The invincible Stan Lee? *Los Angeles Times Magazine*, pp. 18-21.

153. As quoted in Colton, M. (1999, November). Cartooning for Christ. *Brill's Content,* pp. 50-52.

154. French, H. W. (2000, December 10). The rising sun sets on Japanese publishing. *New York Times Book Review,* p. 51.

155. Eiji, O. (1988, July-September). Comic book formula for success. *Japan Quarterly,* p. 289.

156. Adams, K. A., & Hill, L. Jr. (1991). Protest and rebellion: Fantasy themes in Japanese comics. *Journal of Popular Culture, 25*(1), 99-127.

157. From Friend, T. (2001, July 30). Comics from underground. *The New Yorker,* pp. 26-29.

158. Stated in an article by Orenstein, P. (2001, August 5). A graphic life. *New York Times Magazine,* pp. 26-30.

159. Reported in the *New York Times,* Nov. 12, 2001, media section, C8.

160. Quoted by Handelman, D. (2001, November 12). Like other monthlies, *Esquire* dances to a new rhythm. *New York Times,* p. C8.

161. Ibid.

162. Statistics provided by *Media Industry Newsletter,* a monthly industry trade publication, in November 2000.

163. Quoted in an article by Van Hoffman, N. (2000). Lion of the line. *Civilization: Magazine of the Library of Congress,* pp. 36-40.

164. The origin of this quote is unknown, however, it is posted on several Web sites, including www.sios.com/hfowlkes/voice.php3

165. Music consumer trends report. (1996). Conducted by the Recording Industry Association of America. Accessed December 5, 2002, at www.riaa.org/MD-Cons-5-96-MCT.cfm

166. Cited in Boucher, G. (2001, February 11). The bubble pops: Radio stations are beginning to turn a cold shoulder to teen acts. *Star Tribune,* Minneapolis, MN (Metro Edition), p. 10F.

167. Gundersen, E. (1992, December 4). Hyperkinetic techno music wins dance floor raves // Blasts from Belgium // Innovators struggle to keep ahead of the clones. *USA Today,* p. 04D.

168. Dunaway, M. (1999). James Brown is dead. *Pif Magazine* (online), vol. 20, accessed December 5, 2002, at http://pifmagazine.com/vol20/duna.shtml

169. A history of country music. Accessed December 9, 2002, at www.cduniverse.com/asp/university/cy/cy_origin.asp

170. Blow, C. *History of Rap: Vol. 1: The Genesis* posted at http://rap.about.com/gi/dynamic/offsite.htm?site=http%3A%2F%2Frhino.com%2FFeatures%2Fliners%2F72851lin.html

171. Cited on Davey D's Hip Hop Corner, What is Hip Hop Directory Web site. Accessed December 8, 2002, at www.daveyd.com/whatiship.html

172. Erlewine, S. T. All music guide. Accessed December 10, 2002, at www.24-7rap.com/drdre/

173. Sandler, A. (1999, August). Ames takes Warner reins. *Variety,* pp. 23-29.

174. Cited in Stark, P. (1994, November 1). A history of radio broadcasting. *Billboard.* Accessed December 5, 2002, at www.kcmetro.cc.mo.us/pennvalley/biology/lewis/crosby/bilboard.htm

175. Ibid.

176. Ibid.

177. Ibid.

178. Statistics and sources cited from Gliniewicz, L. Big summer concerts mean big prices. Accessed December 5, 2002, at www.bankrate.com/brm/news/advice/20000509b.asp

179. Ibid.

180. Cited in Fritz, J. (1999). *Rave culture: An insider's overview.* Victoria, B.C., Canada: Small Fry Enterprises. Accessed December 5, 2002, at www.raveculture.cjb.net/

181. Soeder, J. (2001, August 1) MTV's revolution—20 and still evolving. *Plain Dealer,* Cleveland, Ohio, p. A1.

182. See for review Hansen, C., & Hansen, R. (2000). Music and music videos. in D. Zillmann & P. Vorderer (Eds), *Media entertainment: The psychology of its appeal* (pp. 175-196). Mahwah, NJ: Lawrence Erlbaum Associates.

183. Reprinted with permission from the Combined Law Enforcement Agencies of Texas. Accessed December 5, 2002; full text available at www.cleat.org/remember/TimeWarner/

184. For review see, Hansen, C., & Hansen, R. (2000). Music and music videos. In D. Zillmann & P. Vorderer (Eds)., *Media entertainment: The psychology of its appeal* (pp. 175-196). Mahwah, NJ: Lawrence Erlbaum Associates.

185. Ibid.

186. Ibid.

187. Ibid.

188. Rock 'n' Roll's Holy War. (1994, June 20). *Time,* pp. 48-49.

189. On the Appeal of Ticketmaster. (1999, February 15). American Antitrust Institute Activities Web site; accessed December 8, 2002, at www.antitrustinstitute.org/recent/21.cfm

190. From Litman, B. R. (2000), Windows of exhibition. In A. N. Greco (Ed.), *The media and entertainment industries.* Boston: Allyn & Bacon.

191. Corliss, R. (1997, May 12). Cartoons are no laughing matter. *Time Magazine,* p. 88.

192. Hochman, D. (1998, November 20). Epics and insects. *Entertainment Weekly,* pp. 27-28.

193. From Heller, S. (1994, February 16). Dissecting Disney. *The Chronicle of Higher Education,* p. A-1.

194. King, T. (2000, December 1). Nickelodeon comes of age. *Wall Street Journal,* p. W8.

195. For more on the psychology of humor, see Goldstein, J. H. and McGhee, P. E. (Eds.). (1972). *The psychology of humor.* New York: Academic Press.

196. From Platinga, C., and Smith, G. M. (1999). *Passionate views: Film, cognition and emotion.* Baltimore, MD: Johns Hopkins University Press.

197. Mitchel, E. (2001, July 11). [Film review of *Final Fantasy: The Spirits Within*]. *New York Times,* p. B1.

198. Tasker, Y. (1993). *Spectacular bodies: Gender, genre and the action cinema.* London: Comedia/ Routledge, p. 149.

199. From Baker, A. (2000, December). A new combination: Women and the boxing film. *Cineaste,* pp. 22-26.

200. Munoz, L. (2000, November 19). Women on the verge of a breakthrough. *New York Times Calendar,* cover story.

201. Gladstone, V. (2000, December 3). When battle and ballet become synonymous. *New York Times,* Arts, p. 6.

202. Ibid., p. 8.

203. Ansen, D. (1995, March 13). The return of a bloody great classic; *The Wild Bunch* still pushes our buttons about violence. *Newsweek,* pp. 70-71.

204. From Zillmann, D., & Vorderer, P. (Eds.) (2000). *Media entertainment: The psychology of its appeal.* Mahwah, NJ: Lawrence Erlbaum.

205. See Zuckerman, M. (1996). Sensation seeking and the taste for vicarious horror. In J. B. Weaver III & R. Tamborini (Eds.), *Horror films: Current research on audience preferences and reactions.* Mahwah, NJ: Lawrence Erlbaum, pp. 147-160.

206. From Tartar, M. (1992). *Off with their heads! Fairy tales and the culture of childhood.* Princeton, NJ: Princeton University Press.

207. Watson, M. W., & Peng, Y. (1992). The relation between toy gun play and children's aggressive behavior. *Early Education and Development, 3,* 370-389.

208. Lagerspetz, K. M., Wahlroos, C., & Wendeline, C. (1978). Facial expressions of preschool children while watching televised violence. *Scandinavian Journal of Psychology, 19,* 213-222.

209. Zillmann, D. (1991). Television viewing and psychological arousal. In J. Bryant & D. Zillmann (Eds.), *Responding to the screen: Reception and reaction processes.* Hillsdale, NJ: Lawrence Erlbaum.

210. See Goldstein, J. H. (Ed.). (1998). *Why we watch: The attractions of violent entertainment.* New York: Oxford University Press, p. 232, Table 10.1.

211. Monaco, J. (2000). *How to read a film: Movies, media, multimedia.* New York: Oxford University Press, p. 264.

212. Menand, L. (1997, March 24). The iron law of stardom. *The New Yorker,* pp. 36-40.

213. Dyer, R. (1998). *Stars.* London: British Film Institute, p. 18.

214. Tolston, A. (1996). *Mediations: Text and discourse in media studies.* London: Arnold, Chapter 5.

215. From a notion developed by Klapp, O. E. (1962). *Heroes, villains and fools.* Englewood Cliffs, NJ: Prentice-Hall.

216. King, B. (1985). Articulating stardom. *Screen, 26*(5), 27-50.

217. Mayne, J. (1993). *Cinema and spectatorship.* London: Routledge.

218. Stacey, J. (1994). *Star gazing: Hollywood cinema and female spectatorship.* London: Routledge.

219. See Strauss, W., & Howe, N. (2001, July 15). Youth culture. *Los Angeles Times,* p. M1.

220. From Hoberman, J. (2001, July 15). I oughta be in pictures. *New York Times Sunday Magazine,* p. 13.

221. Russell, C. A. (1998). Toward a framework of product placement: Theoretical propositions. *Advances in Consumer Research, 25,* 357-362.

222. From an item by Marshall Sella in the *New York Times Sunday Magazine,* December 9, 2001, p. 66.

223. Sella, M. (2000, May 21). The electronic fishbowl. *The New York Times Magazine* (May 21), pp. 50-68.

224. Rutenberg, J. (2000, December 6). Outback confidential. *The New York Times Magazine,* pp. 100-102.

225. Quoted in commentary on television by Bill Carter, *New York Times,* July 9, 2001, p. C8.

226. From Flaherty, M. (2000, December 8). Voyage. *Entertainment Weekly,* pp. 49-52.

227. Secrecy and the allure of the hidden is the subject of Sante, L. (2000, December 6). What secrets tell. *New York Times Magazine,* pp. 75-77.

228. James, C. (2000, December 5). Real copy, real crises, and real voyeurism, too. *New York Times,* p. B3.

229. Quoted in Carter, B. (2001, July 17). The land rush to reality island. *New York Times,* p. B1.

230. From an item by Marshall Sella in the *New York Times Sunday Magazine,* December 9, 2001, p. 57.

231. Sardar, S. (2000, November 10). Consumed by voyeurism. *Australian Financial Review.*

232. From Franklin, N. (2001, July 23). Fright nights. *New Yorker,* p. 84.

233. From Meinhof, U. H., & Smith, J. (Eds.). (2000). *Intertextuality and the media: From genre to everyday life.* Manchester, UK: Manchester University Press, p. 110.

234. McQuail, D., Blumler, J., & Brown, J. (1972). The television audience: A revised perspective (pp. 135-65). In D. McQuail (Ed.), *The sociology of mass communications.* Harmondsworth: Penguin.

235. Ballard, C. (2000, November 5). The know-it-alls. *New York Times Magazine,* pp. 54-57.

236. From Greenberg, B. S. & Hofshire, L. (2000). Sex on entertainment television (pp. 93-111). In D. Zillmann & P. Vorderer (Eds.), *Media Entertainment.* Mahwah, NJ: Lawrence Erlbaum.

237. Ibid.

238. Fiske, J. (1990). *Television culture.* London: Routledge, p. 3.

239. From a study reported in Cress, S. L., & Rapert, K. D. (1996, November). *Talk show viewing motives: Does gender make a difference?* Paper presented to the annual meeting of the Speech Communication Association in San Diego.

240. Greenberg & Hofshire, op. cit., p. 106.

241. Santora, M. A. (2000, December 3). Byproducts [a column]. *New York Times,* p. 26.

242. Quoted in a piece in the "Stuff We Like" section by Cohen, L. K. (2000, October). *Brill's Content,* p. 60.

243. Hernandez, E. H. (2000). Lights, camera, spiritual enlightenment? A phenomenology of the TBN viewing experience. Master's thesis completed at California State University, Fullerton.

244. Proclaimed in Gabler, N. (2001, March 4). When every TV show is a rerun [op-ed column]. *New York Times,* p. 15.

245. From Leeds, J., & Boucher, G. (2001, July 22). Rocking the world. *Los Angeles Times,* p. C1.

246. Stated in an article in the "Critic's Notebook" section by Salamon, J. (2001, July 30). *New York Times,* p. B1.

247. From an article by James, C. (2001, October 29). Dramatic events that rewrite the script. *New York Times,* p. E1.

248. Accessed December 12, 2002, from http://extratv/warnerbros.com/dailynews/pop/08_01_22C

249. Graber, D. A. (1988). *Processing the news: How people tame the information tide.* New York: Longman.

250. Gerbner, G., & Gross, L. (1976, Spring) Living with television: The violence profile. *Journal of Communication, 26,* 173-199.

251. Bandura, A. (1977). *The social learning theory.* Englewood Cliffs, NJ: Prentice-Hall.

252. McCombs, M. E., & Shaw, D. L. (1972). The agenda-setting function of the mass media. *Public Opinion Quarterly,* 176-187.

253. See Clausen, J. A. (Ed.). (1968). *Socialization and society.* Boston: Little, Brown.

254. For a summary of this theory, see Severin, W. J. & Tankard, J. W. Jr. (1988). *Communication theories.* New York: Longman, pp. 300-310.

255. Elliott, S. (2000, November 16). Advertising column. *New York Times,* p. C10.

256. Stern, B. (2000, October). *From art to science: Literary theory in the laboratory.* Paper presented to the annual conference of the Association for Consumer Research, Salt Lake City, UT.

257. From Holson, L. (2001, May 27). Bidding to be moguls of a risky business. *New York Times,* section 2, p. 1.

258. From Teachout, T. (2002, March 10). Turning a television into a music box. *New York Times,* television section.

259. See Miller, J. (1978). *Living systems.* New York: McGraw-Hill.

260. From Skyttner, L. (1996). *General systems theory: An introduction.* Houndmills, U.K.: Macmillan.

261. Example from Peterson, R., & Simkus, A. (1992). How musical tastes mark occupational status groups. In Michele, L., & Fournier, M. (Eds.),*Cultivating differences: Symbolic boundaries and the making of inequality.* Chicago: University of Chicago Press.

262. Crawford, D., Jackson, E., & Godbey, G. (1991). A hierarchical model of leisure constraints. *Leisure Sciences, 13,* 309-320.

263. See Tokarski, W. (1985). Some social psychological notes on the meaning of work and leisure. *Leisure Studies, 4,* 227-231.

264. Holt, D. (1995), How do consumers consume? A typology of consumption practices. *Journal of Consumer Research, 22,* 1-16.

265. From Mason, R. (1993). Cross-cultural influences in the demand for status goods. *European Advances in Consumer Research, 1,* 46-51.

266. Historical facts are based on information obtained from www.britannica.com November 2000.

267. See Chapter 1 in Zillmann, D., & Vorderer, P. (Eds.). (2000). *Media entertainment.* Mahwah, NJ: Lawrence Erlbaum.

268. Chenpitayaton, K. (2000, spring). *The temperature of musical: Looking at the audience.* An unpublished paper presented in a graduate class at California State University, Fullerton (spring).

269. This is the term used by New York dance critic Arlene Croce, as cited in Pasles, C. (2001, December 4). [Her column]. *Los Angeles Times,* p. B8.

270. Dalva, N. (2000, November 5). One-time only dances, in the Cunningham style. *New York Times,* Arts section, p. 13.

271. www.britannica.com, op. cit.

272. Pollak, M. (2000, November 9). Web is a new stage for vaudeville. *New York Times,* p. D15.

273. From Goldberg, R. (1998). *Performance: Live art since 1960.* New York: Harry N. Abrams, Inc.

274. From Plato's *Sophist,* written in 360 B.C. Accessed December 12, 2002, at www.formalontology.it/plato-sophist.htm/

275. Eakin, E. (2000, December 9). If it's funny you laugh, but why? *New York Times,* p. A23.

276. Factual information accessed from http://lookd.com/magic/ December 1, 2002.

277. From Jameson, M. (2000, November 19). The Houdini of the hoi polloi. *Los Angeles Times,* p. E1.

278. From www.magiccastle.com, accessed December 1, 2002.

279. Silverman, R. E. (2000, December 15). The old magic store is no more, not the one Houdini used to run. *Wall Street Journal,* p. 1.

280. Furchgott, R. (2000, March 12). Taking its brand beyond the center ring. *New York Times,* p. B4.

281. Gurwitt, R. (2000). Circus Smirkus. *Doubletake, 6* (4), 47-58.

282. Van Gelder, L. (2000, December 7). Topsy-turvy, wacky, zany and funny. *New York Times,* p. B5.

283. As characterized by Riding, A. (2001, July 5). Not exactly new, not exactly circus, but a magical mix. *New York Times,* p. B1.

284. Gerard, M., Abdel-Baset, M., Allen, A., Reitzer, N., & Gonzales, E. (1966, November). *Performing arts research project.* Conducted for a class at California State University, Fullerton.

285. Huizinga, J. (1955). *Play theory of communication.* Boston: Beacon Press, p. 4.

286. Ibid., p. 8.

287. From "game theory" *Encyclopedia Britannica Online* (members.eb.com), accessed September 1, 2001.

288. The Prisoners' Dilemma was formulated by mathematician Albert W. Tucker.

289. Information for this section was provided by a paper, "Video Gaming," written by Keerati Chenpitayaton in September, 2001, as part of a Master of Arts program at California State University, Fullerton.

290. From Poole, S. (2000). *Trigger happy: Video games and the entertainment revolution.* New York: Arcade Publishing.

291. For a comprehensive review of video game history, see Kent, S. (2000). *The first quarter: 25-year history of video games.* Marietta, OH: BWD Press.

292. Adapted from Poole, S. (2000). *Trigger happy: Video games and the entertainment revolution.* New York: Arcade Publishing.

293. From Grodal, T. (2000). Video games and the pleasure of control. In D. Zillmann & P. Vorderer (Eds.), *Media entertainment: The psychology of its appeal* (pp. 197-213). Mahwah, NJ: Lawrence Erlbaum.

294. Ibid., p. 21.

295. Hirschman, E. C., & Holbrook, M. B. (1982). Hedonic consumption: Emerging concepts, methods and propositions. *Journal of Marketing, 46,* p. 92.

296. Ibid., p. 138.

297. From www.gamedev.net/reference/business/features/biologhy/page4, accessed May 4, 2001.

298. From Glaser, M. (2001, August 9). Museum raiders. *New York Times*, p. D1.

299. Sales are year to date as of November 2002, United States only. From Keighley, G. (2002, December). The Next Disney? *Business 2.0*, p. 112.

300. Ibid.

301. Ibid., p. 116.

302. From a quote by game designer Bruce Shelley presented in Kushner, D. (2001, September 6). In historical games, truth gives way to entertainment, *New York Times*, p. D6.

303. From Pham, A., & Johnson, G. (2001, July 22). Advertisers play on allure of online games. *Los Angeles Times*, p. C1.

304. Presented in the "gambling" entry at *Encyclopedia Britannica Online*, accessed September 7, 2001, at www.eb.com/bol/topic

305. From Gegun, A., Siegel, M., & Jacob, N. (Eds.). (1998*). The information series on current topics: Gambling, crime or recreation*? Wylie, TX: Ritter Press.

306. From Bolen, D. (1976). *Gambling and society.* Springfield, IL: Charles C Thomas.

307. From www.casinosonline.com, accessed July 2001.

308. From www.lasvegas.com/features.impact.html, accessed March 2001.

309. From Hsu, C. (Ed.). (1999). *Bad bets: The inside story of the glamour, glitz and danger of America's gambling industry.* New York: Basic Books.

310. From www.business.com/directory/travelandleisure/casinosandgaming/profile/, accessed March 12, 2001.

311. From Straymeyer, M. (1997). *The professional gambler.* New York: Davis Publishing.

312. From Schreiner, T. (1986). The West: Who plays California's lottery? *American Demographics, 8* (6), 52.

313. Calculation based on figures from Thompson, N. (1999). Snake eyes. *Washington Monthly, 31* (12), pp. 14-24.

314. Reported in Shafaatulla, S. (2000, April 3). Millions live in hopes of a dream ticket. *The Herald*, p. 23.

315. Geary, R. (1997). The numbers game—State lotteries: A ticket to poverty. *The New Republic, 216* (20), pp. 19-24.

316. From Walsh, J. (1996). Why do people play the lottery? *Consumer Research Magazine, 79* (3), 22-26.

317. Grodal, T. (2000). Video games and the pleasures of control. In D. Zillmann & P. Vorderer (Eds.), *Media entertainment: The psychology of its appeal* (pp. 197-214). Mahwah, N.J.: Lawrence Erlbaum.

318. From Babington, C., & Chinoy, I. (1998, May 4). Lotteries win with slick marketing. *Washington Post,* p. A1.

319. Burton, R., & Howard, D. (2000). Recovery strategies for sports marketers: The marketing of sports involves unscripted moments delivered by unpredictable individuals and uncontrollable events. *Marketing Management,* Vol. 9, No. 1; p. 43.

320. Merriam-Webster Dictionary. (2002). (sport, 2, noun, 1a, 1c) at www.m-w.com.

321. Epstein, K. (2000, December 19). Sound offense, no defense: Today's pro sports events, like much entertainment, assault you with noise; some explosive moments at Redskins games can throw your hearing for a loss. *The Washington Post*, p. Z10.

322. Mandell, R. D. (1984). *Sport: A cultural history.* New York: Columbia University Press.

323. Singer, T. (1998, March). Not so-remote-control. *Sport*, p. 36.

324. Farhi, P. (2002, August 8). Lateral drop; Pro wrestling may be down, but don't count it out. *Record*; Bergen County, NJ, p. F06 (via Washington Post News Service).

325. Lelan, J. (2000, February 7). Why America's hooked on wrestling. *Newsweek*, p. 46.

326. Mazer, S. (1998). *Professional wrestling: Sport and spectacle.* Jackson, MS: University Press of Mississippi.

327. Hickey, J. (2000, November 13). Corporations Love Sports. *Insight on the News,* Section: Nation: Business, p. 22.

328. Simon, M. (2001, December 13). Buying goodwill that'll stick: Big wheel could stop the stadium whining. *San Francisco Chronicle,* p. A19.

329. Johnson, G. (2001, April 20). Some fumbles in arena name game; Marketing: A few companies with their moniker up in lights have faltered since signing the big-money deals. It's bad news for the sports franchises, too. *The Los Angeles Times,* p. C1.

330. Shank, M. D. (1999). Sports marketing: A strategic perspective. Upper Saddle River, NJ: Prentice Hall.

331. Super Bowl ratings better than expected. (2000, February 1). *St. Petersburg Times* [South Pinellas Edition], Sports, p. 3C.

332. Flint, J. (2000, October 4). NBC's low ratings for Olympic Games were enough for it to turn slight profit. *The Wall Street Journal,* Section B; Page 7A, Column 5.

333. Shank, M. D. (1999). *Sports marketing: A strategic perspective.* Upper Saddle River, NJ: Prentice Hall.

334. Cited in Bonfante, P. (1999, September. 29). Hooked on the edge: The old extremes aren't extreme enough for a new brand of athlete. *Boston Globe* [City Edition], p. F1.

335. Yema, J. (2000, July 2). Herd instinct. *Boston Globe* [Third Edition], p. BGM 5.

336. Cited in Bonfante, P. (1999, September. 29). Hooked on the edge: The old extremes aren't extreme enough for a new brand of athlete. *Boston Globe* [City Edition], p. F1.

337. Sullivan, J. (2000, August 19). Extreme's foothold firm in pop culture: Music, filmmaking, ads move to the edge. *San Francisco Chronicle* [Final Edition], p. D1.

338. Merriam-Webster Dictionary. (2002). At www.m-w.com.

339. Perrin, D. (2000). *American fan: Sports mania and the culture that feeds it.* New York: Avon Books.

340. Berger, A. (1982). *Media analysis techniques.* Beverly Hills, CA: Sage, p. 129.

341. Ibid.

342. Rowe, D. (1999). *Sport culture and the media.* Philadelphia: Open University Press. p. 14.

343. Documented at each of the following Web sites, accessed December 19, 2002: www.aef2004.org/ancient_olympics/index.asp, www.enchantedlearning.com/olympics/printouts/Flag.shtml, and www.wsd1.org/earlgrey/Grp3History.htm

344. Elias, N., & E. Dunning, E. (1986). Folk football in medieval and early modern Britain. In N. Elias & E. Dunning (Eds.) *Quest for excitement: Sport and leisure in the civilising process.* Oxford: Basil Blackwell, p. 176.

345. Rowe, D. (1999). *Sport culture and the media.* Philadelphia: Open University Press.

346. Ibid., p. 16.

347. Ibid., p. 22.

348. Guttmann, A. (1986). *Sports spectators.* New York: Columbia University Press, p. 149.

349. See for review Crabb, P. B., & Goldstein, J. H. (1996). The social psychology of watching sports: From ilium to living room. In J. Bryant & D. Zillmann (Eds.), *Responding to the screen: Reception and reaction processes.* Hillsdale, NJ: Lawrence Erlbaum Associates, pp. 355-371.

350. Outrageous behavior: Sportsmanship becomes a casualty of escalating violence on and off field. (2002, January 15). *The Grand Rapids Press, Grand Rapids, MI,* p. A8.

351. Crabb, P. B., & Goldstein, J. H. (1996). The social psychology of watching sports: From ilium to living room. In J. Bryant & D. Zillmann (Eds.), *Responding to the screen: Reception and reaction processes.* Hillsdale, NJ: Lawrence Erlbaum Associates, pp. 355-371.

352. West, W. (1999, April 19). The blurred lines of heroism, Villainy. *Insight on the news,* v15 i14 p. 48(1).

353. Goodman, M. (1993, May-June). Where have you gone, Joe DiMaggio? *Utne Reader,* n57 p. 103(2).

354. As reported in How to be great! What does it take to be a hero? Start with six basic character traits. (1995, November-December). *Psychology Today*, v28 n6 p. 46(6).

355. Cited in How to be great! What does it take to be a hero? Start with six basic character traits. (1995, November-December). *Psychology Today*, v28 n6 p. 46(6).

356. Study referenced in How to be great! What does it take to be a hero? Start with six basic character traits. (1995, November-December). *Psychology Today*, v28 n6 p46(6).

357. Ibid.

358. Ibid.

359. Peters, K. (1998. September 13). Disney's magic works on Angels. *Houston Chronicle*, p. 12.

360. Peters, K. (1998, September 11). Disney's wonderful world: First-place Angels aren't the only attraction at the ballpark. *State Journal Register*[M1, M2 Edition], Springfield, IL, p. 24.

361. Cited in Shaikin, B. (2000, July 8). Angels rally 'round a monkey—and win; Sports: A moment of whimsy at Edison Field sparks a fan craze—and a big morale boost. *The Los Angeles Times* [Orange County Edition], p. 1.

362. Ibid.

363. Cited in Saxon, L. N. (2000, August 13). Angels fans are going bananas. *The Press—Enterprise*, Riverside, CA, p. C02.

364. See Swarbrooke, J., & Horner, S. (1999). *Consumer behavior in tourism*. Woburn, MA: Butterworth-Heinemann.

365. Horner, S., & Swarbrooke, J. (1996). *Marketing tourism, hospitality and leisure in Europe*. London: International Thomson Business Press.

366. From Matley, I. M. (1976*). The geography of international tourism*. Resource Paper 76-1. Association of American Geographers, Washington.

367. Urry, J. (1990). *The tourist gaze*. Thousand Oaks, CA: Sage.

368. Adapted from a list by Cohen, E. (1972). Towards a sociology of international tourism. *Social Research, 39*, 64-82.

369. See Boorstein, D. (1961). *The image: A guide to pseudo events in America*. New York: Harper & Row.

370. Ritzer, G., & Liska, A. (1997). "McDisneyization" and "post-tourism": Complementary perspectives on contemporary tourism. In Rojek, C., & Urry, J. (Eds.), *Touring cultures: Transformations of travel & theory*. New York: Routledge.

371. A view found in MacCannell, D. (1989). *The tourist: A new theory of the leisure class*. Berkeley: University of California Press.

372. From Nash, D. (1981). Tourism as an anthropological subject. *Current Anthropology, 22* (5), 461-481.

373. Urry, op. cit.

374. See a discussion in Pearce, P. L. (1982). *The social psychology of tourist behaviour*. London: Pergamon.

375. From Dobb, E. (1998). Where the good begins: Notes of the art of modern travel. *Harper's Magazine*, v297 n1778, 59.

376. Gladstone (1998). Tourism urbanism in the U.S. *Urban Affairs Review, 34* (1), 3-27.

377. MacCannell, op. cit., p. 41.

378. Robbins, T. (1995). *Half asleep in frog pajamas*. New York: Bantam Books.

379. From Lippard, L. (1999). *On the beaten track: Tourism, art and place*. New York: The New Press.

380. From Galant, D. Guides finger *Sopranos* sites. (2001, July 22). *New York Times*, p. T5.

381. From Gordon, B. (1986). The souvenir: Messenger of the extraordinary. *Journal of Popular Culture, 20* (3), 135-46.

382. See Love, L., & Sheldon, P. S. (1998). Souvenirs: Messengers of meaning. *Advances in Consumer Research, 25*, 170-175.

383. Sayre, S. (2000, October). *Tourism, art stars and consumption: Wyland's whales*. Paper presented to the annual conference of the Association of Consumer Research, Salt Lake City, Utah.

384. From Chambers, E. (2000). *Native tours: An anthropology of travel and tourism*. Berkeley: University of California Press.

385. MacCannell, op. cit.

386. Swarbrooke & Horner, op. cit., Chapter 16.

387. From Hughes, R. (2002, April 19). Adventures at summer camp. *Wall Street Journal*, p. 2.

388. From Schmitt, B., & Simonson, A. (1997). *Marketing aesthetics: the strategic management of brands, identity and image*. New York: The Free Press.

389. See Severin, W. J., & Tankard, J. W. Jr. (1992). *Communication theories: Origins, methods and uses in the mass media*. New York: Longman.

390. Terms used by Weiss, W. (1971). Mass communication. *Annual Review of Psychology, 22*, 309-336.

391. Swarbrooke & Horner, op. cit., p. 98.

392. From Cook, R. A., Yale, L. J., & Marqua, J. J. (2002). *Tourism: The business of travel*. Upper Saddle River, NJ: Prentice Hall.

393. Adapted from Inskeep, E. (1991). *Tourism planning: An integrated and sustainable development approach*. New York: Van Nostrand Reinhold.

394. See Hamblen, M. (1992, April). Frontierland. *Planning, 58*, 17.

395. From Gottdiener, M. (1997). *Themed environments*. Boulder, CO: Westview Press, p. 3.

396. From Pine, B. J., & Gilmore, J. H. (1999). *The experience economy*. Boston: Harvard Business School Press.

397. Philip Kotler, author of *Principles of Marketing* and marketing professor at Northwestern's Kellogg School of Management, is credited with the idea of combining education with entertainment.

398. Pine & Gilmore, op. cit., pp. 49-52.

399. Firat, A. F., & Venkatesh, A. (1993). Postmodernity: The age of marketing. *International Journal of Research in Marketing, 10* (3), 227-249.

400. Csaba, F. F., & Askegaard, S. (1999). Malls and the orchestration of the shopping experience in a historical perspective. *Advances in Consumer Research, 26*, 34-40.

401. See Brown, S. (1995). *Postmodern marketing*. London: Routledge.

402. Reese, W. (2000). *Shoppertainment: The Ontario Mills Mall*. Unpublished paper, California State University, Fullerton.

403. Hetzel, P. L. (2000, October). *Authenticity in public settings: A socio-semiotic analysis of two Parisian department stores*. Paper presented at the annual meeting of the Association for Consumer Research, Salt Lake City, Utah.

404. From Sherry, J. (Ed.). (1998). *ServiceScapes: The concept of place in contemporary markets*. Chicago: NTC Business Books.

405. From Sharkey, J. Business Travel (2001, May 30). *New York Times*, p. D4.

406. From Beardsworth, A., & Bryman, A. (1999). Late modernity and the dynamics of quasification: The case of the themed restaurant. *Sociological Review, 47* (2), 228-257.

407. Name applied to retailers in Sherry, J. (2000). The soul of the company store: Nike Town Chicago and the emplaced brandscape. In J. Sherry Jr. (Ed.), *ServiceScapes: The concept of place in contemporary markets* (pp. 11-12). Chicago: NTC Publishing.

408. In Mandel, D. (1967). *Changing art, changing man*. New York: Horizon Press.

409. O'Guinn, T., & Belk, R. (1989). Heaven on earth: Consumption at Heritage Village. *Journal of Consumer Research, 16* (1), 147-157.

410. Sherry, J. (1985). *Cereal monogamy: Brand loyalty as secular ritual in consumer culture*. Paper presented to the 17th annual conference of the Association for Consumer Research, Toronto, Ontario, Canada.

411. See Csaba, F. F., & Askegaard, S. (1999). Malls and the orchestration of the shopping experience in a historical perspective. In A. Arnould & L. Scott (Eds.), *Advances in Consumer Research,* 26, 34-40.

412. From Kling, R., Olin, S., & Poster, M. (Eds.). (1991). *Postsuburban California.* Berkeley: University of California Press, p. ix.

413. From Loja, E. W. (1992). Inside exopolis: Scenes from Orange County. In M. Sorkin (Ed.) *Variations on a theme park: The new American city and the end of public space* (pp. 94-122). New York: Noonday Press.

414. From Huxtable, A. L. (1997, March 30). Living with the fake, and liking it. *New York Times,* Arts & Leisure, p. 1.

415. Ibid.

416. Gottschalk, S. (1995). Ethnographic fragments in postmodern spaces. *Journal of Contemporary Ethnography,* 24 (2), 195-228.

417. From Belk, R. (1998). Las Vegas as farce, consumption as play. *Advances in Consumer Research,* XXV, p. 8.

418. See Weinstein, R. (1992, summer). Disneyland and Coney Island: Reflections on the evolution of the modern amusement park and cultural innovation. *Journal of Popular Culture,* 26 (1), 131-164.

419. From The Imagineers. (1996). *Imagineering. A behind the dreams look at making the magic real.* New York: Hyperion.

420. Carson, T. (1992, March 27). To Disneyland. *Los Angeles Weekly,* 27, 16-28.

421. From Goodheart, A. (2001, February 25). Theme park on a hill. *New York Times Magazine,* pp. 13-14.

423. From *Nation's Restaurant* News, December, 10, 1999, p. 4.

424. Solomon, M., & Englis, B. (1994). Reality engineering: Blurring the boundaries between marketing and popular culture. *Journal of Current Issues and Research in Advertising,* 16 (2), 1-18.

425. Solomon, M (2000, October). *But is it true blue mate? Cross-cultural perceptions of authenticity.* Paper presented at the annual conference of the Association of Consumer Research, Salt Lake City, Utah (October).

426. See Baudrillard, J. (1983). *Simulations.* New York: Semiotext(e).

427. From Denzin, N. K. (1991). *Images of postmodern society.* London: Sage, p. vii.

428. From Featherstone, M. (1991). *Consumer culture and postmodernism.* London: Sage, pp. 7-8.

429. Baudrillard, op. cit., p. 10.

430. Ibid., p. 95.

431. From Cumming, R. D. (1965). *The philosophy of Jean Paul Sartre.* New York: Random House.

432. From Ewen, S., & Ewen, E. (1982). *Channels of desire.* New York: McGraw-Hill, pp. 249-51.

433. Quoted by Downey, R. (1999, February 19). Experience this! *New York Times,* p. E21.

434. Quoted by Verhovek, S. H. (2000, May 17). He's turning Seattle into his kind of town, *New York Times,* p. D12.

435. A term used by Jamison, F. (1991). *Postmodernism or the cultural logic of late capitalism.* Durham, NC: Duke University Press, p. 115.

436. As described by Macrae-Gibson, G. (1985). *Secret life of buildings.* Cambridge, MA: MIT Press, p. 12.

437. See Jameson, F. (1991). *Postmodernism.* Durham, NC: Duke University Press, Chapter 4.

438. From Thornburg, B. (2001, December 16). Suites of San Francisco. *Los Angeles Times Magazine,* pp. 26-32.

439. Ibid., p. 27.

440. Ibid., p. 31.

441. Quoted in Goldberger, P. (2002, March 25). High-tech emporiums. *New Yorker Magazine,* p. 56.

442. Excerpted from Root, D. (1996*). Cannibal culture: Art, appropriation and the commodification of difference.* Boulder CO: Westview Press.

443. From Kimmelman, M. (2001, August 26). Museums in a quandary: Where are the ideals? *The New York Times,* p. AR2.

444. Said by art and culture critic Dave Hickey in Kinzer, S. (2001, September 5). Las Vegas's museums play to type. *New York Times,* p. B1.

445. See Muscamp, H. (2000, October 20). Where ego sashays in style. *New York Times,* p. B33.

446. See Tannen, M. (2000, April 19). Art world tries on fashion and finds that it fits. *New York Times,* p. D6.

447. Smith, R. (2000, December 3). Memo to art museums: Don't give up on art. *New York Times,* Arts p. 35.

448. Remark of art critic Hilton Kramer, quoted in Puente, M. (2001, January 5). What is art? *USA Today,* p. D1.

449. Ed Able as quoted in Puente, M. (2001, January 5). What is art? *USA Today,* p. D1.

450. From Ferrell, S. (2000, November 12. Famous faces, all in wax. *New York Times,* p. TR31.

451. From a piece written by Tanner, M. (2000) in the museum catalog of the "In Smog and Thunder: Historical Works from the Great War of the Californias" exhibition in Laguna Beach, California, p. 45.

452. Ibid., p. 48.

453. See Delp, L., Ryan, C., & Sanders, L. (2000, November). Museum smackdown, *Travel Holiday,* pp. 106-113.

454. From Baudrillard, J. (1983). *Simulations.* New York: Semiotext(e), p. 130.

455. From Kael, P. (1986, September 22). [Review of *Blue Velvet*]. *New Yorker,* p. 101.

456. From a Simon, J. (1986, November 7). On film. *National Review,* p. 36.

457. From Barthes, R.(1977). *Image, music, text.* New York: Noonday Press.

458. See Heim, M. (1987). *Electric language: A philosophical study of word processing.* New Haven, CT: Yale University Press, p. 217.

459. Cited in Brown, W., & Boxer, S. (1999, December 30). Connected—Millennium Issue: Entertainment. *The Daily Telegraph,* London, p. 13.

460. The phrase "sounding like a broken record" has been used to describe a person who says the same thing over and over again; the reference is to old records that would skip and repeat due to scratch marks on the vinyl.

461. The phrase "taking an E-ticket ride" was a metaphor for a great, exciting—often whirlwind—experience; the reference was to Disney theme park's ticketing practices up until the mid-1980s. At that time, people bought individual tickets for park attractions with E-tickets, which were designated for Disney's most exciting and popular attractions, such as the Space Mountain and the Pirates of the Caribbean rides.

462. Copeland, P. (2000). Foreword to new media f@ctfile Brighton Wired Sussex. Cited in Perrons, D. (2001). *Understanding social and spatial divisions in the new economy.* Paper prepared for presentation at Regional Transitions. European regions and the challenges of development, integration and enlargement, Regional Studies International Conference University of Gdansk 15th through 18th September. Accessed December 15, 2002, at http://secure.rogerbooth.co.uk/rsa/gdansk/Perrons.doc

463. Accessed December 17, 2002, at www.dabra.com/newmediaskills.pdf

464. New Media Survey: PricewaterhouseCoopers (1999, June). Public policy review: A review of recent policies, regulations and announcements. 99(6), p. 3 [An online publication of the Institute of Chartered Accountants of BC]. Accessed December 17, 2002, at www.ica.bc.ca/pdf/june99.pdf

465. New media: Communicating in the new media to promote teamwork. Accessed March 9, 2002, at www.lc.capellauniversity.edu/~thamilton/NewMediaSite/newmedia2.htm

466. Reported in Allen, K. (2000, July 28). Net used for entertainment, not info. *Advertising and Marketing.* Accessed March 9, 2002, at www.digitrends.net/ena/index_10402.html

467. Arlidge, J. (2002, March 3). Focus: Naked capitalism: The dirty secret that drives new technology: it's porn. *The Observer,* London, p. 20.

468. Ibid.

469. Ibid.

470. Cornell, D. (1997, winter). Edutainment and girls. *CPSR* [Computer Professionals for Social Responsibility] *Newsletter,* Vol. 15, no. 1, p. 6.

471. New study by SRI Consulting maps consumer use of new media. (1997, February 4). Accessed December 15, 2002, at www.sri.com/news/releases/2-5-97.html.

472. Cited in Kerber, R. (2000, April 24). New media: Changing demographics. *Boston Globe.* Available December 15, 2002, at www.roundtablegroup.com/about/article.cfm?ID=1

473. Amos, B., Cameron, T., Mesko, J., Smith, K., & Tuinstra, K. (2001, June 4). Techno kids: An injured breed. *Grand Rapids Press,* Grand Rapids, MI, p. B3.

474. Information derived from the following articles, which appeared in the *New York Times* on September 11, 2002. Kakutani, M. And now, back to our regularly scheduled programming (p. 35). Nelson, C. The old days never looked so good" (Arts, p. 1),

475. Budick, A. (1999). Exhibiting a little pizzazz. *Future.Newsday.Com,* paragraph 1. Accessed December 18, 2002, at http://future.newsday.com/8/ftop0801.htm#museum

476. Proceedings of the Third International Entertainment-Education Conference for Social Change. (2000) Accessed December 15, 2002, at www.jhuccp.org/ee/eeHTML/intro.htm

477. Advertisement for Ken Davis's video, *Is it Just Me?* Accessed December 18, 2002, at https://www.kendavis.com/video/vt013.cfm

478. The slogan of the Christian Comedy Index. Accessed December 17, 2002, at http://christiancomedy.tripod.com

479. Excerpted from Pricewaterhouse Coopers press materials. Accessed March 9, 2002, at www.pwcglobal.com/extweb/ncpressrelease.nsf/DocID/F1FF8047FDBC67C3852568470070389B

Index

About the Authors

Shay Sayre is a professor of advertising and director of the graduate program for the Department of Communications at California State University, Fullerton. She received her Ph.D. from the University of San Diego. Recipient of a Fulbright to study in Hungary, Sayre has taught in Brussels and traveled extensively in Europe, China, Turkey, and Russia. She is the author of *Qualitative Methods for Marketplace Research* (Sage) and *Campaign Planner for Promotion and IMC* (Southwestern) as well as numerous book chapters and journal articles in publications such as the *Journal of Advertising*; *Consumption, Markets and Culture*; *Journal of Professional and Business Ethics*; *Advances in Consumer Research*; and *Research in Consumer Behavior*. She lives in Laguna Beach, California.

Cynthia King serves as the director for the Center for Entertainment and Tourism Studies at California State University, Fullerton, overseeing programs in education, research, and policy regarding entertainment and tourism in Orange County and the greater Southern California region. She is also an associate professor in Cal State Fullerton's Communications Department, where she teaches and conducts research in the areas of entertainment, media effects, and public relations. Her professional background includes experience in audience research, corporate public relations, and integrated marketing communication. She earned her Ph.D. in mass communications theory, processes, and effects at the University of Alabama; she received her master's degree in political science and her bachelor's degree in general communication, *summa cum laude*, from Florida State University.